News from Other Worlds

Studies in Nordic Folklore,
Mythology and Culture

THE WILDCAT CANYON ADVANCED SEMINARS

OCCASIONAL MONOGRAPH SERIES

Volume 1

News from Other Worlds

Studies in Nordic Folklore, Mythology and Culture

In Honor of John F. Lindow

Edited by

Merrill Kaplan
&
Timothy R. Tangherlini

NORTH PINEHURST PRESS
BERKELEY • LOS ANGELES

Library of Congress Cataloging-in-Publication Data

News from other worlds : studies in Nordic folklore, mythology and culture : in honor of John F.
  Lindow / edited by Merrill Kaplan and Timothy R. Tangherlini.
    p. cm. — (The Wildcat Canyon Advanced Seminars occasional monograph series ; vol. 1)
    Includes bibliographical references and index.
    ISBN 978-0-578-10174-3 (cloth : alk. paper)
    1. Old Norse literature—History and criticism. 2. Mythology, Norse, in literature. 3. Folklore—Scandinavia.   I. Title. II. Series. III. Kaplan, Merrill. IV. Tangherlini, Timothy R.
PT7113.N49 2012
839.6'09--dc22

COVER PHOTOGRAPHY BY MERRILL KAPLAN
COVER DESIGN BY CHRIS SELLERS
ADDITIONAL COVER PHOTOGRAPHY
BY   TOBBA JÓNSDÓTTIR (FRONT FLAP) &
GERRY PAILLE (TUCHODI ON FLICKR)

North Pinehurst Press
Berkeley and Los Angeles

Printed on acid-free paper

ISBN: 978-0-578-10174-3

Vask árvakr, bark orð saman
með málþjóns morginverkum;
hlóðk lofkǫst þann's lengi stendr
óbrotgjarn í bragar túni.

John Lindow
(*photo by Kitty Lindow*)

Contents

Tabula Gratulatoria

MARIA TERESA (MABEL) AGOZZINO
THEODORE M. ANDERSSON
ANDERS ANDRÉN
INGUNN ÁSDÍSARDÓTTIR
KIMBERLY A. BALL
KAREN BEK-PEDERSEN
ÚLFAR BRAGASON
CHARLES L. BRIGGS
STEFAN BRINK
ANTHONY B. BUCCITELLI
CENTER FOR FOLKLORE STUDIES, THE OHIO STATE UNIVERSITY
CENTER FOR FOLKLORISTIK, KØBENHAVNS UNIVERSITET
MARTIN L. CHASE
MICHAEL CHESNUTT
CAROL J. CLOVER
MARGARET B. CLUNIES ROSS
GERDA COOK-BODEGOM
JOANN CONRAD
MARGARET J. CORMACK
DEPARTMENT OF ESTONIAN AND COMPARATIVE FOLKLORE,
    UNIVERSITY OF TARTU
THE DEPARTMENT OF SCANDINAVIAN, UNIVERSITY OF
    CALIFORNIA, BERKELEY
THOMAS A. DUBOIS
THE DUNDES FAMILY
JÜRG GLAUSER
TERRY A.GUNNELL AND TOBBA JÓNSDÓTTIR
VALDIMAR TR. HAFSTEIN
RICHARD HARDACK
JOSEPH C. HARRIS
LINDA HAVERTY RUGG
ELDAR HEIDE
VERENA J. HOEFIG

GARY HOLLAND
INSTITUT FÜR SKANDINAVISTIK, GOETHE-UNIVERSITÄT
MOLLY JACOBS
ÁRMANN JAKOBSON
MARIANNE KALINKE
MERRILL KAPLAN AND CHRIS SELLERS
HENNING KURE
CAROLYNE LARRINGTON
HANNE P. LARSEN
ANNETTE LASSEN
JAMES P. LEARY
LARS LÖNNROTH
ARNE O. LUNDE
MATS MALM
JAMES MASSENGALE
TONY MAXWELL
JOHN S. MCKINNELL
RORY MCTURK
DANIEL F. MELIA
TODD MICHELSON-AMBELANG
WILLIAM IAN MILLER
TOMAS MILOSCH
STEPHEN A. MITCHELL
RAGNHEIÐUR MOSESDÓTTIR
ELSE MUNDAL
JOSEPH FALAKY NAGY
JOHN D. NILES
GUÐRÚN NORDAL
MARY KAY NORSENG
DOROTHY P. NOYES
HEATHER O'DONOGHUE
VÉSTEINN ÓLASON
CARL OLSEN
ELLIOTT ORING
ULF PALMENFELT
VIÐAR PÁLSSON
RUSSELL POOLE
NEIL PRICE
JUDY QUINN
CATHARINA RAUDVERE

ALISON DUNDES RENTELN
CHIP ROBINSON
MARK B. SANDBERG
KENNY AND KARIN SANDERS
TRACEY SANDS
THE SCANDINAVIAN SECTION, UNIVERSITY OF CALIFORNIA, LOS
    ANGELES
JENS P. SCHJØDT
STEFANIE VON SCHNURBEIN
KLAUS VON SEE
ROSS SHIDELER AND KATHY KOMAR
GÍSLI SÍGURÐSSON
RUDOLF SIMEK
SIDNEY SIMS
STOFNUN ÁRNA MAGNÚSSONAR Í ÍSLENSKUM FRÆÐUM
NIELS TANGHERLINI
TIMOTHY R. TANGHERLINI AND MARGARET KONG
KIRSTEN THISTED
TOK F. THOMPSON
BERGUR THORGEIRSSON
ÜLO VALK
AURELIJUS VIJUNAS
ERIC J. WAGNER
SUSAN E. WALIMA
KEVIN WANNER
ELISABETH I. WARD
MORTEN WARMIND
ANDREW WAWN
ERIC WEAVER AND SARAH HOLCOMBE
JONAS WELLENDORF
KENDRA WILLSON
KIRSTEN WOLF
JULIA ZERNACK
RÓSA ÞORSTEINSDÓTTIR

Acknowledgements

A project of this nature relies on the eagerness and goodwill of many people. We were fortunate that asking people to pitch in on a book to celebrate John was not a hard sell. We would like to thank all of the contributors who met our deadlines with good cheer, and who assisted in the endless tasks of proofreading, checking citations and rechecking citations. We would also like to thank our two anonymous reviewers who provided thoughtful and timely suggestions for our contributors. Chip Robinson did a spectacular job of bringing rough versions of the bibliography—and all of the other apparatus that goes into a work of this nature—up to a high scholarly standard. His skill as bibliographer and library scientist is rivaled only by his amazing ability with languages. Chris Sellers came to the rescue transforming our initial clumsy attempts at a cover into an eye-catching book design. Try as we might to avoid mistakes, we are sure there are errors in these pages—we take full responsibility for these.

Tim would like to thank Margaret, Isabella and Magnus for their endless patience during many evenings of editing, proofreading and formatting, and for enduring his general grumpiness during the process. Merrill thanks Chris for every kind of support, and she extends humble gratitude to all the editors of other projects who have been waiting on her while she has worked on this one.

Timothy R. Tangherlini &
Merrill Kaplan

Introduction[1]

Merrill Kaplan &
Timothy R. Tangherlini

The current volume was produced to honor John Lindow on his sixty-fifth birthday and to capture, in some small way, the profound influence that he has had over the course of his forty-year career on the fields of Old Norse-Icelandic literature, Scandinavian folklore and mythology, and the broader field of Nordic studies as a whole. While this volume was in preparation, John unexpectedly announced his retirement. Consequently, the volume also serves to celebrate his move from the regular faculty ranks to that of Professor *emeritus*. There can be little doubt that John will continue to be active in research, teaching, and mentoring, and so this volume stands more as a mile post marking his transition from one scholarly status to another. Given John's long-standing interest in mythology and ritual, the transitional nature of this volume is only fitting: it is hard not to read the performative aspect of this *festschrift* as a van Gennepian rite of passage, providing some ritual protection for the journey across the limin of retirement, a fraught space betwixt and between where the normal rules might not always apply.

If the normal rules had applied to John, it is unlikely that he would have ended up as a professor of Scandinavian languages and literatures in California. A far more likely career trajectory would have been that of a banker, attorney, physician or engineer. John was raised on Long Island, the eldest of two boys and spent his high school years at the well-regarded Manhasset High School where he excelled academically, played football, and ran track. A great deal of his time was spent on the waters of the Long Island sound where he became an expert sailor, teaching youngsters to sail at the Point Washington Yacht Club. John's burgeoning knowledge of sailing and navigation were probably his first meaningful connection to the world of the Vikings, however tenuous that connection may have been. Indeed, for all the kids who learned to sail on the Long Island sound in the 1960s very few—apart from John—became experts in medieval Scandinavia and authored articles on Viking ships, picture stones, and sailing (see Lindow 1993.1).

Besides academics and sports, John dabbled in film during high school, producing two memorable, yet relatively unknown, shorts—the retrospectively titled "The Godfather, Part ½" and the slightly more experimental "Pumping Tin". These films became the foundation for later work that has delighted Old Norse graduate students for many years. Best known of these films is the now classic philological short, "Umlaut and Breaking," produced, like another famous film, using a Super-8 camera on a grassy knoll (this time on the Berkeley campus) and screened repeatedly since.

John's teen-age interest in film and the visual arts were easily indulged in the vibrant arts scene of New York City in the 1960s. Unlike many of his contemporaries who became denizens of East Village coffee houses, his attention lay farther north along Central Park West. John had become intrigued by Wagner's Ring Cycle, parts of which were performed at the Metropolitan Opera ("The Met") during the 1961 and 1962 seasons. Although one would like to imagine him sailing down to Manhattan after commandeering a skiff from the yacht club marina and then perhaps scaling the walls of the opera house to peer in through a skylight on these productions, it is far more likely he simply took the train, walked up the front steps, bought a ticket and sat down in the audience. This youthful exposure to the early Nordic heroic literature had a profound and lasting effect and doubtlessly sowed the seeds for his later scholarly endeavors.

John left Long Island in 1964 to attend Harvard, a small liberal arts college outside of Boston. While there, his mentors included Albert Lord and Einar Haugen. Although John had initially expressed some interest in studying Slavic languages and literatures, perhaps an unconscious nod to the masters of avant-garde film to whom he must on some level have been attuned, Albert Lord insisted that he major in something else. "Mr. Lindow," he said, "do not major in Slavic! You will never get a job!" John took this advice to heart and went off to search for a new major with better employment prospects. One cannot help but imagine the scene where John walks past the buildings housing Economics, Law, Medicine, and other profitable majors and instead turns into the one housing obscure and less commonly taught subjects. Of course it is the great fortune of our profession that he passed those earlier buildings by and became a Scandinavian major.

Used to hard work from grueling workouts as a member of Harvard's freshman track squad, John continued straight on to graduate school after receiving his A.B. in 1968. Four years later, including a yearlong stint in Uppsala, John was a newly minted Ph.D. in Scandinavian. In the fall of 1972, he moved with his wife Kitty to California. There he joined the faculty of UC Berkeley as the newest member of the Scandinavian Department, having been recruited by Lars Lönnroth. John has been at UC Berkeley ever since, challenging students with his lively lectures and rigorous seminars, contributing immensely to the running of the university and pushing the boundaries of knowledge in his voluminous and engaging research. And occasionally dabbling in film.

Myth in all its manifestations has been one of John's very favorite subjects: myth in saga (*Bandamanna saga*, for example), saga as myth (including *Íslendingabók*), myth as history (as in *Ynglinga saga*), and—always—myth as a meaningful system through which people structure knowledge and experience. John has brought individual myths of Thor, Loki, Njǫrðr, Bragi, Skaði, and others under the loupe, and he has written an astonishing array of reference articles on gods and monsters and the prose and poetry they inhabit. His longest study of myth, *Murder and Vengeance Among the Gods* (1997.1), ransoms Baldr from the perennial desire of scholars to make him the god of rebirth. He shows that "Baldr the Dying God" is most significant for dying, the god whose death paralyzes the community because it cannot be avenged, settled, or undone. He restores Baldr's death to the society for whom it was meaningful.

Snorri has fascinated John because myth fascinated Snorri. John shows great respect for Snorri as an author and mythographer, one who, while he may not always have understood the most original and pagan form of the myths he retells, always understood something. That is, Snorri had a specific understanding of his material that he was interested in communicating to his readers in a sophisticated, artistic way. John, unlike some of his oldest intellectual forebears, has always valued that understanding of myths as highly as any reconstructed original, if not more highly.

Poetry was long the medium of privileged knowledge, of *frœði*, in the North, and perhaps for that reason has attracted John's attention again and again. He has looked for narrative in supposedly static skaldic verse and excavated some of its art. His article "Riddles, Kennings, and the Complexity of Skaldic Poetry" (1975.1) is one way of answering the question *how is skaldic poetry like riddles?* It is also an exploration of what the difficulty of skaldic verse was good for in the context of its performance. Elsewhere, he examines the relationship between poem and patron, whether that patron was St. Óláfr or Thor, and between poetry and audience. He is intrigued, too, by the poetic duel, perhaps especially when it involves an otherworldly opponent—perhaps a dwarf (as in *Alvíssmál*) or a mound-dweller (as in *Kumlbúa þáttr*).

The Otherworld intrigues John where it intersects with ours, and the field benefits as a result. His essay on *Þorsteins þáttr skelks* (1986.2) is one of the best articles written about the supernatural in saga and whether its original audience found it realistic or fantastic. It is also an exemplary application of modern folklore scholarship to an Old Norse problem that has nothing to do with orality. Though so much of John's work is about the Otherworld, all of it is ultimately about historical worlds and human societies. The Other contrasts with the "We", whether the Other is supernatural or just another ethnic group (a hazy distinction, it turns out), and the "We" is the real object of study. The concerns of the Æsir upon Baldr's death are the concerns of a particular society with a particular legal system—law being the other meaningful system through which people structure an existence among like beings. (And like myth, law involves rituals like those that make blood brothers or that manumit slaves.) An ethnographic sensibility runs through John's scholarship from the very beginning. He reads sagas, eddas, *þættir*, and *vísur* for what they say about the concerns, beliefs, and understandings of actual human beings at specific moments in time. He listens for the voice of a society talking to itself and talking sometimes in verse and often about trolls, but always talking about itself.

Trolls, of course, are a common supernatural feature of the folkloric landscape of Scandinavia, and so it is no surprise that John's folklore scholarship focuses on supernatural beings and interactions across the boundary between this world and the Otherworld. John's engagement with the Nordic region is far ranging, including considerations of folk belief and folk narrative from Iceland in the west to Finland in the east, from Denmark in the south to Sámi land in the north. Thousands of students of Scandinavian folklore have, over the years, learned about Swedish legends and folktales on the basis of John's influential annotated collection of tales (1978.1). His annotations—mini articles in their own right—situate the stories in the lived experiences of the storytellers, bringing the historic context of the telling into the interpretation of their stories while, at the same time, linking these stories to earlier tradition and scholarship. John's abiding concern with understanding the stories in the context(s) in which they emerged is a strong corrective to the overly normative and largely National Romantic approach to the study of national folklore traditions that tend to creep into studies of such traditions. John's approach, in contrast, links the stories he presents to many of the concerns of the tradition groups themselves. His collection still stands, after thirty years, as the gold standard for annotated and translated editions of national folk narrative traditions.

John's ongoing research on understanding how stories—particularly legends—create meaning for the tradition participants runs as a red thread through all of his folkloric essays and links this work inextricably to his work on mythology and the sagas. In one of his earliest articles, John considers the personification of the threat of the Black Plague in Nordic legends (1974.2), reading this personification as a representation of the capricious nature of the disease as it ravaged Scandinavia. In another article, John reveals convincingly how supernatural encounters tend to cluster around significant life events (birth, marriage, death) (1978.3). Using the model of rites of passage, John explains how the intrusion of the supernatural into the everyday—and the response to that intrusion—helps people narratively structure these liminal events. Indeed, this focus on the limin is a hallmark of John's folkloristic work. These studies range from a convincing explanation of the male focus of Scandinavian household spirits (*nisse* and *tomtar*) (1985.3) to an exploration of the motif of the strong wife in Nordic legend (2009.1).

Ideas concerning economic exchange and the shifting economic terrain of nineteenth-century Scandinavia also inform a great deal of John's work on Scandinavian legendry. In an article about legends of buried treasure in Sweden (1982.1), he resists the standard interpretation of these legends as an expression of the structure of peasant economies based on the notion of limited good and instead proposes shifting the focus of the analysis to the economic demands confronting the storytellers themselves. In a later article, he explores the economic challenges posed by disabled children and their manifestation as changelings in narrative tradition (2008.2). John's work reveals a deep appreciation for the lives and experiences of the storytellers and a wide-ranging knowledge of the social, political, and economic demands confronting these men and women. In his work, John strives to understand the stories as meaning-making narratives for the tellers and their audiences.

As a logical development of this concern with the contemporaneous meanings of folk narrative expression, John has written several important works that link earlier folklore traditions to contemporary traditions. Perhaps best known of these is his work on Swedish legends, tracing the motifemic equivalence of different classes of threat over the course of many centuries (1989.2). Here, John shows that motifemic slots such as villain that had been occupied by supernatural beings in earlier traditions are, in contemporary tradition, occupied by ethnically marked outsiders. This substitution reveals the narrative strategies of ethnocentrism and xenophobia that have increasingly begun to mark the political landscape of the Nordic region. John's deep knowledge of the earliest folkloric expressions—perhaps best reflected in his co-edited work, *Medieval Folklore* (2000.3)—allows him to trace these developments with authority and see connections that might elude others. In all of John's work, one finds an exceptional ability to meld distant reading to close reading: he traces continuities across time and space, while simultaneously providing historically sensitive close readings of the texts under question. The supernatural, the uncanny, the unusual is made familiar, while the familiar is put under question. The end result is that a student of John's scholarship can access a nuanced, complex understanding of folklore, mythology, and culture across the Nordic region through history.

The first half of this volume is dedicated to essays that consider Old Norse literature, mythology, and other Icelandic subjects. In the opening essay, Margaret Clunies Ross investigates the mysterious *reginnaglar* mentioned so fleetingly in the prose of *Eyrbyggja saga* and the verse *Glælognskviða*. In *Eyrbyggja saga*, they are nails driven into the high-seat pillars of a pagan hof. In Þorarinn loftunga's poem, they are part of a difficult kenning in a stanza exhorting the king, Sveinn Álfífuson, to pray to St. Óláfr Haraldsson. Clunies Ross argues that the eleventh-century Christian poet knew enough about paganism to see a parallel between high-seat pillars studded with metal and saints' relics ornamented with gold and to use his realization to poetic ends.

In the next essay, Jens Peter Schjødt explores Dumézil's three functions in relation to the Æsir, ideas with which John has also worked. Dumézil himself thought the tripartite scheme fit the Norse mythological material less than perfectly: Odin has rather a lot to do with war for a god of sovereignty, for example. This imperfect fit is the way in, and Schjødt shows us that the model becomes more illuminating when we look at the big three—Odin, Thor, and Freyr—as pairs opposed to a third. The point is not whether Dumézil's theory as a whole is right or wrong, rather the point is that we have learned something about the Æsir.

Anders Andrén turns his attention to the archaeological record and addresses Thor and evidence of his veneration on the island of Gotland. Gotland has long been a place to itself, and it is not always adequately represented in studies of Scandinavian paganism. Andrén fills this gap and argues convincingly from place names, archeological finds, and *Guta saga* that Thor was foremost in the Gotlandic pagan mind.

In her essay, Merrill Kaplan returns to a hoary problem that has long vexed scholars of the mythology: the significance, if any, of the mistletoe in the myth of Baldr. When Frigg says that she thought the plant too young to make swear, Kaplan hears legal language and looks to *Grágás* for confirmation. She shows how saga and heroic verse portray boys too young to make a legally binding oath as threats to peacemaking and argues that the mistletoe in *Gylfaginning* is Snorri's articulation of a cultural anxiety about the legal system.

Carol J. Clover, John's colleague in Old Norse-Icelandic literature at UC Berkeley, turns a legal eye on *Njáls saga*, looking for evidence of fact-finding in the complicated legal proceedings that characterize that saga. She finds this evidence not in court, where historians of law have looked for it, but rather as implicit in saga scenes that fill in who could have known what and why. Careful reading reveals a literary work at pains to explain, unobtrusively, how anyone could know what happened inside the burning farmhouse at Bergþórshváll after the last eyewitness escaped. Lars Lönnroth also examines saga, but in this case it is a missing one. A *Saga of Þorgils Hǫlluson* is mentioned in passing in *Laxdœla saga*, but no such work survives. Lönnroth teases apart the prosimetrum in search of the shape of the vanished narrative and a different take on Þorgils.

Two contributors shed light on eddic poetry, but from surprising angles. Gísli Sigurðsson comes by way of recent folklore and gives us a fascinating glimpse of a corpus of Icelandic language folktales, poetry, and other material collected in North America during the early 1970s. Male and female repertoires are markedly different. If subject matter can vary so dramatically within the oral lore of a single, small community at one time and place, could the contrast between the eddic poems about heroic exploits and those about family conflict and high emotion be attributable to gender too? Kendra Willson also provides a new perspective on eddic poetry in an investigation of how translators make the Poetic Edda sound like a national epic in ears tuned to Kalevala meters and vice versa. Though national epic is an international genre (and very much a constructed one), the elements that signal a work's epic status vary considerably from tradition to tradition. Meter, Willson shows us, can make a work suitable for presentation to foreign dignitaries as an expression of a specific nationality or, failing at that task, damn it to endless parody.

The modern construction of epic is not far from the construction of modern myth, and Úlfar Bragason introduces us to the mythmaking and mythbreaking Rasmus B. Anderson, founder of Nordic studies in the United States. In *America Not Discovered by Columbus*, Anderson offered an alternative, counter-Columbian foundation myth for the United States, one with ample credit assigned to the Norse.

The second part of this volume is dedicated to aspects of Nordic folklore, belief and culture. In the first essay, Ulf Palmenfelt weds concerns of the contemporary folklorist with those of the narratologist. He considers personal experience narratives of Gotlanders and shows how these narratives intersect with the concept of the "Grand Narrative." Palmenfelt provides us with a method for understanding the interrelatedness between an individual's narrated world and the more collective grand narrative that constitutes the shared experienced world of individuals encapsulating the historical fabric of a period. He concludes with the suggestion that this same framework may help us understand the world(s) of early Scandinavian mythology in a more nuanced fashion.

Thomas Dubois, in his essay, offers a cross-cultural analysis of folktales classified as ATU 710, "Our Lady's Child". Working with three tales—one Northern Sámi, one Finnish, and one Norwegian—Dubois provides a series of culturally sensitive readings that help explain the culturally- and historically-based variations across these tales. He reveals how these tales created meaning for the individual tellers, emphasizing that first and foremost, even the most traditional of tales have to be meaningful for the tellers and their audiences for them to persist in tradition. Terry Gunnell, in an article that focuses on local legends about ghosts, emphasizes the importance of the local meanings created by these stories. He decries the normalizing tendencies of "national" folklore scholarship and instead strives to situate the expressions in the communities and local histories in which they emerged. Timothy Tangherlini, in his essay, echoes this theoretical premise and uses it as the basis for his effort to understand stories and storytelling in the context of contemporaneous economic and social change. In a close reading of a series of tales from late nineteenth-century Denmark, he reveals the deeply transgressive nature of selling something on the way to market—a common occurrence in folk tales, but one that also violated the law. This understanding of the law would have been immediately available to contemporary audiences, but is largely unknown to contemporary scholars.

JoAnn Conrad explores the representation of folklore as "national" culture in her examination of the illustrations accompanying the well-known folktale collections of the Norwegian scholars Asbjørnsen and Moe. She provides a detailed history of the development of these collections as well as an analysis of the processes by which the famous illustrations of trolls that accompany them came into being. The next essay, by Hanne Pico Larsen, also remains rooted in the visual. She uses a painting of the main street of Solvang by Thomas Kinkade as a means to interrogate questions not only of ethnicity and belonging but also of the representation of traditional culture in a contemporary society marked by consumerism. She proposes the theoretically rich concept of the "third gaze" as a means for understanding the overlapping and at times contradictory meanings available to the audience of Kinkade's painting.

In the next essay, Tok Thompson offers an examination of the ritual practices of the Sámi, exploring the complex site of belief and worship represented by the *seite*. A similar interest in the idea of "cultural property" and "ownership" animates Valdimar Tr.

Hafstein's exploration of United Nations cultural policies related to traditional and minority cultures. He also considers the dynamic processes that are a hallmark of contemporary cultural production. His astute theoretical reading of the political dynamics of this global phenomenon is brought down to the level of a specific case study in the volume's final article by Kirsten Thisted. Focusing on the recent victory of a Greenlandic choir in a Danish television talent competition, Thisted follows the *Julie AllStars* choir as it progresses through the stages of the competition, revealing how the choir accesses, represents, and negotiates aspects of traditional Greenlandic culture as part of their public expression of Greenlandic identity. The result of their triumph is one that aligns well with the shifting political terrain of Denmark-Greenland relations, where Greenland emerges out from under the colonial shadow of Denmark as an independent and competent—indeed triumphant—cultural group.

John is curious about other worlds—be they conceptual such as the worlds of spirits and the supernatural, or be they actual, such as the diverse and varied groups that constitute the Nordic region— and so are his students. They have flocked to his classes, eager for *frœði* [wisdom] from beyond (or if not from beyond, at least from John). They have all learned more than they expected, and his popularity among his students is well known. In 2006, UC Berkeley's graduate student government, the Graduate Assembly, selected John for the Distinguished Faculty Mentor Award, the highest graduate teaching award at Berkeley. On the basis of dozens and dozens of letters from students and former students supporting his nomination. His dedication to his students has been marked in other, smaller ways. Late in the spring of 2005 a student left an envelope in John's office mailbox. It turned out to contain a playing card—not one from a normal four-suited deck but from a card-based game that allows players to pit heroes of history and legend against each other: Achilles vs. Grettir the Strong, Miyamoto Musashi vs. Beowulf, the armies of Amazonia vs. Freydís Eiríksdóttir. This particular card bore the name Canute the Great. John has never consumed much of the pop culture expressions of his subjects of study, though he has always had students who do. The accompanying note explained the intent of the giver.

King Canute—Knud or Knútr—held a North Sea Empire from 1017 to 1035 that included England, Denmark, Norway, and some of Sweden, maintaining an Anglo-Scandinavian court where skaldic art and Christian learning flourished, a site of hybrid *frœði*. John, in a similar manner, has supported, taught, and mentored students in multiple disciplines—not just Scandinavian Studies and Folklore, whose close ties at Berkeley owe much to John, but Celtic Languages and Literatures, Religious Studies, Medieval Studies, and others. He has helped make possible several *ad hoc* interdisciplinary degrees and allowed students of Folklore to continue their studies at the Ph.D. level within the Scandinavian Department. In 2005, when his own friend and mentor Professor Alan Dundes unexpectedly died, John, ever generous with his time and support, stepped in mid-semester to teach Alan's classes and ensure that his students were not forgotten. As the student who left him the playing card put it, these were all chieftainly acts, all the more so for being carried out quietly. Thus the card was a light-hearted but deeply felt token of appreciation. We hope that this small volume is received as a similar token of appreciation. We feel that the essays presented here capture the some of the excitement, the vibrancy, and the inquisitiveness that is a hallmark of John's scholarship.

Notes

[1] References to John Lindow's work throughout this introduction refer to the bibliography of his work at the back of this volume. The format is year followed by a period and then a number designating the order in the list for that year of the referenced work.

A. Studies in Old Norse and Nordic Mythology

Reginnaglar

Margaret Clunies Ross

There are only two recorded uses of the compound noun *reginnaglar* in Old Norse literature, one in poetry, the other in prose. Both have connections with religious ritual, but the referent of the word in both its manifestations is obscure. This study, offered to one of the foremost modern interpreters of Old Norse religion and myth, John Lindow, attempts to throw light on the vexed but fascinating question of how the new religion of Christianity may have used the concepts, terminology and even the material culture of the old religion to adapt Christianity to local customs and ways of thought and then how such adaptations could be focused backwards in time to make sense of the religious customs and rituals of the past. Such a study assumes that people in early Scandinavia, particularly in Iceland, had a special interest in their pagan past and sought to understand it within the Christian interpretative framework of their present. In line with the now commonly-adopted view that the presentation of paganism within Old Norse texts has to be understood as a medieval Icelandic *interpretatio christiana* of phenomena and beliefs of the past, this study begins with the early Christian period in Norway and Iceland and works forwards in time but backwards in terms of culture to Icelandic representations of the religion of the pre-Christian past.

Þórarinn loftunga, Glælognskviða 10/3

Very little is known of the skald Þórarinn loftunga [Praise-tongue]. He is said to have been an Icelander according to several later prose sources including *Heimskringla*, and to have composed poetry for the Anglo-Danish kings Knútr inn ríki and Sveinn Álfífuson.[1] The ten surviving stanzas of his poem *Glælognskviða* [Sea-Calm *kviða*] have a strong claim to have been composed during

3

the very early period of the Christianisation of Norway and Iceland, although they are recorded only in manuscripts of Snorri Sturluson's *Óláfs saga helga* in both the Separate version and the version in *Heimskringla*, with the first stanza alone quoted in *Fagrskinna*.[2] It is often claimed that this *kviðuháttr* poem is one of the very earliest witnesses, if not the earliest witness, to the cult of St. Óláfr, the Norwegian king Óláfr Haraldsson, who died at the battle of Stiklastaðir in 1030 and came to be regarded as a saint shortly afterwards. Hallvard Magerøy argued (1948, 43-4) that the poem probably dates from c. 1032, not long after the translation of the saint's body to St. Clement's church in Trondheim (Niðaróss), and this date was earlier also proposed by Finnur Jónsson in his 1912-15 edition in *Den norsk-islandske Skjaldedigtning*. It must certainly date from the period 1030-1034, as it addresses Óláfr's successor Sveinn Álfífuson, whose reign spanned those years. Sveinn was the son of Knútr inn ríki and his Anglo-Saxon concubine, Ælfgifu of Northampton. Snorri claimed in *Heimskringla* that Þórarinn was an eyewitness to the events surrounding Óláfr's translation and the earliest manifestations of his sanctity (Bjarni Aðalbjarnarson 1945, 409).

In the form we know it, *Glælognskviða* begins by focusing upon Sveinn, and the first two stanzas tell of his Danish retinue's journey with the new king to take up the Norwegian throne in Trondheim. In stanzas 9 and 10 Þórarinn addresses Sveinn directly, urging him to pray to Óláfr that, in Óláfr's capacity as [God's man] (*goðs maðr* 9/3), the saint grant him [his ground] (*grundar sinnar* 9/4), the land of Norway, as its legitimate Christian ruler. The stanza that is usually numbered 10 is placed between lines 1-4 and 5-8 of stanza 9 in some manuscripts, because syntactically it is a dependent clause, and it directs Sveinn to pray to Óláfr:

> *þás þú rekr*
> *fyr reginnagla*
> *bóka máls*
> *bænir þínar.*

It is this enigmatic clause that I shall attempt to understand in what follows.

Snorri quotes stanzas 2-10 of *Glælognskviða* as evidence that St. Óláfr was performing miracles after the translation of his incorrupt body from its original burial place in a sandbank along the river Nið (Nidelven) into St. Clement's Church. According to most early lives of Óláfr and Einarr Skúlason's *Geisli* stanza 25[3] this event took place a year and five days after Óláfr's body had been first buried and was an important stimulus for the development of his cult, because it made visible to many people the saint's body and his shrine with accompanying holy relics. The translation of the saint's remains on 3 August 1031 is said to have been initiated and superintended by the English bishop Grímkell.

If we leave aside later hagiographical and historical texts and images, of which there are many (cf. Introduction to Phelpstead 2008), there is little reliable evidence surviving about the nature of the very first group of relics associated with Óláfr's cult in the 1030s. In fact *Glælognskviða* and the slightly later *Erfidrápa Óláfs helga* by Sigvatr Þórðarson are our principal contemporary or near-contemporary witnesses. *Glælognskviða* mentions Óláfr's incorrupt body, whose hair and nails still grew (stanza 5), implying that the body was open to public view. It also describes bells that rang by themselves placed in a wooden structure above the saint's bed (stanza 6)[4] and candles burning above the altar (stanza 7). In stanza 3 there may be an allusion to a shrine in which his body or part of it lay, if the word *kykvasettr* [enshrined alive(?)] in line 7 can be so understood. Stanza 8 tells that a host of people come there, where the holy king himself is, both *beiðendr máls* [petitioners for speech], that is, the dumb (8/5, 7), as well as the blind, and that all are cured (8/6, 8). We find a similar statement in stanza 24/5-8 of the slightly later *erfidrápa* [memorial *drápa*] for Óláfr composed by Sigvatr Þórðarson, usually dated to c. 1040.[5] This stanza states that many men, who had come there blind, go from the king's *leiði* [resting-place, tomb] with their vision cured. Sigvatr also mentions in the same stanza that a gilded shrine (*gollit skrín* 24/2) has been made about (or over) his lord (*gollit skrín es gǫrt of dróttni mínum* 24/1, 2, 4), seeming to imply that what remains of Óláfr's body is either in the shrine or that the shrine rises above him.

The cult of royal saints in eleventh-century Norway seems to have been inspired by Anglo-Saxon models, and many of the leading clergy in Norway at the time *Glælognskviða* was composed were English, including Bishop Grímkell. Both the missionary kings Óláfr Tryggvason and Óláfr Haraldsson had spent considerable periods of time in England, and several of their poets, including both Þórarinn and Sigvatr, had worked for patrons with English connections or had travelled there themselves. Much of what we know of religious observance and cult in early eleventh-century Norway suggests the dominant influence of the English church, even though administratively the Norwegian church formed part of the archbishopric of Hamburg-Bremen at this time. Thus in our evaluation of the evidence for the early cult of St. Óláfr, it is logical to turn to English evidence as well as what we can find in Old Norse sources to interpret the scanty information that Þórarinn and Sigvatr provide.

It is possible to deduce from their poems that Óláfr's body, apparently incorrupt, was on public view in the church of St. Clement and that sick people seeking cures were able to approach it and be made whole, possibly by touching it. Depending on its physical condition (disregarding for a moment the hagiographical notion of bodily incorruption as evidence of spiritual sanctity), Óláfr's body or what remained of it is likely to have been displayed in some kind of open coffin or bed (Sigvatr's *leiði*, Þórarinn's *sæing* [6/3]).[6] According to *Glælognskviða* there was a wooden structure (*borðveggr* 6/1) above the bed in which bells hung, that miraculously rang by themselves, probably to mark the canonical hours, while candles burnt [up from the altar there] (*þar upp af altári* 7/1-2). Sigvatr (possibly supported by Þórarinn) also describes a *gollit skrín* [gilded shrine] that extended over the saint's body.[7]

It is reasonable to infer that the words *leiði*, *sæing* and *gollit skrín* all refer to the same structure, which must therefore have been large enough to accommodate what remained of Óláfr's body. This information suggests that the object was a body-sized reliquary or shrine, rather than a small capsule (*sepulchrum*) or portable reliquary. Large reliquaries capable of containing the whole of a saint's body appear to have been common in Scandinavia during the Middle

Ages, although only three such reliquaries have survived into modern times, two in Odense cathedral in Denmark, and a third, the shrine of St. Birgitta, in Vadstena, Sweden (Liebgott 1993). Both the surviving Danish body-shrines were made of oak and "mounted with gilt-copper plates in repoussé technique" (Liebgott 1993, 525). An Icelandic shrine, commissioned by Bishop Páll Jónsson for the relics of St. Þorlákr, is said to have been more than three ells long and decorated with gold, gems and silver (Kristján Eldjárn 1974). The Anglo-Saxon saint Cuthbert's shrine is another example of a wooden tomb chest, into which precious relics were deposited both shortly after his death and at later intervals (Lapidge 1999, 132). If we are to give credence to Sigvatr's words in his *erfidrápa*, Óláfr's shrine may also have been covered with gilt-copper and it is certainly likely to have been made of wood. Both Þórarinn's and Sigvatr's poems indicate that people seeking cures were able to gain direct access to the saint's body, Þórarinn stating that a crowd of people (*herr*) comes to where the king himself is and *krýpr at gangi* [prostrates itself for access] (8/4), indicating their veneration of the saint.[8]

Whether the wooden structure with its self-ringing bells above the saint's bed (*of sæing hans*) that Þórarinn describes in stanza 6 formed part of the shrine or was a separate object it is not possible to say with certainty, though in all likelihood it was separate. It is described as a *borðveggr* (6/1), a wall made of planks, a word that occurs in Old Norse only in poetry and only here and in the eddic poem *Vǫluspá* 24/4, where it is used of the wall of the Æsir's stronghold (*borg*) broken down during the first war in the world, usually understood to refer to the war between the Æsir and the Vanir. Such a structure is likely to have been substantial. In *Glælognskviða*, however, it is the bells (*bjǫllur borðveggs*, 6/1-2) as well as the *borðveggr* itself that command attention. Throughout the early medieval Christian world, bells were important objects of Christian cult, especially closely connected with the foundation of churches and the persons of saints. Kock (1923-44, §1130) suggested that the *borðveggr* and its bells in St. Clement's church might have been an early example of a bell-tower and this is very plausible in the context of the strong Anglo-Saxon influence on the early church in Norway. Some surviving late Anglo-Saxon churches, such as Earls

Barton in Northamptonshire, have bell-towers, and an illustration
of the dedication of a church in the Benedictional of St. Æþelwold,
usually dated c. 971-84, clearly shows at least two bells, possibly
more, hung in a bell-turret surmounted by a weathercock (Prescott
2002, folio 118v, discussion on p. 19). John Blair (2005, 425) has
made the interesting suggestion, relevant to the present context,
that "the thegnly tower-naves of central and eastern England
exemplified by Earls Barton, may... reflect distinctive tastes of the
Norse and Anglo-Danish nobility." It is possible, then, that St.
Clement's church in Trondheim had its own bell-tower or louvre
and that this formed one of the relics associated with St. Óláfr and
his shrine.

The evidence we have, although somewhat meagre, allows us to
see that the early cult of St. Óláfr, like many early medieval cults of
northwest European saints, depended on a secondary exhumation
of the saint's body for the definitive assertion of his sanctity. That
is, the saint's body is first buried (in this case, legend tells, hurriedly
after the battle of Stiklastaðir), buried again, and then exhumed,
after it had risen once more, in order to be translated to another
and holier place, thereby exposing the physical remains to
verification as holy (because they can be seen to be incorrupt) and
at the same time enabling them to become the focus of a cult
supervised by figures of authority, the clergy. The early stages of the
cult of St. Óláfr seem to have formed around the translation of his
physical body, its exhibition in St. Clement's church inside some
kind of body-sized, gilded shrine, above which was a wooden wall
or tower to which bells were attached. The precise physical
relationship of these relics to the (or an) altar above which candles
were said to burn (*Glælognskviða* 7/1-4) is not clear but the
proximity of the poem's description of the *bjǫllur borðveggs* and the
altar (*altári*) in stanzas 6-7 implies the proximity of the objects
themselves.

Having established the evidence for the nature of the earliest
relics of St. Óláfr from near-contemporary sources alone, we can
now turn to ask what Þórarinn is urging Sveinn Álfífuson to do
when he addresses him in stanzas 9-10 of *Glælognskviða*. His first
message is clear enough: [pray to Óláfr, that he grant you his

ground (Norway)] (*Bið Óláf, at unni þér grundar sinnar*, 9/1, 2, 4). Óláfr's capacity to do this is sanctioned by God (*hanns goðs maðr* [he is God's man] 9/3; *hann of getr | af goði sjalfum | ár ok frið | ǫllum mǫnnum* [he obtains from God himself prosperity and peace for all men] 9/5-8). The stanza which editors usually present separately as number 10, but which may be a *helmingr* forming a clause subordinate to the first part of stanza 9, *Bið Óláf, at unni þér grundar sinnar*, is the enigmatic four lines presented untranslated above, here given in prose word order as: *þás þú rekr bænir þínar fyr reginnagla bóka máls*. The first part of the clause, *þás þú rekr bænir þínar*, is reasonably straightforward, the only difficulty being the verb, given here as *rekr*. It may mean to perform (from *reka*) or to present (from *rekja*).[9] So these words may be translated as "when (one manuscript has *þar* [where]) you perform (or present) your prayers." The poet's voice thus urges Sveinn to pray to Óláfr to grant him his land of Norway when he performs or presents his prayers.

The final phrase of this clause contains the enigma towards the solution of which this discussion is directed. Editors have been puzzled by *fyr reginnagla | bóka máls* (10/2-3) and there is no agreed understanding of these words, although several interpretations have been suggested. All are agreed, though, that whatever the referent of the phrase, Sveinn is being encouraged to present or perform his prayers to Óláfr before a particular object or person and the most likely scenario for such an action would be that Sveinn prays to something or someone imbued with Óláfr's (and so God's) numinous power in order to obtain legitimated rule over the kingdom of Norway, something he could not expect to receive on his own account, as the son of the Anglo-Danish Knútr and his Anglo-Saxon concubine Ælfgifu.

The most likely meaning of *fyr reginnagla bóka máls*, in the context of *Glælognkviða*'s concentration on Óláfr and his relics, is that this phrase also refers to a relic, and one of particular efficacy. The linguistic form of the phrase, containing two genitives, follows the normal structure of the skaldic kenning. As such, it must be a two-part kenning, with *mál bóka* constituting the first, subordinate kenning and its referent, together with *reginnagla*, forming the second and main kenning. Another possibility is that the word-group constitutes a kenning-like phrase, similar in structure to a kenning but not conforming to the standard conventions of kenning formation and thus not having a standard kenning referent. The use of such kenning-like phrases is common in Christian skaldic poetry.[10]

Interpretation is not helped by the fact that both *reginnagla* and *mál*, maybe also *bók*, have several possible meanings; further *reginnagla* may be singular or plural.[11] It is logical to begin construing *bóka mál* first, as the meaning of this phrase conditions or circumscribes the interpretation we can put upon *reginnagla*. The majority of editors and scholars who have considered the meaning of this passage have thought that *bóka máls* means "of the language of books" and that the kenning or kenning-like phrase refers to Latin, presumably the Latin language in contrast to the vernacular, Old Norse, or alternatively to the contents of a particular Latin book.[12] The word *mál*, however, may have other meanings besides "speech, language", including "measure, meal, portion of time" and "mark, inlay", especially when used of inlaid ornaments on weapons such as spear heads and the hilts and guards of swords.[13] This third sense of *mál* requires consideration because books, particularly holy books, were often covered with metal or had leather covers inlaid with precious stones or metalwork in early medieval Europe.

What then of *reginnagla*? The only other instance of this compound noun occurs in the Old Icelandic *Eyrbyggja saga*, whose anonymous composition is generally dated to the middle of the thirteenth century, though that date is imprecise. There the reference to *reginnaglar* comes as part of the saga-narrator's extensive description of a pagan temple (*hof*) that the Norwegian settler Þórólfr Mostrarskegg [Moster-beard] built at his new home in Iceland.[14] This description, which is unparalleled in saga texts, has been much discussed in the scholarly literature, and has often been seen as a piece of antiquarianism purporting to show that the structures of worship and the rituals carried out by priests in pagan times corresponded in essential details to the churches and forms of worship familiar to medieval Christians. Following the Danish archaeologist Olaf Olsen's influential study *Hörg, hov og kirke*, published in 1965-6, it became customary for some time for scholars to discount the possibility that there was any underlying "reality" to medieval claims that pagan worship was carried out in special cult houses or *hof*, let alone any veracity attaching to the detailed descriptions of such places. All these issues will be discussed further later in this study.

Eyrbyggja saga says relatively little about the *reginnaglar*, a term normally translated as "sacred nails," assuming the first element to derive from *regin*, neuter plural "powers, rulers, gods," so by extension "sacred."[15] The narrator tells that Þórólfr's *hof* was a *mikit hús* [large house] with a door in one of the side walls near one end. Just inside stood the settler's *ǫndvegissúlur*, a term usually translated as "high-seat pillars" (on this subject and their importance in Icelandic settlement myths see most recently Wellendorf 2010). These pillars, sacred to the god Þórr, and with an image of Þórr carved on one of them, had previously stood in Þórólfr's *hof* in Norway and had been brought to Iceland and thrown into the sea so that Þórr could guide the settler to his new dwelling-place. The narrative then informs us: *þar fyrir innan stóðu ǫndvegissúlurnar, ok váru þar í naglar; þeir hétu reginnaglar; þar var allt friðarstaðr fyrir innan* [Inside there (i.e. the door) stood the high-seat pillars, and there were nails in there; they were called *reginnaglar*; everywhere inside there was a place of sanctuary.]

If for the moment we accept that the narrator of *Erybyggja saga* was conveying reliable information about what *reginnaglar* were in the pre-Christian past, and then return to *Glælognskviða*, we must also entertain the idea that Þórarinn was using a comparison between a cult object of the past, which he knew about, and one of the Christian present in order to convey the essential characteristics of the referent he was urging Sveinn Álfífuson to pray before. Aside from both texts' use of the lexical term *reginnagla(r)*, there are at least two other general points of similarity between the *Eyrbyggja saga* description and the situation Þórarinn represents: both Þórólfr Mostrarskegg and Sveinn Álfífuson are intruders in a new land, to which they do not have hereditary rights. Although their situations are different, each requires, or is urged to seek, divine intervention and support to assist them, Þórólfr from Þórr, Sveinn from God through "his man" Óláfr. Further, in each case the texts assert that the sacred relics are associated with peace or sanctuary (*frið* in *Eyrbyggja saga*, *ár ok frið* in *Glælognskviða* 9/7), which can perhaps be construed as the calm that obedience to divine authority bestows on those who observe its cults.

If, as we surmised above, Þórarinn intended an analogy between the *reginnaglar* used in the old high-seat pillars and those "of the language (or possibly ornament) of books," can this help to narrow down the possible referents of the phrase whose meaning we seek? I think it can. Three possible interpretations have been canvassed by previous scholars and editors. The first is, taking the second element of the compound to be the accusative plural of *nagli* [nail, spike] (as it must be in the *Eyrbyggja saga* example) that *reginnaglar bóka máls* refers either to the altar Þórarinn mentions in his poem or to Óláfr's shrine, assuming this to be a case of *pars pro toto* and, presumably, that there were ornaments on these sacred objects that could be compared to the high-seat nails. In this case, though, the defining phrase *bóka máls* must be understood very generally indeed to refer to any sacred object from the sphere of the Church, whose official language was Latin. The second and third interpretations are variations on the same theme: in each case the *reginnagl/nagli* is a person, not an object, associated with the use of Latin, the language of the Church; if *reginnagla* is plural, it refers to priests, who read and speak Latin (as Finnur Jónsson interprets it in *Skjaldedigtning* B); if singular, it has been taken to refer to Óláfr himself as "the sacred nail of the language of books," and this last as been the most frequent understanding.[16]

If we examine these three interpretations both in the light of the context of use of the phrase *fyr reginnagla bóka máls* and the general syntax and semantics of *Glælognskviða*, they fail to convince. The poem as we have it concentrates on two themes: Sveinn and his status as an intruder into Trøndelag who needs to pray to Óláfr for help in regularising his position; and the sacred power of Óláfr's body and other relics associated with it, including his body-sized reliquary or shrine, his still-living remains, with his still-growing hair and nails, the *borðveggr* with its bells, and the altar over which candles burn. The first interpretation is certainly attractive, particularly if it refers to Óláfr's shrine, the locus of his sanctity, which we presume to have been made of wood, like the high-seat pillars of old, and to have been decorated with gilding, which could have been formed of gilt-copper plates like the decoration of the surviving Danish body-reliquaries. Such plates might have suggested an equivalence to the *reginnaglar* of pre-Christian high-seat pillars to an early Christian like Þórarinn. If the reference is to the *borðveggr*, then presumably the bells would constitute the *reginnaglar*. No detail is available of the decoration of the altar except that candles burned above it. The weakness of the first theory, however, lies in the delimiting genitival phrase *bóka máls*, which has to be applied very generally in this instance to refer to anything associated with the Christian Church. By contrast, the application of the normal rules of interpretation of skaldic poetry would indicate that this phrase ought to lead the hearer (and in our modern situation, the reader) to a special sense of the word *reginnaglar*. What kind of "sacred nails" can be associated with "the language of books" (or possibly "the ornament of books")?

Theory two, that the *reginnaglar bóka máls* are priests, conforms more clearly to the normal rules of Old Norse kenning formation in that priests were closely associated in early Scandinavia with the knowledge and use of Latin, but, on the other hand, both this and the third theory are unconvincing because they require the hearer or reader to substitute a human referent (priests/Óláfr) for the material objects that it appears the pagan *reginnaglar* were. After all, there has to be a convincing analogy to explain why Þórarinn used this special term. Another argument against the referent of the whole phrase being Óláfr himself is that, again, the phrase *bóka máls* would have to be applied in a very general sense, because even his greatest admirer would find it difficult to imagine this Norwegian warrior king as proficient in Latin.

It is not possible, of course, to give a definitive answer to the question of what the *reginnaglar bóka máls* actually were. If the parallel with the *reginnaglar* described in *Eyrbyggja saga* has any force, and I see no reason why this detail should have been invented, particularly as it fulfils no narrative function, we are looking for special, nail-like decorations, probably thought to have been imbued with numinous power, inserted into an object made of wood, and associated in some way with books. We cannot rule out Óláfr's shrine or the bell-turret as possible referents, but much more plausible, and answering all the criteria we have established, is a particular kind of liturgical book, either a gospel book or a mass book, both of which could be referred to simply as *bók*.[17]

These Latin codices, containing the various services of the Christian liturgy and intended for the use of priests and bishops, were often lavishly decorated because they were designed as display objects. Both in Scandinavia and elsewhere in medieval Europe such books were often used for the swearing of oaths (*bókareið*) and the recording of vows, so directing Sveinn's prayers towards such a holy object would be an appropriate recommendation for Þórarinn to make. Usually the covers of medieval codices were made of wooden boards, attached to the manuscript quires by cords, and covered with dampened leather folded over the edges. Sometimes jewels or precious metalwork were set into the covers of liturgical books, though few of these have survived, and sometimes individuals had books so ornamented for the good of their souls.[18] Although *Glælognskviða* does not mention a liturgical book among the sacred objects associated with St. Óláfr, Bishop Grímkell would undoubtedly have had at least one within the church. Its ornamentation of metal or jewel upon a wooden base could have been fittingly referred to as *reginnaglar bóka máls*.[19]

Eyrbyggja saga, Chapter Four

Þórarinn's *Glælognskviða* is probably more than two hundred years older than *Eyrbyggja saga* and much closer to the time when people still had some direct knowledge of pre-Christian ritual and the material structures within which it was performed. It seems reasonable to assume that Þórarinn knew what *reginnaglar* were when they were used in the pre-Christian sacred spaces of western Norway and what they signified. Presumably, because he saw a parallel between pre-Christian cults and those of Christianity, he applied the term *reginnaglar* to objects associated with the cult of St. Óláfr. Even if we cannot be sure what they were, we can be fairly certain that this early Christian poet recognized the similarities between the sacredness of old and new cult objects and the way or ways in which they functioned ritually. In considering the likely nature of the *reginnaglar* embedded in *ǫndvegissúlur*, therefore, we can legitimately draw on the knowledge that for Þórarinn, an early Christian witness, these objects had numinous power (cf. Böldl 2005, 174, 259).

In recent decades Olaf Olsen's approach to the *Eyrbyggja saga* passage describing Þorólfr Mostrarskegg's *hof* has not so much been discredited as modified by an approach that has come to view the historical truth of such descriptions as evidence of a later medieval creation of a reconstructed pre-Christian past that has value in its own right (cf. among others Meulengracht Sørensen 1993, 87-96). At the same time, recent archaeological excavations in both mainland Scandinavia and in Iceland have produced evidence that throws some doubt on the universal applicability of Olsen's main arguments, that pagan cults were carried out in people's homes, not in specially built cult houses (*hof*), and that Christian churches were not built on sites of pre-existing pagan worship, as had previously been argued. Much evidence has now been unearthed from excavations of so-called "central places" in Denmark and Sweden, such as Tissø, Lejre, Gudme and Uppåkra, which points in the direction of the existence of separate cult-places in pre-Christian settlements there (Larsson and Lenntorp 2004, Larsson 2006), and, from Trøndelag and the neighbouring (now Swedish) province of Jämtland, there is also now good evidence of cultic continuity from pagan into Christian times (Lidén 1969, Brink 1996). On the other hand, there is also good evidence that sometimes cultic activities took place in private houses or royal halls, as seems to have happened at Uppsala (Nordahl 1996).

It is not central to our consideration of *Eyrbyggja saga*'s representation of Þorólfr's *ǫndvegissúlur* and their *reginnaglar* to judge the accuracy of the saga-writer's insistence that the *hof* in which they were found paralleled a Christian church and its parts in all essential particulars, as well as the functions performed there. In fact, the saga-writer does not claim that the *ǫndvegissúlur* and the *reginnaglar* corresponded to any particular part of a Christian church. They are mentioned at the beginning of the account when the outside of the *hof* is described and are said to be located just inside the entrance

door. They are said to define the beginning of the area of sacred
space (*þar var allt friðarstaðr fyrir innan*), and presumably themselves
were thought to embody numinous power, a hypothesis given
credence by certain details presented earlier in the same chapter,
when the saga-writer describes how Þorólfr was particularly
attached to the cult of Þórr, whom he regarded as his *ástvinr* [loving
friend]. It was Þórr's advice that led him to undertake the voyage to
Iceland and settle there. We are told that, back in Norway, Þorólfr
dismantled his *hof*, and took most of the timber from it with him to
Iceland, including the *ǫndvegissúlur*, as well as some earth from under
the pedestal upon which Þórr had been placed (*ok svá moldina under
stallanum, þar er Þórr hafði á setit*). Later we are informed that þórr
(presumably an image of the god) was carved on one of the
ǫndvegissúlur (*þar var Þórr skorinn á annarri*). All this information seems
to suggest that, for Þorólfr at least, as the saga-writer understood it,
there was an intimate connection between the significance of his
high-seat pillars and the power of the god Þórr, although several
other accounts of the importance of high-seat pillars to the early
settlers in Iceland in guiding them to their proper land-takings
indicate that these pillars had a more general significance as divinely
authorized symbols of chieftainly authority (Strömbäck 1970[1928];
Clunies Ross 1998, 122-57).

From what we know, it is not hard to discern at least the general
symbolic significance of high-seat pillars, which seem to have come
in pairs. They presumably connected the household master's *ǫndvegi*
or high-seat to both earth and, at least, symbolically, to heaven. We
cannot know this for certain, but, as many scholars have speculated,
it is possible that they were considered to be representations of the
world-ash, Yggdrasill, linking all worlds, and that they reproduced in
the microcosm of the hall (or *hof*, if that was a separate building) the
imagined structures of the Old Norse mythic world.[20] The
significance of the pillars' anchorage in the earth (which comes
through in *Eyrbyggja saga*'s detail about Þorólfr taking earth from
under Þórr's pedestal - and we remember that this god's mother
was Jǫrð) has been underlined in recent times by the discovery of
very small pieces of gold foil stamped with human images (the so-
called *guldgubber*) in the earth below wooden post-holes, as in the
Viking-Age building excavated underneath the church of Mære in

Trøndelag, at the site of Borg in Lofoten (Nielsen 1997; Munch 1991), and at a number of other places. These and other objects found in similar locations do suggest that ritual activity of some kind took place at and around wooden pillars. Larsson (2006, 251) has proposed that the distribution of gold foil figures in direct association with heavy roof-supporting posts "suggests that they had been fastened on the posts as decorations." Alternatively, the *guldgubber* and other objects found in or near post-holes may have been votive depositions rather than fixed adornments on the *ǫndvegissúlur*.

It is possible, if we accept Larsson's hypothesis, that the *guldgubber* themselves functioned as *reginnaglar*, but this seems unlikely, given the use of the term *naglar* [nails, spikes], which the *guldgubber* certainly are not. The closest similarity in early Scandinavian material culture is likely to be with inlaid ornaments on weapons, such as spearheads or on the hilts and guards of swords. There is also evidence from the language of skaldic poetry that the adjective *naglfari* [studded or decorated with nails] could be applied to a sword or a ship or a shield and that studs or nails were also used to decorate belts.[21] Thus the *reginnaglar* set into high-seat pillars are most likely to have been nail-like decorations of metal, possibly gilt-bronze, set into the *súlur*. We have no information on how they were arranged, whether along the length of the pillars or in particular places, nor do we have information on what their significance might have been. They may have been purely decorative, although the evidence of *Glælognskviða* argues against that. It supports the probability that the *reginnaglar*, as the first element of the compound suggests, were regarded as manifestations of the power of the specific deity to whom the pillars may have been dedicated, arguably Þórr, or to the pre-Christian Norse gods in general. Given the analogy we have been pursuing with the cult of St. Óláfr, one might surmise that in most cases the pillars were dedicated to a particular god, and that they could be seen by a Christian as analogous to a saint's holy relic, especially if some manifestation of the god or an image of him were carved or inlaid into the wood. The fact that Þórarinn specifically mentions that Óláfr, through God, grants all people *ár ok frið* [prosperity and peace] (9/7) mirrors the expectation of these same benefits that pre-Christian Scandinavians appear to have anticipated as the outcome of their own rituals. This is the only use of the formula *ár ok frið* in the whole corpus of skaldic poetry, making Þórarinn's usage quite pointed and strongly suggesting that he recognized basic similarities of purpose between the old and the new religions in medieval Scandinavia.

Notes

[1] Bjarni Aðalbjarnarson 1945, 307. Cf. the discussion (apropos Þórarinn's listing in *Skáldatal*) in Jón Sigurðsson *et al.* 1848-87, III, 727-32.

[2] In the Separate Saga (Johnsen and Jón Helgason 1941, 594 and 603-4) and in *Óláfs saga helga* in *Heimskringla* (Bjarni Aðalbjarnarson 1945, 399 and 406-8), Stanza 1 is quoted and then a short while later stanzas 2-10. I am grateful to Matthew Townend of the University of York for giving me access to a draft of his as yet unpublished edition of *Glælognskviða*, which will be forthcoming in Volume I of the new edition of the skaldic corpus, edited by Diana Whaley. He is not to be held responsible for any errors on my part in understanding this text. The poem has been separately edited by Finnur Jónsson 1912-15, IA, 324-7 and IB, 300-1, as well as by Kock 1946-50, I, 152-3.

[3] For a discussion of these sources and the information they provide, see Chase 2005, 38 and references given there.

[4] Following Kock, Magerøy, Bjarni Aðalbjarnarson and Townend, I understand the word *borðveggs* (6/1), discussed in more detail below, to go with *bjǫllur* [bells] (6/2) not, as Finnur Jónsson would have it (1912-15 IA, 300), with *of sæing hans* [above his bed] (6/3), which is syntactically awkward. He translates (*loc. cit.*) *over hans skrin af træ* [above his shrine of wood].

[5] Cf. Finnur Jónsson 1912-15, AI, 324 and BI, 300.

[6] Such an object is represented in detail in the much later upper right-hand panel of the Trondheim frontal depicting events from Óláfr's life (dated c. 1300-1330), now in the Oldsakssamling, Oslo.

[7] Øysteinn Ekroll 2007, 152-3, in the course of a discussion of the various shrines made for St. Ólálfr over time, supposes that over the ten years between Þórarinn's and Sigvatr's poems "[the shrine] was transformed from a plain wooden coffin to a golden shrine," but he bases this understanding on Finnur Jónsson's interpretation of stanza 6 of *Glælognskviða*; see Note 4 above. It is not necessary to understand such a transformation from the evidence provided by the two poems.

[8] Compare Anǫn *Líknarbraut* 30/1, ed. George Tate in Clunies Ross 2007, Part 1, 260 and Note 1. There has been some debate about how to construe *at gangi* (cf. Magerøy 1948, 29 who understands the phrase *at gangi* to refer to the restoration of lame suppliants' ability to walk), and it must be noted that the majority of mss here read *at gagni* [for gain, benefit].

[9] Finnur Jónsson 1931, 463, s. v. *rekja* favours this verb in the sense [to unwind, recall, present (one's prayers) one after another].

[10] See Introduction to Clunies Ross 2007, Part 1, lvi-lxi.

[11] The second element *-nagla* may be accusative plural of the strong masculine noun *nagl* [nail] (of the body) or accusative or dative singular or accusative plural of the weak masculine noun *nagli* [nail, spike]. In the case of the citation from *Eyrbyggja saga* discussed below, the form *reginnaglar* must be nom. pl. of *nagli* and it is very likely that the instance in *Glælognskviða* is also from this noun.

[12] So Finnur Jónsson 1931, 58, s.v. *bók* 3). In its earliest usage in Old Norse, *bók*, a loan-word from Old English, meant [textile, tapestry].

[13] See Fritzner 1883-96. II, 625, s. v. *mál* 14) and examples, as well as the compounds *málaspjót, málajárn, gullmál*.

[14] *Eyrbyggja saga*, ch. 4, ed. Einar Ól. Sveinsson and Matthías Þórðarson 1935, 8.

[15] Cf. entries under *regin* and its compounds in La Farge and Tucker 1992, 213; other uses in compounds have the more general sense [mighty], [powerful] rather than [divine], [sacred]. See "Gods, Words for" in Lindow 2001b, 147-8.

[16] So Kock 1923-44, §2017; Magerøy 1948, 32-6; Bjarni Aðalbjarnarson 1945, 408-9, note; Townend forthcoming. A fourth view is that the phrase refers to the crucified Christ (see Magerøy 1948, 71, Holtsmark 1968, col. 713), but this seems far-fetched in the context of the stanza in which it occurs.

[17] For the usage, see Fritzner 1883-96, I, 163, *bók* 3) and Degnbol *et al.* 1989-, II, *bók*, senses 1)-6). Very few early Scandinavian liturgical books have in fact survived from before 1100, though the oldest, neither of them from Norway, are a fragment from a missal of the Anglo-Saxon Winchester School and a gospel book (Petersen 1992a, 216-17, 361)

[18] An example from late Anglo-Saxon England is the dedicatory poem *Þureð*, prefaced to the benedictional British Library MS Cotton Claudius A. III, which tells how, for the good of his soul, a man named Þureð *me fægere þus frætwum belegde* [thus decorated me (the book) beautifully with ornaments]. For a text and discussion, see Ronalds and Clunies Ross 2001.

[19] Lars Boje Mortensen (2002, 1015) has made the interesting suggestion that emerging narratives of Óláfr's miracles, turned into Latin and overseen by the Trondheim clergy, may have been entered into an official book; if so, that book is likely to have been a liturgical book of the kind described here.

[20] There is a wealth of literature on the subject of the symbolic significance of the *ǫndvegissúlur* and the *reginnaglar*, including the possibility that the *súlur* represented the *axis mundi* and that the *reginnaglar* may correlate with post-medieval descriptions of a Saami custom of embedding an iron nail symbolizing the pole star as the centre of the world at the top of a wooden beam. For a summary see Holtsmark 1968 and, for the most recent discussion, Böldl 2005, 163-76. Two obscure skaldic *heiti* for nails or spikes are listed right at the end of the *heiti* section of the early fourteenth-century manuscript AM 748 I b 4° on fol. 22r line 8 (Jón Sigurðsson *et al.* 1848-87, II, 494): *Regingaddi* [divine spike/nail] and *veraldar nagli* [nail of the world]. These appear to support the theory that the *reginnaglar* and *ǫndvegissúlur* once had cosmic significance, but a context for these words is absent.

[21] Cf. skaldic uses of the compound adjective *naglfari* [something studded or decorated with nails], considered to refer to a sword, a shield or a ship, in Gamli gnævaðarskáld Fragment 1/2-3 (Finnur Jónsson 1912-15, BI, 132), Bragi Boddason *Ragnarsdrápa* 5/3 (Finnur Jónsson 1912-15 BI, 2) and the island-kenning *nagla holmgjarðar* [(let us hold) the stud of the islet-belt [SEA > ISLAND] in the eleventh-century Einarr þveræingr Eyjólfsson's Lausavísa 1/8 (Finnur Jónsson 1912-15, BI, 285).

"West-Icelandic" Women's Tales and the Classification of the Edda Poems[1]

Gísli Sigurðsson

During the winter of 1972-3 the Icelander Hallfreður Örn Eiríksson and his Czech wife Olga María Franzdóttir made a journey through the "West-Icelandic" settlements in North America collecting ethnological material in Icelandic. These travels produced approximately sixty hours of recorded material, from which can be extracted twenty or so hours of actual stories and poems related by eighty-seven respondents, thirty-one of them women. The material is highly varied, and includes reminiscences from Iceland, stories about the pioneer years and early life in the new settlements, accounts concerning Native Americans, notable characters and famous strongmen, as well as descriptions of hunting, dreams and supernatural phenomena. The material also includes poetry and traditional folktales. Within this wide-ranging corpus the material collected from the female informants stands apart to some degree in that their contributions (excluding poetry) are restricted almost entirely to traditional folktales and tales about dreams and the supernatural (Gísli Sigurðsson 2002b).[2]

An interesting aspect of this collection is that, in most cases, the respondents had no formal education in Icelandic nor had they played any active part in the literary culture of the language. The stories collected by Hallfreður and Olga were to a large extent bound to West-Icelandic society, families, friendship groups and local communities and were told in Icelandic. Consequently, it is fair to regard these stories as representative of an oral culture that flourished independent of public or official structures or the mass media. The stories and their subjects are not influenced by contemporary trends and fashions in literature or the wider society. They reflect a "peasant" outlook and express ordinary people's ideas about life at the time when Hallfreður and Olga made their journey – or at least how their respondents chose to represent such ideas when these guests from far-away Iceland turned up on their doorsteps. The value of the collection is further increased as it was made before the explosion in contact between the Icelanders and West Icelanders that followed in the wake of both the 1100th anniversary of the settlement of Iceland in 1974 and the centenary celebrations in 1875 of the establishment of the New Iceland colony on the banks of Lake Winnipeg. After these watershed events, contact between the West Icelanders and the parent country grew considerably. Ideas and customs from the latter have exerted an ever-stronger influence on both the West Icelanders' linguistic idiom and the stories they tell among themselves. The stories in the collection reflect either people's personal experiences or material they had learned from others and "made their own." The corpus constitutes an excellent source for an examination of the informants' outlook on life and a window onto a cultural world little touched by the homogenizing forces that formal education and the mass media exert on cultural groups.

Commentators have often remarked on how long it took for women with literary aspirations—those who wanted to engage in a field traditionally dominated by men—to build up enough self-confidence to be able to write on their own terms rather than on the terms of the received male-created written tradition (Svava Jakobsdóttir 1980, 226). From the start of the age of literacy it is men who have been both the bearers and principal inheritors of book culture. At the same time, it appears women had easier access to the poetic and narrative oral traditions, as was also the case for folktales and popular verse (ballads, etc.). This suspicion is confirmed by collections undertaken in later centuries (Vésteinn Ólason 1979, 82). It can thus be illuminating to read or listen to Hallfreður and Olga's collection through "gender" glasses or headphones, and consider particularly the kinds of stories that women told and contrast them with those told by men. In short, the goal is to look for distinctions on the basis of gender within a tradition that we are more accustomed to lump together as a single homogeneous entity under the label of West-Icelandic folk culture.[3]

The following breakdown of the material requires various caveats. First, the material collected owes much to the collectors themselves, both in regards to whom they talked and the kinds of questions asked. Second, we can assume that the respondents reacted to the collectors in some particular way and selected material from their repertoire that they felt suited to the specific occasion, in this case the visit from Iceland of an Icelandic/Czech husband and wife team with tape recorder in hand in search of stories in Icelandic among Icelandic Canadians/Americans. One may imagine that the material offered might have been different if, for instance, Hallfreður or Olga had been traveling alone. Third, the form in which the material appears in the collection is partly the product of the editor's decision to restrict the published collection to "finished" stories: stories that could be considered "whole" or "complete." Our conclusions might well be fundamentally different if the interviews were presented in full. The selection has been filtered first through Hallfreður's reading of the material and subsequently my own, which without doubt introduces an element of masculine taste into the equation. Someone else might well have selected differently. Allowing for these qualifications, the following describes the picture that emerges.

The group I label *Memories from the Old Country* comprises thirteen stories from six men and three women. The men relate things like the quantity of verse that people used to know, their resourcefulness in the face of danger and adversity, how hard life was in Iceland, how strong the Icelanders were and how they were able to struggle on in savage weather, regardless of heavy drinking. One of them tells a remarkable story about a dog that foresaw its own death in a dream. In contrast, the women – Sigríður Kristjánsson (one story) and Sigrún Jónsdóttir Thorgrímsson (four stories) – tell about Icelandic ghosts (Sigríður) and dreams (Sigrún) foretelling marriage, offspring, recovery from sickness, the professional success of her husband, and death. Indíana Sigurðsson offers a "true" story about an avalanche that engulfed some men who bore false witness before the minister that a stranded whale belonged to his church. Indíana knew of this story in print but claimed she was telling it as it had been told orally to her.

Nine stories, told by eight men and one woman, center on the early years of the "New Iceland" settlement. The men tell about the founding of the colony when the first settlers landed in their flatboats and about their first contacts with the native Americans, the origins of placenames, farming problems, a plague of locusts, smallpox, religious disputes, droughts and economic hardship, and how Icelandic culture gained a foothold in the new country. The only woman in this group, Anna Sveinsson, tells a story about a couple who got married even though they were on either side of the quarantine line during the smallpox epidemic that ravaged the settlement in its early years.

A further group of fourteen stories describes *Memories of life and farming in the New Country*. Nine male respondents provided recollections of the heavy rains of the summer of 1907, the abundance of food during the Great Depression (despite the crushing poverty), infestations of flies, a horse that fell into a well, the first dances and how people procured alcohol, slaughtering in the home, children's fear of the forests, *Íslendingadagurinn* (The Icelandic Festival), and general accounts of the struggle to survive, working practices and relations with the Big Neighbor to the south who refuses to let a cow across the national frontier though its owner is welcomed as a guest. Two of the stories in this group are from women: Hólmfríður Daníelsdóttir recalls how she and the other girls were scared of bears and tried, in vain, to get the boys to shoot them for them, and Guðrún Olgeirsson tells about some children that were saved after their mother perished in a terrible snowstorm near Mountain, North Dakota.

Sixteen stories collected from ten men and one woman deal with *Perilous journeys*, mostly about people losing their way in bad weather in the northern wastelands or out on the lake. This group also includes the only story told by a woman, Ólína Benson, who describes how her husband got into difficulties on the lake. He managed to save himself and his crew through his undaunted courage, driving his men to keep bailing their boat.

One hundred and eighty-eight stories are classified as *Tales of notable individuals and miscellaneous humorous anecdotes*. A large proportion of them come from 44 male interviewees (on the most prolific of these, Eddi Gíslason, see Gísli Sigurðsson 2002a) and their contributions provide us with general insights into storytelling as a form of entertainment. The favorite subjects are Kristján Geiteyingur, Tryggvi Halldórsson, Snæbjörn Johnson, Guðmundur the Strong, Elías the Strong, "Bible Sigurður", Óli Vigfússon, Guttormur Guttormsson, Hálfdan the Runner, Baldi Andersson, Björn Hjörleifsson, Doctor Hjaltason and a certain Fúsi, plus various others, named and unnamed. There are stories about strongmen and the tellers of tall tales; missionaries, eccentrics and book learning are all mocked, while poetry, independence, feats of strength and narrow escapes from tight corners, through brains or brawn, are held up for admiration.

The tellers of this large and colorful group of stories are mostly men. Of the women contributors, Anna Nordal tells or plays a part in two stories about Kristján Geiteyingur and Sigríður Kristjánsdóttir tells another, but otherwise the Kristján stories are a strictly male preserve. Aðalbjörg Sigvaldason knows of a clever comeback attributed to Guttormur the Poet and Bergþóra Sigurðsson tells two stories about "Bible Sigurður" in connection with her father. The situation is thus similar to that of a tale about Tryggvi told by Erla Gunnarsdóttir Sæmundsson, occasioned by a tale told by one of the men. Guðrún Stefánsson refers to another story about Tryggvi that she had heard and considered "a fearful pack of lies" (óttalega lygileg). Lóa Finnsson also mentions Tryggvi more or less in passing but makes more of a story about a woman who swallowed a diamond that she had happened to pick up at an auction and needed to hide from the police. She recovered the diamond a couple of days later and was able to sell it – unlike the man who swallowed a gold coin and only got silver, five cents and ten cents in return. Þóra Árnason interrupts a stream of stories from her husband Einar with three of her own, all self-contained comic anecdotes: one about an Icelander who adopts a highly idiosyncratic approach to his shopping; another about an Icelander who hollered at his car in the same way as he had his horses; the third about a Ukrainian who refused to settle his account at Sveinn Þorvaldsson's store in Riverton on the grounds that, according to the bill, he had bought lots of "ditto", a commodity of which he knew nothing. The storekeeper Sveinn plays a minor part, anonymously, elsewhere in Icelandic literary history for his somewhat extreme reaction to a reading given by Halldór Laxness of his story *Nýja Ísland* ("New Iceland"), as recalled by Halldór in his collection of essays *Skáldatími* ("The Time of the Poets"): "When I read my newly written story New Iceland in the settlement where it takes place, the village of Riverton, present at the reading was the local grocer, considerably the worse for drink, a great jingoist, as is often the case with rural grocers. He became so worked up at the story that as the reading progressed he had to be held back from climbing onto the platform and laying hands on this pale and gawky author from outside the district who had come there to disparage the people of his own."[4]

The six *Tales of other people* come entirely from four male interviewees. These stories mostly concern the squalid drinking habits of the Finns, the home-brewing activities of the Ukrainians (known to the West Icelanders as "Galls"), and an Icelandic-speaking Native American. Women are better represented among the contributors of the fifteen *Tales of translation errors and language mixing*. Hólmfríður F. Daníelsson tells two stories, one about a woman with toothache who goes to a quack doctor complaining of being "sick in *tönn*" (EF 72/3), the other about a man who is teaching others how to load their things (*gripir*) onto a train: "If you go with the wagon *á undan*, the *grips* will come much better walking *á eftir*." (EF 72/3) Bergþóra Sigurðsson has a story about a West Icelander at a hotel in Iceland who asks the man at the desk to make sure his wife is knocked up at 10 o'clock and his daughter at 11.[5] There is a similar mild *double entendre* in Rannveig Guðmundsson's tale of some Icelanders who late one night ask for somewhere to stay and say to their host "To lady tonight" instead of "Too late tonight" (EF 72/40). For whatever reason the men do not seem to go in for stories based on this kind of unintentional intralingual double meaning, except perhaps for the oft-repeated tale of the boy who tells some people who turn up that his father is down at the shop "að sjúa" the mare (i. English "shoeing", in Icelandic *sjúga*, "sucking") (EF 72/39).

Twenty-two men and eight women provided stories in which *Verse* constitutes a central theme. This however gives a somewhat misleading picture of the interviews as a whole, since the material as published only contains verse that was associated with some narrative piece. In addition, the editors chose to omit any seriously indecent verses and verses that were disparaging of particular individuals. The interviews also elicited a fair amount of uncontextualized verse – rhymes, mnemonics, odd stanzas, whole poems, etc. – often known to the informants from printed books or newspapers, which the collectors originally intended to cover in a second selection.

The most prolific of the women contributors to the section on verse was Margrét Sæmundsson, who had a sizeable body of verse she had learned from her grandfather Baldvin Halldórsson (in a similar way to many of the male informants). Her repertoire also included a verse about disappointed childhood dreams that she had learned from her mother. The verses Margrét had had from her grandfather covered subjects as diverse as the morning frost patterns on a window pane, the death song of an old mare, lampoons about the meanness of neighbors and rampant inflation, patter verses about smoking, drinking and parenthood, and a satire on shallow consumerism. Aðalbjörg Sigvaldsson knew some verses by Lúðvík Kristjánsson and said he had often taught her new ones when they met; several of the men also knew verses of Lúðvík's. Ólína Benson recited two verses by Einar Guðnason about lost joys and a broken clothes peg, and Petrína Þórunn Soffía Árnason knew a verse about a filthy fish that was "both little and useless, like him who gave it me." (EF 72/11) Both she and Guðrún Pálsson recited a poem contrasting Iceland and Mikley (Hecla Island in Lake Winnipeg), opening with the lines (EF 72/12 and EF 72/32) for Mikley:

> Þú flóa víða flæmi,
> Þú flugnaparadís,
> Þitt úldið vatn og willow,
> Á vetrin allt er frýs.

> [You wide expanse of marshes,

You paradise of flies,
Your choppy streams and willow,
In winter all is ice.]

As opposed to the following for Iceland:

Þú fannafaldur hvíti,
Þú fossinn silfurgljá,
Þú dalur dýrðargræni,
Þú dimma fjallagjá.

[You pure white veil of snowdrift,
You silver-shining falls,
You green and glorious valley,
You gorge of dim-lit walls.]

Indíana Sigurðsson recited a well-known quatrain from
Skagafjörður, northern Iceland ("Grundar dóma hvergi hann..." EF
72/29)). And finally there are some verses from Sigríður
Kristjánsson that she ascribed to her grandmother, Sigurbjörg
Gísladóttir, both concerning the position of women (EF 72/18):

Ketil velgja konurnar
Og kaffið svelgja forhertar,
Ófriðhelgar alls staðar,
Ítum fjölga skuldirnar.

[The women heat the coffee
And they shameless gulp the coffee
Nowhere are inviolate
The debts mount up apace.]

and

Heldur gerir hug minn þjá
hreinlæti fær rýrnað,
sokkaleistum sínum á
Sigríður mjólkar kýrnar.

[A sinking feeling fills my heart
She filth and dirt allows
When in her socks Sigríður goes
Outside to milk the cows.]

The latter verse is addressed by Sigurbjörg to Sigríður when, as a
little girl, she went out in her socks to do the milking. These two
verses and the poem by Margrét Sæmundsson's mother are the only
ones in the group that are said to have been composed by women.
This tallies with Magnús Elíasson's observation about women's
verses not being generally well known. Magnús cultivated poetry
throughout his long life and knew large quantities by heart, but he
remarks: "...there were women who could turn out a good verse
but I didn't actually know any, didn't know much about it. Of
course, there were Icelandic women poets. Yes, but I'm just not
familiar with it." However, a little later he recalls that there was "a
man in the Árnes settlement called Hjörtur Goodman who was
really pretty handy at making verses and many people said he must
have got it from his mother, that she had had something to do with
it." He then recites an election jingle that "some people were saying
his mother Guðrún, now dead, maybe had had something to do
with." Magnús ends his reflections thus: "But I simply don't
remember there having been any women in New Iceland that – you
heard very very little about it. No, I just don't remember. Of
course, there were lots of incredibly clever women but I don't
actually recall any poetry by them. No." (EF 72/2)

Women are, however, conspicuously well represented among
the tellers of the 104 tales of *Dreams and the supernatural* – fourteen
women sources compared to twenty men. Hólmfríður Daníelsson
recounts a well-known story about the native American Ramsay
who appeared in a dream to a man and asked him to tend his wife's
grave, and repaid him with a gift of fish. Guðrún Þórðarson tells
twenty-four stories – more or less in a single go, clearly indicating
that they formed part of a well-rehearsed repertoire – about the
dead appearing in dreams, dreams foreboding death, cures and
assistance "from the other side", telesthesia, the "mark of death"
and visitations from beyond the grave, visions, the power of prayer,
hauntings, predictions, second sight and fate. Many of these stories

involve Guðrún herself or her family, in which there was a strong tradition of psychic involvement. Ólína Benson tells three tales about a child with second sight, a dream predicting longevity and other dreams foretelling the birth of children. Þuríður Þorsteinsdóttir tells five stories concerning premonitions of her mother's death, spiritual cures and the deaths of her husbands. Valdheiður Sigurðsson tells two stories about omens presaging news of accidents and the death of a young girl. Salome Johnson knew of a dream that had saved the lives of some people out on the ice. Steinunn Guðmundsdóttir Daníelsson relates a vision she had of the Lutheran church at Árborg being carried up into the heavens, and Málfríður Einarsson tells of a dream in which she saw the mark of death on her brothers some time before the end of the First World War. Margrét Sæmundsson and her daughter Erla Gunnarsdóttir Sæmundsson provided a group of eleven stories, including a "naming dream," a dying father who appears in a dream, signs and portents of recovery from sickness, a dead father who returns in a dream to interfere in Margrét's love life, child care from beyond the grave, predictions, telesthesia, second sight and paranormal goings-on among children. Magnúsína Helga Jónasson describes how God sent her father home one day when an unknown and suspicious visitor turned up at the house. Margrét Sigurðsson's father, mother and sister all came to her in dreams at the time of their deaths to say goodbye, and Sigrún Jónsdóttir Thorgrímsson includes an account of a mischievous female ghost that acts as a *doppelgänger* and turns up in advance of people to announce their arrival, as well as telling her about a haunting outside Lund. Finally, Anna Sigfússon tells about her mother seeing her father's death prefigured in the clouds.

The men interviewed also told many stories about dreams and the supernatural, to some extent comparable with those told by the women. Common themes include telesthesia, premonitions of death and contact with the dead, often associated with family members but more usually concerning unrelated people and far-away events, in the forests or on the Lake, even involving native Americans.

In only three stories, all told by men, do we get any mention of native American beliefs, and women are less in evidence when we come to ghost stories *per se* than with stories concerning other kinds of supernatural phenomena. The collection contains forty-five stories that can be categorized as *Ghost stories*, collected from seventeen men and eight women. Valdheiður Sigurðsson tells the story of a girl called Rauðpilsa ("Red-skirt") who haunted a man in Iceland but missed the boat when he emigrated and was left behind. Along with her husband Lárus, Anna Nordal tells about a girl who was killed in a shooting accident and returned from the grave to haunt the man responsible. Hólmfríður Daníelsson and Lára Mýrdal Daníelsson both tell of a malevolent female ghost that harassed the people of Borgfjörður. Margrét Sæmundsson describes a ghost woman seen by a little girl at a birthday party. Erla Gunnarsdóttir Sæmundsson, whose family remained particularly strongly attached to traditional Icelandic customs and beliefs had had dealings with the "hidden people" in her childhood and her brother Ómar had seen the fearsome ghostly "minotaur" Þorgeirsboli. The celebrated story of Þorgeirsboli dragging a pair of ghosts behind it on its hide was also known to Indíana Sigurðsson, who said she had got it from a certain woman storyteller. Bergþóra Sigurðsson provided three ghost stories: about a haunted native Indian burial plot, about a harmless Indian ghost once seen by Guttormur the Poet, and about the time when she and her sister fled from a ghost that jumped out at them from a burial ground but on closer inspection turned out to be "a man who was a bit tipsy." (EF 72/44) This jokey tone is rare among the women: it is much more often the men who poke fun at belief in ghosts and spirits in this way. The men, for instance, have all kinds of tales about tricks and pranks played by ghosts – a tone that however largely disappears when it comes to native American ghosts out in the wilds, presumably reflecting their experience of dark nights spent alone in the great unknown.

The collection includes three well-known traditional Icelandic folktales, all collected from women interviewees: Ólína Benson tells the tale of the magical cow Búkolla, Margrét Sæmundsson the story of Loðinlappi ("Hairy Paw"), and Indíana Sigurðsson is the only informant I know of to provide a version of the tale of the Hall of

Glass at Glerhallavík behind the mountain Tindastóll (Gísli Sigurðsson 2002b, 176-77).

So what lessons can we draw from this brief outline of a large body of material? How justified are we in focusing specifically on tales told by women when discussing the self-image and story repertoire of immigrants in a new society – in this case, the "West Icelanders"? From the analysis above there appears to be a clear difference between the kinds of stories that the women told and those that the men told. It seems reasonable to explain this difference on the basis of the gender roles that these people occupied in their society and the home. In their stories the men identify themselves much more strongly with events outside the family and the West-Icelandic community, for instance in the interest they show in the Ukrainian settlers and Native Americans. They tell about strangers and eccentrics, about hunting trips and dangerous ventures into the unknown, while the women's stories tend to revolve largely around people and situations associated with family life – marriage, child-rearing, the comforts of religion, sickness and the death of family members. On the rare occasions that women tell stories from the male domain they tend to identify them as men's stories, specifying their sources by name and without making them "their own" in the way that men do; or they tell about men from their own families as a tribute to their excellence. Emotional subjects, loss and regret and nostalgia for the beauty of "the Old Country" feature more strongly in the verses women introduce into their stories than is the case with men. The traditional folktales occupy a special position in "women's culture". Margrét and Indíana both mention having passed them on to their children. Ólína, to be sure, heard the tale of Búkolla from a fifteen year old boy in Iceland when she was herself seven; but Margrét learned the story of Loðinlappi from her mother and Indíana the story of the Hall of Glass from "an old woman". The status of folktale adventures as children's stuff is in all probability linked to the fact that men do not tell them and that childrearing was largely the responsibility of women.

It is therefore possible to account for the differences in story material and selection on the basis of gender, which to a

considerable extent determines the status and roles of individuals in
the society from which the stories arise. If we lacked the names for
these stories' sources, as happens for example with the ancient
Edda poems, scholars might be tempted to attribute the differences
between the West-Icelandic stories to differences of age.
Explanations along these lines have enjoyed considerable currency
in the field of Edda studies—an early dominant taste for stories
celebrating the exploits of great warriors was later superseded by a
taste for sentiment and family issues (Gísli Sigurðsson 1990 and
1998). The example of the West-Icelandic women's tales acts as a
corrective to such thinking: stories emanating from more or less the
same cultural environment can in reality vary widely and reflect
different outlooks depending, in this case, on the gender of the
person who tells the stories, rather than some all-inclusive taste
shared by every member of the cultural unit under investigation.
The findings here tend therefore to support the view that the
differences in the ancient poems are better explained through the
gender of those who preserved, transmitted and performed them
than by the age of the poems.

Notes

[1] Nicholas Jones translated this essay from the Icelandic.

[2] Direct references below are identitfied by catalogue numbers in the
sound archive of the Árni Magnússon Institute for Icelandic studies.
Transcriptions are made by Gísli Sigurðsson for a forthcoming edition of
the extractions from the collection. References to individual stories are
based on decisions made for that edition.

[3] For a gender-based analysis of a large corpus of collected folklore
material, see Tangherlini 1994, 145-162; also Rósa Þorsteinsdóttir
(forthcoming).

[4] Translated by N.J. from Halldór Laxness 1963, 82-83. About the
reception of Halldór Laxness's readings in New Iceland, see Gísli
Sigurðsson 1988b.

5 The pun in the original is untranslatable. Literally the man asks the receptionist to send his wife and daughter a *kall*, "call", but homophonous with *karl*, "man" (EF 72/44).

Once More on the Mistletoe[1]

Merrill Kaplan

What should we make of the mistletoe in Snorri's myth of Baldr? John Lindow has convincingly argued that the myth of Baldr, as we have it from the thirteenth century, is about a fatal flaw in Commonwealth Iceland's dispute resolution system, namely, the devastating implications of a slaying within a family (Lindow 1997). This essay is a footnote to Lindow's larger argument, an attempt to fit the mistletoe of Snorri's version of the myth into an existing and compelling interpretation of the central tragedy of Old Norse mythology. If the Baldr complex as expressed in the sources surviving from the thirteenth century explores the legal system's fundamental inability to cope with kinslaying (and I believe it does), Snorri directs us to another weak point. One who owes another a blood debt may attempt to pay it in silver before further violence takes place, but a potential avenger may be too young to be effectively bound by any such settlement. Accordingly, any given generation's ability to broker lasting peace is limited. This is a serious flaw, and Snorri is not the only one to reflect on it. The danger posed by a young son's future self is a recurrent theme in Old Norse literature, and it is articulated elsewhere in the mythology. *Mistilteinn*, I will argue, is part of a story about the impossibility of consensus and inevitability of exceptions. Teasing out its significance will lead us, through saga and lay and, ultimately, to Fenrir, whose tale is about fosterage as a strategy for dealing with the too-young son as exception. Snorri's *mistilteinn* will be our pass not to the Underworld, as in the Æneid, but into a sprawling complex of ideas with clear urgency in the medieval Icelandic mind.

Traditionally, those who have wrestled with the mistletoe have taken on simultaneously all the material that relates to the Baldr myth (and much that does not) and attempted either to reconstruct an original that will make sense of the often contradictory extant sources or to reveal in those sources a gestalt of meaning that we can assign to the thirteenth century.[2] My subject is the *mistilteinn* alone, and that word appears in only two texts: *Vǫluspá* and *Gylfaginning*. Reading it into other textual sites assumes that this perennially vexatious lexical detail is implicit in all versions of the Baldr myth, and of this I am not convinced. In any case, investigating how it generates meaning in individual works seems to me a valid endeavor. As *Vǫluspá* and *Gylfaginning* present the interpreter with very different problems, I will treat Snorri's version only and leave *Vǫluspá* for another occasion.

Ungr at krefja eiðsins

Snorri knew a version of *Vǫluspá* very like that in the Codex Regius of eddic poetry, and his use of the rare word *mistilteinn* suggests that he knew stanzas like 31 and 32, in which the slender and very fair (*mjór ok mjǫk fagr*) tree (*meiðr*) that is *mistilteinn* proves the death of Baldr. However, Snorri does not quote them and so avoids making the oddities of their depiction of the physical nature of the plant part of his narrative. Snorri is not much interested in the size and appearance of *mistilteinn*.[3] He is interested in a story about the exception to what should have been a universal rule, and this motif is absent from *Vǫluspá*. The crux is this: Baldr ought to be invulnerable. Hearing about his dreams, the Æsir take counsel, decide to seek immunity against all dangers for Baldr (*at beiða griða Baldri fyrir alls konar háska* (Faulkes 2005, 45)), and send Frigg to collect oaths from a long list of things that are probably meant to stand for everything. Loki comes to her in disguise. Has absolutely everything sworn? Frigg's answer is well known but not well understood:

> *Vex viðarteinungr einn fyrir vestan Valhǫll; sá er mistilteinn kallaðr; sá þotti mér ungr at krefja eiðsins.* (Faulkes 2005, 45)

> [A woody stalk grows west of Valhǫll, that one that is called mistletoe. It seemed too young to have the oath demanded of it.]

These lines have generated much gnashing of scholarly teeth but little discussion of the crucial second sentence to ends other than making it go away. Detter had already complained in 1894 that Snorri's explanation made no sense: there would have been many things as young as the mistletoe (Detter 1894, 495). For Liberman, "youth" is nonsensical as a vegetable attribute, for "a plant is young today and mature tomorrow" (Liberman 2004, 34). De Vries doesn't find the adjective significant enough to render and leaves it out of his summary altogether (de Vries 1956, II 215, 225). Bellows' paraphrase (in a note to *Vǫluspá*) makes mistletoe "too weak to be worth troubling about" (Bellows 2004, 14n32) rather than too young. Many translations, reworkings, and retellings in English replace "youth" with insignificance and weakness: "the weak mistletoe bough" (Wägner 1917, 14); "[t]oo small and weak to be feared" (Guerber 1895, 188); "too insignificant to harm [Baldr]" (Nicolson 1892, 90); or simply "too small" (Gjerset 1915, I 102). Even handbooks may characterize the mistletoe as "a tiny plant which had gone unnoticed" (Ellis Davidson 1964, 184). Already in Oehlenschläger's *Baldur hin gode*—not a scholarly work but likely to have influenced others' understandings of the myth—Frigga points out the *mistilteinn* to Loke as "et afmægtigt Skud | ... | Som kraftløs hen for Vinden sveier hid og did; | Den holder ubetydeligt af alt paa Jord" (Oehlenschläger 1807, 162) [a frail shoot ... that sways hither and thither, weak before the wind; all the world thinks it insignificant]. Deliberately reading *ungr* as if it were a synonym for small, weak, or harmless helps align Snorri's description with the nature of real mistletoe and some of the more forced readings of *Vsp* 31-32, but it does not help us understand why Snorri chose it over words that more straightforwardly mean small, weak, or harmless. *Ungr* is the only adjective Snorri applies to the *mistilteinn*, and that should move us to discover exactly what that word brings to the myth.

O'Donoghue is exceptional for finding the mistletoe's youth not just significant but aesthetically pleasing. Carrying on from Dronke, who sees the slender beauty of *mistilteinn* in *Vǫluspá* (*mjór ok mjǫk fagr*) as an attribute of youth (Dronke 1997, 53), O'Donoghue hears an echo with the proverbial *mjór er mikils vísir*, which she renders as "tiny is the tendril of a mighty growth." As she reads it, Snorri has Frigg pass over the mistletoe because "she failed to foresee the dramatic though long-term future of the Norse equivalent of a tiny acorn" (O'Donoghue 2003, 89). I like O'Donoghue's concluding image better than her line of reasoning, which requires us to bounce back and forth between *Vǫluspá* and *Gylfaginning* until we hear the word *mjór* in the text in which it does not appear. Nonetheless, I agree that we have here something like a tiny acorn, except that the Norse equivalent is rather more grim.

The physical description of *mistilteinn* in *Vǫluspá* is beside the point if our subject is Snorri's text. For the plant too young to make swear, let us read a boy too young to make an oath. We find such a boy (really a young man) in a *fornaldarsaga*: in *Þorsteins þáttr bæjarmagns*, the king of Jǫtunheimar cannot ask a subordinate king's son to pledge him obedience, for *ekki er þat lög at krefja svá unga menn til eiða* [it is not lawful to demand oaths from men so young] (*Þorsteins þáttr bæjarmagns*, 331). He is not just a motif of fantastic literature. Youth also had legal ramifications in the world in which Snorri and his contemporaries operated: the medieval laws confirm that there was an official category of young men too young to swear. *Kristinnalaga þáttr* 38 in the Staðarhólsbók redaction of *Grágás* has this to say about pledging tithes:

> *huer maðr scal eið vinna at fe sino oc er scylldr þes þa er hann er .xvi. vetra gamall* (*Grágás*. Staðarhólsbók 48)

> [Every man shall pledge his share of wealth, and the obligation to do so starts when he is sixteen winters old.]

Under sixteen, we are to understand, he is too young to have the oath demanded of him. In *Vígslóði*, too, the section on homicide, a paragraph requires anyone acting legally on behalf of a man unfit to appear in court on a panel of neighbors to be at least twelve years old and of sufficient mental capacity to have command of both word and oath (*ráða fyrir orði oc eiði*) (*Grágás*. Staðarhólsbók, 322). In other words, the precocious twelve-year-old who can act as an adult is one precocious specifically in the realm of the powerful language that includes oaths.[4] Numerous paragraphs in *Grágás* show that boys under sixteen have little or no control over their own affairs and finances. (Boys between twelve and sixteen have some control, with the permission of their guardians.) These passages make explicit that the obligation and privilege to swear oaths starts at a specified age of majority and not before. The oath motif in Snorri's narrative is not just an afterthought to give some nominal logic to the associated motif of exceptionality, as per (Lorenz 1984, 561): it makes *mistilteinn* the perfect abstraction of the thing left out of a legal agreement on a technicality. The technicality in question is youth.

The oath Frigg collects is not just any oath and certainly not a tithe pledge. It is meant to prevent future violence, a seal on an agreement like an official friendship or *vinátta* (made with the same verb with which one swears an oath: *binda*) or a settlement after a slaying. The words *sáttareiðr* or *sættareiðr* [settlement-oath] attest to the importance of oaths in making legal settlements. By gathering this sort of oath from everything that might harm Baldr, Frigg brokers a pre-emptive settlement among potential disputants.[5] Neither passage quoted above directly concerns settlement, but both suggest that a thirteenth-century consumer of Snorri's version of the mythology might have understood Frigg's phrasing in just the way suggested here: the plant who was not made to swear is like the boy too young to be an independent party to legal settlement, whether because too young to be required to do so (as the passage in *Kristinna laga þáttr* implies) or too young to command the power of legal language (as the passage in *Vígslóði* implies). The point, then, of Frigg's failure to collect an oath from this being is not that she overlooks it or the potential threat it poses (per Dronke and many others) but that she knows no meaningful oath can be extracted from it. In this way, it is like the boy too young to be the principal (*aðili*) in the case of his father's slaying. It is unlike that boy in that there is no father to avenge, no triggering event, no case. *Mistilteinn* stands simply for the essence of the thing unavoidably left out of a violence-limiting agreement because it is too young.

A legal interpretation of the mistletoe would not be out of place here. Snorri's version of the myth is saturated with legal detail. Not only does Frigg collect oaths (*svardagar*), but they are made official through publication (*vitat*). The scene moves then not to a hall, the expected site for entertainments (*skemtun*), but to the Æsir's assembly, the *þing*, and it is there that Baldr is killed. The little Snorri tells us of Baldr elsewhere in *Gylfaginning* also connects him to the law. His judgments never hold (*sú náttúra fylgir honum, at engi má haldask dómr hans*),[6] which is a pity, since he may be the wisest of the Æsir (*vitraztr*, though *hvítaztr*, "whitest," in the Uppsala manuscript) and most merciful (*líknasamaztr*). Of Breiðablik, where he lives, we are told that no unclean thing is permitted (*í þeim stað má ekki vera óhreint*) (Faulkes 2005, 29). Maybe the place is simply as shining as he, but the phrasing recalls how the thing-sites of saga are described as sites of ritual cleanliness. For example, the guardians of the Þórsnes assembly grounds in *Eyrbyggja saga* will not tolerate human waste on the site, but when they bring arms against those who refuse to go elsewhere, the blood they shed despoils the land anyway, and the site must be moved. The Æsir's own *þing* is so great a place of legal assurances (*svá mikill griðastaðr*)—the same assurances the oaths granted Baldr—that revenge cannot be taken at once when Baldr is slain there. Thing-sites are sensitive to defilement by the unclean. Perhaps Breiðablik is also an assembly ground, the place where Baldr hands down his wise and unheeded judgments.[7] Ineffectual though he may be, Baldr's purview would appear to be a legal one.[8]

Even a few odd details of Baldr's final moments at the *þing* take on additional meaning when legal matters are kept in mind. The Æsir have at Baldr with weapons of all kinds, but Baldr is not hurt, and everyone thinks this a great honor for him (*hvat sem at var gort, sakaði hann ekki, ok þótti þetta ǫllum mikill frami*). It is easy to see the scene as a breakdown of the proper functioning of the assembly, where weapons are to be sheathed and conflicts conducted with words,[9] but we might better read it as a performance of the efficacy of the oaths collected by Frigg. By casting weapons at Baldr, the Æsir call on every thing that has sworn to grant Baldr *grið* to make good on that promise, and every edge and stone that fails to bite or bruise affirms its oath in the public forum of the *þing*. This is appropriate: it is at the *þing* that alliances, loyalties, and settlements are tested officially. In this context, it begins to make more sense that the Æsir should think their sport gives Baldr fame (*frami*) and that Loki should try to coax Hǫðr into shooting him by urging him to do his brother honor (*sœmð*). Taking part contributes to a demonstration that this is the man to whom no one bears ill, and who has maximal social worth because he has the legal backing of all. The Æsir do Baldr honor by calling the roll of his sworn supporters, and Baldr gains honor by having them called. Given Baldr's associations with law and judgment and the wealth of legal detail in Snorri's narration of his death, it is fitting that the missile that kills him is shot through a discernable weak point in the law.

It could reasonably be objected that the laws in fact account for this weak spot. Were *mistilteinn* a young human being, laws would provide for an *aðili* who would act on his behalf. *Vígslóði* specifies that a man is principal in the case of the slaying of his father (*sonr manz er aðile vig sacar xvi. vetra gamall. eða ellre*), but if he is not of age, the role of *aðili* passes to the slain man's nearest male kin of age (*ef maðr er eigi fulltiði enda gøriz söc sv er hann er aðili at ef hann eigi alldr til. þa asa karl maðr soc er nanastr er fulltiði*). The succession of next of kin is clearly outlined, passing from the boy's grandfather, to his paternal uncle or uncles, to his maternal uncle or uncles, and so on (*Grágás. Konungsbók*, 167). A settlement reached by the principal would seem to bind even his underage kinsmen. The Truce Speech (or *Griðamál*) in *Baugatal* is very clear on this point:

> *Nu selr N. N. N. N. grip til sattar stefno þeirrar er þeir hafa a quepit firir sic oc sin erfingia oc alla þa men er hann agriðom fyrir at selia. En N. N. tecr grið af N. N. ser til handa oc sinom erfingiom oc öllum þeim monnum er hann þarf grið til handa at taca* (*Grágás*. Konungsbók, 204).

> [Now A, on behalf of himself and his heir and all the people for whom he has the right to give truce, gives truce to B until the settlement meeting they have appointed, and B accepts truce from A for himself and his heirs and all the people for whom he needs to accept truce] (Foote 1980, 183).

Properly speaking, the *Griðamál* guarantees only the peace leading up to the settlement meeting (or between settlement meetings, if more than one is required to reach an agreement) rather than the final settlement, but the Settlement Speech or *Tryggðamál* takes similar care:

> *Nu haldit þit báþir abóc einni enda ligr nu fe aboc er N. N. bøtir fyrir sic oc in erfingia alin oc o borin. getin oc ogetin. nefndan oc onefndan. N. N. tecr trygðir en N. N. veitir ævintrygðir þar æ scolo halldaz meþan molld er oc menn lifa.* (*Grágás*. Konungsbók, 206)

> [Now the pair of you hold the same book – and on the book now lies the money which A pays in compensation for himself and his heir born and unborn, conceived and unconceived, named and unnamed. B. takes guarantees of peace and A gives everlasting guarantees of peace which shall be kept while mold and men last.][10]

Oddly, only the heirs and descendants of the man paying compensation are explicitly mentioned. I hesitate to read too much into this omission by itself: surely the laws are meant to bind the heirs of the man receiving compensation as well as those of the man giving it. In any case, anyone breaking the peace so arrived at is to suffer God's wrath (*hafa sa hylle guðs er helldr trygðir. en sa reiðe er ryfr rettar trygþir*), and that, at least, must include any young man who could have demanded compensation himself, had only he been older.

Elsewhere in the laws, however, other paragraphs spell out that young men retain some rights even after their guardians have reached agreements on their behalf. Unsurprisingly, perhaps, *Vígslóði* ensures that if the guardians of a young man fail to prosecute a case belonging to him or bungle it, the young man retains the right to sue when he comes of age (*Grágás*. Konungsbók, 168-69; *Grágás* 1980, 157). The law goes further, however. *Baugatal* specifies that a man whose representatives settled on his behalf for too low a sum can demand the balance of rightful payment from the killer's family upon reaching majority:

*Ef men ero eigi fulltiða eða af landi farnir þeir er bötr eigo at
taca. þa scolo þeir heimta sit at þeim er þeirra lut tóco. En ef
þa var scerðom bottom bøtt oc scolo veganda frædr þat giallda
er afurðe.* (*Grágás.* Konungsbók, 203)

[If men who have the right to atonement are not of
age or have left the country, then they are to claim
what is theirs from those who took their share. But
if atonement was made with reduced sums, then the
kinsmen of the killer are to pay what was deducted]
(*Grágás* 1980, 183).

No procedure for determining whether the amount of
compensation paid was a "reduced sum" is specified.[11] No matter:
the passage makes clear that the rights of a young man might
extend beyond the terms of a settlement reached by others on his
behalf. Upon attaining his majority, he may yet have a claim on
further compensation from the killer's family, if not in the form of
outlawry or blood vengeance then at least in silver.

Silver, however, will always be too low a sum in the mind of
someone. The sagas, at least occasionally, place a higher value on
blood than anything else, and some characters express offense at
being asked to accept monetary compensation for a slain kinsman,
as when Franmar challenges his brother's slayer to a duel in *Sturlaugs
saga starfsama*, saying *ek uil ei bera brodr minn j siodi* [I do not wish to
carry my brother in my purse] (*Sturlaugs saga starfsama* 1969, 15).[12]
Moreover, the laws favor the rights of an *aðili* who would prosecute
aggressively over those of one who would not. Among a group of
brothers with equal claim to a case, for example, the one who wants
to sue instead of settle prevails.

*Ef sumir vilia søkia en sumir sættaz á oc a sa at raða er
søkia vill til fullra laga* (*Grágás.* Konungsbók, 168;
compare *Grágás.* Staðarhólsbók, 335).

[If some want to prosecute and some to settle, then
whoever wants to prosecute to the limit of the law
is to have his way] (*Grágás* 1980, 156).

The limit of the law in a homicide case is, of course, full outlawry, as close to a death sentence as the system afforded. In this way, the laws skate close by valuing blood over silver.

Were we ignorant of the passage in *Baugatal* explicitly binding heirs, we might have expected a man newly come of age to be able to bring his own, independent suit against his father's killer – perhaps even to be within his rights to slay his father's killer had his guardians settled for anything less than blood vengeance. This is, of course, exactly what the language about heirs is meant to prevent, and without it minors would simply not be bound by settlements at all. This would have been a legal loophole through which all manner of deadly missiles would have flown. Of course the law is meant to close that gap. To that end, the laws of the Icelandic Commonwealth have endless provisions for how one individual may act on another's behalf, including on behalf of those without direct access to the legal system: women, the feebleminded, the infirm, and the insane, as well as minors. Officially, everyone can be bound by settlement because everyone has a legal representative of one kind or another. Minors, however, unlike women and the insane who never have full access to the law, grow up and achieve majority. There is no loophole here but a sort of soft spot. The laws here are a patch over a naturally weak point that, if the literary sources are any indication, remained a source of anxiety in the minds of who lived under those laws.

The laws offer a solution to the problem of the youth too young to swear: that is what laws are about. They are compendia of matter-of-fact *if this* … *then that*, where *that* provides clarity, structure, peace, a return to the order that preceded *this*. Lack—lack liquidated; complication—resolution. In literature, the same youth is a recurrent motif, a problem chewed over again and again in narratives that twist, swerve, and double back on the path from complication to resolution. Different literary genres articulate ideas in different ways. *Íslendingasögur* are grounded in a world in which human beings, as a rule, would just as soon not have their conflicts destroy society as a whole and act accordingly. The legendary-heroic sagas and poems can be tragic and antisocial: the pure heroic ideal trumps any interest in limiting violence. The mythology reads like the theory of which the sagas are praxis (Lindow 1994, 80). Myth itself is less about human motives and more about social and symbolic structures, and it explores the implications of those structures through resonant image and narrative. Some of the symbolic language of myth echoes across genres. The legal problem outlined in Snorri's version of the Baldr myth arises also in the legal masterpiece of *Brennu-Njáls saga* and in the catastrophic Burgundian material. A closer look at these shows that, whatever the letter of the law, the young man who could not be sworn was sufficiently urgent a problem in the social imagination of medieval Icelanders to be worthy of repeated treatment. It should therefore not be surprising that Snorri would have chosen to articulate it in abstract form using the heaviest conceptual machinery available to him, the matter of myth.

Finna þá alla, er gjǫld áttu at taka

The *Íslendingasögur* are full of boys whose youth makes them potential future threats because they cannot be compensated in the immediate wake of a slaying. The extreme case is the son not yet born, as in *Laxdæla saga* 55, where Helgi Harðbeinsson, having taken part in the slaying of Bolli, wipes his bloody sword on the robe Guðrún has tied around her waist. His companion Halldórr tells him this was poorly done and: *ek hygg þat … at undir þessu blæjuhorni búi minn hǫfuðsbani* [I think … that under the corner of this robe dwells my own killer] (ÍF V, 168). Halldórr has second sight (i.e., he is *skyggn*) and discerns that Guðrún is pregnant (*Laxdæla saga*, 165). Of course Guðrún will raise her son to avenge his father, and there is nothing that his killers can do in the present to prevent it, especially as Guðrún is careful to raise him at a safe distance. The young Helgi Þorgilsson of *Þorsteins saga hvíta* 7 (not yet Brodd-Helgi) will be a danger to his father's slayer when he is older, and his grandfather does not need second sight to know it. Wanting to prevent further violence, he sends the potential target out of the country. These boys are not overlooked, too slender to be considered threats. Rather, they are understood to be dangerous because they will not be young forever.

For a closer parallel to the Æsir's plan to avert Baldr's prophesied doom, a narrative that contrasts the class of those who can make a legal settlement with those too young to do so and thus dangerous, we can look to *Njáls saga*. In chapter 93, Njáll seeks to settle the slaying of Þráinn Sigfússon before it blows up into large-scale revenge killings. The gods dispatch Frigg to collect oaths; Njáll sends Þráinn's brother Ketill riding out in search of support, not to sue but to settle: *Var þat þá ráð þeira, at Ketill skyldi fara at finna þá alla, er gjǫld áttu at taka, ok koma á griðum* [It was their plan that Ketill should find everyone who had the right to compensation and bring them to truce] (*Brennu-Njáls saga*, 235). Frigg's task is greater than Ketill's, but the method and goals are the same. Both Frigg and Ketill identify the future expiators of violence, approach them, and ask them to grant the person or persons under threat a legal guarantee of peace. The same technical term is used: *grið*. Ketill can rely on *Baugatal* (or its equivalent) to determine who is due compensation for the death of his brother—they are also his potential avengers. Frigg knows only that her son is in danger from an unknown source and so must approach everyone and everything.

In *Njála* as in *Gylfaginning*, there is a loose end even after legal steps have been taken. His name is Hǫskuldr Þráinsson, the slain man's son, and in chapters 93 and 94 he is not yet nine years old.[13] Accordingly, he is too young to have been rounded up in the group assembled by Ketill in the chapter previous and too young to have taken *gjǫld* and sworn a settlement oath. Technically, Ketill should be the principal in the case, Hǫskuldr being underage and Ketill being the eldest of the surviving brothers, and the settlement he reaches with Njáll should bind Hǫskuldr as Ketill's ward and heir[14]. Nevertheless, it is clear from Njáll's actions that faith in the practical efficacy of the relevant formulas is limited.

While on a visit, Njáll calls the young Hǫskuldr to him and offers him a gold ring from his own finger as a gift. The boy accepts it. Only then does Njáll sound him out as to whether he considers himself aggrieved. *"Veiztú,"* segir Njáll, *"hvat fǫður þínum varð at bana?"* ["Do you know," says Njáll, "how your father was killed?"]. The boy answers: *"Veit ek, at Skarphéðinn vá hann, ok þurfu vit ekki á þat at minnask, er sætzk hefir á verit ok fullar bœtr hafa fyrir komit"* ["I know that Skarphéðinn killed him, but we don't need to talk about that, because a settlement has been made and full compensation paid"] (*Brennu-Njáls saga* 236). Njáll does not offer him compensatory silver labeled as such, but Hǫskuldr accepts the gift in the same spirit as his kinsmen accepted *bætr* and *gjǫld* from Njáll just lines above. The observant reader will note that only once the ring is on his own finger does the boy say that full compensation has been made. Njáll's gift is charming, certainly, but it is also a strategic attempt to compensate preemptively the adult Hǫskuldr who might consider Njáll's payment to have been too low a sum and decide to take sword in hand to reach more favorable terms. Njáll takes the extra step that Frigg does not: he approaches a minor to ask (guardedly and obliquely) for an assurance that future violence will not take place. The situation remains dangerous because the assurance of a child cannot be legally binding: he is too young to swear.

As it turns out, Hǫskuldr never goes after the Njálssons. Horribly, many chapters later, it is they who kill him. The full literary effect hinges on the audience's understanding that Hǫskuldr should be the point where the settlement breaks, and in Snorri's narrative, the peace breaks at the point corresponding to Hǫskuldr. Snorri's myth of *mistilteinn* articulates the theory that makes the art of *Njála* at this juncture possible.

Al eigi upp úlfhvelpinn

The forward-thinking Frigg and conciliatory Njáll have few counterparts in Old Norse heroic poetry and prose, the great men and women of the *fornǫld* not being much for moderation and settlement. The dangerous young son is a commonplace in the Burgundian material, but the proposed solutions to the problem are bloodier. Brynhildr plans Sigurðr's death, but she knows that his and Guðrún's young son will be dangerous to her when he is grown, and so in *Vǫlsunga saga* 32 she orders Gunnarr to kill them both:

Þú skalt láta bæði ríkit ok féit ok mik ... nema þú drepir Sigurð ok son hans. Al eigi upp úlfhvelpinn (Vǫlsunga saga, 190)

[You will lose your lands and riches and me ... unless you kill Sigurðr and his son. Do not raise the wolf cub.]

Brynhildr says much the same thing in *Sigurðarkviða in skamma* 12 (Neckel and Kuhn 1962, 203):

> *Lǫtum son fara*
> *feðr í sinni,*
> *skalat úlf ala*
> *ungan lengi;*
> *hvem verðr hǫlða*
> *hefnd léttari*
> *síðan til sátta*
> *at sonr lifit*

The first half of the verse is clear:

> Let the son go
> the same way as his father,
> do not raise
> a wolf cub for long;

The second half is vexed, and scholars differ as to whether it is easier to prevent revenge being taken if no son remains alive (Gering 1896, 229) or if the act of revenge comes to no one more naturally than to the son (Larrington 1999, 183, compare Hollander 1986, 254). There is general agreement on the overall sense of the lines, however: the son of a slain man will grow up to be bad news for those who did the slaying. Revenge is involved (*hefnd*) and settlement of grievances (*til sátta*).

The language of wolves, sons, and oaths is not specific to youngsters of the Vǫlsung clan. Brynhildr is worried about Sigurðr's son, but Sigurðr himself was warned by the valkyrie Sigrdrífa about such situations in the abstract (*Sd.* 35) (Neckel and Kuhn 1962, 192):

> *Þat ræð ek þér*
> *eitt tíunda,*
> *at þú trúir aldregi*
> *várum vargdropa,*
> *hverstu ert bróðrbani*
> *eða hafir þú feldan fǫðr;*
> *opt er úlfr í ungum syni*
> *þótt hann sé gulli gladdr*

> [I advise you on a tenth thing,
> that you never trust the oaths
> of an enemy's son (lit. "wolf-drop")
> whether you are the slayer of his brother
> or have felled his father.
> There is often a wolf in a young son,
> though he be gladdened by gold.]

The general nature of the advice strongly suggests that the young wolf is proverbial. The *vargr* in *vargdropi* has quasi-legal meanings to do with outlawry, but I agree with both (Sijmons and Gering 1931, 221) and (Boer 1922, II 199) that in this case we should read *vargdropi* as the offspring of a slain enemy rather than the son of an outlawed man, as (Hollander 240) and (Larrington 1999, 172) have it.[15] The legal meaning appears in *Grágás*, but lines 5 and 6 make clear the sense of the word here, whether or not they are themselves interpolated. Sijmons takes them as a helpful gloss for readers unclear on just this point (Sijmons 1906, 348). Sigrdrífa uses *vargr* again in stanza 23, there in a more obviously legal sense (Neckel and Kuhn 1962, 190):

> *Þat ræð ek þér annat,*
> *at þú eið ne sverir*
> *nema þann er saðr sé;*
> *grimmar símar*
> *ganga at tryggðrofi,*
> *armr er vára vargr.*

[I advise you on a second thing,
that you swear no oath
unless it be a true one;
ill fate follows
a breach of peace,
a wolf of oaths makes for a poor man.]

Vára vargr, which I render here as a "wolf of oaths," would appear to be a man guilty of breaking legal peace or *tryggð*, the equivalent, one would think, of the *griðbítr* ["peace-biter"] referred to in the *Baugatal* of *Grágás*—the animal imagery is striking. The similarity of the alliterating phrases *vára vargr* and *várar vargdropa* suggests that *vargr* might have had specific associations with oathbreaking. If so, those associations would only have amplified the sense that the oaths of an *ungr úlfr* would not be valid.

Brynhildr calls for the death of Sigurðr's young son. In st. 35, Sigrdrífa makes explicit that one might try other strategies when dealing with the loose end that can grow up into an avenger. Oaths might be taken; gifts might be made. A gift of gold is part of Njáll's strategy for dealing with Hǫskuldr. In the world of heroic legend, however, those strategies will fail. Sigrdrífa's advice expresses the pessimism that pervades the world of the Vǫlsungar and Niflungar. In *Njála*, the problem of the young son is used to set up the poignancy of Hǫskuldr's death. In the Vǫlsung material, it is an opportunity to engineer the climactic moment of horror when a woman orders the murder of a child. The effect is the more chilling because Brynhildr's act is not one of random bloodthirst. The audience familiar with the social and legal problem posed by boys too young to swear will be acutely aware of the pressures under which Brynhildr operates. The saga and the poem show society unraveling from the weak point: Brynhildr's solution is destructive of herself as a social female (who should probably not be harming children) and of the social contract in general (according to which children are off-target). As usual in the world of the Vǫlsungar, the actors' motives are perfectly understandable, but the consequences of their actions will drag everyone to their deaths.

Úlfinn fæddu Æsir heima

Symbolic language echoes across genre lines. As it happens, the dangerous young son appears in wolf form in the mythology as well: he is the most famous wolf in the mythology. When the Æsir learn from prophecies that Loki's son Fenrir will grow up to do them harm, they take him back to Ásgarðr and put Týr in charge of him: *Úlfinn fæddu Æsir heima* (*Gylf.* 32). But why raise the wolf at home? Lorenz, not to mention many of my students, thinks this is an odd thing to do (Lorenz 1984, 425), but he has the answer when he calls Týr a *Pflegevater* and *Ziehvater*. For Lorenz, reading Týr as a foster father would at least help make sense of why Fenrir would allow Týr to approach him with fetter in hand (Lorenz 1984, 426). In fact, the text supports our understanding the relationship between the Æsir as a whole and the wolf as fosterage. The verb is *fæða*, which can mean not only "to feed" and "to give birth to" but "to raise or foster." The last is the sense in which it appears in the Codex Regius redaction of *Grágás* when the word *lǫgfóstr* [legal fosterage] is defined:

> *Þat er lögfostr er maðr tecr við manne .viii. vetra gömlum eða yngra oc foðe til þes er hann er xvi. vetra gamall* (*Grágás.* Konungsbók, 161)

> [It is legal fosterage when an individual takes on a person eight years old or younger and raises (*fæða*) him until he is sixteen years old.]

Snorri chooses a legal term. He could have sounded another, closely related chord by using the verb *ala*, and a reader might then have heard an echo of the voice of Brynhildr: *skalat úlf ala ungan lengi* [do not raise the wolf cub for long]. Perhaps he is avoiding the sense of futility that association might bring. The legal term, on the other hand, might signal that the Æsir's actions are strategic and not without parallel in the world of humans.

Njáll has his own young wolf to deal with in the form of Hǫskuldr Þráinsson, and he does not rely on gold alone to turn him from future foe into enduring ally. He adopts him as a foster child, thereby weakening a blood kinship tie and creating a fictive one, all to change the allegiance of the foster child. [16] Njáll is lucky, we might say, that Hǫskuldr is young enough to foster though too young to swear.[17] He removes Hǫskuldr from an environment where he might be groomed to avenge his father on Njáll's sons and into one in which his ties and obligations to Njáll's family will be strengthened. The act is not merely, if even at all, one of atonement (Lönnroth 1976, 28), and it is not a triumph of his good will over his intellect (Einar Ól. Sveinsson 1971, 168). Rather, the adoption is an attempt to graft Hǫskuldr, if the reader will allow the metaphor for the time being, to the family tree. The graft takes: the chapter skips ahead to when the adult Hǫskuldr the other sons of Njáll are thick as thieves.

The Æsir attempt the same strategy in an analogous situation: Fenrir is Loki's son. One might protest that Loki is still alive and that the Æsir have not yet felled his father (*feldan fǫðr*), but mythological time is not simplistically linear, as in *Ls.* 28 where Loki appears simultaneously to threaten to kill Baldr and to boast of having done so already (Lindow 1997, 129). Perhaps Fenrir is already obliged to avenge the death of his father at Heimdallr's hand at Ragnarǫk. If so, he is a direct parallel to the young Hǫskuldr Þráinsson and the *vargdropi* of *Sigr.* 35. Though Fenrir is fed and fostered in Ásgarðr rather than Jǫtunheimar, the wolf sides with the giants at the end of time. The bonds with which the Æsir attempt to bind Fenrir—first the fictive kinship bond of fosterage that ought to bind him to them and then literal *bǫnd*[18]—will not hold. The myth is a straightforward playing-out of the failure of the adoption strategy.

Why should the Æsir not have killed Fenrir at the outset? Gangleri asks this very question, and Hár gives the frustrating answer that the Æsir did not want to sully their sacred place of truce (*griðstaðir*) with his blood (*Gylf.* 34). If the wolf is like a boy who might be fostered, then perhaps still more cultural norms visible in the laws would have been understood to apply. A boy under twelve (already over the age at which he might be fostered out) is not only unable to bind himself to a settlement with oaths, but for the present he is off target. Should he attack you, you are to dodge and parry without hurting him:

> *a maðr at fœra hann or havfði ser sva sem þa mundi ef hann vœre fóstri eða faþir* (*Grágás*. Staðarhólsbók, 333)

[one should fend him off as one would if he were one's foster-father or father][19]

You are to behave, perversely, as if you had taken an oath not to harm him—a settlement oath, even, for the *Tryggðamál* specifies that two men who have settled a dispute between them are to treat each other thenceforth *sem frœndr en eigi sem fiandr* [as family and not as enemies](*Grágás*. Konungsbók, 206; *Grágás* 1980, 184). Any minor who swings at your head is under the protection of the law, whereas you yourself are bound.

Another answer to the question of why the Æsir do not kill Fenrir is more symbolic than legal: he is the wolf, and *oft er úlfr í ungum syni*. Fostering him literalizes the poetic commonplace attached to the dangerous young sons of enemies. There is also the possibility that it is Hǫskuldr and the *vargdropi* who resemble him and not the other way around. Fenrir might be the quintessential wolf raised at home that all orphaned sons resemble. Whichever way the arrow points (and I tend to imagine such arrows as circular), I cannot help but see a connection between the *úlfr* from whom Brynhildr and Sigrdrífa foresee a threat and Fenrisúlfr whom the Æsir raise despite prophecies. Whatever else Fenrir's story is about, it is also about how another strategy for dealing with the dangerous young son may fail.

The legal system of Commonwealth Iceland was by no means perfect—no such system is. It could not deal with kinslaying, for example, for when the class of potential expiators collapses with the class of potential targets, society collapses as well. That this worried medieval Icelanders (and that they worried it) is signaled throughout the literature and, pointedly and heartbreakingly, in the Baldr complex. Neither do all bonds made with oaths hold. Blood-brotherhood, for example, is a fictive kin tie forged between unrelated individuals of the same sex and roughly equal status, adult men of legal majority. But blood-brotherhood between Óðinn and Loki will not save the world of men and gods from a crashing descent into flood and fire (Lindow 1994, 64). Settlement oaths, in their way, make kin of non-kin inasmuch as the parties are sent away having agreed to treat each other thenceforth as *frændr*, but only adult men of legal majority can enter into such settlements. The little slice of the Baldr myth that is Snorri's tale of *mistilteinn* points us to the danger posed by a man not yet of legal age in the context of settlements and points onward to articulations of potential solutions to the problem across Old Norse literature. The young son from whom future violence is easily foreseeable can only be dealt with in one of three ways, none of them wholly satisfactory: slaying, fosterage, and legal settlement. *Íslendingsögur* frequently demonstrate the consequences of no action, which is that the young son takes revenge once grown: Vésteinn's sons return to kill their father's (likely) slayer in *Gísla saga*, and Bolli's unborn son, once grown, does similarly in *Laxdæla*. *Njáls saga* spins art from the reader's expectations, articulated in heroic poetry and embodied by Fenrir, that neither settlement speeches nor fostering will avail. In the world of dragon slayers and shield maidens, Brynhildr confronts us with the horror of the extreme strategy of slaying a helpless child. That way lies the road to total social destruction. Youth, the only quality Snorri assigns to the deadly *mistilteinn*, is the quality that links the sources of danger across these genres. Law holds out hope, an ideal practical structure for containing the threat posed by a young man who may yet commit violence but against whom no violence can be committed. In the world of men, any bereaved boy will have a guardian somewhere who can settle on his behalf. Snorri's narrative of the *mistilteinn*, however, presents the legal problem in its most abstract and insoluble form. There are no kin and no *aðili*, and even after legal steps are taken, the only remaining potential source of the prophesied and thus inevitable danger is too young to swear. Just as Þokk's refusal to cry Baldr out of Hel shows that "grief can never be universal" (Lindow 1997, 130), the legal exception represented by *mistilteinn* shows that settlement can never be unanimous. If this reading is correct, it adds another dimension to the Baldr complex—already deeply concerned with another flaw in the legal system—and it increases our appreciation of Snorri's skill with the weighty and resonant stuff of myth. My hope, too, is

that it go some way towards solving the conundrum of the *mistilteinn*
in Norse myth, if only in Snorri's *Edda*.

Mistilteinn

So far, I have left an old and obvious question unexamined. Did
Snorri picture *mistilteinn* as we do mistletoe? Did he have in mind a
little plant that made its home in the branches of trees, relying on
the roots of its host for any connection to the ground and sprouting
leaves and flowers quite unlike those around it? If we are to make
the actual nature of mistletoe part of our interpretation of Snorri's
version of the myth, he would have had to. He might have: the
debate on this point has been lengthy and inconclusive. If we
entertain, for a moment, the possibility that he did, it is tempting to
imagine him musing on the odd little plant in its arboreal context.
Trees appear frequently in Old Norse sources as symbols of
families, especially in dreams.[20] They appear in *Heimskringla* in
Magnússona saga 25 and *Hálfdanar saga svarta* 6, where different
branches stand for offspring and descendants of different natures.
Kennings, too, attest to the age of this image: *ættar ask*(r) [ash of
lineage] and *kynvið kvánar minnar* [kin-branch of my wife], both in
Egill's *Sonatorrek* (*Egils saga Skalla-Grímssonar*, 255). It is tempting to
imagine Snorri, creative etymologist that he was, rolling the word
viðarteinungr over in his mind, now as *viðar-teinungr* [woody stalk] and
now as *viðartein(n)-ungr* [young woody stick?].[21] It is tempting to
imagine him imagining mistletoe as the branch sprung from the
same root but unlike its brothers or even as the graft that does not
take—pondering this and thinking of Fenrir, the foster son who
bites the proverbial hand clean off his foster father's arm, and
thinking of Loki, numbered among the Æsir but not, in the end, of
them. These were beings of unclear kinship, and dangerous despite
oaths sworn and *grið* given. Snorri might have known mistletoe. I do
not believe we can be certain. But if he did not, then, in the context
of his writing, the biology of the plant whose name we use to
translate his word *mistilteinn* is, at least, a fantastic and fitting
coincidence.

Notes

1 The epiphany that inspired this essay found me in 1998, sitting in the Runearkivet in Oslo while working on something completely different. I had a new M.A. from the University of California, Berkeley, and I was headed into the Ph.D. program with John Lindow as my primary advisor. I knew instantly that the only proper venue for an exploration of the idea would be a *festschrift* in his honor. It is with great pleasure that I am finally able to give it its due in just that context.

2 Lindow takes the latter approach, but says little of the mistletoe, more-or-less satisfied with the leafy little parasite as the sort of uncategorizable thing to which symbolic systems frequently attribute great power (Lindow 1997, 61). Compare (Clunies Ross 1994, 274). For references to the truly vast scholarship on all things Baldr, see (Lorenz 1984), (Lindow 1997), and (Liberman 2004).

3 For the record, Snorri's *mistilteinn* is a woody stalk (*viðarteinungr*) pulled up by Loki, a wand (*vǫndr*) pressed into the hand of Hǫðr and shot through Baldr. There is perhaps a hint of irony when the *vǫndr* pierces Baldr's body, for though *vǫndr* is common enough in sword kennings, "when a sword bites 'no better than a *vǫndr*' … proverbial usage seems close at hand" (Lindow 1997, 65; Fritzner 1973 [1883-96], III 985). Still, if Snorri understands a *vǫndr* to be an unlikely murder weapon, he does not dwell on it. The notion of *mistilteinn* having a deceptive appearance is mostly in the poetic sources; noted by (Clunies Ross 1994, 271n39).

4 The formula *fyrir orði ok eiði* appears multiple times in the laws of both medieval Iceland and medieval Norway with verbs like *ráða* and *hyggja*; for examples see the Dictionary of Old Norse Prose (Degnbol 1989). It frequently appears, along with *fulltíða* [of legal majority] in lists of competencies and qualities required of a man to serve in on or another legal role.

5 Lindow wonders if Frigg's collection of the oaths is strange, if we understand those oaths to belong to a legal sphere in which women do not normally act (Lindow 1997, 49). It would not be the first violation of gender roles in Baldr's immediate family, and it is difficult to imagine Óðinn, unmanly fomenter of strife that he is, rising to this occasion. Further, that a supernatural female might occasionally govern oath-taking is not a foreign concept to Snorri, since he includes the goddess Vár among the Ásynjur (*Gylf.* 35) who supposedly has responsibility for men's

oaths (*eiðir manna*). That she may be little more than Snorri's own extrapolation of a *heiti* in *Þrymskviða* does no violence to an argument primarily about Snorri's version of the myth.

[6] See Holtsmark (1964, 72-74) for variant readings.

[7] Baldr's affinities extend to his son, Forseti, who lives at Glitnir – *dómstaðr beztr með guðum ok mǫnnum* – all parties who come to him with trouble leave at peace with each other (*sáttir*) (Faulkes 2005, 33-34)

[8] Holtsmark (1964, 74) has explored this at somewhat greater length, connecting Baldr with *Kristus judex*.

[9] Certainly, it is a weird instance of dumbshow entertainment from a god one might have expected to have offered more typically verbal *skemtun* (Lindow 1997, 51).

[10] Very slightly revised from the translation in (*Grágás* 1980, 185).

[11] Compare the land claims section (*Landbrigðapáttr*), where we learn that if the guardian of a young man not yet of age to have claimed his property sells the land for anything less than the best price, the entire transaction is void and the land reverts (*Grágás*. Konungsbók, 78; *Grágás* 1980, 99). He who sold it can be sued by both the man he sold to and his own ward.

[12] Þorsteinn hvíti uses the same words in his own saga in refusing self-judgment: *kvazk eigi vilja bera son sinn, Þorgils, í sjóði* (*Þorsteins saga hvíta*, 17). This example is complicated, as Þorsteinn accepts service from his son's killer, Þorsteinn fagri, instead of either silver or blood, and later hustles him out of the country to save him from being killed by his grandson (Brodd)-Helgi, who is coming into an age at which he could avenge his father.

[13] The text does not specify Hǫskuldr's age, but he cannot be older than eight here, for he is fostered out in the same chapter, and boys nine and older are too old for fosterage, as per Grágás (*Grágás*. Konungsbók, 161; *Grágás* 1980, 151).

[14] Hǫskuldr is an heir: Staðarhólsbók's *Erfðapáttr* specifies that a dead man's brother's son may inherit from him, though he is seventeenth in line to do so (*Grágás*. Staðarhólsbók, 64). Compare *Arfapáttr* in Codex Regius (*Grágás*. Konungsbók, 219).

[15] It amounts to the same thing for the person or persons responsible for having the father outlawed. Revenge is due them as well.

[16] Lindow mentions fosterage exactly as a strategy for "chang[ing] the realities of kin reckoning" (Lindow 1994, 80). Miller notes the complexity of "the affective ties within the Icelandic farmhouse," also in the context of discussing fosterage (Miller 1990, 124). Njáll successfully creates affective ties by adopting Hǫskuldr: Njáll loves Hǫskuldr as least as much as he does his own sons; and Hǫskuldr's affectation for his foster-brothers and—father make him resistant to Mǫrðr's lies.

[17] The particulars of Njáll's pan for making it happen are complex, as is often the case with Njáll. After he and Ketill have brokered a settlement with those legally due compensation for the slaying of Þráinn, Njáll rides to Mǫrk and confers with Ketill. The reader is left to put together that when Ketill then rides to Þorgerðr, he does so on Njáll's instructions. Ketill offers to foster Hǫskuldr. He loved his brother greatly, he tells Þorgerðr, and wants to show it in this way. Nothing explicit is said about raising the boy to seek revenge for his father's death, but mentioning his fraternal affection is suggestive without being a promise – perhaps exactly the sort of equivocal pronouncement a clever lawyer like Njáll might formulate. In any event, Þorgerðr immediately agrees to let Ketill foster her son. Not until Ketill is Hǫskuldr's legal guardian does Njáll approach the boy, first with gold ring in hand and then with the offer of fosterage. The boy accepts. Njáll's strategy eliminates the possibility that Þorgerðr might refuse his offer to foster her son, which after all he probably does more out of love for his own sons than for Þráinn.

[18] Admittedly, Snorri uses the word *fjǫtr* [fetter] more than *band* [band or bond] here. Play on physical bonds and kinship bond in the mythology has been discussed recently by (Tranum Kristensen 2007).

[19] *Fóstri* can mean either foster son or foster father. I have chosen foster father here, both for the parallelism and because a law that explained how one would treat a minor in terms of how one would treat another minor seems less than helpful.

[20] Georgia Dunham Kelchner lists several examples of trees or other plants standing for the family and comments that the tree is the most common symbol of descent in dreams (Kelchner 1935, 56-61).

[21] Such play would parallel that implicit in *Rígspula*, in which the name *Konr ungr* [Konr the young], a young man who seems destined to rule, is obviously derived from *konungr* [king]. In both cases, a compound is either made or broken with the subtraction or addition of a nominative singular masculine ending on the first element.

Óðinn, Þórr and Freyr:
Functions and Relations

Jens Peter Schjødt

This article will deal with a certain aspect of Old Norse mythology, namely the functional relations between the three mightiest gods in the pantheon, Óðinn, Þórr and Freyr. The functions of these three gods apparently overlap, even though the gods themselves, at the same time, seem to be very different, both from a psychological point of view, and from their roles in the various myths in which they play a role.

Speaking of functions of the various gods most scholars within the Old Norse field will get associations to the theories of Georges Dumézil. The great French mythologist has no doubt had an enormous impact for the research within Scandinavian mythology, both because he inspired a great many scholars, but also because even many more were provoked by his theories, and did not accept them, arguing that they were 'wrong'.[1] However, no matter whether the individual scholar belongs to the first or the second of these categories, he or she has to take a position on his theories; and thus a lot of discussions, new perspectives and new theorising have taken place as a consequence of Dumézil's work. It is definitely not my intention here to go through the theories of Dumézil. This has been done many times, also by myself (Lundager Jensen & Schjødt 1994). Neither is it the purpose here to judge whether his 'tri-functional' or tripartite theory is right or wrong. The way Dumézil will be 'used' here is simply as a platform from where I shall attempt to demonstrate that, although – when we are dealing with the Scandinavian variant of the tripartite structure – the three functions sometimes overlap and do not seem to fit too well into the Indo-European structure, the division into sovereignty, war, and fertility is still an important classificatory tool and may help to

illuminate some questions that can be hard to grasp, in any other
way.

When we are dealing with the sources for Scandinavian
mythology, everybody who is the least acquainted with the subject,
will know that we are facing all sorts of source critical problems: for
many of the sources we do not know their date of composition,
whereas for others we know with certainty that they are composed
more than two centuries after the religion, and hence the
mythology,[2] was substituted by another, namely Christianity; we do
not know, either, to which extent information given in a certain
source can also be applied to areas of Scandinavia far from the
place of composition, since we often have only one version of a
myth, from one single source. Further, it is clear that the
information that we do have, whether reliable or not, constitutes
only a minor part of the various mythic traditions that must have
existed once as 'a living tradition'. This can be seen from the fact
that in several places we have hints of myths that we do not know
from other sources. Other problems are also at stake, but those
mentioned will suffice to show how complicated it is to
'reconstruct' a pre-Christian Scandinavian mythology.

The obvious analogy to the field of problems would be a jigsaw
puzzle where we have only a small number of pieces, and the pieces
that we do have do not constitute a coherent picture. Some of them
may not even belong to the original picture, although we cannot tell
exactly which. There are parts of various motifs, but not enough to
give us an idea of the overall picture. Unless we have some idea of
what that overall picture would have been like, it would make no
sense to try to reconstruct the puzzle. On the other hand, if we do
recognize in the various pieces that are at hand some patterns that
we do know from other jig-saw puzzles, from which we have more
pieces, it may make sense to try to reconstruct our own along the
same lines using the others for comparison. This may turn out to be
wrong, because our own pieces simply cannot be placed in
positions where they necessarily fit together, or it may prove to
make sense, since most of the individual pieces can be placed in
positions that our better-preserved puzzle would suggest. Of course
we will never know whether our reconstruction is "right," but it

makes good sense to suppose so, until someone, later on, suggests another solution, perhaps inspired by another comparison, which can place even more pieces in meaningful positions. Thus our reconstruction makes sense, if we have chosen our parallel carefully: it must be a jig-saw puzzle from the same period, perhaps made by the same manufacturer, and at least in the same style.

If we are going to reconstruct Old Norse mythology we are, therefore, somewhat in the same position as our puzzle maker: the information from the extant sources do not constitute the whole picture, and we do not know whether some of the picture can be attributed to Christian ideas of the Middle Ages. The only way we can make sense of these pieces of information is by having an idea beforehand of how the picture might have been. And this idea must by necessity come from comparative material, i.e. religions and mythologies that are comparable in regard to material and occupational level, extent of religious centralization, social stratification, etc. It is in this light I prefer to see the general theories of Dumézil, and from this perspective I believe he is very useful. This does not mean that the picture he delivers cannot (and should not) be criticized and perhaps altered, but it certainly should be taken into consideration. It could turn out that it does not make sense, or maybe it does. The only way to find out is by trying.

Now, this may sound as if nobody has ever applied the Dumézilian theoretical framework to Scandinavian mythology which is, of course, not correct, for Dumézil himself and many who may more or less be labeled his disciples, have for decades been occupied with the pre-Christian mythology of Scandinavia. And as mentioned, it has been evaluated in very different ways by different scholars. Personally I think that Dumézil's model has proved its value in relation to Scandinavia. It certainly does not explain everything which was never maintained by Dumézil, either, but it does explain something. In that sense, as was stated above, it is neither right, nor wrong, but it makes sense. However, there are some 'pieces' which are hard to make compatible with the tripartite ideology, as it was formulated by Dumézil. And one of these pieces is exactly the relation between the three gods mentioned before, on the one hand, and on the other hand the relation between this relation and the parallel relation in the tripartite ideology.[3]

Dumézil's view of the gods Óðinn, Þórr and Freyr in the tripartite scheme and some related problems

Dumézil has dealt with these three gods in many connections, and naturally it did not escape him, that the division of the three functions in the North was not exactly parallel to most other Indo-European cultures, and thus not to the model, as it 'ought to be'. This is obvious from much of the information in the sources, but the problem is perhaps expressed most clearly in Adam of Bremen's account of the three gods in Uppsala.[4] Adam says (IV, 26-27):

> 26 In hoc templo……..statuas trium deorum venerator populus, itaut potentissimus eorum Thor in medio solium habeat triclinio; hinc et inde locum possident Wodan et Fricco. Quorum significations eiusmodi sunt: 'Thor', inquiunt, 'presidet in aere, qui tonitrus et fulmina, ventos ymbresque, serena et fruges gubernat. Alter Wodan, id est furor, bella gerit hommique ministrant virtutem contra inimicos. Tercius est Fricco, pacem voluptatemque largiens mortalibus'. Cuius etiam simulacrum fingent cum ingenti priapo. Wodanem vero sculpunt armatum, sicut nostril Martem solent; Thor autem cum sceptro Iovem simulare videtur…

> 27 Omnibus itaque diis suis attributos habent sacerdotes, qui sacrificial populi offerant. Si pestis et fames imminet, Thor ydolo lybatur, si bellum, Wodani, si nuptiae celebrandae sunt, Fricconi…
> (Lund 1978, 47-9).

> [In this temple…the people worship the statues of three gods in such wise that the mightiest of them, Thor, occupies a throne in the middle of the chamber; Wotan and Frikko have places on either side. The significance of these gods is as follows:

> Thor, they say, presides over the air, which governs the thunder and lightning, the winds and rains, fair weather and crops. The other, Wotan – that is the Furious – carries on war and imparts to man strength against his enemies. The third is Frikko, who bestows peace and pleasure on mortals. His likeness, too, they fashion with an immense phallus. But Wotan they chisel armed, as our people are wont to represent Mars. Thor with his sceptre apparently resembles Jove...]

> [For all their gods there are appointed priests to offer sacrifices for the people. If plague and famine threaten, a libation is poured to the idol Thor, if war, to Wotan, if marriages are to be celebrated, to Frikko...] (Tschan 2002, 207-8)

From this it seems quite clear that the three gods cannot in any easy way be classified according to the Dumézilian functions. The second and third functions are present, but immediately there seems to be no hint to anything connected to the first function. Óðinn (Wodan), representing the magical aspect of the first function, according to Dumézil, is clearly portrayed as a god of war: it is in connection with the threatening of war he will receive sacrifices, and his attribute is a weapon, probably a spear or a lance. This means that according to the tripartite ideology, he should be a second function figure. And all through the mythological texts, we see that war and warriors are related to Óðinn (cf. Schjødt 2007) in various ways. Þórr on the other hand is portrayed exclusively as a god of agriculture and fertility. Although he is mentioned as the mightiest of the three gods, he is thus clearly related to neither the first nor the second function. Fricco, or Freyr,[5] also seems to be a god of fertility, but with a clear twist towards sexuality, as opposed to the agricultural aspect that we saw in Þórr.

So how is this description, which is probably the most precise characteristic, but, as mentioned, far from the only one relating these functions of the three gods, to be seen from the perspective of the Dumézilian tripartite scheme? Almost as a refutation, most people would probably mean. On the other hand, in most of the Old Norse sources, apart from Óðinn's obvious connections to war, it is at least just as obvious that he is also connected to magic and numinous knowledge, and thus seems to be a 'traditional' first function god.[6] And similarly with Þórr: apart from his relation to the crops, the majority of myths in which he is a main character, are concerned with – perhaps not war – but fighting. He is constantly going to giant land to kill giants, and the most auspicious characteristic of Þórr is definitely his physical strength. So, judged from many - probably the majority - of the sources, it makes good sense to connect Óðinn and Þórr, respectively, to the first and the second functions. But what can we do with Adam's description and the other sources connecting the two gods with war and fertility, respectively?

As mentioned, Dumézil was naturally aware of the problem, and he tried to solve it in various ways, the main idea concerning Óðinn being that the role of war in Germanic society had become more important than in earlier Indo-European cultures (Dumézil 1971, 88). Concerning Þórr his main argument was that the god's fertility aspect was a sort of 'by-product', when he was going through the air on his way to fight giants, swinging his hammer, he would cause thunder and lightning, and eventually rain (Dumézil 1959, 117). This may all be true, although it is hard to see exactly why the Germanic peoples were more occupied with war than for instance the Romans who were almost constantly at war, and the Celts fighting the Romans for centuries, and probably many other Indo-European peoples who fought for new land and afterwards had to defend it. Anyway, Dumézil's explanation of this *glissement* that appears to have taken place in Scandinavia (and perhaps in the whole of the Germanic area) is purely historical and linked to historical events. But it seems natural in the light of the undoubtedly structural framework within which Dumézil is most often working to ask whether these possible historical explanations could also be viewed from a structural point of view. Thus, the hypothesis to be investigated here is simply whether it is possible to integrate this *glissement* (which was perhaps not a *glissement* after all) into such a structural framework. This may be more or less in contradiction to the way Dumézil himself saw it, although I am not so sure of that, and under all circumstances it must be the aim of any interpretation to explain more, and more adequately than has been done before, and this is exactly what I believe is the case with the following analysis.

My main argument is that what we are facing is not a *glissement* but a consequent overlap of the three gods in regard of functions, this overlap being structurally productive and not only redundant, as we shall see below. And further the structure that can be analyzed has a sort of 'family relationship' to the three functions of Dumézil, it is just that there are two gods representing each of the three functions in various ways as we shall see. I will thus analyze the functional overlap between the three 'couples' Þórr and Freyr, Óðinn and Þórr, and Óðinn and Freyr.

Fertility and Pleasure: Þórr and Freyr

Let us start with one of the two problems that we meet in Adam's description, from the bottom of the scheme, so to speak. If Adam is right, why is it, then, that there seems to be two gods of fertility in Uppsala, and probably in the whole of Scandinavia? Apart from Adam we do have other sources indicating that Freyr was a god of fertility. The myth of Freyr and Gerðr, related in *Skírnismál* and by Snorri has, since Magnus Olsen (1909), been viewed as evidence of rituals concerned with fertility rituals.[7] The story, related in *Gunnars þáttr helmings*, in which Freyr, together with a priestess, drives around in a wagon to different landscapes in Sweden, although it is definitely young in the version we have (from *Fláteyjarbók*), seems to go back to old traditions, not least because of similar stories related about Frotho by Saxo (Friis-Jensen 2005, 258-60) and Nerthus by Tacitus (Bruun & Lund 1974, 72), Frotho probably being identical with Freyr (cf. Schier 1968) and Nerthus, although not a variant of Freyr, still a representative of the Vanir gods. The importance of this driving around lies apparently in the idea that the god has to be present in the landscapes or in the fields to which he is supposed to distribute his power. As has been suggested by several scholars (e.g. Ström 1983; Steinsland 1991, 313; North 1997, 271; Røthe 2010, 19-20) the god (and the god-king) were supposed to fertilize the land which was thought of as their female counterpart during a ritual that included some kind of *hieros gamos.* [8] In other words the god or his incarnation has to go to the centres of the various landscapes to perform an act with sexual connotations which secures fertility. The incest theme, related in *Ynglinga saga* chap. 4 and hinted at in *Lokasenna* st. 32 also supports the fertility theme in connection with this god.[9] And the same applies when we take into consideration the way his sister Freyja is portrayed. She is constantly related to sexuality which in itself would indicate that her brother who is probably a twin has the same characteristics. The ritual in which the fertility god is driven around also indicates that he is a god who at certain ritual occasions lives among the mortals.

Thus it seems as if the portrait Adam relates of Freyr is in agreement with the evidence that we have from the West Norse sources: Freyr is connected to fertility, especially the sexual aspect of it, because it is through sex he bestows fertility; and we could add that this relation is established in a metaphorical way: Just like sexual relations will produce fertility, the crops will flourish when it is fertilized by the rain. So Freyr and the woman (Gerðr or some priestess) are related in the same way as the fertilizing power of the rain is to the land. Further it seems as if Freyr is characterized as a non-warrior; there are hardly any myths in which he fights with arms (although he does fight in Ragnarǫk like all the gods); and this characterization as a non-warrior seems to be emphasized, as Snorri tells us that he had to fight the giant Beli with an antler (Faulkes 2005, 31): he is not a warrior with a proper warrior outfit. This incident may also be related to Saxo's version of the death of Frotho who is killed by the horn of a sea cow (Friis-Jensen 2005, 258). Saxo himself noted in this connection that this was a kind of disgraceful death, or in other words, not the death of a true warrior.

Looking at Þórr we get quite a different picture. This god is hardly ever involved in anything that has to do with sexuality, so whatever his relation is to fertility, it is not a matter of sexuality. As Dumézil maintained it seems rather to be a function of his fighting. Now, fighting is in some way the opposite of sexuality: whereas fighting produces death, sexuality produces life. But how can death be associated with fertility, then? If we imagine a religion like that of the pre-Christian in which spirits of all kinds (*vættir, dísir, álfar* etc.), good and evil, were part of nature, everything outstanding, or just unusual, whether in a positive or a negative way would be ascribed to such powers. The world was basically good because there existed a kind of order (cosmos) since there was a sort of contract between this and the other world, between humans and gods, manifested in the rituals,[10] and among them rituals with a sexual content in which, as we saw, Freyr probably did play an important role. A bad happening would therefore logically be ascribed to spirits that would ruin that order and create chaos. In the mythological language of Scandinavia such beings could be called giants.[11] They were probably imagined in many different and unspecific ways, but there can be no doubt that the knowledge that threatening spirits did exist was part of the pre-Christian worldview, as it is in all religions. These spirits had to be fought with all means, but since they are representatives of another world with powers that are beyond those of men, it would be a necessity to invoke strong powers from the Other world to fight such negative forces. And it is in this connection that we must view Þórr: he is fighting to protect the cosmos.

In that sense he is to a much lesser extent an ambiguous figure from an ethical perspective, than is Óðinn, and probably also Freyr. Both of these gods have certain functions which they have to fulfill, but they are not clearly positive or negative. Óðinn, for instance, like political leaders, sometimes has to do things which, from a moral and ethical perspective, are problematic, in order to fulfill his overall function to which we shall return. As an example his use of *seiðr* can be mentioned. As far as we can judge from the sources this kind of sorcery was not accepted as an art performed by men, as we are told in *Ynglinga saga* chap. 7 (Bjarni Aðalbjarnarson 1979, 19), but nevertheless, this is exactly what Óðinn does when he must create an avenger for the murder of Baldr, as is related by Kormákr (Finnur Jónsson 1908, 69): In order to secure success in the more important matter, he has to do things that should not be performed even by men from the lowest strata of society. And the same applies to Freyr in his wooing of Gerðr in *Skírnismál* (although through Skírnir): he threatens her with magical means to accept his proposal. Even if we do not know the ethical standards of the pre-Christian period in any detail, these sort of threats were probably not accepted during an act of wooing. But they were necessary in order that the more important function could be fulfilled, i.e. the fertility of the land, and fertility in general. This sort of ambiguity is hardly ever seen by Þórr who is always on the side of cosmos.[12] And this means that even if Þórr kills, he kills to prevent negative forces from giant land from creating chaos in the world of humans, including ruining the crops. He thus kills to secure life. In my opinion this is the perspective from which we primarily have to understand Þórr as a god of fertility: he does not actively take part in the creation of fertility, but he is the defender of fertility, just as he is the defender of everything else that represents the cosmic order.[13] And he is a great defender because he is a great warrior, possessing the mightiest weapon of all, the hammer Mjǫlnir. Further, the fights of Þórr take place in the cosmic sphere, as we will return to in the next section.

If this analysis is accepted, it seems as if we have a set of oppositional pairs analogous to the two gods Þórr and Freyr in their relation to fertility. As we saw the one kills, while the other is having sex; while sexuality is almost[14] absent in the Þórr-myths, fighting is almost absent in the Freyr-myths; Þórr is the defender of order which is the prerequisite for having fertility, whereas Freyr is the aggressive creator of fertility; Þórr works on the periphery (preventing evil forces from coming in), while Freyr is in the center, maybe expressed in a kind of *hieros gamos* ritual in various sacred places or otherwise.

War and Fighting: Óðinn and Þórr[15]

The next function to be treated here is Dumézil's second function, that of war. As we saw, both Adam of Bremen and many other sources clearly indicate that Óðinn is the god to whom the Scandinavians turned in connection with war. This is not to deny that Þórr could be invoked here, too, which may be indicated by some of the European chroniclers (cf. Dumézil 1959, 115), but these sources do not tell in any detail of how this happened. Therefore it seems reasonable, or at least possible, to explain such invocations in accordance with the above mentioned function of

Þórr: as the defender of right order,[16] and not necessarily because he was a god of war, specifically. The right order must here be understood as 'the natural order', and so Þórr seems to be connected to 'nature' in its broadest sense.

Like Freyr, Óðinn himself does not usually fight mythological battles; in fact he only fights on two occasions: in the first war of the world, where he throws his spear across the enemy army consisting of the Vanir (*Vǫluspá* 24), and in the last war, Ragnarǫk, where Fenrir devours him. Otherwise Óðinn's role in war and fighting is not physical but rather mental, just like his connection to natural phenomena, such as the wind and the sea, which, according to Snorri, he calms with words, i.e. a kind of magical or mental activity. In relation to war it is Óðinn's role to bring warriors into ecstasy and equip them with supernatural abilities, and to advise the military leaders on deployment of troops and strategy. Therefore such strategic teaching is almost always directed at rulers,[17] and it is therefore usually armies or groups of warriors connected to kings, such as *berserkir* or *úlfheðnar* (cf. Schjødt 2007) who benefit from Óðinn's help, such as we shall see below. Thus, besides the affiliation to the mental side of war, Óðinn is also a representative of the *collective* aspect of the war: the warrior bands, the existence of which has been demonstrated by many scholars (Weiser 1927, Höfler 1934, Kershaw 2000, Røthe 2010, 33-62), and the kings who are by definition representatives of the people. It must, however, also be emphasized that Óðinn, as we just saw, is not a mythological warrior. He does not participate in cosmic battles, except for the two just mentioned, whereas he is often present on the battlefield when human kings and armies are fighting, most often in order to take 'home' his chosen men to Valhöll (for instance in relation to Haraldr Hilditǫnn and Sigmundr, cf. note 17 above). He is thus not, like Þórr, a defender of the natural order, and thus certainly not a 'nature deity'; his enemies are clearly a product of the 'cultural' order, i.e. they are defined by the society, most often represented by the king, to whom, as we shall see in the next section, he has a special relationship. Finally it is worth mentioning that the heroes that are supported by Óðinn are not in any way 'better' from an ethical point of view than are their opponents. They may be greater warriors, but there is no evidence that there ever was an idea of fighting for a higher moral course. The reason why Óðinn supports some kings and warriors and not some others seems to be that they 'belong' to him, either because he is seen as their first ancestor, or because they are initiated to him (Schjødt 2007), but they are certainly not chosen because of particular moral standards. This is probably what is emphasized in *Grímnismál* in the conflict between Agnarr and Geirrøðr, maybe, as Jere Fleck has suggested, as a part of exactly an initiation ritual (Fleck 1970). We thus may speak of a kind of 'moral indifference'.

Þórr, on the other hand, usually fights singly. He may be accompanied by Þjálfi or Loki, but the physical fighting itself is done by Þórr alone. Further, the majority of the narratives in which Þórr is the main actor describe his fights against giants and beings of every kind representing chaos, and they are, therefore, purely mythological. There is also, as we just saw, a clear distinction in the manifestation of power: Óðinn participates in fights through mental means, while Þórr is explicitly physical. As was noticed above Þórr is also in opposition to Óðinn in regard to the ethical opposition positive vs. negative. He is always and unambiguously on the side of the 'good guys' as the defender of the 'natural' order.

Thus we get the oppositional pairs collective vs. individualistic, intellectual power vs. physical power, earthly setting vs. cosmic setting and 'moral' indifference vs. 'moral' actions. In addition there is one other, and I believe important, difference, namely offensive versus defensive. These terms require some explanation. On the one hand it is obvious that Óðinn can also be called upon, if war threatens from abroad; on the other hand Þórr usually travels to the lands of the giants in order to fight them. In the greater context, however, the constellations in which Óðinn participates are *potentially* offensive. If his chosen ruler wins he can subjugate new lands and thus do what any good king should be able to do, namely gain new riches for the people as a collective. Óðinn is thus the helper of the king (as representative of the people), and thus of the world, understood as an ethnic or social unity. By contrast Þórr's wars against the giants are always elements in the defence against potential threats to the world, understood as cosmos.[18] From that opposition we may also see the periphery-centre opposition, as Þórr defends against intruders from outside, whereas Óðinn is in the political as well as the religious centre (the kingly halls). Further, as was mentioned, it seems as if we can also discern an opposition between culture and nature, Óðinn is at the cultural centre (i.e. with the king) while Þórr always travels on the periphery, fighting for the natural order. This analysis shows that a discussion whether Óðinn or Þórr is a 'god of war' in the Nordic pantheon is futile. Both gods are clearly associated with war and fighting, but each in his own way.

Finally it should be mentioned that, compared to the analysis above, concerning Þórr and Freyr, we notice that, even though the relation between Þórr and Óðinn is of another kind and concerned with other themes than that one, it seems clear that the semantic center of Þórr is quite stable. He is first and foremost a 'defender', of fertility as well as of any other part of the natural order. His means are physical strength and killing. Whether such a distinction is also possible to draw for other Indo-European religions cannot be discussed here – but a priori it does not appear unrealistic. Suffice it to mention the example of Indra, whose enemies are remarkably similar to those of Þórr.

Sovereignty and Kingship: Freyr and Óðinn

In an article published more than twenty years ago, in 1990, I argued that the way divine 'luck' was transferred to the king-to-be was during his initiation. At that time, I did not discuss the relation between descent and initiation; nor did I discuss the fact that there may seem to be two gods involved in the descent of the pagan kings, i.e. Freyr and Óðinn. It is my aim in this section to bring these two discussions together and to propose a solution to the seemingly incidental choice of ancestor. I am fully aware that the evidence is scanty, but nevertheless, I do believe that the theory proposed will be able to create a more comprehensive model by which to understand the various (and sometimes, from a logical point of view, mutually exclusive) statements in the sources. At the same time it will be possible to argue that the relation between the three gods that is the subject of this article is not a just matter of historical and political development, although such a development has, of course, also taken place.[19]

I still think that I was basically right in proposing that the king's 'luck' was imposed on him during initiation. And there can hardly be any doubt that the god involved in such an initiation was Óðinn, whom I have shown in several publications to be, primarily, a god of rulers and a god of initiation.[20] This would make it natural to think of Óðinn as the ancestor of the kings, too, especially as he is mentioned directly as the progenitor in the traditions of the earls of Hlaði, and so also in most of the genealogies of the Anglo-Saxons. Nevertheless, we have evidence, from perhaps the most famous of all genealogies, namely that of the *Ynglingar*, showing that Freyr – probably the same as Seaxneat (the continental Saxnot, cf. Dumézil 1959, 29) who is mentioned as progenitor of the royal house of Essex – is the god from whom the kings descended in Uppsala. Naturally, this could be explained by the trite fact that traditions may evolve differently in different areas. However, in 1997 the English philologist Richard North published a very interesting and much learned book *Heathen Gods in Old English Literature*, in which he argues that originally Ing (eponymous forefather of the Ingaevones [*Germania* chap 2]) or Freyr was the ancestor of all the Germanic royal houses, and that the Woden-sprung kings in England were a later development, having in turn influenced the Norse tradition (North 1997, 118-24). The same issue was addressed two years later by the Danish historian of religion Morten Warmind in a small article that, apparently independent of North, reaches almost the same conclusion (Warmind 1999, 234-6).

Now, it is of course possible that North is wrong, but he seems to have a good case,[21] and if we accept his basic arguments, at least hypothetically, we are left with the puzzling fact that Freyr as well as Óðinn played a role in the religious legitimacy of the rulers. North and Warmind explain this historically, North proposing that the conflict between Vanir and Aesir was some sort of 'cult war', and a sign of an 'older type of paganism in which the Vanir ruled' (North 1997, 42). This sort of 'historicist' explanation does not seem to be convincing in the light of Dumézil and his followers' structural theories in which it is shown, beyond doubt, that the conflict must be viewed as a common Indo-European theme. But whether or not such historical explanations are true or false, they also have to be explained at another level to make real sense. Even if North proposes some historical-political explanations, in which Woden was used as a sort of parallel to Christian figures such as Jacob and Abraham (North 1997, 114-7), it never becomes clear what caused the shift from Ing-kings to Woden-kings. My point here is that the two were from the very beginning (whenever that was) both connected to the kings, but in very different ways, and this connection appears to be part of the explanation of why Óðinn can be seen as a forefather to the kings in the North as well as among the Germanic peoples in general.

Before proceeding, we have to look briefly at the two gods and the semantic fields they cover. Firstly, they are both apparently connected with kings, which we will return to below. Second, they are both involved in the wellbeing of the land; Freyr, as we saw, is worshipped for *ár ok friðr*, and Óðinn has as his mistress the goddess Jörð, suggesting some sort of *hieros gamos*.[22] However, it is definitely Freyr who is mostly attached to fertility and sexuality in the Old Norse sources,[23] as we saw in Adam of Bremen. Mention of Óðinn's connection to the land and to fertility is sporadic at best. We will never know for sure, but this may be a later development sprung from the fact that Óðinn was always very closely related to the kings who in due time came to be strongly associated with the land (Steinsland 1991), whereas in previous times, he may have been primarily the ruler of a *people*, and not of a land. As I have argued elsewhere, it seems quite certain that Óðinn's relation to the kings was related to his role in initiation,[24] and there is no reason to believe that this role was only late. There are at least three possible explanations why there is no definitive evidence. First, most authors of antiquity and early medieval Christianity dealing with the pagan Germanic peoples did not relate many myths to us in a reliable way. Second, large parts of the whole complex of myths and rites that surrounded the consecration of kings were probably more or less secret; and third, it is a fact that, during the process of Christianisation, the kings were among the first to accept the new religion. This would imply, therefore, that rituals and narratives connected to paganism were able to survive among the lower classes, but among the kings and noble classes, they could only survive as vague memories in fantastic narratives of the past, such as in the *fornaldarsögur*. On the other hand we know from Tacitus' *Germania* (Bruun and Lund 1974, 44) and other antique and medieval sources that Mercurius was the most venerated among the Germans. And from their perspective it was hardly the god of farmers and commoners that was in focus, but rather the one of the nobles, the chieftain and the warriors, so that a priori it seems reasonable that the god, acknowledged as the major Germanic god would be Mercurius whom most scholars would identify with Woden or Óðinn.

Therefore, it is not farfetched to maintain that, ever since the early Iron Age (and possibly also earlier), Óðinn (or a god of the Óðinn type) was viewed as the god to whom rulers were initiated because of the numinous knowledge he possessed. This, however, does not exclude the possibility that the kings were thought of as being the offspring of Freyr – or Ing (Sundqvist 2002).[25] On the other hand, it may be an important element when we attempt to explain why Óðinn came to be seen as the main progenitor in Anglo-Saxon England as well as in parts of Scandinavia, such as is proposed by North: he already was connected to the kings, although they may not, during the time of Tacitus, have believed that they actually descended from him.[26]

Freyr, on the other hand, was probably closely connected to fertility at all levels right from the start.[27] According to *Ynglinga saga* and North's theory, he was the ancestor king from whom later kings descended and, in the same way as he produced welfare and prosperity, his descendants would secure welfare and prosperity. If this reconstruction of the characteristics of 'Óðinn kings' and 'Freyr kings' comes close to reality, one may well ask how these two complexes were related. Even if it could be proven that the Freyr kings (Ing kings) were prior to the Óðinn kings, which I doubt was the case, it seems as if there must be some sort of logical relation as well.

In relation to the ruler, we then have two types of gods: one being the ancestor and the other being the guardian god to whom the ruler is initiated.[28] The Freyr aspect would probably[29] represent the king as fertilizer of the land in a very physical way, as we saw above, perhaps in a symbolic *hieros gamos*[30] with the female pendent of the god of fertility representing the land. This would then form part of a configuration of ideas maintaining that we are 'like' the ancestors: just as Freyr (and Fróði) were able to fertilize the land, both as living and dead, so is the present king – at least ideally. And this, of course, is part of the sacrificial complex surrounding the dead king.

The relation between Óðinn and the ruler is of quite another kind. He is not primarily 'fertilizer' of the land but instead 'personal' guardian god of the ruler. We have, especially in the *Fornaldarsögur* and in *Gesta Danorum*, many descriptions of Óðinn acting as protector and adviser of the ruler, and in most cases it is possible to analyze an initiation-like structure, previous to this relation (Schjødt 2008). So, Óðinn seems to be the god who gives the ruler the sort of numinous knowledge necessary in order for him to rule, creating the right relations between this and the other world. Structurally, we could maintain that the relation between the two gods, the ruler and the god of the rulers, consists in a mediating process with the god approaching this world, walking into the kings' halls, going to the battlefields, and meeting the hero in order to give him advice. On the other hand, the hero will, during the rituals, be approaching the other world as a sacrificer, and perhaps in extreme cases as a sacrificial victim himself. And, as we know from skaldic poems (e.g. *Eiríksmál*), the dead kings may act as inhabitants in Valhöll, being very close to having godly status. The two worlds will thus mingle as the king, representing this world, and Óðinn, representing the other, will meet in different situations. This is substantially different from the relation between Freyr and the ruler. We do not know about Freyr's walking about in this world, helping people or rulers with anything. He is simply a god, or perhaps rather a godly ancestor who seems to be present among humans only on ritual occasions, but not in their myths. In the rituals he may promote fertility, if the king acts according to certain rules and performs certain rituals *and if he acts as did his first ancestor*. So, even if Freyr, as we saw, is strongly connected to the land he is only present, perhaps as a statue, but he does not move about in this world, disguised as a human being which is a characteristic of Óðinn – the wanderer – taking part in battles and giving advice on how to fight.

We can thus view the opposition between Óðinn and Freyr concerning rulership as an opposition between, on the one hand, psychic or intellectual aspects and, on the other, the physical aspects. This would be in accordance with the fact that the main relation between Óðinn and the ruler is ritualized during initiation rituals, characterized as a transference of numinous knowledge from the god to the king to be, whereas that between Freyr and the ruler is ritualized during some sort of fertility ritual in which the king acts as Freyr, the fertilizer, perhaps involving the rite of *hieros gamos*. In structural terms we may see the relations between the ruler and the two gods Óðinn and Freyr respectively as metonymic and metaphorical.

At the structural level, it thus seems reasonable to assume that the model for Germanic kingship involved two gods: one who takes care of the fertility of land and people and who is also seen as the ancestor of the present ruler, symbolizing the continuity of the relation between ruler and land. Whether the female representative of the land was originally a giant woman, as was suggested by Steinsland (Steinsland 1991) or some other female being, perhaps a woman of the same kin as the god himself (e.g. his sister) cannot be determined with any certainty, and there may have been various traditions, the main feature being that there was a female consort to the ruler who was identified with the land. Sexuality is then the symbolic means of Freyr for bringing *ár ok friðr* to the land, with the king, the representative of the people, as the medium. The other god, Óðinn, would transfer numinous knowledge to the ruler and thus bestow him and his army with the mental abilities necessary for success in war, including strategic skills and warlike ecstasy.

Moreover, the function as a personal guardian god probably also implied that the ruler could communicate with the god when it was needed. This communication was important for the whole 'luck' of the land, including fertility. But fertility, understood as a physical phenomenon, was, as far as we can see, not taken care of by Óðinn who, as his primary function would have 'luck' and ability in war. In reality, however, we should hardly expect such clear-cut limits between the various ideological configurations. There has no doubt been room for variation, and, just as we know from the Anglo-Saxon regal lists, and notwithstanding the arguments of Richard North, Óðinn (Woden) may have played an important part from very old times in the complex of ideas surrounding royal ancestors. One could easily imagine how a guardian god would also be associated and eventually mixed up with the progenitor.

As a hypothesis we may also mention the distinction made by Tacitus in *Germania* chap. 7 (Bruun and Lund 1974, 42) between *reges* and *duces*. The first are taken as kings because of their family relations whereas the others are taken because of their personal abilities such as courage and skills in war. Could it be that at the time of Tacitus we did not only have two gods connected to kingship, but also two 'kings' each being related to one of two gods - a Freyr (or Ing)-king and an Óðinn-king – perhaps related as kings of peace time (we remember that Freyr is called upon for *ár ok friðr*) and kings of war time? Could it be, further, that just as these two kings were eventually turned into one, so were the gods – in some parts of the Germanic area resulting in kings (probably mostly of the '*duces*' type) who were not only protected by Óðinn, but also believed him to be their ancestor?[31]

To conclude this section, we can state that Óðinn and Freyr in their relation to kingship are related to each other as are the diads mental vs. physic, war vs. fertility,[32] and people vs. land which partly correspond to the opposition culture vs. nature. As I have demonstrated elsewhere, this is also the case with the relation in general between the Æsir and the Vanir who are also related to each other, as are culture and nature (Schjødt 2008, 392-3). Thus, it is not surprising that the terms culture and nature would also be part of the dichotomy involving Óðinn and Freyr. Further it is of some interest that whereas Óðinn in his relation to Þórr was characterized as the god taking care of the king, and thus of the collective aspect of war, in his relation to Freyr, on the contrary, he is characterized as the guardian god of the individual king, because Freyr is a representative of the kingly lineage.

Conclusion

Where does all this take us, then? Before I shall propose a model that will comprise all the elements that we have analyzed above, it would be relevant to begin this conclusion with Dumézil, whose basic argument was the point of departure for the whole article. If the analysis above is meaningful, what consequences does it have for our evaluation of Dumézil's theory of a tripartite ideology in the mythology and theology of the Indo-Europeans?

The three functions have definitely proven to be a useful device. This is not to say that there is no other meaningful way to view the three gods who have been treated here. Rather, as a point of departure, the tripartite structure as a classificatory principle is surely relevant. It is important to remember that structural analyses are about relations. So, what Dumézil was aiming at was a description not of the three gods individually but the relations between them. His proposal that there were three gods (or rather five, since both Týr and Njǫrðr, in the Scandinavian version, were part of the tripartite structure as well), who each took care of one function may be exemplary concerning other Indo-European cultures. It does not fit too well, however, with the tendencies in the Nordic sources.[33] It is not that Dumézil's catergories do not fit at all—after all Óðinn *is* a magician, Þórr *is* a fighter, and Freyr *is* a fertility god—but rather that each individual god is more than the tripartite scheme would suggest. When Óðinn is a god who takes care of not only the first function, defined as sovereignty, but also the second, defined as fighting (which is perhaps more appropriate than 'war'), and Þórr, although certainly a fighter and thus a second function figure, also plays a role in connection with the third function, defined as well being and fertility, and Freyr who, apart from his sexual aspects, is also seen as a god connected to the kings, then this can be interpreted in two mutually exclusive ways.

On the one hand it could be taken to be a sign that Dumézil's overall theory is simply wrong, the various gods being more or less scattered around at random in relation to the three functions which have no different status in Scandinavia (or among the Indo-Europeans, for that matter) than in any other society in the world.

On the other hand, because of the trifunctional tendency that we *do* find in the material, we could decide to investigate whether the way Dumézil described this tendency could be refined in order to bring it in better accordance with the sources. I have chosen the second option here, confirming the heuristic value of the three functions as a model for analyzing the theology of the pre-Christian Scandinavians. The structural framework within which we have to view the three functions is more complicated than was suggested by Dumézil and most of his followers, at least when applied to the Scandinavian material.

How can we interpret this structural framework, and what are the elements that have to be taken into account in order to define the themes that are treated with it? The functions and characteristics of the three gods seem to be part of a vast semantic network. We have noticed that the relations between the two gods in each function partly overlap in the sense that some of the oppositional pairs can be applied to more than one function. For instance culture vs. nature can be seen in the relations between both Óðinn and Þórr, and Óðinn and Freyr, Óðinn being representative of culture, whereas Þórr as well as Freyr in their relation to Óðinn, in different ways, are representatives of nature. In other instances the oppositional pairs are specifically connected to a certain function. For instance the relation between land and people appears to correspond exclusively to the relation between Freyr and Óðinn.[34] The terms in both kinds of oppositions are important elements in the characterization of each individual god. The fact that Óðinn is a representative of the collective in his relation to Þórr, whereas of the individual in his relation to Freyr, demonstrates the basic idea in the structural perspective, namely that the individual elements can be defined only in relation to other elements, and not in any essentialist way. This is one of the reasons why some gods may seem to be characterized in mutually exclusive ways: they participate in various relations, and these relations are often concerned with different clusters of problems. Consequently, the relation between Óðinn and Freyr concerns two different kinds of leadership, while that between Óðinn and Þórr is concerned with two different aspects of fighting. The various characteristics of each individual god, therefore, will contribute to the general character of the god that form the frames to which every statement concerning this god has to stick. On the one hand there is a great freedom to juggle the individual elements, yet on the other hand there is no such thing as absolute freedom. For instance it would make no sense to present Óðinn as unintelligent, or Þórr as physically weak, or Freyr as a great warrior. Apart from that, however, new motifs can be added as long as they are in accordance with the general character of each god.

The terms that we have been able to depict in the three relations are the following:

> *Þórr and Freyr:* killing vs. sex, and periphery vs. centre.

> *Þórr and Óðinn:* individual vs. collective, physical vs. mental, periphery vs. centre, cosmic vs. societal, clear morals vs. moral indifference, defensive vs. offencive, and nature vs. culture.

> *Freyr and Óðinn:* physical vs. mental, peace vs. war (more or less equivalent with sex vs. killing), land vs. leader, collective vs. individual, and nature vs. culture.

It should be noted that some of these pairs are clearly derived from others, as is the case in the Freyr-Óðinn opposition with the last three mentioned pairs. Although all such pairs are important for our understanding of the individual god it is also to some extent possible to reduce them into a few, very significant terms. These may not cover the whole spectrum of semantic content but, conversely, they may express the basic traits that distinguish the three gods. For the sake of simplicity I shall illustrate this with two diagrams that will act as a final conclusion. Figure 1 illustrates the relationship between the three functions and the three gods:

Óðinn

fight   sovereignty

Þórr ——————————————— Freyr

fertility

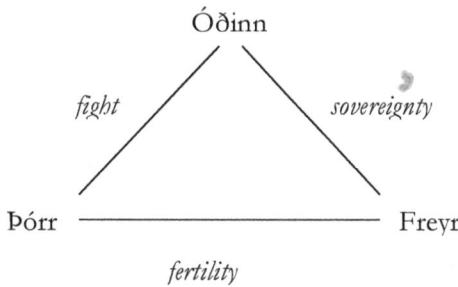

Figure 2 shows how the three gods are related in a way that connects them in pairs as opposed to the third god in the triangle. I believe this to be a useful device for understanding that, although the formal logic of myths can often be hard to find, both in the individual narratives and in the cluster of narratives that we normally call *mythology* (elements do not fit together, they contradict each other, apparently unimportant information is repeated again and again, etc.), at another level, that of the concrete, there certainly is a logical order as was demonstrated many years back by Lévi-Strauss in what he called *mythologique*. Here certain basic categories are treated in order to cope with the fundamental questions of culture such as for instance: what is culture and how is it to be distinguished from nature? I believe that by reducing the above mentioned oppositional pairs (for the sake of simplicity not all the pairs are present in the figures), to some of these fundamental categories it will be possible to acknowledge the importance of the three gods of Adam of Bremen on the one hand, and on the other hand the 'tripartite structure' of Dumézil:

Mental/Culture		*Periphery*		*Peace/Sex*	
Óðinn		**Þórr**		**Freyr**	
—	—	—	—	—	—
Þórr	**Freyr**	**Óðinn**	**Freyr**	**Óðinn**	**Þórr**
Physical/Nature		*Center*		*War/Killing*	

Notes

[1] "Wrong" is probably not the right word in this connection. Theories like those of Dumézil are neither "wrong" nor "right"" (at least not at the more general level). To postulate that in proto-Indo-European times people had a tri-functional ideology cannot be wrong: because these tri-functional figures can be found in all sorts of sources, including modern folklore and cartoons. The important question is thus not: "right" or "wrong", but how important this tri-functional figure is in the various mythologies. Dumézil thought that it was extremely important for the Indo-European view on society, whereas others would deny that. Some have argued that the figure of tri-functionality is so general that it cannot be seen as exclusively Indo-European. This is a legitimate objection and has been discussed ever since the theory was first argued (see for instance Scott Littleton 1982, 198-201). However these sorts of objections, even if they are relevant, only concern a part of the theory, namely that tri-functional thinking was a way of thinking practiced only by the Indo-Europeans. I would argue that this part of the theory is not the most important in Dumézil's work. It is certainly interesting but it is not nearly as important as is the fact that this principle of organization (the tri-functional division) can help us understanding many particular mythic features. Other critics, like for instance Belier (1991, 228-39), argue that the theory is invalidated since neither verification nor falsification is possible. Criticism such as this is, in my opinion, attributable to pure naïveté concerning the formation of theories in the humanistic disciplines, since whenever we are dealing with textual (or archaeological) interpretations, whether historically, structurally, hermeneutically etc. it is hardly ever possible to "verify" or "falsify" anything, in the way that it is (sometimes) done within the natural sciences. What we can hope for is that our "models" of interpretation may help us in grasping important and characteristic features, leading to new and convincing theories about, for instance, the Indo-Europeans. Whether these are true or not we will probably never know, but their quality would consist in that they "make sense" for the scholarly community in the beginning of the third millennium (see also Schjødt, forthcoming a and forthcoming b)

[2] It will take us too far away from the subject of this article to discuss the notions of "religion" and "mythology". Very briefly, in my view mythology is part of religion (when we are dealing with religious societies). Mythology is the description of the "Other world", in most societies

constituted by many different narratives (and not by "dogma", as is primarily the case in other types of religions). From these narratives it will, then, be possible to construe a "world view" (for a more comprehensive outline of my understanding of "mythology," see Schjødt 2008, 62-72).

³ This already suggests that what I am going to do in the following will be a structural analysis. This means that we are occupied primarily with relations between elements. Dumézil did not see himself as a structuralist, but it is hard to escape the impression that in comparing relations between gods (eg. the relation between Varuna and Indra compared to the relation between Óðinn and Þórr, and *not* (in the first place, at least) a comparison between Varuna and Óðinn), we certainly witness a structuralist at work.

⁴ The question about the source value of Adam's description has been heavily debated (see for instance the articles in Hultgård 1997). However, it seems more important to evaluate the individual piece of information than the source as such. This goes for Adam as well as for other sources: To argue, for instance, that *Vǫluspá* is unreliable because it is late (how late is still a question, however) does not help us in any way. It may be so that the poem is unreliable concerning many pieces of information, but not in other respects. It is important to be aware of this distinction, the source as such and the individual piece of information. If it can be argued that Adam's description of the three gods fits well in with what we are told in other sources, there seems to me to be no reason for rejecting it.

⁵ Even if the two names are not etymologically connected there seems to be no reason to doubt the identity (cf. Simek 1984).

⁶ This has been acknowledged by all scholars, and there is no doubt that this intellectual or "mental" aspect of Óðinn is also the reason why some scholars (e.g. Hedeager 1997, Solli 2002, and Price 2002) have seen a connection to the phenomenon of shamanism, and why the description of Óðinn in *Ynglinga saga*, chapters 6 and 7 can hardly be distinguished from that of a shaman, as John Lindow has shown (Lindow 2003).

⁷ Scholars have, of course, had different opinions on the details in the myth, and *Skírnismál*, especially have been interpreted in various ways, not all of them having to do with such rituals (for instance Lönnroth 1977, Mitchell 1983, and Bibire 1986). Gro Steinsland (1991) has very convincingly related the myth to a sort of *hieros gamos* between the king to

be and a giant woman, representing the land (p. 313). And even if the theory of Steinsland is particularly related to the ideology of rulership, it certainly admits some fertility aspects, too.

[8] There has been a heated debate about this relation between the goddess and the land which I shall not deal with in any detail here. For a recent overview see Frank 2007 (although I disagree substantially with Frank). The subject will be touched upon below in discussing the relation between Óðinn and Freyr.

[9] Again: we can easily cast doubt on the individual pieces of information, but taken together they seem to form a pattern. But of course, confronted with hyper criticism, we can never "prove" anything.

[10] This is perhaps expressed most strongly in the Roman religion with the term *pax deorum* – peace with the gods.

[11] I do not distinguish between different terms, such as *troll, jotnar, þursar* etc. The semantic content of these terms is not certain. It is possible that they were imagined in different ways, and it is also possible that they were not all related to chaos; but it seems that at least some of them were (they are living in the periphery, they are threatening, and in the end, at Ragnarǫk, they will destroy the world).

[12] This could well be the reason why Þórr to a much higher extent than Óðinn became the direct opponent of Christ during the Christianization process.

[13] There can be no doubt, in my opinion, that this is the reason why Þórr is the god who is called upon as protector of the rune stones: This is not because he is connected to the runes in any special way, but he is simply the one who takes care of the destructive forces.

[14] "Almost" because myths and theologies are never "consequent" – yes, Þórr must have had sex, since he is the father of several children, and yes, Freyr has fought a giant (but the most interesting about it apparently was that he did not use a proper weapon). What we have to go after in characterizing the various gods, however, is exactly the differences which – even if they are not consequent, but only appear as tendencies – constitute the role and position of the individual god.

[15] This part of the article is an elaboration of parts of two earlier articles (Schjødt 2004 and 2011).

[16] And, of course, we must also bear in mind the diversity, and the lack of stability in oral religions. So what we can hope to draw is a general picture of the tendencies that can be found in the sources.

[17] The examples are almost legion in which Óðinn helps his chosen heroes, most of them kings or outstanding warriors, for instance Haraldr Hilditǫnn by Saxo (Friis-Jensen 2005, 520-2), Sigmundr, Sinfjǫtli, and Sigurðr, all of the Vǫlsungr dynasty (Guðni Jónsson 1954, I, 111-37 and 140-65), and many others.

[18] Just as we were pointing to a difference between center and periphery related to Freyr and Þórr respectively, it may be worth noticing that another cosmological difference or opposition can also be found between Óðinn and Þórr, namely between the horizontal and vertical: whereas the myths in which it is possible to point to a certain cosmological setting, and in which Þórr is the protagonist, are almost always played out in a horizontal scenario (including the opposition between center and periphery), the myths with Óðinn as the protagonist are usually played out in a vertical scenario, Óðinn approaching the underworld in order to acquire numinous knowledge. The poles in this opposition are thus up vs. down. The interesting thing here is that "up" and the "center" are both identified as the world of man and the gods, and thus of "culture"(Schjødt 1990b).

[19] Basically I believe that there has been a tendency within the study of Old Norse religion that scholars are much too eager to accept interpretations that are based on one, and only one, model. In my opinion historical reality is mostly formed by a combination of many features, including historical development as well as structural traits, based on biological, psychological, sociological, cultural, and other facts that are at stake in religious worldviews.

[20] Cf. Schjødt 2008, in which there are further references including some of my own articles.

[21] I certainly do not agree with North on all points as, sometimes, he seems to be a victim of his own systematization. But on the whole and in his basic argument, he definitely seems to have proven that an Ing-figure,

at least in some places, has originally been seen as the ancestor, and he is thus able to explain many puzzling issues in the sources.

22 Cf. Steinsland 1991, 119-29. The relation between Freyr and his sister Freyje could also be interpreted as some sort of *hieros gamos*. The problems concerning the relation between the Vanir gods of the medieval sources and the Nerthus of Tacitus (*Germania* chap. 40; Hutton 1970, 196) are too complicated to be treated here. However, there can be little doubt that Nerthus and the Vanir gods are related somehow, and that they are both connected to the fertility of land as well as of man and beast.

23 Óðinn certainly do have sexual affairs, but in most cases, they seem to be due to a desire for numinous knowledge, rather than a question of lust and sexual desire.

24 In Schjødt 2008 I have argued that it is Óðinn's double role as initiate and initiator – which we come across in many myths – that makes him especially suited for being the guardian god of kings and rulers. I will not go further into this material, but it can hardly be doubted that Óðinn was first and foremost conceived as the *knowing* god, i.e. the one who has acquired numinous knowledge and eventually is able to pass it on to his chosen heroes - that sort of numinous knowledge which is necessary, in a religious society, in order to keep up good relations to the other world. This is probably the main reason why Óðinn was so closely connected to the initiation of kings, and thus to the position of the rulers, as we see in the source material.

25 Sundqvist's book contains all the available material concerning the Ynglingar of Uppsala with many valuable discussions.

26 Once again: we cannot be sure (probably rather the opposite) that all the various Germanic peoples always held the same ideas about who their progenitor actually was. It seems more likely that, right from the beginning, there were differences according to different tribes and traditions. I am not proposing some ideological complex held by all tribes. Ideological structures will always be in flux, sometimes slow and sometimes faster, but they change all the time. Different tribes influence each other until, perhaps, some newcomers come in and separate them; also internal changes may occur because of mutual influences from one ideological complex to another. In this connection it should be mentioned that a scholar like Eve Picard, writing more or less in the same tradition as

Walter Baetke, is wrong when she writes that a basic problem for the "Sakraltheorie" is the chaos that stems from the different versions of the genealogy, where there is no agreement (Picard 1991, 199). Of course it would be nice if there were some crystal clear system, but unfortunately, this is not the case, which is probably not due to the medieval authors but rather to an inherent "chaos" going back to the beginning of humanity. Why Picard (and most other mythologists) have the idea that in the old days human thought was always systematic and coherent (especially those scholars writing in the period after structuralism, discourse theory, and cognitive science – theories that have proven things not to be so [see for instance Boyer 2001; especially 4-11 and 297-312, and Whitehouse 2000; especially 54-98]), is quite a riddle.

[27] We have only very limited evidence that the Vanir gods, as they are known to us from the West Norse sources, were worshipped in the pre-Viking periods. We do, however, have the famous description by Tacitus of Nerthus, which seems to show beyond doubt that some sort of continuity must have existed (see, however, Picard 1991, 85-92).

[28] It is quite interesting that North leaves room for Óðinn being "the adoptive father of kings, princes or warriors slain in battle" (p. 131). This role as "adoptive father" suits the role of "initiator" perfectly. Just as blood brothers during the ritual of forming a blood brotherhood *become* brothers (Schjødt 2008, 355-72), it is frequently expressed during initiation rituals that the initiates have become children of the god or goddess to whom they have been initiated.

[29] "Probably" because this must remain hypothetical. We must assume that behind the scattered information, there could easily have been an ideological complex, but a reconstruction of it must necessarily involve reasoning based on analogy and hypotheses. One could argue, then, that we ought to leave the subject all together because our interpretations will remain uncertain (and some would say: random). This viewpoint is legitimate since it is impossible to draw any sharp limits between what can be the object for scholarly reconstruction and what cannot. Just like in most archaeological interpretations, the degree of uncertainty is considerable, but nevertheless, they (or at least some of them) "make sense" (whether they are "true" is quite another matter). A problem, however, arises when some scholars on the one hand, reject the possibility of reaching any knowledge about Old Norse and Germanic religion and,

on the other hand, spend all their time showing that scholars that aim at saying, at least, something are completely stupid. Some may find such a procedure boring, and the time of these scholars might be spent in a more productive way dealing with other subject fields.

[30] And once again: Frank (2007) does not believe in a *hieros gamos*; other scholars do; and we will probably never know with certainty. But the point is that our sources actually do suggest that, in the figure of thought concerning ruler and land, there would be room for such a ritual – it could have been there. Whether it was ever carried out in reality is not quite the same, and is certainly a question to which we will never get a final answer.

[31] In this connection I should like to refer to a couple of articles by the Danish archaeologist Kristian Kristiansen (2001 and 2004) in which he has many interesting ideas concerning the "twin-kings" of Bronze Age Europe. Even if I disagree with Kristiansen on several points, his results may be of interest, also in this connection.

[32] Whereas it makes good sense to characterize the opposition between Þórr and Freyr as homologous with the "killing vs. sex", then the proper characterization of this opposition between Óðinn and Freyr would rather be "war vs. peace" (cf. the *ár ok friðr* formula).

[33] I use the term tendencies deliberately. The sources for Old Norse religion are of such a heterogeneous nature that regardless of which interpretation a scholar proposes, there will always be some pieces of information that lead in other directions. And apart from the sources, the diversity which we must expect *a priori* in dealing with a religion such as the Old Norse or Old Scandinavian (as has been stated from various perspectives by scholars as e.g. Andrén 2007; Schjødt 2009; Brink 2007; Gunnell 2000 and forthcoming; Wellendorf 2006) and with various influences, various political developments, various historical circumstances, etc. will inevitably lead to different myths and different rituals, even in neighbouring tribal communities. Therefore, what we may hope to find to be stable features will be the discourse, i.e. the frames within which a god could act. There were many possibilities for expressing mythical incidents, but there was not totally free choice (cf. Schjødt forthcoming a).

[34] It is necessary to proceed with caution here since we have access to only a tiny part of the oral traditions that once existed. It could well be that certain functions, in the course of history could be applied to other gods.

Servants of Thor?
The Gotlanders and Their Gods

Anders Andrén

In recent years, the idea of a homogenous Old Norse religion has been challenged by many scholars. In archaeology, the distinct character of rituals in different regions has been emphazised such as in the investigations of burial rituals in southern present day Sweden by Fredrik Svanberg. Svanberg has shown how these rituals varied considerably even between regions situated only 100-150 kilometers apart (Svanberg 2003). In place-name-studies, Stefan Brink has renewed an old discussion about the regional character of sacred place-names. The selection of gods and goddesses in relation to place-names differs considerably from one region to another. For instance, the god Ull is present in parts of Sweden and Norway, but not at all in Denmark (Brink 2007; cf. de Vries 1957, 53, 116-7, 155, 194-5, 201 and 309). In similar ways, Terry Gunnell has argued that Odin was not necesserally viewed as the highest god in all regions of Scandinavia, even though he is portayed as such in the skaldic poetry and by Snorri Sturluson. Instead Gunnell stresses the importance of Thor, especially in many parts of Norway and Iceland (Gunnell *forthcoming*).

Recently, Olof Sundqvist has contributed to the discussion on the diversity of the early Scandinavian religious traditions by studying how the relations between humans and the divine world were understood (Sundqvist 2011). He emphasizes that variations in the social order was expressed by different views of the relationships to the gods. In the central parts of Scandinavia, where one found families of kings and jarls, the aristocratic families were portrayed as the heirs of the gods. Families such as the Ynglings of Old Uppsala and the Jarls of Lade claimed a divine descent from Freyr and Odin respectively. In Iceland, on the other hand, the society was deliberately organized without kings and jarls. Instead the local chieftains regarded themselves as friends of the gods. For instance, the chieftains of Þórsnes were viewed as "very good friends of Thor" (Sundqvist 2011). These social aspects of the relation between humans and gods are important. Probably other relations between humans and gods existed in various parts of Scandinavia, although the possiblities to investigate them are limited by the lack of distinct sources. However, on Gotland, which Sundqvist does not include in his study, it is possible to make further investigations.

Gotland, the large island in the middle of the Baltic Sea, stands out as a special region in the Viking Age and earlier periods. The island had a distinct local identity, expressed above all through unique picture stones (Lindqvist 1941-42; Andrén 1993; Nylén and Lamm 2003). In addition, Gotland had an area-specific female dress, with special brooches used only on Gotland (Carlsson 1983; Thunmark-Nylén 1983). The island is best known for its enormously rich silver hoards, with significant finds of silver dress ornaments and tens of thousands of silver coins minted in a wide range of geographic areas, from central Asia in the east to England in the west (Stenberger 1947/1958). Much of this silver reached Gotland by trade and plunder. This means that Gotland was a society with a distinct local identity built up in relation to long-distance cultural encounters.

The social order of Gotland in the Viking Age and the early Middle Ages is highly disputed (Andrén 2010). In the thirteenth and fourteenth centuries, Gotland was ruled by the *Gutnalting*, the Gotlandic allthing situated at Roma in the middle of the island, and by twenty smaller assemblies distributed over the island (Yrwing 1978, 80-88). Gotland clearly differed from mainland Scandinavia, because no land-owning aristocracy can be traced on the island. Several researchers have proposed that Gotland was a "peasant republic" (cf. Siltberg 1989), but this idea is certainly too Romantic. There existed clear social differences on the island, with families of *seniores* or judges that ruled the assemblies for generations (Lerbom 2003). However, the social hierachies were not as pronounced as in mainland Scandinavia.

In contrast to many other regions in Scandinavia, a myth of origin is also preserved from Gotland. In a text adjacent to the *Guta Lag*, the provincial code from the first half of the thirteenth century, it is told how the island was inhabited and organized (Holmbäck and Wessén 1943, 291). According to this text, which is known since the nineteenth century as the *Guta Saga*, the island was uninhabited for a long time, since it sank into the sea every day. Only at night was the island above sea level . Eventually Gotland was found by a man called Tjälvar, who brought fire to the island. After that it never sank into the sea again. Tjälvar had a son named Havde, who married a woman named Huitastierna (Whitestar). They had three sons, Gute, Graiper and Gunnfjaun, each of whom were given one third of the island. From these three brothers all Gotlanders are descended (Holmbäck and Wessén 1943, 291-292).

The Gotlandic myth of origin follows a common pattern of north European descent myths. In several cases three sons, with alliterating names, descend from a couple. One further generation is sometimes mentioned. Good examples of this mythological motif are Mannus and his three sons, mentioned by Tacitus in CE 98; the Anglo-saxon tradition of Wictgils, Witta and Wecta; and the Icelandic tradition of Burr and his sons Odin, Vili and Vé (Simek 1993, 224-5). According to Snorri in *Gylfaginning* 5, Burr was licked out of the ice by the primordial cow Auðumla. This event is interesting since the name Huitastierna (Whitestar) from the *Guta Saga* was also a typical cow's name in later periods (Löffler 1908).

The most interesting aspect of the Guta Saga is that the Gotlanders in the thirteenth century saw themselves as descendants of a man called Tjälvar. Already during the nineteenth and early twentieth centuries several scholars noted that the name Tjälvar (Þieluar) is a parallel to the name Þjálfi, which appears in several Icelandic texts (overview by Läffler 1908; Holmbäck and Wessén 1943, 301) According to *Þórsdrápa* and *Harbarðsljóð* 39, Þjálfi was a companion to the god Thor, whereas Snorri Sturluson portayed him as a servant of Thor in *Gylfaginning* 43-44 and *Skáldskaparmál* 4. This linguistic link between Tjälvar and Þjálfi has never been fully explored, but with inspiration from Sundqvist's study it is possible to go one step further. The possible link between Tjälvar and

Thjálfi, and the role of Þjálfi as companion or servant of Thor, indicate that the Gotlanders regarded their relations with the gods in similar ways as the Icelanders (Sundqvist 2011). The Gotlanders may consequently have viewed themselves as decendants of Tjälvar/Þjálfi, that is decendants of the companion or servant of Thor.

Sacral place names also indicate that Thor played a major role on Gotland. In contrast to mainland Scandinavia very few sacral place names are known from Gotland (Olsson 1996, 136-138; Blomkvist 2002, 157-170). However, among these few place names are some names with the compound *Tor-*. Although place names with the compound *Tor-* also may refer to a personal name Tor, at least nine place names may refer to the god Thor. These names include three places called Torslunde, two places called Torsburg/en, two places called Torsvät, one place called Torsåker, one place called Torsänge, one place called Torsbrunn and one place called Torssaud. Since no other god or goddess is represented by more than two place names on the island, these possible place names associated with Thor point towards his importance on Gotland.

Among these place names, Torsburgen is of special interest (fig. 1). Torsburgen is the name of the largest hill fort on Gotland—and in Scandinavia—situated in the eastern part of the island (Engström 1984). It is located in the outland between several settlement regions, the nearest farm being situated one and a half kilometers away.

The hill fort is placed on a natural limestone plateau, with a circumference of four and a half kilometers. To the north, the plateau ends with steep cliffs of ten to twelve meters, whereas the edges are less pronounced in the south. Instead a limestone wall of up to six and a half meters height is built along two kilometers of the southern border of the hill fort (fig. 2).

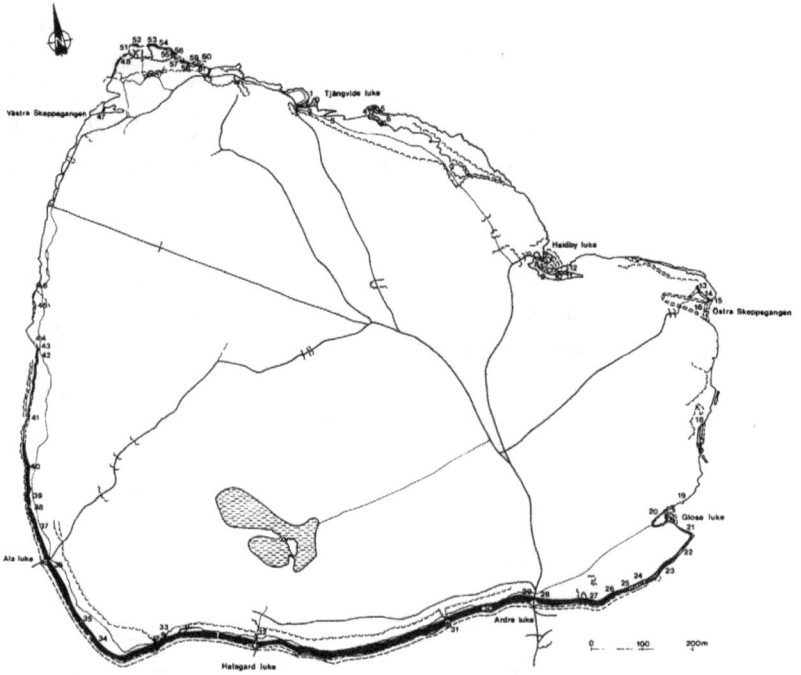

Fig. 1. Plan of Torsburgen (after Engström 1984, 6).

There are at least twelve entrances to the hill fort, seven through gates in the built wall and five via narrow gorges in the cliffs, which have been partly blocked by built walls. No traces of settlement have been found inside the hill fort, but there are a few cairns and a small bog, which was described as a small lake at the end of the eighteenth century (Engström 1984; Gislestam 1994, 225-230). Today the hill fort is covered by pine forest, but pollen analysis from the bog shows that the plateau was an open landscape with only hazel and juniper bushes in the Iron Age. Part of the high wall was excavated in 1977-78, and Carbon-14 dating show that the wall was built and subsequently and repeatedly rebuilt from the third century to the tenth century CE. These dates can be partly corrobated by a few objects found by the wall (Engström 1984).

Fig. 2. The south wall of Torsburgen (photo by the author).

Torsburgen is very distinct in size, form and location in comparison to the other eighty or so recorded ringforts and hillforts on Gotland. Most ringforts are small, usually with a diameter of only seventy-five to 125 meters (although some are even smaller). They are mostly situated in settlements or at the edges of settlements from the Iron Age. Another group of hillforts that are placed on limestone outcroppings are generally larger with diameters ranging from 100 to 200 meters. Most of these forts are located at a short distance from the nearest settlements. The walls of the ringforts as well as the hillforts are modest, seldom rising above half a meter in height. Peter Manneke has suggested that the walls were the foundations for taller wooden palisades. Very few of the forts have been dated, but a few finds and Carbon-14 dates point toward building dates in the early and middle Iron Age (500 BCE - 650 CE) (Manneke 2005). In contrast to the other forts, Torsburgen stands out as a special place. It is enormous in size, has high walls, is situated in a peripherial location, and was in continued use into the late Iron Age and through the Viking Age (650-1000 CE). These marked differences from all of the other ring forts suggest that Torsburgen was built and used by the island as a whole (cf. Engström 1984).

Torsburgen is unusual in another sense as well: it is the only prehistoric hill fort in Scandinavia that is mentioned in a medieval source. According to the *Guta Saga*, Gotland eventually became so overpopulated that one third of the Gotlanders had to leave their homes. They did not want to go far away and so they settled in Torsburgen. However, the Gotlandic Allthing (general assembly) did not allow this, and forced the population away from the island. First they settled on Fårö, a small island northeast of Gotland, then on the Estonian island Dagö (Hiiumaa), and finally they moved through Russia to Greece, where they finally settled. The saga notes that these Gotlandic emigrants "still today they have traces of our language in their speech" (Holmbäck and Wessén 1943, 291-292)

This story of the emigrating Gotlanders has been interpreted as a narrative based on a classical *exodus* motif, used by for instance Herodotus, Paulus Diaconus and Saxo Grammaticus (Weibull 1943). What is important in this context, however, is the information that the Gotlandic Allthing did not permit the emmigrants to settle in Torsburgen. This fact indicates that the general assembly of the island was in control of the hill fort. A possible interpretation of the Allthing's action is that the enormous hill fort was the central fortification for the whole island during a span of six to seven hundred years (cf. Engström 1984). The association with the god Thor also indicates that the organization of war was inscribed in a local cosmology as were other contemporary forts (Andrén 2006). That Torsburgen remained in use during the Viking Age indicates that the collective nature of this hill fort remained more or less intact on the island. In contrast to Gotland, hill forts in many other parts of mainland Scandinavia went out of use in the sixth and seventh centuries, when families of kings and jarls reorganized societies around halls and central places (Andrén 2006). Instead a more collective, but still hierachical, society remained on Gotland, being based on legal assemblies that were dominated by families of *seniores*. Such a society provides the social grounding for the Gotlanders to perceive themselves as the servants of Thor.

Several other finds contribute to the conclusion that Thor occupied a special role on Gotland. A grave from the first part of the eight century CE at Hallbjärns on southern Gotland was excavated and in the grave, the archaeologists discovered a piece of copper tin with the runic inscription "ÞunurÞurus…" This text has been interpreted as a combination of two words: "Thunarr", an older form of Thor, and "thurs", meaning giant or demon (Gustavson and Snædal Brink 1981; Snædal 2002, 43-45). If this interpretation is correct, it is the only time that an Old Norse god is mentioned in a text from Gotland. Intriguingly—and again if the reading is correct—Thor is mentioned in connection with his mythological enemies, the giants. As in other parts of Scandinavia, several pendants found in hoards and in one grave on Gotland have been interpreted as Thor's hammer (Stenberger 1947/58; Trotzig 1983; Thunmark-Nylén 2006, 162-3). In addition, miniature chairs of silver or amber have also been found in some hoards and female graves and these chairs have also been interpreted as symbols of Thor, since he is depicted as sitting on a small chair in two figures from Lund and Iceland respectively (Trotzig 1983). Finally, a man holding a large hammer-like object on a picture stone from Alskog has been interpreted as an image of Thor (Trotzig 1983).

It is quite reasonable to imagine that Thor was the major god on Gotland, as Gunnell has proposed for other regions of Scandinavia. Apart from Thor only a couple of other divinities can by traced via the few sacral place names on Gotland (Olsson 1996, 136-138; Blomkvist 2002, 157-170). These include a small and limited set of gods: Freya (Fröjel), Ull (Ullvi and Ullviar) and the disir (Disaker, Dishagen and Disrojr). Some of the images on the late Gotland picture stones also seem to depict gods, heroes and other mythological motifs that are known from the Icelandic narratives. These motifs show that ideas concerning Valhall, the valkyries and Odin with his eight-legged horse were known on Gotland, as were stories about Vǫlund and the Vǫlsungs such as Sigurd Fafnisbani (Lindqvist 1941-42; Buisson 1976; Andrén 1993; Staecker 2004).

Several observations support the notion that Thor had an important role on Gotland in the pre-Christian religious traditions. He may have been regarded as the high god by the Gotlanders, although Odin and other gods and goddesses were certainly known. Given the island's social order, the Gotlanders did not view themselves as the descendants of Thor. Instead, they saw themselves as companions or servants of Thor, claiming descent from Thor's companion or servant Þielvar/Þjálfi.

The Saga of Thorgils Holluson

Lars Lönnroth

One of the beautiful Gudrun's many suitors in *Laxdæla saga* is a somewhat dubious character by the name of Thorgils Holluson, described as "mikill maðr ok vænn ok inn mesti ofláti; engi var hann kallaðr jafnaðarmaðr " [a large, handsome man, extremely vain, and not very fair in his dealings] (*Laxdæla saga* 170).[1] Since he is a tough warrior who could possibly help her take revenge for her husband Bolli's death, Gudrun finds it convenient to accept Thorgils as a frequent visitor at her farm, Helgafell. She also accepts Thorgils' offer to teach law to her oldest son, Thorleik, but she certainly does not want to marry this rather bumbling and self-important suitor. Thorgils then offers to lead a revenge expedition against Bolli's killer on the condition that Gudrun promises, in the presence of witnesses, to accept him as her new husband.

At the advice of her friend and protector Snorri the Godi, who is an enemy of Thorgils, Gudrun then makes a plan to fool her suitor into believing that she will indeed accept him as her husband, even though she is actually planning to marry another man, Thorkel Eyjolfsson, who at this time happens to be travelling abroad. In the presence of witnesses Gudrun makes a solemn promise to "marry no other man in this country than Thorgils," provided that he carries out the revenge. Thorgils declares himself satisfied with this promise and promptly carries out the revenge. But when he returns to collect his prize, Gudrun reminds him of the exact wording of her promise and declares that she intends to marry Thorkel Eyjolfsson, who is not now "in this country" but will soon return to Iceland. Needless to say, Thorgils is furious but cannot do much about the situation except exclaim that Snorri the Godi must be behind this devious plan to trick him. He leaves Helgafell in haste and never comes back.

101

Somewhat later we learn that Thorgils is bullying a poor chieftain in the neighborhood into giving up his chieftainship. The mistreated chieftain's son is assisted in his efforts to take revenge by Snorri the Godi, who gives him an axe, scornfully describes Thorgils as *Hǫlluslappi* [Halla's layabout] and says that it is time that his bullying comes to an end. The young man makes an attack on Thorgils and chops off his head while he is counting money at the Althing. The last thing we hear about Thorgils is that "Sæzk var á víg þessi, sem í sǫgu Þorgils Hǫllusonar segir" [a settlement was reached after this killing, as is related in the saga of Thorgils Holluson] (*Laxdæla saga*, 199).

My purpose here is to discuss what this lost "saga of Thorgils Holluson" may have contained. It was evidently one of the sources of *Laxdæla saga*, but was it a written or an oral source? In the introduction to his edition of *Laxdæla* for Íslenzk Fornrit, Einar Ólafur Sveinsson (1934, XXXVII f.) assumes that it was a written saga, and that is indeed possible though by no means certain. Einar Ólafur is also of the opinion that this lost saga presented a much more favorable picture of Thorgils than *Laxdæla* does, since he is treated with respect in other texts, particularly in *Hávarðar saga Ísfirðings*, where he is characterized as "inn mesti ágætismaðr ok fullhugi" [a most excellent man and a hero] (*Vestfirðinga sǫgur*, 312). Even in *Laxdæla saga* Thorgils is said to be "lǫgkænsti maðr" [a most clever lawyer] (*Laxdæla saga*, 171).

On the other hand, Thorgils is presented in *Eyrbyggja saga* (180) as one of the *stórbokkar* that made life difficult for Snorri the Godi at the beginning of this great chieftain's career. The word *stórbokki* [big buck] may suggest that Thorgils was thought of as not only a powerful but also an overbearing and arrogant man. Perhaps *Laxdæla* was not completely alone in its critical view of Thorgils Holluson's character. However that may be, Einar Ólafur is probably right in assuming that there must have been different opinions about Thorgils, depending on whether people sided with him or with his main adversary, Snorri the Godi. *Laxdæla* obviously sides with Snorri, and one possible reason for that may well be, as Einar Ólafur suggests, that this saga was written under the influence of the Sturlungs who counted Snorri the Godi as an important and highly respected ancestor.

Let us now turn to the chapters in *Laxdæla* where Thorgils appears, namely chapters fifty-seven through sixty-seven. What is first interesting to note is the reason given in chapter fifty-seven for Thorgils being named after his mother, Halla, and not after his father, Snorri Alfsson from Dalir. According to *Laxdæla*, the reason was that his mother outlived his father: "því var hann kenndr við móður sína að hún lifði lengr en faðir hans" [He was named after his mother because she lived longer than his father] (*Laxdæla saga*, 170). This explanation is not trustworthy, since it is much more likely that Thorgils, like King Sven Estridsson of Denmark, was named after his mother because she came from a higher ranking family than his father. The mother of Thorgils, Halla, was the daughter of Gest Oddleifsson, who was one of the most respected chieftains in Iceland, described in *Laxdæla* as an extremely wise, Christian and almost saintly character, Gudrun's noble and benevolent adviser.

In chapter sixty-six of *Laxdæla* we are told in detail how Gest took ill and was buried at the church that Gudrun had erected at Helgafell, after having made a prophecy that this place would one day become a great monastery. Yet Thorgils Holluson is not at all mentioned in this connection or in any other chapter that concerns his grandfather, in spite of the fact that he was undoubtedly Gest's most important heir and trusted helper (cf. *Hávarðar saga Ísfirðings* in *Vestfirðinga sǫgur*, 171 f). *Laxdæla* is evidently playing down the close relationship between Thorgils and Gest, making it almost invisible. This relationship must have been more clearly emphasized in the lost saga of Thorgils, since it is obviously the main reason why he became a powerful man in the region and a frequent visitor at Helgafell.

Chapters sixty-five through sixty-seven in *Laxdæla* differ from the rest of the saga in that they contain some interesting and rather peculiar verses that are either about Thorgils or spoken by him. Apart from these verses *Laxdæla* is almost completely devoid of poetry. It is then natural to conclude that the verses formed part of the lost saga and may give us a clue to its content. The first of these verses is recited by Thorgils at Helgafell in Gudrun's presence after he has returned together with her two sons, Thorleik and Bolli junior, from the revenge expedition, where the older Bolli's killer, Helgi Hardbeinsson, lost his life together with two of his men:

> Sóttum heim at Helga;
> hrafn létum ná svelga:
> ruðum fagrröðuls eiki,
> þás fylgðum Þorleiki.
> Þría létum þar falla,
> þjóðnýta görvalla,
> hjálms allkæna polla.
> Hefnt teljum nú Bolla.

[We came home to Helgi,
letting the raven swallow corpses;
we reddened the oak of the shining shield[2]
as we followed Thorleik.
There we felled three
of great excellence,
three great helmet-trees.[3]
We tell you: Bolli is now avenged]
(*Laxdæla saga*, 194)

This is a fairly conventional skaldic stanza as far as the poetic language is concerned, but it is composed in *runhenda* with end rhymes in each half line, a meter that may not have been very common in the early eleventh century when Thorgils Holluson is supposed to have lived. Regardless of whether the poem is indeed from that time or not, it indicates that the lost saga of Thorgils contained a story about the revenge expedition and the death of Helgi Hardbeinsson.

There is, however, one interesting difference between the manner in which this story is told in the poem recited by Thorgils and the manner in which it is told in chapters sixty-three through sixty-four of *Laxdæla*. In the prose of these chapters Thorgils is the formal leader of the attack but Gudrun's younger son, Bolli junior, is the most prominent hero and the one who makes the most important decisions: it is he who actually manages to kill Helgi Hardbeinsson, and it is also he who nobly decides to spare the life of Helgi's innocent son, Hardbein. Gudrun's older son, Thorleik, is also presented as an able member of the revenge expedition, but his role is subordinate to that of Bolli, and this is in general accordance with the way *Laxdæla* presents the relationship between the two brothers: Bolli is always the greater man, in spite of being the youngest, and he is always Gudrun's favorite. In the poem, on the other hand, Bolli is not even mentioned but Thorleik is presented as the actual leader of the expedition. Since the poem must be older than the prose, and Bolli junior was actually too young to have been present when Helgi Hardbeinsson was killed (Einar Ól. Sveinsson 1934, LV), there are good reasons to conclude that the poem is closer than the prose to the historical facts. *Laxdæla* has reversed the order between the two brothers, expanding Bolli's role at Thorleik's expense.

A mysterious large woman encountered by Thorgils while he is on his way to the Althing where he will soon be killed recites the next poem. As Thorgils approaches her she turns away from him and says:

> *Kosti fyrðar*
> *ef framir þykjask*
> *og varisk við svá*
> *vélum Snorra.*
> *Engi mun við varask,*
> *vitr es Snorri.*

[May people who think highly of themselves watch out for the plots of Snorri. Nobody can escape, for Snorri is shrewd] (*Laxdæla saga*, 198)

Thorgils then makes the following mysterious remark: "Sjaldan fór svá, þá er vel vildi, at þú færir þá af þingi, er ek fór til þings" [It seldom happened when my future looked bright that you were leaving the Thing as I arrived] (*Laxdæla saga*, 198). The wording, which is unusually poetic (note the rhythm and the alliterations!), implies that Thorgils has met his fetch or *fylgja*, and that in turn indicates that he has lost his luck and is now a doomed man (Mundal 1974, 98). This whole scene has a tragic atmosphere which seems to prepare us for the fall of a hero rather than the fall of an oppressive fool, even though the words of the woman suggests that Thorgils has thought too highly of himself in his dealings with Snorri the Godi.

The third and last poem is recited shortly afterwards by a blue hooded cloak which belongs to Thorgils and had been hung out to dry on the wall of his booth at the Althing. People heard the cloak speak this verse:

> *Hangir vát á vegg,*
> *veit hattkilan bragð,*
> *þvígit optar þurr,*
> *þeygi dylk, at hún viti tvau.*

> [It hangs wet on the wall,
> the hood knows of wiles,
> will not dry again,
> I don't hide that she knows of two.]

These puzzling words should probably be understood as follows: Thorgils had been wearing the blue hooded cloak when he attacked Helgi Hardbeinsson and was wounded by him (see *Laxdæla* 187, 192) and he is going to wear it again when his head is chopped off at the Althing. Both times the cloak is bloodied and wet as a result of Snorri the Godi's "wiles" (cf. Lindow 2004). The verse is thus an ominous warning of the same kind as the verse spoken by the *fylgja* as Thorgils was riding to the Althing. In both cases Thorgils is seen as the victim of Snorri the Godi and as a doomed man deserted by Fate and his own luck.

We may conclude that the lost saga of Thorgils described the dealings between Thorgils, Gudrun and Snorri the Godi in a way that differed from the prose of *Laxdæla* in at least three important respects:

1. The close relationship between Thorgils and his great grandfather, Gest Oddleifsson, would have been more clearly emphasized than in *Laxdæla*.
2. Gudrun's oldest son, Thorleik, not his brother Bolli, was described as the most prominent hero of the revenge expedition against Helgi Hardbeinsson.
3. Thorgils himself was described as a tragic victim of Snorri the Godi's shrewd and devious machinations.

The lost narrative about Thorgils was not necessarily a heroic tale but it was evidently a tragic story of a man who came from a prominent family and was once a great lawyer and chieftain but at the same time a bit too arrogant for his own good and therefore destined to fall, brought down by the machinations of a ruthless rival by the name of Snorri the Godi.

Why did then *Laxdæla* favor Bolli Bollason and Snorri the Godi rather than Thorleik Bollason and Thorgils Holluson? Einar Ólafur Sveinsson may be right in assuming that the general influence of the Sturlungs on saga-writing may have played a role here, but I think a more precise answer may be found at the end of the saga where the descendants of Gudrun are listed and described.

The last we hear of her older son Thorleik is that he stays with Olaf the Saint in Norway, and he does not seem to have left any offspring in Iceland. Her younger son Bolli, on the other hand, marries Thordis, the daughter of Snorri the Godi, and becomes the most powerful man in the area after having returned with great wealth from Miklagard. Among the many prominent descendants of Bolli and Thordis the saga mentions Ketill Hermundarson, who was the abbot of Helgafell monastery between 1217 and 1220 (*Laxdæla* 227). There are reasons to suppose that *Laxdæla* was written at Helgafell or in its immediate neighborhood around that time or somewhat later. If Ketill Hermundarson did not actually write the saga as has been suggested (Hannes Þorsteinsson 1912, 348-50) he is at least likely to have had an influence on the way *Laxdæla* was told.

The saga of Thorgils Holluson would perhaps have had a better chance of survival if either Thorgils or his protegé and law-student, Thorleik Bollason, had left any descendants in the Helgafell area. Unfortunately they did not, and it was instead the version favored by the descendants of the powerful Snorri the Godi and his successful son-in-law, Bolli Bollason, that prevailed in the tradition. This version, which is still preserved in *Laxdæla*, is not only, as Rolf Heller puts it, "eine dichterische Konstruktion" [a literary construction] (Heller 1976, 144). It is also a story designed to serve the interests of the people who ruled Helgafell and its environment in the earlier part of the thirteenth century.

Notes

[1] The translations are my own to a large extent but I have sometimes borrowed phrases from the translation of *Laxdæla* by Keneva Kunz in *The Complete Sagas of Icelanders*, ed. Viðar Hreinsson, vol. 5 (Reykjavík: Leifur Eiriksson Publishing, 1997), pp. 1-120.

[2] Oak of the shining shield = warrior

[3] Helmet-trees = warriors

Composing Facts:
Evidence and Narrative in *Njáls Saga*

Carol J. Clover

To judge from the sagas, the early Icelanders didn't deal much with facts and evidence in their courts of law. It's not that "trial of questions of facts, in anything like the modern sense, was unknown," as Pollock and Maitland said of Anglo-Saxon law (1898, 38). It's that in the sagas' formal trials, fact-finding, if there at all, can seem thin or casual or both. Recent work has gone a long way in exposing a fact-finding system more developed than it may seem at first glance, especially if one turns one's eyes from the descriptions of trials proper to dispute processing more broadly.[1] It's with the contextual model in mind that I want to take another look at facts, evidence, and proof—though less as legal matters than as compositional ones, particularly as they play out in the textual span between an actionable deed (a killing, say) and its payback in law or in kind. I proceed, that is, not as a legal historian, but as someone with an abiding interest in the Icelandic sagas' species of prose narrative and the problem of its origins.

I also proceed on the very limited basis of just two passages from just one saga. The saga is *Brennu-Njáls saga*; the passages, an episode in the feud between Gunnar and the two Þorgeirs (chapters 67-70) and the account of the Bergþórshvál burning (especially chapters 127-132). With more than a half-dozen formal lawsuits, just one of which takes up about a tenth of its 300-some pages in modern edition, *Njála* is by a large margin the trial-heaviest of the *Íslendingasögur*. It is no less exceptional in its extravagant concern with formalities of law and procedure and its eccentric medley of legal sources. *Njála* is an outlier, in short, and its singularities very much qualify its value as a source on matters legal in early and medieval Iceland.[2] What I want to suggest here, however, is that it is exactly *Njála*'s arrant obsession with legal reasoning that puts fact-finding into such clear relief as a compositional force, and, in doing so, invites us to attend, with its patterns in mind, to corresponding sequences in other of the Icelandic sagas, as well.

This essay has two parts. The first examines facts and evidence in *Njála* and notes the text's systematic, almost urgent, concern with proof—as though neither the feud nor the saga itself can go forward without the assignment of culpability. The second part takes a closer look at proof scenes and considers the possibility that they are of later manufacture. I conclude by speculating on why accounts of proof might be particularly susceptible to fabrication.

Facts and the Burning Trial

Because the question has to do with "trials of fact in…the modern sense," I begin with some definitions culled from two standard Anglo-American handbooks.[3] "Fact" is defined as "anything cognizable by any of the senses," those things being "matters, circumstances, acts, and events," either mental or physical, which may have "legal implication or which may be a matter of enquiry as a basis for a conclusion of law." In legal controversy, "facts are determined by admission or by evidence," and the "process of fact-finding is one of reconstruction of what was said and done." Evidence, then, is "testimony, writings, material objects, or other things presented to the senses that are offered to prove the existence or nonexistence of a fact." And proof "is the result of the effect of evidence, while evidence is the medium or means by which a fact is proved or disproved," although "the words 'proof' and 'evidence' may be used interchangeably." In the Anglo-American system, the usual "trier" or "finder" of fact is the jury.

Let's look first at a *Njáls saga* passage in which we moderns might expect to find facts under consideration, but don't, or do only barely: in the trial of the men who attacked Bergþórshvál and killed, among others, Njál, his wife Bergþóra, and their sons Skarpheðin, Grím, and Helgi—Helgi by blunt force, others by burning. The leader of the thirty-some attackers is Flosi Þórðarson.

The specific killing with which Flosi is charged is that of Helgi Njálsson, beheaded while trying escape the burning house. Here is just one passage from the very long trial that ensues.[4]

> Mǫrðr nefndi sér vátta;-- "nefndi ek í þat vætti," segir hann, "at ek lýsi lǫgmætu frumhlaupi á hǫnd Flosa Þórðarsyni, er hann hljóp til Helga Njálssonar á þeim vættvangi, er Flosi Þórðarson hljóp til Helga Njálssonar ok veitti honum holundar sár eða heilundar eða mergundar, þat er at ben gerðisk, en Helgi fekk bana af. Tel ek hann eiga at verða um sǫk þá sekjan skógarmann, óalanda, óferjanda, óráðanda ǫllum bjargráðum; tel ek sekt fé hanns allt, hálft mér, en hálft fjórðungsmǫnnum þeim, er sektarfé eigu at taka eptir hann at lǫgum. Lýsi ek vígsǫk þessi til fjórðungsdóms þess, er sǫkin á í at koma at lǫgum; lýsi ek lǫglýsing; lýsi ek í heyranda hljóði at lǫgbergi; lýsi ek nú til sóknar í sumar ok til sektar fullrar á hǫnd Flosa Þórðarsyni. Lýsi ek handseldri sǫk Þorgeirs Þórissonar." At lǫgbergi var mikill rómr at því gǫrr, at Mǫrðr hefði mælt vel ok skǫruliga. Mǫrðr tók til máls i annat sinn; – "nefni ek yðr í þat vætti," segir hann, "at ek lýsi sǫk á hǫnd Flosa Þórðarsyni um þat, er hann særði Helga Njálsson holundar sári eða heilundar eða mergundar, því sari, er at ben gerðisk, en Helgi fekk bana af á þeim vættvangi, er Flosi Þórðarson hljóp til Helga Njálssonar lǫgmætu frumhlaupi áðr..." etc. (141)

[Mǫrd named witnesses—"to testify that I give notice of an action against Flosi Þórðarson for unlawful assault, inasmuch as he assaulted Helgi Njálsson at the place where he assaulted Helgi and inflicted on him an internal wound, brain wound, or marrow wound, which did cause Helgi's death. I demand that Flosi be sentenced to full outlawry on this charge, not to be fed nor forwarded nor helped nor harboured. I claim that all the possessions be forfeit, half to me and half to those men in the

Quarter who have a lawful right to receive his confiscated goods. I refer this manslaughter action to the proper Quarter Court. I give lawful notice of it, in public, at the Law Rock. I give notice of an action, to be heard at this session, for full outlawry against Flosi Þórðarsson, as assigned to me by Þorgeir Þórisson."

There was loud approval at the Law Rock for the eloquent and forceful way Mǫrd had spoken.

Mǫrd continued: "I call upon you to testify that I give notice of an action against Flosi Þórðarson, inasmuch as he inflicted on Helgi Njálsson an internal wound, brain wound, or marrow wound, which did cause Helgi's death, at the place where Flosi had previously made an unlawful assault on Helgi…"etc.]

The language is legal-formulaic, of course, the part about the wounds—that Flosi inflicted on Helgi "holundar sári eða heilundar eða mergundar, því sari, er at ben gerðisk, en Helgi fekk bana af"—an almost verbatim resounding of the laws' concern with, in the words of *Grágás*, "hvarz er heilvnd eða holund. eða merg und. eða þa er hann særðe hann því sáre er at ben gerðiz þa er hann fec bana" ["brain wound or internal wound or marrow wound; or that he wounded the other with a wound which proved mortal when he [got] his death"] (*Grágás*, I:88; *Laws of Early Iceland*, 148). In all, there will be nine iterations, in the space of some two dozen pages, of the wound-formula against Flosi; these are the fifth and sixth.[5]

The legal fact in the above passage is that Flosi struck Helgi with a wound that proved mortal. According to Miller, it is of the kind that "attained the status of fact by formal procedures," in this case Mǫrd's pleading and the absence of counterpleading by the other side (250). Although fact-finding of this type may not be as irrational as ordeals, oaths, compurgation, and the like (to which the Icelandic system was in any case little given), it is far from a formal "trial of questions of facts in anything like the modern sense," either.

Also worth noting is that despite its many repetitions, this fact does not stand out as an especially dramatic element in the trial, Like its few fellow facts, it is all but drowned out by other concerns: claims, notices, referrals, disqualifications, invalidations, challenges, citations, and so on. The burning trial's most operatic moments have nothing to do with facts or evidence and everything to do with clever coups and the performance skills with which they are delivered. But does that mean that fact-finding in "anything like the modern sense" didn't exist, or that it happened in another place, time, and form?

Witnessing Helgi's Death

Let's consider the possibility that Helgi's beheading by Flosi needed no further consideration because, as an open event fully witnessed by men of standing on both sides, it was subject to consensus pretty much on the spot. As Miller writes, "the Icelandic system of proof was remarkable for its almost total reliance on the knowledge and witness of neighbors, at the expense of more irrational modes of proof" (250). Most killings in the sagas either happen in public or are soon made known by the killer's admission or publication (*lýsing*) to neighbors. "The honorable killer always admitted his act. How else was the world to know that the repayment owed had been made, that honor had been satisfied? The proper functioning of the legal system and even the feud itself required wrongs to be made openly." Given the ethos of openness, it comes as no surprise that what few secret killings do turn up in the sagas tend to be processed by irrational means (249).

The "proper functioning of ... even the feud itself" is an important codicil. To accept that "legal process is stylized feud," in Andreas Heusler's formulation, is to accept that formal process and feud, both prodigiously rule-driven, were not only alternatives, but reciprocals—as the laws clearly contemplate and as the sagas repeatedly show.[6] (This complicates our terminology; I'm going to be using the term "legal" for both formal process and feud, but "law" for formal process only.) In that case—if, that is, redress could take the form of feud reprisal as well as a legal judgment— then something like good-enough facts must have served for both and therefore must have been in place sooner rather than later. That could be soon indeed, to judge from the swiftness with which, according to the sagas, the aggrieved party could start organizing a feud response. (Because trials took place at Thing meetings, the wait for formal resolution could be considerable.) I'll call these good-enough facts "serviceable facts" to distinguish them from the formally-tried ones of the usual definition.

With an eye to serviceable facts, let's look again at the most public of the Bergþórshvál killings: that of Helgi, the first of Njál's family to die. Urged by people in the house to escape when the women and servants are offered egress, the narration says, Helgi dons a woman's cloak and joins them. Flosi spots him for the man he is and calls for his comrades to grab him. Then:

> En er Helgi heyrði þetta, kastaði hann skikkjunni; hann hafði haft sverð undir hendi sér ok hjó til manns, ok kom í skjǫldinn, ok af sporðinn ok fótinn með. Þá kom Flosi at ok hjó á háls Helga, svá at þegar tók af hǫfuðit. (130)

> [When Helgi heard this, he threw off the cloak; he was carrying a sword under his arm, and now he struck out at one of the men, slicing off the bottom of the shield and severing his leg. Then Flosi came up and struck at Helgi's neck, cutting off his head with one blow.]

That's it; the following sentence turns to another matter. Until the trial, months and chapters later, Helgi's death is scarcely mentioned in the text; the saga offers no discussion, no appraisal, no colloquy of any kind. Yet Flosi is presumably among the burners on whom, only hours after the event, Kári plans to retemper his sword (see below), so serviceable facts of the killing must fall into place here pretty quickly.

Witness testimony is at the heart of Icelandic fact-finding, and we are given to understand that there were witnesses aplenty on this occasion——a veritable crowd of people who saw the attack leader himself decapitate Njál's son in the fire-bright courtyard. The eventual trial as the saga tells it includes no direct witness testimony, however. Perhaps that absence points to a less-than-modern legal process. But perhaps, together with the absence of counterpleading, it says something about the legal robustness of the serviceable facts. Perhaps, that is, the presence of so many trusty citizens sufficed to stipulate, as it were, something like facts pretty much then and there—in which case no further proof was forthcoming because none was required.

Then there is the language: "Þá kom Flosi at ok hjó á háls Helga, svá at þegar tók af hǫfuðit." Like other reports of public deaths, this one is chillingly blunt. The sentence registers exactly the intelligence needed to launch a lawsuit or a feud response: who struck whom with what kind of wound and that the blow was fatal. Although the point of view here is the sagas' usual third-person objective, its informational compass—what it registers and what it ignores—seems decisively determined by legal relevance. The narrative voice in this passage is not that of just any third person; it's that of a third person with consequences on his mind. Of course this has to be something of a pose, given *Njála*'s distance from the historical events, but it's a revealing one. It draws our attention to just how legally instrumental the reporting is or claims to be in this passage and others like it, testifying to the facts—nothing less, but also, tellingly, nothing more. It draws our attention, that is, to the extent to which saga style can be an effect of legal purpose. "Third-person legal objective" might be a more fitting term for the narrative mode of large tracts of *Njáls saga*'s narrative.[7]

Murky Matters

Thus outdoor events with lots of observers. But what of things that don't happen in plain sight and are neither publicly witnessed nor admitted to? For an answer to this question, we need only follow the saga as it turns from the courtyard to the contained and virtually private happenings inside the burning buildings. The narration tells how Njál charges the steward, who is about to leave the flaming house with the women and other servants, to take note of where and how he, Bergþóra, and the child Þórð were arranging themselves to die in bed. It then tells how the steward agrees, covers them with an ox-hide, and goes outdoors, whereupon Ketil "tók í mót honum ok kippti honum út ok spurði vandliga at Njáli , magi sínum " [seized his arm and dragged him clear and questioned him closely] and the steward "sagði allt it sanna " [told everything that had happened] (129). As if this witness relay were not enough, Skarpheðin (back indoors) will confirm it when he tells Kári "Nú mun faðir minn dauðr vera, ok hefir hvárki heyrt til hans styn né hosta" [Now my father must be dead, and not a groan or a cough has been heard from him"] (ch. 129). That leaves Skarpheðin, Grím, and Kári. After a bit more fight-back, they set about trying to escape the smoke and flames. With some heroic help from Skarpheðin, Kári gets out through a back way. That leaves Grím and Skarpheðin. Then:

> Skarpheðinn gekk þá til Gríms, bróðir sins; heldusk þeir þá í hendr ok tráðu eldinn. En er þeir kómu í miðjan skálann, þá fell Grímgr dauðr niðr. Skarpheðinn gekk til enda hússins; þá varð brestr mikill; reið þá ofan ǫll þekjan. Varð hann þá í millum þess ok gaflaðsins; mátti hann þaðan hvergi hrœrask. (130)

> [Skarpheðin went over to his brother Grím. They joined hands and stamped on the fire. But when they reached the middle of the room, Grím fell dead. Skarpheðin went to the gable-end of the house; then, with a great crash, the whole roof fell in. Skarpheðin was pinned between roof and gable, and could not move an inch.]

But how can we know this? Neither of the two will live to tell the tale, and of course there is no public here, nor Kári nor a handy steward, to register their *in extremis* actions.

Almost as if to preempt that question, the burning narration's very next sentence brings us back outdoors to the following scene.

Þeir Flosi váru við eldana, þar til mjǫk var morgnat. Þá kom þar maðr ríðandi at þeim. Flosi spurði hann at nafni; hann nefndisk Geirmundr ok kvezk vera frændi Sigfússona ok mælti: "Þér hafið mikit stórvirki unnit." Flosi svarar: "Bæði munu menn þetta kalla stórvirki ok illvirki. Ok þó má nú ekki at hafa." Geirmundr mælti: "Hversu mart hefir hér fyrirmanna látizk?" Flosi svarar: "Hér hefir látizk Njáll ok Bergþóra, Helgi ok Grímr ok Skarpheðinn Njálssynir, Þórðr Kárason ok Kári Sǫlmundarson, Þórðr leysingi. En þá vita vér ógǫrla um fleiri menn, þá er oss ókunnari." Geirmundr mælti: "Dauðan segir þú þann mann, er vér vitum, at á braut hefir komizk ok ek hefi talat við í morgin." "Hverr er sá?" segir Flosi. "Kára Sǫlmundarson fundi vit Bárðr, búi minn," segir Geirmundr, "ok fekk Bárðr honum hest sinn, or var brunnit af honum hárit ok svá klæðin." "Hafði hann nǫkkut vápna?" segir Flosi. "Hafði hann sverðit Fjǫrsváfni," segir Geirmundr, "ok var blánaðr annar eggteinnin á, ok sǫgðu vit, at dignat mundi hafa, en hann svaraði því, at hann skyldi herða sverðit í blóði Sigfússona eða annarra brennumanna." Flosi mælti: "Hvat sagði hann til Skarpheðins eða Gríms?" "Á lífi sagði hann þá báða, þá er þeir skilðu," segir Geirmundr, "en þó kvað hann þá mundu nú báða dauða." (130)

[Flosi and his men stayed by the blaze until broad daylight. Then a man came riding towards them. Flosi asked him his name, and he replied that he was Geirmund, a kinsman of the Sigfússons.

"You have taken drastic action here," said Geirmund.

"People will call it a drastic action, and an evil [malicious] one, too, said Flosi, "But nothing can be done about it now."

Geirmund asked, "How many people of note have perished there?"

Flosi said: "Among the dead here are Njál and Bergþóra, their sons Helgi, Grím, and Skarpeðin, Kári Sǫlmundarson and his son Þórd, and Þórd Freedman. We are not sure about those others who are less well known to us."

"You have listed among the dead a man who to my certain knowledge has escaped," said Geirmund, "for I talked to him only this morning."

"Who is that?" asked Flosi.

"Kári Sǫlmundarson," said Geirmund. "My neighbour Bárð and I met him with his hair burnt off and his clothes badly charred, and Bárð lent him a horse."

"Had he any weapons with him?" asked Flosi.

"He was carrying the sword Life-Taker, said Geirmund, "and one of its edges was blue and discoloured. "We said that the metal must have softened, but Kári replied that he would soon harden it again in the blood of the Sigfússons and other of the Burners."

'What did he tell you of Skarpheðin and Grím?" asked Flosi.

"He said that they were both alive when he left them," replied Geirmund, "but that they must be dead by now."]

To which Flosi responds that his fellow attackers would soon pay with their lives.

This sounds for all the world like a fact-settling process. To Geirmund's observation that the attack on Bergþórshvál is a "major act" (*stórvirki*) here, Flosi acknowledges that it will be deemed both a major act and a "evil," "malicious" one (*illvirki*, a term also found in *Grágás* , e.g., I:64; Beck 1993, 143). To Geirmund's question about the dead, Flosi names eight known in addition to some unknown others. Geirmund corrects him on three, all of whom were in the murky interior: Kári was certainly not dead, because Geirmund had just encountered him in person and from him had learned that Grím and Skarpheðin were alive when he himself escaped, "en þó kvað hann þá mundu nú báða dauða" ["though, he said, they must both be dead by now"] (ch. 130). Even this last assessment may be only half right, for just moments later, somewhere down amongst the flames, they hear a poem being uttered ("Þar heyrðu þeir í eldinum niðri, at kveðin var vísa")—a poem that makes little sense in the form we have it. (Flosi declines to guess whether Skarpheðin was alive or dead when he spoke it.) Four witness accounts thus come into play here: Flosi's overall one about the loss of life as far as he has been able ascertain it from his outdoors vantage; Geirmund's about Kári's having escaped, with Bárð's help, not only alive but revenge-fit; according to Geirmund, Kári's about the condition of Grím and Skarpheðin when he last saw them in the burning house; and the aural perception of several of the burners as to Skarpheðin's liminal state even at that late hour.

There will be more fact-settling later as Kári, Hjalti, and others excavate the site and examine the corpses. The discovery of the bodies of Njál, Bergþóra, and the boy Þórð in bed covered by a hide confirms both the steward's testimony to that effect and, of course, the burning narration's own earlier statement. The condition of Skarpheðin's corpse—e.g., upright with odd burn marks—is open to interpretation, but at the very least it confirms his position at the gable. And the location of Grím's body at the "middle of the main room" substantiates the narration's earlier report that he fell dead as he was traversing just that space. The saga narrator uses the remains as a modern prosecutor might to establish the particulars.

That the passage reads like a brief for Njál's canonization as a martyr saint should not detract from its other, plainly secular purpose: to confirm who died where and in what circumstances. Religiously motivated though it may be, the excavation is also a combination crime-scene investigation and inquest.[8]

In the end, there is no significant—that is, legally relevant—information in the as-it-happens narration of these indoor events that has not been or will not soon be reported second-hand (by Geirmund, the steward, and others) or inferred by Kári and Hjalti from the physical evidence of the crime-scene investigation. Witness testimony appears to be just as crucial in circumstantial-evidence scenes as it is in publicly-witnessed ones. The evidence-vetting in this sequence amounts to a proof process of which the result, I suggest, is a stout set of serviceable facts that will soon serve as the basis of some retaliatory gestures, then some actions, and eventually the Alþing trial. Once again, though, *Njála* never has these serviceable facts proclaimed as such: no character offers a recital, nor is there one at the trial. It is as though we are yet again expected to trust the as-it-happens narration when it tells us that Njál and Bergþóra died in bed (covered, by the steward, with an oxhide), Skarpheðin got pinned at the gable, Grím fell at the center of the room, and so on.

Note how different this compositional strategy is from that of the plain-view events. In plain-view events, things seem to become legal facts by mere virtue of their having been directly witnessed—which process makes them narratable without further tests, demonstrations, outlier testimony, and the like. If public onlookers are sufficiently numerous and credible, the narrator can evidently adopt their testimonial voice without further ado. Because saga killings are by and large public, most of them are told in this way. But when there is no witnessing public, as in the indoor events, the as-it-happens narration must instead be synced to circumstantial evidence witnessed in later scenes. Thus what may seem an unsubstantiated detail on one page—that Grím fell in the middle of the room—emerges, paragraphs or pages or chapters later, as a fact proved by the circumstantial evidence of the inquest. To be sure, there are a few unbuttressed or "free" details, like the one about

Grím and Skarpheðin's handholding and fire-stamping, but these are notably few and more by way of pathetic ornament than of legal substance. We are more struck by the methodical care with which the as-it-happens narration works to adduce facts that are, or soon will be, established by witnesses and thus subject to response via feud or law. Or, to reverse the formulation, we are struck by how the later proofs enable the earlier as-it-happens narration to proceed as though the details ("Grim fell in the middle of the room") are facts already. As the narrator might explain himself: "How do I know the facts of what happened indoors? Just wait a while and you'll see: I got them from the excavation evidence, from Geirmund, from those who heard the steward," and so on.

Of narrative time and sequence, Vésteinn Ólason observes that "[S]aga writers do not try to play tricks with or falsify time, as is often the case with novelists; instead they are content to follow the chronological flow of events in the saga" and that "every possible attempt seems to be made to present [the events] in their proper chronological order" (1998, 98-99). As "every possible attempt" hints, however, proper chronological order can be hard-won. The syncing operation outlined above may be seen as such an "attempt"—actually, a complex solution to the conflicting imperatives of proceeding chronologically (even in legally charged contexts like the burning) and proceeding factually (that is, on the basis of facts proved by evidence). This solution involves the apparent elaboration of the as-it-happens narration ("Grim fell in the center of the hall") from matters that could only later emerge as facts (the location of his corpse at the inquest). The brilliance of *Njála*'s narration in chapters 127-32 has long been appreciated. A good deal of that brilliance lies in its syncing operation, which is a compositional tour de force.

Backformation

Crucial to that operation, it would seem, is the process of backformation. Like linguistic backformation (e.g., 'shoplift' from 'shoplifter,' Swedish 'utland' from 'utländsk'), narrative backformation entails the development of a new element from an existing one, often in such a way that the existing one appears secondary and the newer one original. As it happens, some of the most conspicuous examples of backformation in our own narrative culture have also to do with law: the reverse-engineering, from real trials, of the crime and detection stories that lead up to them. This process has long been at the heart of especially Anglo-American detective and courtroom stories. Take, as a pertinent example, the television series *Law & Order*, famously "ripped from the headlines." As producer and head writer Rene Balcer clarifies, a real-life case "with interesting legal issues" provides the basis for the episode's "back half" (the lawsuit part, which is related second), and then the "front half" (the cop part, which is related first) is elaborated from it.[9] When Balcer says, "We don't make up laws and we don't make up decisions," he is referring to the back or lawsuit part, the implication being that the front or detection part *is* more or less "made up"—if not invented from scratch, then reshaped or adjusted or amplified to serve the immediate purposes of the privileged "back half." In his words, "quite often it's the tail wagging the dog."

The sagas are no strangers to such dog-wagging tails. Their stories of place-name origins—some men eat breakfast on a ness; that place is thereafter called Breakfast Ness—are routinely suspected of having been elaborated after the fact from the names themselves. Likewise the prose context of certain skaldic verse, which spells out the circumstances of the poem's production: one theory of transmission (put "forgeries" aside for the moment) has it that the poem is the historical nail from which the later prose explanation is hung.[10] The process in both cases is rather like reconstructing a joke's set-up from its punchline. It has been argued that entire sagas, or good chunks of them, have been elaborated from punchlines of a sort—*Hrafnkels saga*, for example, from mentions in written sources, notably *Landnámabók*.[11] Backformation, real or apparent, and textually positioned before or after the (temporally) "original" element, seems a key part of the saga makers' compositional stock in trade.

With that process in mind, let's have another look at the Geirmund-Flosi conversation, which occupies such a central place in the saga's parsing of evidence regarding the burning. The scene is odd on the face of it. Geirmund appears nowhere in *Njála* but here; after another quick mention a half-page later, he evaporates from the saga without further ado. A *Fornrit* footnote observes that "Geirmundur er annars ókunnur og slíkt hið sama Bárðar..." [Geirmund is otherwise unknown; likewise Bárð, his neighbor]. Nor does Flosi seem to recognize this Geirmund, for he must ask his name. Nor does Geirmund offer a patronymic, which would have identified him more specifically than the vague "frændi Sigfússona." His job in the saga, as we have seen, is not trivial: he corrects and supplements Flosi's faulty understanding of who was and was not killed in the attack. All the more reason to wonder why a bearer of such significant news should be so spectral. Maybe his scene reflects some memory-shred in the oral tradition; maybe it is distilled from other information; or maybe it was just invented at some later point along the way, even the moment of writing. In any case, its job in the burning narration is clear: to give its recital of serviceable events the source footnote it seems to need. The problem to which the Geirmund scene is the solution is essentially that there was only one witness to the indoor happenings, Kári, and he left early. That raises the question of whether like situations—situations in which direct evidence is missing—might be especially prone to creative solutions.

Such may be the case in an earlier passage in *Njáls saga*: the failed attempt on Gunnar's life recounted in chapters 68-70. The murkiness here has to do not with literal visibility, but with a mental matter, namely state of mind and the question of intent.[12] (Under "intent," Black's has "Design, resolve or determination with which a person acts. A state of mind in which a person seeks to accomplish a given result through a course of action" [Black's 1991].) In chapter 68, we are told that the "two Þorgeirs often met, and became intimate friends." According to Kolskegg, it's a bond with a purpose:

> Kolskeggr mælti till Gunnars: "Sagt er mér, at mikil sé vinátta þeira Þorgeirs Otkelssonar ok Þorgeirs Starkaðarsonar, ok er þat margra manna mál, at þeir muni vera ótrúligir, ok vilda ek, at þú værir varr um þik."(68)

[Kolskegg said to Gunnar, "I hear there is great friendship between Þorgeir Otkelsson and Þorgeir Starkaðarson; many people are saying that they are planning some treachery. I want you to be on your guard."]

Egged on by Mǫrd Valgardsson, the saga tells us, the Þorgeirs agree that they want to pay Gunnar back for his earlier deeds. At the end of chapter 68, in a one-on-one conversation, they get down to business:

Ok semja þeir þat með sér at fara at Gunnarri; segir þá Þorgeirr, at Gunnarr myndi á fara nátta fresti einn heima vera;--"skalt þú koma við inn tólfta mann til móts við mik, en ek mun hafa jafnmarga." Síðan reið Þorgeirr heim. (Ch 68)

[They agreed to make an attack on Gunnar. Þorgeir Starkaðarson then said that Gunnar would be alone at home in a few days' time. "Meet me with eleven men," he said, "and I shall bring the same number." After that, Þorgeir rode home.]

The attack is thwarted in the following chapter (69), but in the chapter after that (70), Njál, on Gunnar's behalf, brings a charge of conspiracy to an arbitration hearing at the Alþing.

Ríða menn nú til alþingis at vanða; eru nú hvárirtveggju á þingi. Njáll kvaddi sér hljóðs, spurði alla ina beztu menn, er þar váru komnir, hvert mál þeim þœtti Gunnarr eiga á þeim nǫfnum fyrir fjǫrráðin. Þeir svǫruðu, at þeim þótti slíkr maðr mikinn rétt á sér eiga. (70)

[People now rode to the Alþing as usual, and both parties attended. Njál asked for a hearing, and then asked all good men present what claim, in their opinion, Gunnar had against the Þorgeirs for the conspiracy against his life; they answered that in their opinion a man of Gunnar's standing had claims for heavy compensation.]

How did the private plan to kill became a public fact? As Kolskegg's warning makes clear, rumors of a plot against Gunnar had been about the district for a while. But it is not until chapter 69—i.e., the chapter between Kolskegg's warning (68) and the arbitration hearing (70)—that the conspiracy gets outed as such. Njál is over at Þórólfsfell talking with his daughter-in-law Þorhild. It's late at night, and a shepherd has been out looking for some missing sheep. Then, the saga says, the shepherd returned. He rides up to the door, dismounts, knocks, and enters.

[Þorhild] mælti: "Fanntu sauðina?" "Fann ek þat, er meira myndi varða," segir hann. "Hvat var þat?" segir Njáll. "Ek fann fjóra ok tuttugu menn," segir hann, "í skóginum uppi; þeir hǫfðu bundit hesta sína, en sváfu sjálfir; þeir hǫfðu fest skjǫldu sína í limar." En svá hafði hann gǫrla at hugat, at hann sagði frá allra þeira vápnabúnaði ok klæðum. Njáll vissi þá gǫrla, hverr hverrgi var... (Ch. 69)

[Þorhild asked, "did you find the sheep?"

"I found something much more important," he replied.

"What was that?" asked Njál.

"I found twenty-four men up there in the wood," he replied. "They had tethered their horses and were fast asleep, and had hung their shields in the branches."

He had observed them so closely that he could describe the weapons and clothing of all of them, and Njál could tell exactly who each one was.]

Njál thanks the shepherd, sends him to warn Gunnar, and then mounts a horse himself and rides out to the woods, where he finds the party of men lying asleep. He rouses them:

> "Óvarliga liggið þér," segir hann, "eða til hvers skal fǫr sjá gǫr hafa verit ? ok er Gunnarr engi klekktunaramaðr. En ef satt skal um tala, þá eru þetta in mestu fjǫrráð. Skuluð þér þat ok vita, at Gunnarr er í liðsafnaði; ok mun hann hér brátt koma ok drepa yðr, nema þér riðið undan ok heim." Þeir brugðusk við skjótt, ok varð þeim mjǫk við felmt, ok tóku vápn sín ok stigu á hesta sína ok hleyptu heim undir Þríhyrning. (Ch. 69)

> ["You are careless, lying about like this," he said. "What was the point of this expedition, anyway? Gunnar is no man to be pushed around, and this is truly the worst form of conspiracy to kill. You should know that Gunnar is gathering forces; he will be here soon and will kill you, unless you flee back home."

> They jumped to their feet in panic, grabbed their weapons, mounted their horses, and fled back to Thrihyrning.]

It's in this scene that the private matter of intention gets "cognized" into a serviceable fact. The shepherd was the first witness: he observed the men so nearly that he could describe them all—so he sees *who*. Njál is the second witness, and in addition to confirming who, he gets at the tricky matter of intent. "Intent," in Black's, "can seldom be proved by direct evidence but must ordinarily be proved by circumstances from which it may be inferred" (Black's 1991). Njál provides just such a circumstance when he accuses the band of men with having plotted to kill— which pronouncement, together with the threat that Gunnar is on his way to crush their undertaking, produces a reaction that serves as circumstantial evidence that they indeed do have just such a plan. To this grand forensic test of sorts, the only eyewitness on our side is its maker, but he's after all a respected man of law; and that, together with the presence of some two dozen others, however motley, appears to make the scene public enough to "factualize" the charge of conspiracy. (*Njála*'s taste for forensic tests turns up elsewhere in the saga, most ostentatiously in chapter 49, when Mǫrð Valgarðsson establishes Hallgerd as a food-thief by cleverly tracking chunks of the stolen cheese and fitting them to a neighbor's cheese mould.) With his proven fact in hand, Njál goes then to Gunnar and suggests bargaining with the Þorgeirs now that they've been caught out. Gunnar agrees and Njál gets the Þorgeirs to consent to arbitration with himself as one of the arbitrators. It works: at the Alþing, Njál wins a handsome sum for Gunnar (and, later, a light sentence when he is tried for the killing of Þorgeir Otkelsson). Of course the matter doesn't end there; after some more back-and-forth conflict over the coming months, Gunnar will be killed after all. But the immediate outcome of Njál's midnight ride is proof enough to do the legal job for the moment.

But this episode, too, is a little odd on the face of it. There's something unconvincing, almost comical, about the idea of a sixty-year old Njál charging solo into the woods in the middle of the night, waking two dozen would-be killers, and driving them to flee. There's also, to my mind, something a little too legally convenient about both this scene and the prior one with the shepherd. Could they be contrived to justify, most immediately, the charge of *fjǫrráð* that Njál will bring against them at the coming court confrontation (chapter 70)? If so, virtually all of chapter 69 can be seen as a narrative backformation from that eventuality—thus making the Alþing arbitration a half-page tail that wags a two-page dog.

Proof Segments and Saga Composition

Njál's forest scene and the Geirmund-Flosi conversation have more in common than a loud ring of inauthenticity. They are functional and compositional equivalents. Both serve to bring fresh evidence into the public record, thus evincing facts that work on the story front to warrant what actions the characters will take next and, on the discourse front, to capacitate the earlier as-it-happens narration. Both strike a pointedly formal tone, as in Njál's declaration of *fjǫrráð* in the forest encounter and in the crafted questions and answers of the Geirmund-Flosi exchange; in this they echo, in the burning sequence, the solemn instruction and then interrogation of the steward; and, at the excavation, the careful comparison of "verdicts" [*atkvæði*]. And of course both passages appear to be the products of unclarity: smoky invisibility on one hand and, on the other, secret dealings and the question of intent.

It's as though, following every murky fact, there's a slot marked "proof segment" that needs filling with conclusive evidence. The obvious example here is the publication of a killing to someone nearby. Discussed in the laws and richly attested in the sagas, formal admissions of this kind appear to constitute unequivocal proof; some take the form of full scenes, but it is also appears that a one-sentence report will do.[13] The saga's heftiest proof segments, however, are the ones like Njál's forest scene and, in the burning chapters, the Geirmund, steward, and inquest episodes—passages in which the saga must turn to circumstantial evidence. Needless to say, circumstantial reasoning requires fuller accounts. In *Njáls saga*, at least, the rule would seem to be that the scarcer the data, the longer and more elaborate the proof segments (and the less credible they may seem). But the discursive implication of all proof segments, especially but not only the unlikely-sounding ones, is that without some such evidence, neither feud retaliation nor lawsuit (nor saga) can go forward.

What interests me here, though, is not so much the authenticity or inauthenticity of the proof segments themselves as it is the power of the slot. Njál's forest scene may be a later invention, but the fact that a teller or writer along the way knew there had to be evidence at this moment in the text says a lot about the customary necessity of evidence in the lead-up to a counteraction. Fabricated proof segments are not unlike those skaldic poems believed to have been composed not by the claimed poet at the claimed time, but by another person at a later date: that someone saw fit to put a certain kind of poem at just that point tells us something about the traditional role of skaldic verse in saga prose.[14] (No wonder certain poems—like the one ascribed to an otherwise-unknown Þorkell Elfaraskáld after the death of Gunnar—feel a lot like proof segments: they look to be manifestations of the same compositional habit.) Even when we suspect *everything* of being pseudo—the as-it-happens narration, the proof segment, *and* the action it looks forward to--we are still looking at a pattern whereby potential lawsuits and acts of revenge were expected to be justified by facts in evidence. We are looking, in other words, at a compositional enterprise in which legal expectations govern narrative even to the point of generating it. The implication of this in the ongoing discussion of saga origins clear enough: in long sections of the text, law is prior.

If *Njáls saga's* fact-finding is to be counted as premodern or prerational, it's not because facts weren't examined or didn't matter. It's that they were found by the wrong people (the participants) at the wrong time (too soon) in the wrong place (not in court). Again, though, it could hardly be otherwise in a stateless world in which feud and lawsuits were legal alternatives. However, if we look past the "wrongs" in the above sentence and focus instead on the text between the deed at hand and the payback action that lies ahead, we find an almost compulsive consideration of facts. Things happen; evidence is adduced; and a somehow-proved fact provides the basis for a counteraction in law or feud. This protocol is not occasional; lining up facts, one way or another, is the regular narrative business of *Njála* from its beginning to about a dozen chapters of the end.

It is of course unclear which of these narrative pieces are older and which younger, and which stem from oral tradition and which are writerly artifacts. What is clear, though, is that even in the late thirteenth century, the author of *Njáls saga* knew, and apparently knew that his audience knew, that proof, real or imagined, was needed in order for a tale even to be told. So, presumably, did earlier generations and the authors of the other sagas.[15] I take it as a given that for all its singularity where law is concerned, *Njála* is not unique in its fundamental narrative-building practices. No other saga may match its urgent sense of fact-finding, or the elegance of its evidence-driven narrative syncing, or what looks to be an over-the-top predilection for backformation in legal matters. But the probative or evidentiary protocol itself is hardly unique to *Njála*. Like the legal-objective voice, with which it is obviously of a piece, the probative mode is a basic condition of saga composition—such a familiar feature of the discursive landscape that we scarcely register it for what it is.

Let me say, in closing, what a privilege and a pleasure it has been to have worked all these years at a university able and willing to support two faculty members in the field of early Scandinavian culture. And to have had as a partner in this venture such a fine colleague and scholar as John Lindow has been nothing short of a gift.

Notes

1 I am particularly indebted here to William Ian Miller's 1990 *Bloodtaking and Peacemaking*, especially chapters 6, "Feud, Vengeance, and the Disputing Process" and 7 "Law and Legal Process." I have also learned from Gísli Sigurðsson's (2004) *The Medieval Icelandic Saga and Oral Tradition: A Discourse on Method*, especially chapter 1 ("From Lawspeaker to Lawbook"), which explores, among other things, the relation of lawspeaking and oral literary tradition and, more particularly, the tension between the tradition of speaking the laws and the church-associated push to write them down; and Tommy Danielsson's *Hrafnkels saga* (2002), especially the chapter "Domen" (see note 19, below).

2 As Miller concludes his discussion of *Njála*'s problematic status as a legal source, "Once the saga concerns itself with processual structures and disputing style, rather than with procedural technicality, it falls well within the range of patterns described in earlier sagas. But in matters of courtroom procedure the saga is to be used with caution, if at all" (Miller 1990, 364).

3 See *Oxford Companion to Law* and *Black's Law Dictionary* under "fact," "evidence," and "proof." I have used Anglo-American sources here in part because of the historical similarities between the early Icelandic trial and the present-day Anglo-American one (i.e., adversarial structure with jury-like body, as opposed to the Roman-canonical or "inquisitorial," top-down form that came to dominate all of Europe but England, which would later import it to its colonies. An early and enthusiastic student of the relation between English legal process and that of early Scandinavia, notably Iceland, was Þorleifur Guðmundsson Repp (1794-1857). That relation is a burden of his extraordinary *A Historical Treatise on Trial by Jury*,

Wager of Law, and Other Co-Ordinate Forensic Institutions, Formerly in Use in Scandinavia and in Iceland (especially pp. 5, 20, 42-3, 59-60,106, 129, 136, 152-63). In his election address to the voters of Árnessýsla, Repp was loud and clear in his view that the top-down inquisitorial Danish legal system was not suited to Iceland's long tradition and that the Icelanders should be inspired by the English example to urge revision of their Danish trial along English lines in order to recapture the spirit of the Commonwealth. "Forfeðr vorir höfðu fullt frelsi ok neyttu þess vel um ríð, ok var þá Íslands blómi mestr," he wrote. "Nú vil ek þat því till leggja við Íslendinga, er ek hefi áðr til lagt við Dani, at vér leggim alla stund á at nema vel lög Íslands, en fornu, en þar at auk lög Engla, sem þeim erum líkust ok upp runnin af sömu rót, ok at vér semjim vor lög öll sem mest má verða at þeirra dæmum" (Repp 1849, 2). See also Wawn (1991), especially 97 and 203-4.

[4] I have used the Íslenzk fornrit version of *Njáls saga* as my basis. Numbers refer to chapters, not pages. Translations are mostly from Magnusson and Pálsson with some silent adjustments of my own. I have generally preferred this translation because of the specificity of its legal terminology. On the literary function of the trials in *Njáls saga*, see Ordower 1991.

[5] On this and other legal formulas in *Njála*, see especially Lönnroth (1976, 241-48).

[6] "Denn der Gerichtsgang ist eine stilisierte Fehde" and "Der altisländische Prozess...ist eine Fehde, aber eine stilisierte, durch bestimmte Formen gebundene" (Heusler 1911, 103 and 108). Miller (1911, 232) adds that "Heusler's view of law as feud was not solely a function of the law's vengefulness; it also depended on the combativeness of the legal process itself." And "there was no state making the claim that law and feud were antithetical. No one understood law and feud to be necessarily opposed. But these facts do not so blur the line between legal process and self-help that we are entitled to dismiss the law as little more than an obfuscatory style of vengeance-taking. Legal process was not the feud itself" (235-36).

[7] For a recent discussion of narratological matters in the sagas of the Icelanders, see Vésteinn Ólason (1998, especially "Telling the Tale," 95-110). Vésteinn notes such matters as the sagas' "view with an unprejudiced eye the unfolding events," and their adoption of "the same tone of voice whether major or minor events are being described." This

"measured approach," he observes, "serves often to create a powerful contrast with the fateful events being described" (101). To some extent, I suspect, this contrast is an effect of the legal-objective voice. On legal language even in non-court contexts in *Hrafnkels saga*, see Danielsson 2002, 113-117.

[8] Consider the easy coexistence, in one and the same episode, of evidence-parsing on both the secular legal front (e.g., the location of Grím's corpse) and on the religious front (e.g., such canonizable qualities as the relatively incorrupt quality of Njál's body). Some of the evidence on the religious side is intriguingly equivocal: the state of Njál's body, which, as the singed nature of Thord's extended finger suggests, may be the effect of the oxhide's preservative qualities; the question of how Skarpheðin's body came to have burn marks in the shape of a cross (because of his position when he died?), and so on. Similarly on the secular side: was the cough really Njál's? Was the garbled poem really uttered by Skarpheðin?

[9] Rene Balcer, interview on National Public Radio's "Talk of the Nation," September 29, 2009. Balcer is here speaking of the "mother ship" *Law & Order* (not *Special Victims Unit*, *Law & Order Criminal Intent*, etc.). See http://allthingslawandorder.blogspot.com/2009/10/rene-balcer-on-producing-law-order.html

[10] For an account of this and other transmission models, see Frank (1985) and Guðrún Nordal (2001 and, with specific reference to *Njála*, 2005 and 2008).

[11] The locus classicus here is Sigurður Nordal's *Hrafnkatla* (1940). For an opposing view (and a valuable history of scholarship on that touchstone text), see Tommy Danielsson (2002). Especially useful for present purposes is his chapter "Domen" (113-24).

[12] Under "Intent," *Black's Law Dictionary of Law* has "Design, resolve, or determination with which person acts. A state of mind in which a person seeks to accomplish a given result through a course of action." On state of mind in *Grágás*, see Miller (1990, 248).

[13] *Grágás*'s extensive rules on confessions before witnesses give the impression that the act of publishing was itself something of a mini-trial of the facts. As well it might be, given the effect it could have on the outcome.

[14] As Guðrún Nordal (2005 and 2008) has pointed out, tracking the history of the inclusion of skaldic verse in the (unusually numerous) manuscripts of *Njáls saga* provides a picture of changing tastes with respect to saga's prose-verse practices.

[15] This seems even likelier given the connection Gísli Sigurðsson posits between law in practice and the larger oral tradition. "Judging from the writings ascribed to him," Gísli writes, "Snorri was fully at home in the oral heritage of stories and poems, and it is not improbable that oral knowledge of the law went hand in hand with other kinds of oral learning and the rhetorical use of language implicit in oral poetry" (117). Danielsson (2002) also stresses the significance of such a massive public-sphere oral tradition for such a long time and during such a formative period. "De gamla lagarna förmedlades muntligt, och den uppgiften ålåg lagsagomannen, ett ämbete som vi sett inrättas i och med alltinget och som ägde bestånd ända fram till år 1271. På grund av recitationskraven— helt lagen under tre allting—kan man bara föreställa sig den tid och den kraft som måste ha lagts ned för att kunna bli lagsagoman, och *Þórðarbók* nämner—antagligen efter *Mélabók*—att Úlfljótr var den förste på Ísland att undervisa i lagkunskap. Samtidigt måste den allmänna insikten om lagarnas utformning då, innan paragraferna gömdes undan i svåråtkomliga handskrifter, ha varit betydligt större än längre fram i tiden" (117). Further: "Tanken att man automatiskt föreställde sig att omständigheterna på 1100-talet var annorlunda än dem på 900-talet förutsätter ju en historisk grundsyn som dröjde til romantiken att växa fram. Samtidigt kan det inte uteslutas att äldre konventioner levt kvar i muntliga sidokällor eller knutna till själva berättelsen, till den muntliga sagan. Vi har således att ta hänsyn till tree möjliga tidsskikt i sagan. Dels skeendets samtid och de seder och bruk som senare undergick förändring eller helt och hållet försvann. Dels mellanperiodens lagar, speciellt då det faktum att en skriftlig kodifiering ägde rum genom *Grágás*-manuskipten. Dels samtiden lagar och konventioner" (2002, 122). Although Danielsson is speaking of *Hrafnkatla* here, his observations (with which I agree) may be extended to the Íslendingasögur more generally. Finally, Theodore M. Andersson includes, in his list of six aspects of saga narrative that must have had precedents in the oral period, "traditions about lawsuits, which we find almost everywhere…" (2006,16).

Rasmus B. Anderson and Vínland: Mythbreaking and Mythmaking[1]

Úlfar Bragason

Rasmus Bjørn Anderson (January 12, 1846 – March 2, 1936) may be called the father of Nordic studies in the United States: not only did he introduce courses in Scandinavian Languages as soon as he became an instructor at the University of Wisconsin in Madison in 1869, and continue with them after being appointed to a professor's chair at the university in 1875 until his retirement in 1883 (Hustvedt 1966, 89–122); he was also untiring in his efforts, in the spoken word and in print, to increase awareness of Nordic culture. Professor Einar I. Haugen wrote of Anderson's work:

> He was a man with a brilliant memory and unflagging determination, whose originality consisted rather in doing the things he did at all than in the manner of his doing them. In a pioneer community he was the focus of important cultural influences, and his gift for popular presentation and narrative made him a highly pertinent instrument for the dissemination of these influences. In a country utterly unaware of Scandinavian culture he broke the ground for a wider appreciation and more exhaustive study. (Haugen 1937, 261)

Anderson's interests focused not least on the sagas that recount the discovery and settlement of Vínland, and other sources, true and suppositious, on the discovery of the New World. His book *America Not Discovered by Columbus: A Historical Sketch of the Discovery of America by the Norsemen, in the Tenth Century*, first published in 1874, undoubtedly contributed to greater awareness in America of the ocean journeys of Norse seafarers, while also disseminating dubious theories and claims; the book was reissued a total of eight times, most recently in 1930. But its main impact was to make Leifr Eiríksson more widely known in the USA, to counteract the reputation of Christopher Columbus. With respect to Leifr "the Lucky," Anderson was a mythmaker, and for Columbus he was a mythbreaker. The intention here is to discuss the book, the reasons why it was written, the facts presented there, and also dubious assertions and their provenance. Last but not least, the writing of the book will be viewed in the context of the circumstances of Anderson's life, and his relationship with Norwegians and Icelanders on both sides of the Atlantic.

In his biography, *Rasmus Bjørn Anderson: Pioneer Scholar*, Lloyd Hustvedt recounts that Norwegian violin virtuoso Ole Bull and Rasmus Anderson were keen for a monument to Leifr Eiríksson to be erected in Madison, Wisconsin. With the aim of raising funds for the project, the two men travelled to Norway together in the summer of 1873, and Ole Bull gave six fund-raising concerts. Among those present at the first concert were author Bjørnstjerne Bjørnson, who gave a speech in support of the project, and composer Edvard Grieg, who accompanied Bull on the piano in one of his own compositions. Bjørnson also promised to come to Madison in 1876 to unveil the statue. On his return from Norway, Anderson settled down to write *America Not Discovered by Columbus*, the main purpose of which was to win support and financial backing for the proposed monument. The project, however, never came to fruition, and in due course Ole Bull contributed the funds raised in Norway to a statue of Leifr Eiríksson in Boston, which was unveiled in 1887 (Hustvedt 1966, 130–133).

Rasmus B. Anderson's motivation for writing the book explains to some degree its form. Lloyd Hustvedt's judgment of the book is that "apart from its startling title and bold presentation, nothing in *America Not Discovered by Columbus* was new" (Hustvedt 1966, 354). In the book, however, Anderson mentioned the proposed statue of Leifr only in a footnote, as follows:

> A step toward the vindication of the claims of the Norsemen to the honor of having discovered, settled,

and made America known to the world, has been made, and a movement has been inaugurated for the erection of a monument in the memory of the Norse navigator, LEIF ERIKSON, who visited and explored America in the year 1000, nearly five centuries before Columbus. For the realization of this object OLE BULL has contributed his eminent services. He has already given several concerts, both in this country and in Norway, the proceeds of which go to the monument fund. OLE BULL is President, Senator JOHN A. JOHNSON, Treasurer, and the writer of these pages Secretary, of the monument committee. Norway's famous poet and orator, BJÖRSTJERNE BJÖRNSON [...] has promised to write, for the dedication of the monument, a cantata, to which the eminent Norse composer, EDWARD GRIEG, will write the music. BJÖRNSON has also promised to come to America in person and deliver the dedication oration. (Anderson 1874, 19)

In his foreword to the book Anderson called it a "sketch" (as he also did in the subtitle). Its object, he said, is "to present a readable and truthful narrative of the Norse discovery of America, to create some interest in the people, the literature, and the early institutions of Norway, and especially in Iceland, – that lonely and weird island, – the ULTIMA THULE of the Greek Philosophers" (Anderson 1874, v–vi). In the foreword he also stated that he had "freely made use of such material as he considered valuable for his purpose from the works of Torfæus, C. C. Rafn, J. T. Smith, N. L. Beamish, G. Gravier, B. F. De Costa, A. Davis, William and Mary Howitt, R. M. Ballantyne, P. A. Munch, R. Keyser, and others" (Anderson 1874, v). In other words, Anderson never implied that the book was based upon his own original research, but frankly admitted that it was compiled on the basis of the work of other writers and scholars (Haugen 1937, 259). However, as he rarely cited these sources specifically in the book, it is not an easy task to trace the provenance of specific arguments, or how he developed them.

In truth, the reviewers of the first edition of *America Not Discovered by Columbus* appear to have been quite clear on the significance of the book. Most reviews were favorable. Comments included: "Another image breaker" – "These scholars are fearful fellows. They have destroyed our Wm. Tell, played havoc with Washington, shaken Shakespeare's standing, and now comes another." The review pointed out, however, that: "It deals largely with questions of which the author obviously has no clear knowledge himself, and hence he is incapable of estimating at their right the various authorities which he brings forward with ostentatious impartiality." The book was also seen as propaganda, either for Anderson himself, or for the monument to Leifr Eiríksson (Hustvedt 1966, 315).

Who and what are the sources Anderson claimed to have for the Norse voyages to Vínland? Firstly he mentions Torfæus, otherwise Þormóður Torfason, whose translations of the Vínland sagas into Latin were published in Copenhagen in 1705. The next source cited is C. C. Rafn, whose work *Antiqvitates Americanæ sive scriptores septentrionales rerum ante–Columbianarum in America,* published in Copenhagen in 1837, became hugely influential on both sides of the Atlantic. No doubt this was a contributory factor in the subsequent development that more has been written about the two Vínland sagas than any other saga (see Bergersen 1997). Not only did Rafn publish the texts of *Eiríks saga rauða* (the Saga of Eiríkr the Red) and *Grænlendinga saga* (the Saga of Greenlanders); they were also accompanied by translations into both Danish and Latin. In addition the publication included color facsimiles of several manuscript folios and diagrams of alleged Viking-Age archaeological finds in New England, followed by edited correspondence between scholars in Copenhagen and Boston relating to these finds. In all probability it was this publication that formed the foundation of Anderson's "sketch," and no doubt this was the source of Anderson's knowledge of the Vínland sagas, as well as the credence he placed in alleged archaeological discoveries (see Anderson 1874, 17–18, 60–62). As a matter of fact, *Antiquitates Americanae* has been called "the CD ROM disc of nineteenth-century Vínland scholarship, praised for its production values, but mocked for lending unwonted encouragement to a new breed of cult archaeologists in North America" (Wawn 2001, 193).

The third source mentioned by Anderson is Joshua T. Smith, who published, only two years after *Antiquitates Americanae*, his book *Northmen in New England, or America in the Tenth Century.* Basing his work on Rafn's sources, Smith wrote more than three hundred pages, seeking to convince his readers of the veracity of the Vínland sagas and the authenticity of the Dighton Writing Rock, the Newport Tower, and the purported remains of a Viking warrior found near Fall River, Massachusetts, and maintained that Christopher Columbus had acquired information about America before he undertook his journey (Hustvedt 1966, 313). Anderson was clearly won over by Smith's arguments, as all these items reappear in his book, presented as unassailable truths.

Next Anderson cites North Ludlow Beamish; his *The Discovery of America by the Northmen*, published in 1841, was for many years the "acknowledged authority" on the Norse discoveries in the New World (Hustvedt 1966, 313). Anderson refers to Gabriel Gravier's *Découverte de l'Amérique par les Normands au Xe siècle*, published in Paris in 1874, as a source. As this book was published in the same year as Anderson's own "sketch," it is unlikely to have been of any importance, other than to demonstrate that he was keeping up with the latest scholarship on the Vínland explorations. The same applies to B. F. DeCosta's *The Pre-Columbian Discovery of America by the Northmen*, published in 1868. DeCosta ruled out the Dighton Rock, the Newport Tower and other alleged proofs as having any connection with Norsemen, but Anderson ignored those points (Hustvedt 1966, 313–315). Anderson cites DeCosta directly only once in his book, with respect to the antiquity of America (Anderson 1874, 21).

Another source named by Anderson is Asahel Davis's *Lecture on the Discovery of America by the Northmen, Five Hundred Years before Columbus*. The lecture had been published many times when Anderson wrote his book, and it is still in print today. Anderson borrows Davis's concluding words for his own work, thus demonstrating that they were twin souls (Anderson 1874, 75–76).

Anderson counts among his sources William and Mary Howitt; he cites them to support his view that the Norsemen's "spirit found its way into the Magna Charta" (Anderson 1874, 40). Here Anderson is probably referring to *The Literature and Romance of Northern Europe*, published in London in 1852. The book was much read on both sides of the Atlantic. It contains the assertion that "though Britain had long ago absorbed and smoothed over the rough edges of its Viking inheritance, the people retain 'the old Norse fire in their veins'" (Wawn 2000, 109). R. M. Ballantyne also features on the list of Anderson's sources. The reference is apparently to Ballantyne's novels *Erling the Bold* (1869) and *The Norsemen in the West* (1872). Anderson may here have detected a resonance with his praise for liberty, natural rights and local democracy, and also found his inspiration for his description of a Viking ship in chapter eight. The cover illustration of *Erling the Bold* features just such a dragon ship (Wawn 2000, 321–323). Norwegians P. A. Munch and Rudolf Keyser are mentioned as sources. The reference is probably to Munch's *Det norske Folks Historie*, published in eight volumes from 1852 to 1859, and a two-volume *Norges historie* by Keyser, published in 1866 to 1870. This is probably where Anderson found his ideas on the origins of the Norsemen, expounded in chapter four.

Anderson mentions several other sources in his book. For instance, he quotes at length from Henry Wadsworth Longfellow's poem "The Skeleton in Armor," and refers to Alexander von Humboldt's *Cosmos*, vol. II, and *Nouvelles annales des voyages, de la géographie, de l'histoire et de l'archéologie*, edited by V.-A. Malte-Brun, with respect to the veracity of the Vínland sagas, which he presents as beyond dispute (Anderson 1874, 43). He mentions the medieval manuscript *Flateyjarbók* (the Flatey Book). Its text was edited by Guðbrandur Vigfússon and Carl Richard Unger and was published in Christiania in 1860–1868. According to Anderson there was a copy of the book in Mimer's Library at the University of Wisconsin; he himself had been responsible for putting together this library's collection (Hustvedt 1966, 57, 106, 123). And he clearly makes use of *Flateyjarbók*, as in several chapters of his book he retells the story of *Grænlendinga saga* that is preserved in that manuscript, but gives no account from *Eiríks saga rauða*, nor mentions the discrepancies between the accounts in the two sagas. Anderson makes, on the other hand, no reference to Samuel Laing's English translation of *Heimskringla*, published in 1844. In his discussion of this compilation of sagas, Laing devotes considerable space (I, 141–187) to the question of where Vínland may have been (Wawn 2000, 97–100). Anderson himself would in due course be editor of the second edition of the translation in 1889, and in 1891 he published a pamphlet, *Where Was Vinland?* Laing was thus in all probability among Anderson's sources for his book (Hustvedt 1966, 332–333).

America Not Discovered by Columbus is one hundred and four pages long in small format. The book is handsomely bound by publisher S. C. Griggs in Chicago. Of the one hundred and four pages, an appendix occupies pages 77–104, on the historical, linguistic, literary and scientific value of the Scandinavian languages, including a selection of "quotations from eminent American, English, German and French scholars." Anderson's text is thus accurately termed a "sketch." As witness Anderson's selection of sources of his book, his critics were correct in their assessment of his lack of original investigation and scholarly evaluation of the subject. On the other hand, it was not Anderson's intention to write a work of scholarship, but a "readable and truthful narrative." His aim was "to present the reader with a brief account of the discovery of, early voyages to, and settlements in the Western Continent by the Norsemen, and to prove that Columbus must have had knowledge of this discovery by the Norsemen before he started to find America" (Anderson 1874, 9). The critics were also correct in their inference that the sketch served, in addition, as propaganda for the erection of a monument to commemorate Leifr Eiríksson, while also promoting Anderson himself. At that time he was seeking tenure at the University of Wisconsin in the field of Scandinavian studies, although he was under-qualified. He was in a hurry to publish in his academic field, and thus decided on Vínland, a subject on which he had been lecturing since 1868 (Hustvedt 1966, 57–58, 142–143; Øverland 2000, 154–155). The book is dedicated to his principal patron in his campaign for tenure, Prof. Stephen H. Carpenter (Hustvedt 1966, 98).

Anderson also wanted to draw attention to the fact that Nordic studies were a recognized academic discipline in the Nordic countries and elsewhere, and that they were important for Americans. The first two chapters of the volume are devoted to putting this point across, as is the Appendix in its entirety. In chapter one, the author states the view that the account of the Norse discovery of America must surely be as of much interest to Americans as to the Nordic peoples:

> For those who are born and brought up on the fertile soil of Columbia, under the shady branches of the noble tree of American liberty, where the banner of progress and education is unfurled to the breeze, must naturally feel a deep interest in whatever facts may be presented in relation to the first discovery and early settlement of this their native land; while those who first saw the sunlight beaming among the rugged, snow-capped mountains of mountains of old Norway, and can still feel any of the heroic blood of their dauntless forefathers course its way through their veins, must, as a matter of course, feel an equally deep interest in learning that their own ancestors, the intrepid Norsemen, were the first pale-faced men who planted their feet on this gem of the ocean, and an interest too, I dare say, in having the claims of their native country to this honor vindicated. (Anderson 1874, 11)

These words demonstrate that the tone of the book is, at least in places, anything but scholarly.

Chapter two commences with praise for the New World, on which the eyes of all enlightened men are focused, "from which great revolutions have proceeded, and in which great problems in human government, human progress and enterprise, are yet to be worked out and demonstrated" (Anderson 1874, 15). The author then turns to the Norse discoveries, stating that until recently it has been believed that Europeans knew nothing of the New World before the time of Columbus; too few, he says, have sought out evidence from northern Europe, for in the Nordic countries is to be found "incontestable evidence that the coast of North America was discovered in the latter part of the tenth century" (Anderson 1874, 16). He goes on to propound his theory that Norsemen continued to visit the coast of North America into the fourteenth century, concluding with the assertion that sources show that Christianity was adopted not only by the Norse in America, but also by the aboriginal population!

Anderson discusses the primary sources, mentioning the publications of Torfæus and Rafn, which he showers with praise. He then points out that the Germans and British have realized the significance of Norse sources for their own history, and expresses the wish that the Americans may do so too. The Germans and British, he maintains, are translating saga literature "as fast as they can," and he cites the research of Konrad Maurer and Th. Moebius in Germany. In Great Britain, he says, there are Icelandic professors at the universities of Oxford and Cambridge, and Nordic languages are taught at three US universities: Cornell, Michigan and Wisconsin. He ends the chapter with the hope "that the time is not far distant when the Norsemen will be recognized in their right social, political, and literary character, and at the same time as navigators assume their true position in the pre-Columbian discovery of America" (Anderson 1874, 19).

In chapter three, Anderson turns his attention to the antiquity of America, and in chapter four he considers whether other Europeans may have reached the New World before the Norse; he concludes that there is no reliable evidence of any such discovery. In chapter five Anderson asks: Who were the Norsemen? He traces their ancestry back to Asia, and describes their language as "the Old Norse, which is still preserved and spoken in Iceland" (Anderson 1874, 24). He stresses that they were free: "They were a free people. Their rulers were elected by the people in convention assembled, and all public matters of importance were decided in the assemblies, or open parliament of the people" (Anderson 1874, 24–25). They had an international reputation, he says, as bold adventurers; they conquered territories, formed colonies as far south as Sicily, and took part in the Crusades. Last but not least, he recounts that the

English royal family is descended from Rollo, or Hrólfr, son of Earl Rögnvaldr of Møre.

Chapter six is devoted to Iceland. Anderson places the settlement of the island in the context of the unification of Norway in the time of King Harald Fairhair: "Political circumstances in Norway urged many of the boldest and most independent people in the country to seek an asylum of freedom" (Anderson 1874, 28). He also draws a parallel between the medieval settlement of Iceland and the mass emigration from Europe to the New World in the nineteenth century: "There were as great emigrations from Norway in those days as there are now. The Norse spirit of enterprise is as old as their history" (Anderson 1874, 29). Anderson then draws up a picture of the Icelanders "surrounded the whole year by dreary ice-mountains, the glare of volcanic flames, and the roaring of geysers or boiling springs" (Anderson 1874, 31), and concludes that the Icelanders' interest in Eddic poetry and sagas was a function of the long, harsh winters. He apologizes, admittedly, for devoting so much space to Iceland, but puts forward the justification that "in the first place, Iceland is of itself an exceedingly interesting country; and, in the next place, it is really the *hinge upon which the door swings* which opened America to Europe" (Anderson 1874, 31). It was as a result of ocean journeys between Norway and Iceland, he says, that Greenland and America came to be discovered, and "it is due to the high intellectual standing and fine historical taste of the Icelanders" that accounts of the discoveries were preserved in Iceland, in due course to be passed on to Columbus, and to help in resolving the enigma of Vínland (Anderson 1874, 32). He discusses contemporary Icelandic culture, and Iceland's status as a place where Norse culture has been preserved. Icelandic medieval literature, he says, is superior to all other literature of its time, and it is now being compared with the Greek and Roman classics.

Chapter seven deals with the Norse discovery and settlement of Greenland, and the four-hundred-year history of the colony, and in chapter eight Anderson focuses on the ships of the Norsemen. He says that he himself has crossed the Atlantic four times, and is thus well aware of what was required in order to sail safely on such a long journey. He has also seen with his own eyes, he says, one of the old Viking ships, which is preserved at the University of Norway. Admittedly, he points out, such vessels cannot be compared with the modern ocean liners which ply the waters between New York and Liverpool; but the Norse were, and still are, outstanding navigators, and had fine ships at their disposal. He takes the example of the "Long Serpent," the great ship of King Olaf Tryggvason of Norway, as a magnificent vessel, and concludes with the information that "its stem and stern were overlaid with gold"! He expresses the view that the ships of the Vikings were in no way inferior to the *Nina,* the *Pinta* and the *Santa Maria.* And the Norse seafarers knew how "to calculate the course of the sun and moon, and how to measure time by the stars" (Anderson 1874, 39). Anderson concludes the chapter by voicing his idea that the Norsemen's spirit of freedom and autonomy made its mark on the Magna Carta in England, and the US Declaration of Independence in America: "The spirit of the Vikings still survives in the bosoms of Englishmen, Americans and Norsemen, extending their commerce, taking bold positions against tyranny, and producing wonderful internal improvements in these countries" (Anderson 1874, 40). The Declaration of Independence has traditionally been the central document of the American ideology of liberty, and hence it was important for the immigrants of the 19th century to demonstrate that they too shared in that heritage (Øverland 2000, 133).

In chapter nine Anderson focused on the veracity of the historical sources for the Norse discovery of the America. However, instead of presenting arguments in favor of this view, he simply cites Alexander von Humboldt and V.-A. Malte-Brun as authorities – perhaps because these writers were not themselves from the Nordic countries, and thus the American readership would realize that their views were generally accepted among the European intelligentsia. Anderson then moves on to the *Flateyjarbók* manuscript; this is the source of the next five chapters of the book, which recount the Norse exploration and settlement in the New World. He briefly summarizes the story as told in the *Saga of Greenlanders,* in the *Flateyjarbók.*[2] This is reflected in the chapter headings: chapter 10 is "Bjarne Herjulfson, 986," chapter 11 "Leif Erikson, 1000," chapter 12 "Thorwald Erikson, 1002," chapter 13

"Thorstein Erikson, 1005," chapter 14 "Thorfinn Karlsefne and Gudrid, 1007," and chapter 15 "Other Expeditions by the Norsemen."

Ólafur Halldórsson, who has studied sources on Greenland in medieval writing, and is an editor of *Eiríks saga rauða*, writes of *Grænlendinga saga:*

> Grænlendinga saga er ekki saga einnar persónu, ættar eða héraðs; megninefni sögunnar er frásögn af fundi Vínlands og af Vínlandsferðunum. [...] Frásagnir eru í réttri tímaröð, og tekur ein við af annarri; aldrei er fléttað saman tveimur frásögnum eða meginfrásögn fleyguð með innskotum sem rjúfa rétta tímaröð. Engir ársettir atburðir eru nefndir til viðmiðunar um tímatal, nema hvað þess er getið, að við upphaf sögunnar var fólk heiðið á Grænlandi, en Grænland var kristnað þegar Þorvaldur Eiríksson andaðist á Vínlandi, "en þó andaðisk Eiríkr rauði fyrir kristni" [...]. Að öðru leyti er ekkert sagt frá kristnitöku eða kristniboði á Grænlandi, og kristnitakan er ekki ársett. (Ólafur Halldórsson 1985, 374–375)

> [The Saga of Greenlanders is not a saga of one person, one clan or one region of the country; its principal content is an account of the discovery of Vínland and of voyages to and from Vínland. [...] The events are recounted in chronological order, one after the other; there is no intertwining of two narratives, nor any interpolation of interludes in the main narrative to disrupt the chronological order. No events which can be dated to a specific year are mentioned in the narrative, to provide a clue to the chronology, except for the statement that at the beginning of the saga the people in Greenland were heathens, while by the time of Þorvaldr Eiríksson's death in Vínland Greenland had been converted to Christianity, "but Eiríkr the Red died before

Christian times" [...]. Otherwise, nothing is said of
the adoption of Christianity in Greenland, nor of
Christian missionary efforts, and no date is specified
for the adoption of the new religion.]

From this Halldórsson draws the conclusion that the author of the
saga was not concerned with giving an impression of historicity
through a clear chronological framework.

From the chapter headings in Anderson's book, it is clear that
his dating of the discovery of Vínland and the voyages to the New
World is based on his other sources. He also seeks to pinpoint
where the Vínland voyagers may have gone in North America, in
accord with the discourse of the time. He says, for instance, of the
voyage of Bjarni Herjólfsson:

> It cannot be determined with certainty what parts of
> the American coast Bjarne saw; but from the
> circumstances of the voyage, the course of the
> winds, the direction of the currents, and the
> presumed distance between each sight of land, there
> is reason to believe that the first land Bjarne saw in
> the year 986 was the present NANTUCKET, one
> degree south of Boston; the second NOVA
> SCOTIA, and the third NEWFOUNDLAND.
> Thus BJARNE HERJULFSON was the first
> *European* whose eyes beheld any part of the
> American continent. (Anderson 1874, 47)

Anderson's treatment of the *Grœnlendinga saga* may be seen in his use
of chapters three and four of the saga, in his account of Leifr
Eiríksson's voyage to Vínland.

Anderson briefly summarizes the content of chapter three of
the saga, but omits the story that Eiríkr the Red intended to
accompany his son Leifr on his expedition, but changed his mind
after being thrown by his horse on his way to board the ship.
Anderson states that Leifr's booths were at Mount Hope Bay. After
quoting the saga's statement that the hours of daylight were more

equal at Leifr's booths than in Iceland or Greenland, and the (much-debated) words that "sól hafði þar eyktar stað og dagmála stað um skammdegi" (the sun was visible there both at supper time and breakfast time at the winter solstice), Anderson asserts: "which circumstance gives for the latitude of the place 41°24'10"; hence Leif's booths are thought to have been situated at or near Fall River, Massachusetts" (Anderson 1874, 50). After this Anderson retails the story of why Leifr called the new land *Vínland*, using as his source chapter four of the *Grœnlendinga saga*:

> There was a German in Leif Erikson's party by name TYRKER. He was a prisoner of war, but had become Leif's special favorite. He was missing one day after they came back from an exploring expedition. Leif Erikson became very anxious about Tyrker, and fearing that he might be killed by wild beasts or by Indians, he went out with a few men to search for him. Toward evening he was found coming home, but in a very excited state of mind. The cause of his excitement was some fruit which he found, and which he held up in his hands, shouting: "Weintrauben! Weintrauben!! Weintrauben!!!" The sight and taste of this fruit, to which he had been accustomed in his own native land, had excited him to such an extent that he seemed drunk, and for some time he would do nothing but laugh, devour grapes and talk German, which language our Norse discoverers did not understand. At last he spoke Norse, and explained that he, to his great joy and surprise, had found vines and grapes in great abundance. From this circumstance the land got the name of VINLAND, and history got the interesting fact that a German was along with the daring argonauts of the Christian era. (Anderson 1874, 50–51)

Anderson has both abbreviated the story, and added to it. The saga, for instance, makes no mention of Tyrkir being "a prisoner of war," or of Leifr fearing that Tyrkir "might be killed by wild beasts or by

Indians." Indeed, at this point in the saga neither wild beasts nor Native Americans have made any appearance. And Anderson adds, on his own initiative, Tyrkir's exclamation "Weintrauben! ..." The conclusion that a German was among the explorers is also Anderson's own invention, and entirely typical of him.

At the beginning of chapter twelve, Anderson recounts Leifr Eiríksson's return from Vínland to Greenland. This account is taken from the end of chapter four of the saga, but Anderson omits the story that Leifr rescued shipwrecked people on the way home, after which he was known as "the Lucky." Anderson does not use that well-known soubriquet in his book.

Chapter sixteen of Anderson's book is about "The Discovery of America by Columbus." Here he traces links between the Norse discovery of the New World and Columbus's journey. He lists five factors to support the theory that Columbus must have known about America before he set off: 1) Guðríðr Þorbjarnardóttir's pilgrimage to Rome, after her return to Iceland; 2) The nomination of Eiríkr *upsi* as Bishop of Vínland around 1100 AD by Pope Paschal II; 3) Adam of Bremen's account of Vínland; 4) a Vínland map, which he concedes cannot be definitely authenticated; 5) and Columbus's visit to Iceland in 1477. At the same time, Anderson alleges that Columbus concealed his prior knowledge of the territories he "discovered."

In the final chapter of his book, Anderson summed up as follows:

> Let us remember LEIF ERIKSON, the first white man who planted his feet on American soil! Let us remember his brother, THORWALD ERIKSON, the first European and the first Christian who was buried beneath American sod! Let us not forget THORFINN and GUDRID, who established the first European colony in America! nor their son, SNORRE, the first man of European blood whose birthplace was in the New World! Let us erect a

> monument to Leif Erikson worthy of the man and
> the cause. (Anderson 1874, 74)

He ended the book with a lengthy citation from Asahel Davis, as mentioned before.

With the publication of his book, Anderson wanted to demolish the myth of Columbus as the discoverer of America, and place Leifr Eiríksson on a pedestal. The book was in fact part of fostering a much larger home-making mythology for Norwegians in the United States, to which Anderson made a crucial contribution (Øverland 2000, 147–166). The main points of that mythology, which was intended to demonstrate that Norwegians were as entitled to be in the United States as the Anglo-Saxon element, are stated in the book: that the Norse were the first Europeans to discover America, and that democratic traditions had sprung from Norwegian roots, spreading from there to Normandy, then to England and thence to the New World.

But Iceland too had an important place in that mythology. It was in Iceland that the written evidence for the discovery of America, and for ancient political freedoms in Norway, had been preserved; and it was to Iceland that freedom-loving Norsemen had fled the tyrannical rule of King Harald Fairhair. In Iceland, allegedly, Columbus had learned of the existence of the New World. The section on Iceland in *America Not Discovered by Columbus* is a paean of unconditional praise. In addition, Anderson chooses to use the word *Norsemen* and not *Northmen/Norwegians*: a much broader term, *Norse* could embrace many peoples, and especially the Icelanders, whom Anderson saw as being of Norwegian origin. In the section on the origins of the Norse, Anderson states that Icelandic is the same language as Old Norse: and he ends his discussion of Columbus with these speculations:

> If the communication between Vinland and the
> North could have been maintained say one hundred
> years longer, that is to the middle of fifteenth
> century, it is difficult to determine what the result
> would have been. Possibly this sketch would have

appeared   in   *Icelandic*   instead   of   English.
Undoubtedly   the   Norse   colonies   would   have
become   firmly   rooted   by   that   time,   and   Norse
language, nationality, and institutions might have
played as conspicuous a part in America as the
English   and   their   posterity   do   now-a-days.
(Anderson 1874, 72–73)

The Romanticized image of Iceland was nothing new. Artists and
intellectuals, both in the Nordic countries and elsewhere, had
nurtured and upheld this idealized view of old Iceland. In Europe
there was an intense interest in Iceland and Old Icelandic literature
(see Wawn 2000; Lassen 2008). But Anderson's enthusiasm was
probably genuine. Just as he had collected books for the colleges
where he had taught, he worked with Willard Fiske to collect books
for libraries in Iceland to mark the millennium of the settlement in
1874 (Rögnvaldur Pétursson 1933, 75). That historical landmark is
also mentioned in *America Not Discovered by Columbus* (p. 30).

Icelanders who emigrated to America in the early 1870s
clustered in Milwaukee, and they had become interested in
Anderson, perhaps due to his lectures on Nordic studies and his
articles in the press. The Icelandic immigrants had close links with
Norwegian communities in their early days in the United States, and
received help from their Norwegian "kinsmen." The Rev. Jón
Bjarnason, who had emigrated in 1873, became acquainted with
Anderson, and the two men collaborated on translations of saga
literature   (Hustvedt 1966, 325).   Anderson was invited to a
celebration held by the Icelanders in Milwaukee on 2 August 1874
to mark the millennium of the settlement of Iceland, but was not
able to attend (Rögnvaldur Pétursson 1933). This interaction
between the Icelanders in America and Anderson, together with his
links to Willard Fiske, may explain why he accords Iceland such
important status in his book. And Anderson's new mythology
influenced the Icelanders in the New World as much as the
Norwegians (see Wolf 2001).[3]

Rasmus B. Anderson was keen for his message to reach Iceland
too and, via the Rev. Jón Bjarnason, he contacted poet Matthías

Jochumsson, who was editor of the periodical *Þjóðólfur*. Jochumsson wrote to Anderson, thanking him for sending a copy of *America Not Discovered by Columbus*, in a letter dated 19 October 1875, and on 6 October 1877 he writes another letter to thank him:

> Meðtakið mínar hjartanlegar þakkir fyrir yðar ágætu bækur: Norse Mythologie, Viking Tales and America not Disc. – allar skilvíslega meðteknar, allar í ljómandi bandi – allar ágætlega prentaðar og – allar ágætlega skrifaðar. Mér skal bæði vera æra og ánægja að geta um þær yður til lofs og dýrðar í Þjóðólfi, því 1° eiga ritin það skilið 2° Þér sjáfur sem höfundur þeirra, og 3°er það okkur og okkar bókmentum hin mesta sæmd að hið nýja hið uppyngda mannkyn nýja heimsins eignist hlut í okkar frægu bókmentum.

> [Accept my sincere thanks for your excellent books: Norse Mythologie, Viking Tales and America not Disc. – all received promptly, all handsomely bound – all very well printed and – all very well written. I shall be honoured and delighted to mention them for your praise and glory in Þjóðólfur, for firstly, the books deserve it, and secondly you yourself as their author, and thirdly it is the greatest honour for us and our literature that the newly-rejuvenated humanity of the New World should gain a share in our renowned literary heritage.]

Jochumsson promised that he would mention the publications in *Þjóðólfur*. He and Anderson continued to correspond at least until the 1890s, and Jochumsson thanked Anderson for his admission to the Folk Lore Congress Committee, in connection with the World's Columbian Exposition in Chicago in 1893 (letter dated 6 Oct. 1892). He was sorely disappointed, however, that he was unable to meet Anderson on his visit to Chicago, nor promote Icelandic interests. But he thanked Anderson for sending him the text of his speech delivered to welcome the *Viking*, a replica of Leifr Eiríksson's ship, which sailed from Norway in April 1893 and arrived at Chicago in July that year, to make the point that it was Leifr the Lucky, not Columbus, who was the discoverer of America (letter dated 5 Sept. 1893).

During Rasmus B. Anderson's tenure as a professor at the University of Wisconsin, two editions of *America Not Discovered by Columbus* were published, with appendices, and when he was US Ambassador to Denmark 1885–1889 he arranged for the book to be translated into Danish and German. It was, however, criticized as "propaganda and fanaticism, devoid of academic merit" (Hustvedt 1966, 315–316). But that did not put an end to Anderson's interest in the feats of Leifr Eiríksson. On his return to the USA, he started to campaign for the establishment of an annual Leif Erikson Day, which later became a reality, and also exerted himself in support of a monument to Leifr in Chicago. He drew attention to Vínland, and himself, by engaging in a debate with Prof. Gustav Storm about the location of Vínland, and whether Columbus had known about America before he sailed there. Anderson never wavered in his conviction that Vínland was in New England, while Storm had reached the conclusion that it was located in Nova Scotia. And, unlike Storm, Anderson was always convinced that Columbus had known about America in advance of his journey (Haugen 1937, 259). His pamphlet *Where Was Vinland?* was part of his contribution to these disputes.

For that reason it was a grave disappointment to him that he – the author of *America Not Discovered by Columbus* and a former ambassador in Copenhagen – was not allocated a prominent role in the Norwegian celebrations in connection with the World's Columbian Exposition. He was not invited to be the principal speaker in Chicago on 17 May 1893, but had to settle for delivering a short address in praise of Norway, and when the *Viking* came to Chicago there was no place for him. His address was therefore delivered in Milwaukee when the ship called there (Hustvedt 1966, 222–224). It was thus understandable that Matthías Jochumsson did not meet Anderson in Chicago. On that occasion, neither of the two friends received any recognition for their writings, Norse literature, or their role in maintaining the renown of the Norse

Discovery of America: instead, their thunder was stolen by a replica Viking ship from Norway!

Notes

[1] Translation Anna H. Yates. The letters from Matthías Jochumsson to Rasmus B. Anderson are in the collection of Rasmus B. Anderson material in the Archives of the State Historical Society of Wisconsin, Madison. They have been transcribed by Dennis Auburn Hill, Librarian, Memory Library, University of Wisconsin, Madison.

[2] Anderson emphasized in his pamphlet, "Where Was Vinland?" that he regarded *Grænlendinga saga* as the best account of the Vinland voyages (Anderson 1892, 5–6). One may speculate whether it was due to Anderson's influence that the US government asked for the loan of *Flateyjarbók* for the World's Columbian Exposition. The request was refused (Petersen 1992b).

[3] It was probably due to Anderson's influence that two of the old Milwaukee Icelanders named their sons Leifur and Hrólfur. Leifur Magnusson went on to win fame and fortune in Washington (*Vestur-íslenzkar æviskrár* 4, 195–197), while Ralph Halldorson died of influenza at the end of World War I on a European battlefield, where he had just arrived, having taken up arms in defence of the ideals of freedom which had inspired his parents when they emigrated to the USA (Jón Halldórsson 2005, 194–195)

Literary Diplomacy and
the International Genre of National Epic

Kendra Willson

Texts which are considered "national epic" are charged with a double burden: they are expected, on the one hand, to reflect the supposedly unique national character of the nation which they represent but, at the same time, to be recognizable as examples of this purported international genre. The texts to which this label has been applied vary greatly in their natures, ages and modes of composition. The genre itself is a construction of nineteenth-century nationalism, as are many canonical examples thereof, such as Elias Lönnrot's *Kalevala*. Other texts which have acquired the status of "national epics" in modern times were written, compiled or composed much earlier under circumstances less well-documented. One example is the *Poetic Edda*, compiled in Iceland in the late thirteenth century. In a more extended sense, the sagas of Icelanders have collectively become a kind of "epic." Viðar Hreinsson, the editor of a five-volume English edition of the *Complete Sagas of Icelanders* (1997) has referred to the product as "sex kíló af menningararfi" ["six kilos of cultural heritage"] (Viðar Hreinsson 2005), and pointed out that a significant fraction of the copies sold are presented as diplomatic gifts.

The term *epic* has acquired a number of senses. One dictionary defines "epic" as "a long poetic composition, usually centered upon a hero, in which a series of great achievements or events is narrated in elevated style."[1] Kuusi, Bosley and Branch (1977) describe it as "narrative poetry portraying events larger than life in a serious manner" (Kuusi-Bosley-Branch 1977, 13); the definition can be "extended...to include poetry which applies the characteristics of epic, such as hyperbole, enumeration, stock epithet, to humbler themes" (ibid.).

The *Oxford English Dictionary* (s.v. *epos*) lists as the first definition for *epos* "A collective term for early unwritten narrative poems celebrating incidents of heroic tradition; the rudimentary form of epic poetry," with the transferred meaning, "A series of striking events worthy of epic treatment." The first attestations are from the nineteenth century. The adjective *epic* (s.v.) in the meaning "Pertaining to that species of poetical composition (see epos), represented typically by the Iliad and Odyssey, which celebrates in the form of a continuous narrative the achievements of one or more heroic personages of history or tradition" is attested in English starting in the sixteenth century. The use of *epic* as a noun "an epic poem" dates from the eighteenth century; the transferred use as "a composition comparable to an epic poem" stems from the nineteenth century, with the first attestation from *Carlyle's Heroes* (1840, 267): "Schlegel has a remark on his Historical Plays, *Henry Fifth* and the others, which is worth remembering. He calls them a kind of National Epic." The dictionary's editors add a note:

> The typical epics, the Homeric poems, the *Nibelungenlied*, etc., have often been regarded as embodying a nation's conception of its own past history, or of the events in that history which it finds most worthy of remembrance. Hence by some writers the phrase *national epic* has been applied to any imaginative work (whatever its form) which is considered to fulfill this function.

In the evolution of the term, the element of oral tradition has been deemphasized. A text's status as national epic is determined less by its content or mode of composition than by its reception, as well as the intentions of its author, compiler or editors.

Although nineteenth-century notions of nationhood associated with the compilation of texts such as the *Kalevala* have since been questioned, these texts continue to be read and translated. Editions and translations of these texts are often presented as diplomatic gifts or acquired by libraries as representations of specific cultures. Hence they have an overt role in "literary diplomacy" (to borrow Gauti Kristmannsson's (2005) characterization of one function of translations in general). The double burden of the "national epic" is compounded with the related challenge faced by all translations: they must be intelligible to the literary culture associated with the target language and yet communicate something of the source culture. They are meant to be read by the target language community both as instances of world literature with universal appeal and as iconic representations of the Other from which they stem.

One way in which translators of national epics pursue the diplomatic function is to highlight the similarities between the source and target language poetic traditions in general and between their "national epics" in particular, by means of word choice, specific allusions, or metrical structures evocative of the target culture's "epic" meters. Often the packaging and marketing of these translations further emphasizes cultural affinities or shared history. They may also reinforce the notion of national epic as an international phenomenon.

In this paper I discuss examples involving translation between Finnish and Old Icelandic. Finnish is of course genetically unrelated to the Germanic languages but has been in very close contact with them for as long as they have been around—though not specifically with the variety spoken in Iceland.

The *Kalevala* was compiled by Elias Lönnrot based on folk poetry which he collected on his journeys throughout Finland, particularly Karelia. Nearly all the individual lines found in the published *Kalevala* (97%, according to Kaukonen 1979, 72) occur in Lönnrot's field notes, but the overall shape and design are Lönnrot's, and there are substantial differences between the 1835 and more familiar 1849 editions. Lönnrot documented his textualization process thoroughly, and an extensive archive makes it possible to reconstruct his methods (cf. Hyvönen 2005).

The Codex Regius manuscript of the *Poetic Edda* was compiled in Iceland in the late thirteenth century under conditions much less well documented. The ages and modes of composition of the individual poems and the role of the final compiler have been matters of ongoing research.

Comparisons between *Kalevala* and *Edda* have fascinated many (e.g. Therman 1936; Andersson 1937; Gallen-Kallela 1953). Bjarni M. Gíslason (1940) went so far as to call the *Kalevala* "Edda Finnlands." Despite long-standing interest in these connections, translations of Eddic poetry into Finnish and *Kalevala* into Icelandic were not published until well into the twentieth century. In the afterword to a Finnish translation of Snorri Sturluson's *Gylfaginning* (*Edda: Gylfin harhanäky* 1911) by Liisa Bergius, Ralf Saxén and Kaarle Krohn, the translators note: "Kalevalan, oman suuren kansanrunoelmamme yhteydessä on paljon puhuttu myös islantilaisesta Eddasta, jonka sisällys on kuitenkin suomalaiselle lukijakunnalle ollut verrattain vähän tunnettu" [In connection with the Kalevala, our own great collection of folk poetry, a great deal has also been spoken about the Icelandic Edda, the content of which, however, is relatively little known to the Finnish reading public] (Snorri Sturluson 1911, 60); the prose Edda did not appear in Finnish for another seventy years. One reason for this delay may be the widespread literacy in mainland Scandinavian languages in both Iceland and Finland, so that the texts were accessible to both communities through the many translations into Swedish, Norwegian and Danish.[2]

Translating Kalevala Meter

The *Kalevala* has been translated into more different languages than has any other work of Finnish literature—at least sixty to date. Ilomäki (1998) notes: "It is clear that the parallel drawn between the Kalevala and the epic folk tradition of their own brings it closer to national and ethnic groups interested in shaping their own identity and cultural awareness" (Ilomäki 1998). Hence the work has been selected for translation or adaptation into such languages as Yiddish (1954) and Plattdeutsch (2001), as well as into "world languages" such as Esperanto (1920, 1964) and Latin (1986) and of course many Finno-Ugric minority languages (Udmurt 2001; Veps 2003; Meänkieli 2007 and 2009). As the publication dates above indicate, new translations continue to appear. Those who translate the

Kalevala into minority or stateless languages may wish to see their own group emulate the Finns' successful nation-building enterprise. Plourde (2006, 800) observes that "translation of a book like the Kalevala is probably a lever for minority cultures, and even for linguistic emancipation."

Meter is a central determinant of the impression made by a poetic translation. Inasmuch as translations of national epics are meant to appeal outside a narrow scholarly circle, they must aim to be read as poetry. Poetic translators face the classic metrical dilemma: Should they attempt to reproduce the meter of the source language, insofar as the structure of the target language permits? Should they "translate" the meter to one which has a similar "status" or connotations in the target language culture as the original meter does in the source culture? Or should they follow the "servile path" that Vladimir Nabokov (somewhat disingenuously) espoused (Pushkin 1964, x) and simply translate the meaning as literally as possible with no regard for meter?

Even a non-metrical translation will display allusions to other poetic traditions. Mustanoja (1964, 326) points out that the layout of Magoun's (1963) English translation of the *Kalevala*, with translations of two Kalevala lines printed side-by-side, separated by a long space, resembles the typographic convention for editions and translations of texts in older Germanic languages. Mustanoja also notes that Magoun's irregular lines "muistuttaa paikoitellen vapaamittaista runoa" [are in places reminiscent of free verse] (1964, 326). Free verse was undeniably the dominant and most respected verse form in American letters in the mid-twentieth century, so the prose translation is also a way of assimilating the text to a high-status, serious form.

Henry Wadsworth Longfellow's *Song of Hiawatha* (1855) represents an attempt to adapt a meter associated with epic in another language—Finnish—and make it an international meter for epic, introduced in his "Indian Edda" (Longfellow 1855, 299; cf. Moyne 1963; Schulz 2007). This may be compared to the transfer of Ancient Greek dactylic hexameter to Latin and later to European vernacular languages.[3] Of course, the Kalevala meter in the Finnic languages is not restricted to epic (even defined broadly as narrative verse), but other genres of folk poetry have less often been translated or broadcast abroad, due to the status of the *Kalevala* as (national) epic.

The Finnish Kalevala meter makes use of distinctive segmental length to create a counterpoint between word stress and metrically strong positions, contributing to rythmic variety. Outside the first foot of the line, the stressed initial syllable of a word must appear in a metrically strong position if it is heavy, but in a metrically weak position if it is light. Non-initial syllables can appear in either weak or strong metrical positions. Roughly half of the lines in classical Kalevala meter verse are pure trochees, with word stress corresponding to metrically strong positions, while half are "broken," with a mismatch between word stress and metrically strong positions (Leino 1986, 136).

This is illustrated with the opening lines of the *Kalevala*.

> Miele | ni mi | nun te | kevi,
> aivo | ni a | jatte | levi
> lähte | äni | laula | mahan,
> saa'a | ni sa | nele | mahan,
> suku | virttä | suolta | mahan,
> laji | virttä | laula | mahan.
> Sanat | suussa | ni su | lavat,
> puhe | 'et pu | toe | levat,
> kielel | leni | kerki | ävät,
> hampa | hille | ni ha | joovat

> [It is my desire, it is my wish
> to set out to sing, to begin to recite,
> to let a song of our clan glide on, to sing a family lay.
> The words are melting in my mouth, utterances dripping out,
> coming to my tongue, being scattered about on my teeth (Magoun 1963, 3)]

In this short passage, stressed syllables appear in strong metrical positions fifteen times and in weak metrical positions seven times, or roughly half as often.

In all the modern Germanic languages except Danish, all stressed syllables are heavy. In Kalevala translations into these languages, the meter has generally been rendered as a stress-based trochaic tetrameter, in which lexically stressed positions most often coincide with strong positions in the meter. When the dimension of syllable weight is lost, the result is the monotonous "Hiawatha meter," illustrated with W.S. Kirby's (1907, 1) translation of the same lines:

> I am driven by my longing,
> And my understanding urges
> That I should commence my singing,
> And begin my recitation.
> I will sing the people's legends,
> And the ballads of the nation.
> To my mouth the words are flowing,
> And the words are gently falling,
> Quickly as my tongue can shape them,
> And between my teeth emerging.

The translation of Kalevala meter as a heavily rhythmic trochaic tetrameter in English appears, from the viewpoint of the late nineteenth and early twentieth centuries, to be a failure in relation to the more dignified aspirations of the national epic. Due to a variety of factors shaping American poetic tradition in the English language, the meter and diction of Hiawatha immediately became associated with light verse. (It is easy, however, for modern readers to forget the tremendous popularity of the *Song of Hiawatha* and underestimate the poem's status at the time it appeared.) However, the meter "went viral" in Anglophone comic verse. Hiawatha was parodied before it even appeared, and Hiawatha parodies quickly became a recognized genre (cf. Moyne 1957).

Keith Bosley, in his translations of Finnish folk poetry, adopts a third option: to borrow a meter from yet another epic or folk tradition. Bosley (1977, 18) chooses to "draw on the resources of his own ear to find a corresponding metre in his own language," settling on "a syllable-based metre reminiscent of the Welsh *cywydd*" (1977, 18). The *cywydd* meter, used by Welsh bards of the forteenth to sixteenth centuries and associated especially with Dafydd ap Gwilym, consists of couplets of two lines of seven syllables each which rhyme an accented against an unaccented final syllable, though the order of the two may vary (Rowlands 1976, xx). Each line contains some form of *cynghanedd*, internal rhyme or repeated consonants (xxvii), and it is common for the lines of a couplet or a series of couplets to be linked by *cymeriad*, the repetition of elements (most often a consonant, but sometimes a full word). The rich variety of types of *cynghanedd* (Rowlands 1976, xxvii-xlix) is reminiscent of the variant patterns of *hendingar* in skaldic meters described in Snorri Sturluson's *Háttatal*, while both the rhythm of the couplets and the variety of line-internal sound effects are reminiscent of the later Icelandic *ferskeytla* and *rímur* traditions.

Evoking the *cywydd* meter ties the Kalevala translations to another folk poetic tradition and hence to an international concept of folk poetry. Like the Kalevala meter, *cywydd deuair hirion* was the predominant meter in its tradition, used for a broad range of subject from love poems to descriptive poems to praise poetry and requests. As the *cywydd* was associated with formally trained bards, it may have had a higher social status than the peasant poetry in the Kalevala meter (and hence the translation into this meter may implicitly ennoble the Finnish folk verse). The choice of a medieval meter also implicitly highlights the age of the Kalevala poems, many of which are believed to have old roots despite their late collection date. However, *cywydd* verse was perceived as somewhat less elite than the *awdl* meters used by the bards of the Welsh princes in the twelfth and thirteenth centuries. Although narrative poems are written in *cywydd* form, they are not commonly referred to as "epic."

In his translations, Bosley does not use *cynghanedd* or *cymeriad* systematically—nor Finnish-type alliteration. The allusion to *cywydd* is largely restricted to the overall length and general rhythm of the lines and irregular assonance and alliteration. This reflects the prevailing sensitivities in Anglophone poetic practice in the late twentieth century, which frowns on strict meters and finds alliteration "oft þunglamaleg og áberandi" [often clumsy and obvious], as Cook (2004, 243) states in a review of Ringler's (2002) alliterating translations of Jónas Hallgrímsson's poetry. Bosley's compromise is reminiscent of that adopted by Burton Raffel in translating *Sir Gawain and the Green Knight*: "to reproduce much though not all of the poem's alliteration, with occasional gaps for the relief of the modern reader (who needs a good deal more relief than did the original audience-reader)" but nonetheless "to make it obvious even to an untutored reader that alliteration *mattered* in this poem" (Raffel 1989, 41).

Bosley states, "I was reassured when my metre imposed syntactic patterns similar to those of Kalevala metre" (1977, 18)— hence judging the suitability of the meter or its equivalence to the source meter in part from its interaction with other aspects of language use, which of course also influence the impression the translation makes on the reader.

Kalevala islanniksi

The only Icelandic translation of the *Kalevala* published to date (1959-1962) was done by Karl Ísfeld (1906-1960), who also translated, among others, Tolstoy, Dumas, Maugham, Steinbeck and Hemingway, but is best known in Iceland for his translation of Jaroslav Hašek's *Good soldier Šveik*. Karl based his *Kalevala* translation on F. Ohrt's (1908) substantially abridged Danish version. Lis Holmberg (1959 and 1964) criticizes this choice and the translation in a detailed analysis, though she also writes a kind obituary for Karl Ísfeld (1961).

The first volume of Karl Ísfeld's Icelandic translation of the *Kalevala* bears an inscription: "Af tilefni opinberrar heimsóknar forseta Finnlands herra URHO KEKKONENS í ágústmánuði 1957 eru gefin út af bók þessari 250 tölusett eintök og er þetta... eintakið" [On the occasion of the official visit of the President of Finland, Mr. Urho Kekkonen, in August 1957, 250 numbered copies of this bok are published; this is number...] (5). Hence the diplomatic function of the translation is explicit. I own a "*Kuva-*

Kalevala" in Finnish with illustrations by Aarno Karimo which bears the book plate "Ex libris Ásgeir Ásgeirsson"—presumably presented to the second president of Iceland (who served 1952-1968) on the occasion of the same diplomatic visit. The Icelandic translation job was clearly rushed for the occasion, as only the first part of the translation appeared at that time. The second volume did not appear until 1962, two years after Karl's death, and was completed by his widow, the poet Sigríður Einars frá Munaðarnesi.

Gylfi Þ. Gíslason's preface to Karl Ísfeld's translation is a diplomatic speech, which underscores parallels between the political circumstances of the nations involved as well as shared cultural history. It begins:

> Mörg og margvísleg eru þau bönd, sem tengja Finna og Íslendinga. Báðar eiga þjóðirnar langa sögu að baki, og menning beggja hvílir á gömlum merg. En ríki þeirra eru ung, yngst á Norðurlöndum. Þótt Íslendingar og Finnar séu ekki skyldar þjóðir og tali ólíkar tungur, heyra þær báðar til þeirri þjóðafjölskyldu, sem norræn menning og norrænir þjóðfélagshættir hafa bundið böndum, sem eru jafnvel vináttutengslum æðri og traustari. Og svo margt er líkt í sögu og hefð, örlögum og lyndiseinkunn Finna og Íslendinga, að aukin kynni hljóta að leiða og hafa leitt til sívaxandi samhygðar (7).

> [Many and varied are the bonds which connect Finns and Icelanders. Both nations have long histories behind them, and the cultures of both rest on ancient ground. But their states are young, the youngest among the Nordic countries. Although Icelanders and Finns are not related nations and speak different tongues, they both belong to the family of nations which Nordic culture and Nordic customs have joined together with bonds which are even more exalted and more sturdy than friendship. And there is so much that is similar in the history

and tradition, fate and temperament of Finns and Icelanders that increased familiarity must lead to and has led to ever-increasing affinity.]

This type of emphasis on parallels between Icelandic and Finnish history is common in the presentation of translations between Icelandic and Finnish. In the introduction to the collection of Icelandic folktales *Thorgeirin härkä* [Thorgeir's bull], Hallfreður Örn Eiríksson and Marjatta Ísberg point out that "Islantilaiset itse vertaavat mielellään historiaansa Suomen historiaan ja sanovat näillä kahdella pohjoismaisella kansalla olevan samantyyppisen taustan: kumpikin oli vuosisatoja vieraan vallan alla" [The Icelanders themselves like to compare their history to the history of Finland and say that these two Nordic nations have the same type of background: each of them was under a foreign power for centuries.] (Hallfreður Örn Eiríksson and Marjatta Ísberg 1987, 9) although they recognize that "Suomen ja Islannin historiassa on toki erojakin" [Admittedly, there are also differences between the histories of Finland and Iceland] (9), particularly that Iceland had a period of independence before 1262.

In a brief essay, poet Steinn Steinarr (1964) satirizes the political context of Karl Ísfeld's *Kalevala* translation with typical deadpan irony, stating that Karl has presented a "fimm ára áætlun" [five-year plan] (273) for the translation; "Rússar vildu fyrir hvern mun komast yfir þau [þessi kvæði], þóttust hafa ort þau sjálfir, og þurfa nauðsynlega að brúka þau á móti Bandaríkjamönnum, þegar þar að kæmi" [The Russians wanted to obtain them [the poems] by any means; they claimed to have composed them themselves, and that they absolutely needed to use them against the Americans when the time came] (274). Steinn also says that he was once engaged to a Finnish maiden "og í einfeldni minni hélt ég, að Kalevala væri amma hennar" [and in my simplicity I thought that Kalevala was her grandmother] (273)—likely a reference to the widespread view that the word *edda* originally meant great-grandmother.

The metrical structure chosen for Karl Ísfeld's translation attempts diplomatically to reflect the original while assimilating it to Icelandic practice. Karl renders the Kalevala meter into the trochaic tetrameter which is conventional for Kalevala translations into Germanic languages. His translation is very strongly trochaic, as exemplified by his version of the opening lines (the same lines quoted above) (9).

Ljóðaþrá til kvæða knýr mig.
Kveikt er löngun, sem ei flýr mig,
orðs að leita, söng að syngja,
sögur fornar ljóðum yngja,
láta bragi leika á vörum,
ljóðin gjalla í spurn og svörum,
gómstáls láta glauminn vakna,
í gljúpum huga þræði rakna.

In a sample of the first 300 lines in Karl Ísfeld's translation, I found that only 20% showed any variation on the basic trochaic rhythm, and only 12% if one does not count vowels that can be elided in pronunciation (such as the final *a* of *leika* in line five or *gjalla* in line six); such elided vowels are standard in Icelandic metrical practice. However, Modern Icelandic poetic audiences expect more regular poetic rhythms than do Anglophone readers and I have no evidence that Icelandic readers responded negatively to the regular rhythm of Karl's translation in the way that English readers have parodied the Hiawatha meter.

Icelandic audiences also expect regular structural alliteration (cf. Jón Helgason 1944). Even today almost all metrical verse in Icelandic follows very strict alliteration rules inherited from the skaldic verse of the ninth through thirteenth centuries. As recently as 1996, a translation of Rilke's "Panther" that failed to add structural alliteration sparked a flurry of controversy and alternative translations (Willson 2008). Here too Karl Ísfeld follows the Icelandic convention. While this choice does not appear to have attracted attention from Icelandic critics, non-Icelandic reviewers have questioned it. Alliteration is a particular focus of Holmberg's (1959) critique of Karl Ísfeld's translation, as well as of a later study by Groenke (2005).

Kalevala meter in Finnish involves much but irregular alliteration. Over half of the lines in folk poetry contain "strong" alliteration (CV); roughly one-fifth have weak alliteration (C) and one-fifth none (Leino 1986, 134). An Icelandic audience would likely have perceived a reproduction of this system as technical incompetence or treason toward the Icelandic language, tradition and nationality: "Það þýðir ekki að bjóða Íslendingum upp á óreglulega stuðlun—það þykir bara braglýti" [It won't do to offer Icelanders irregular alliteration—it is simply regarded as a metrical blemish], as Kristján Eiríksson (p.c.) explained to me.

Groenke (2005) views this assimilation of foreign poetry to the Icelandic alliterative tradition as "besserwisserisch":

> In der Übertragung fremder Dichtung greift der isländische Übersetzer gern zum isländischen Stabreim, auch wenn in Original nichts davon zu sehen ist. Der Übersetzer drückt dem fremden Kunstwerk gewissermaßen den isländischen Stempel auf. Vor allem aber tut er es, wenn das Originalwerk alliterierend strukturiert ist oder ungeregelten Stabreim aufweist. Manchmal wirkt es dann so, als wolle der Übersetzer besserwisserisch zeigen, "wie man's richtig macht" (Groenke 2005, 122).

> [In the adaptation of foreign poetry, the Icelandic translator tends to invoke Icelandic alliteration, even when no such is to be seen in the original. To a certain extent the translator impresses the Icelandic stamp on the foreign work of art. However, he does this above all when the original work is alliteratively structured or shows irregular alliteration. It sometimes appears as if the translator wants, like a Besserwisser, to show "how one does it right."]

While Karl Ísfeld regularizes the alliteration in the *Kalevala*, he does attempt to evoke the effect of irregular alliteration in the Finnish

poem by using—increasingly over the length of the poem—
irregular internal rhyme or *hendingar*. This solution can be viewed as
reflecting a notion that internal rhyme in Icelandic and alliteration
in Finnish constitute analogous dimensions of poetic structure or
have a comparable status in the system. Like Old Norse internal
rhyme, Finnish alliteration is also of two types: "short" with
identical initial consonants in two words within a line, and "long" in
which words match in both the initial consonant and in the
following vowel (native Finnish vocabulary has no initial consonant
clusters).

In Finnish, alliteration is a dimension of poetic structure for
which hearers or readers are accustomed to listening but which is
not essential for every verse. Leino describes it as "strukturaalinen"
[structural] (1970, 317), explaining "It is thus a tendency, not a rule;
a poem in the Kalevala metre which contains no alliteration,
however, is nevertheless an anomaly" (Leino 1986, 134). Hence in
Kalevala verse alliteration is a structural element in the way
kennings are a structural element in skaldic verse, rather than in the
very strict sense in which "structural alliteration" is used in
Icelandic (Ringler 2002, 366). *Hendingar* are used regularly in skaldic
verse, though skaldic meters show some variation, but they are not
a general feature of Eddic verse. In later Icelandic tradition, they are
used in *rímur* and *lausavísur* as part of variant meters and the metrical
intricacy valued in the tradition making poetry *"dýrt kveðið"*
[intricately—literally "expensively"—composed], but they are not
essential for well-formed verse.

The four-beat rhythm of Karl's lines is vaguely evocative of the
Eddic *fornyrðislag* meter. Andersson (1937) discusses affinities
between the Kalevala meter and *fornyrðislag*, going so far as to state
that "Runometern och fornyrdislag äro således överensstämmande
inte bara i själva grundschemat utan också i enskildheter" [The
Kalevala meter and fornyrðislag thus correspond not only in their
basic structure, but also in specific details] (Andersson 1937, 97). As
Icelandic poetic practice has generally shifted from strong-stress
meters like *fornyrðislag* to rhythmic ones, there may be a tendency to
interpret *fornyrðislag* as a type of tetrameter. One friend

misremembered Karl Ísfeld's translation as being in *fornyrðislag*, perhaps in part because he thought of the poem as a national epic.

Affinities between *Edda* and *Kalevala* are also emphasized in the language of the translation itself. One particularly pronounced allusion is the couplet: "[V]reiður varð þá Väinämöinen, / vaknar blygðun hans og gremja" [Wrathful was then Väinämöinen / wakens then his shame, resentment] (40), a rendition of "Siitä suuttui Väinämöinen, siitä suuttui ja häpesi," [At that Väinämöinen became resentful, /at that became resentful and ashamed] is an obvious allusion to the opening lines of the Eddic poem Þrymskviða: "Reiðr var þá Vingþórr, / er hann vaknaði" [Wrathful was then Wing-Þórr / when he wakened] (Edda 1927, 107).

All these tactics contribute to impressing on Icelandic readers the notion that the *Kalevala* is indeed "Edda Finnlands" (Bjarni M. Gíslason 1940) and can be invoked as evidence of cultural commonalities between the traditions and the nations.

Eddukvæði á finnsku

The Eddic poems were fairly late in being translated into Finnish. Alku Siikaniemi's (1934) versions of *Þrymskviða* and *Guðrúnarhvöt in fyrri* are the first Finnish-language renditions of Eddic poems of which I am aware.

The poet Aale Tynni, longtime friend and ultimately wife of folklorist and poet Martti Haavio, completed the first full translation of the Codex Regius poems. Tynni's translations of the heroic poems (*Eddan sankarirunot*) appeared in 1980 and the mythological poems (*Eddan jumalrunot*) in 1982. Tynni had extensive philological training and appears to have worked with the original Old Norse sources as well as consulting with experts. She also translated a selection of skaldic poetry (1960).[4] Matti Kuusi (1983, 250) regards Tynni's *Edda* as a major landmark in bringing world literature to a Finnish audience, in a line of translations that starts with Agricola's New Testament (1548) and continues through Päivi Oksala's 1965 translation of Catullus' *Liber carminum*.

The flap copy of Tynni's translation proclaims that "Edda-runosto on koko Pohjolan aarre" [The collection of poems Edda is a treasure of all of the North]. However, emphasis on the shared cultural heritage is conspicuously absent in Tynni's introduction. Indeed, Tynni emphasizes differences between the *Edda* and the *Kalevala*: "Edda ei muodosta yhtenäistä eeposta Homeroksen eeposten tai Elias Lönnrotin Kalevalan tavoin" [The Edda does not form a unified epic in the manner of Homer's epics or Elias Lönnrot's Kalevala] (*Eddan jumalrunot* 1982, 17). She attributes this difference to the lack of a single compiler: "yhtenäisten kansaneeposten syntyyn tarvitaan aina viimeinen kokoonpanija" [for the birth of unified national epics, a final compiler is always necessary] (*Eddan jumalrunot* 1982, 17). This statement is doubtless informed by the Finnish case and may reflect Tynni's self-identification as a translator and philologist involved in bringing works of traditional literature into the Finnish literary canon.

Tynni follows the Old Icelandic meters fairly closely. Here is the beginning of *Vǫluspá* in Tynni's translation (*Eddan jumalrunot* 1982, 19):

> Pyydän: kuulkaa,
> pyhät heimot,
> Heimdallrin ylemmät
> ja alemmat pojat,
> sinä tahdot, Valfödr,
> että tulkitsen taiten
> mitä ihmisten muinais-
> vaiheista muistan.

Here is the Neckel-Kuhn edition of the Old Norse text:

> Hlióðs bið ec allar   helgar kindir,
> meiri oc minni,   mǫgu Heimdallar!
> Vildo, at ek, Valfǫðr,   vel fyrtelia
> forn spiǫll fira,   þau er fremst um man.

Compare Lee M. Hollander's English translation (1962, 2):

> Hear me, all ye hallowed beings,
> both high and low of Heimdall's children:
> thou wilt, Valfather, that I well set forth
> the fates of the word which as first I recall.

In some ways the sound structure of Finnish is closer to that of Old Norse-Icelandic than is that of Modern Icelandic (or Modern English). While the stress is always word-initial in both Old and Modern Icelandic as well as in Finnish, vowel and consonant length are distinctive in both Old Icelandic and Finnish, whereas Modern Icelandic has a proportional length system whereby the vowel is lengthened before a short consonant and all stressed syllables are heavy.

There are, however, rhythmic differences between the two languages. In Old Norse, there is a strong tendency for stressed syllables to be heavy—a pattern which became a rule in Modern Icelandic following the quantity shift (cf. Kristján Árnason 1980). In the passage above, a short syllable falls on a lift only twice in the Norse text (*mǫgu*, line 4, and *fira*, line 7) but four times in Tynni's translation (*pyhät*, line 2, *ylemmät*, line 3, *alemmat* and *pojat*, line 4). The number of unstressed syllables between the first and second lifts is one in lines 1, 2 and 5 of Tynni's translation but elsewhere 2. In the original, five of the eight lines have only one unstressed syllable between the lifts and three have two; however, a vowel at the end of a word may be elided before another vowel. Hence the rhythm in Icelandic is more trochaic, in Finnish, more dactylic. In the translation, four of the eight lines have one or two unstressed syllables preceding the first lift; in the original, only line 8.

The number of distinct consonants in Finnish is small (due to mergers during the proto-Finnic period) and initial clusters do not occur except in very recent loanwords. Hence alliteration is "easy" in Finnish (rather as people say end-rhyme is "easy" in French or Italian) and regular alliteration may not seem as contorted or disturbing as it is sometimes said to be in English (Cook 2004, 243).

In a discussion of Rein Sepp's Estonian translation of the *Poetic Edda*, Lehiste (1983) likewise notes that the quantity system of Old Icelandic "is strikingly similar to the syllable quantity structure that is found in the old Estonian and Finnish folk songs—the Kalevala meter" (180), with the greatest difference being the higher frequency of short syllables in Estonian (182). According to Lehiste, the greater number of short syllables in Estonian means that Sepp's Estonian translation of the *Poetic Edda* produces a different rhythmic effect: "The heavy-stressed syllables of the fornyrðislag beat a massive rhythm—like waves against a rock; the rhythm produced by the short syllables of Estonian, chosen by the translator, is more like a ripple on the surface of a pond" (183). She suggests that this difference may be one reason the Edda uses the resolution of one long into two short syllables so sparingly (184).

Kuusi similarly observes that "Suomentajan erityismurheena on ollut islanninkielen staccaton ja suomen kielen legaton rytminen perusristiriita" [A special difficulty for the translator was the basic conflict between the staccato rhythm of Icelandic and the legato rhythm of the Finnish language] (1983, 251) and that, due to the larger number of longer words with more unstressed syllables in the Finnish version, "sen jambis-anapestinen rytmikuviointi jää kauaksi islannin korthugget-sanonnasta" [its iambic-anapestic rhythm pattern remains far from the 'blunt' Icelandic expression] (1983, 251).

The diminished rhythmic emphasis may be why some Finnish readers experience Tynni's translations as slightly "dry" (Tapio Koivukari, p.c.), although in general they are highly regarded. Without assimilating the eddic poems to Finnish tradition or overtly emphasizing affinities to Finnish poetry, but treating them with the academic distance of world poetry, Tynni renders them in a way that is both true to the original and palatable to the target audience, as noted by Kuusi (1983). The fact that this is possible reflects similarities between the structures of Finnish and of Old Icelandic, as well as of course speaking to Tynni's skill as a translator.

Conclusion

Translators of "national epic" are conscious of the international genre and especially of their own languages' poetic traditions and "epics." They use allusions—metrical, verbal and stylistic—to the target language's epic tradition to help make the translation sound like a national epic to the target language community. The marketing and presentation of these translations emphasizes their diplomatic function, often with reference to current political circumstances at the time of translation.

Notes

[1] http://dictionary.reference.com/browse/epic

[2] An interesting link between the traditions is the Swedish linguist Björn Collinder, who translated both the *Kalevala* (1948) and the *Poetic Edda* (1957) (as well as *Beowulf* (1954)) into Swedish, and who wrote extensively on cultural connections among Finnish, Sámi and the Nordic languages revealed by linguistic evidence.

[3] The dactylic hexameter even reached Iceland through Jónas Hallgrímsson's experiments using it for patriotic poems such as "Ísland farsælda Frón."

[4] An amusing footnote to all these connections may be seen in the fact that Tynni translated parts of the *Song of Hiawatha* into Finnish (1985). Her translation naturally uses the Kalevala meter as well as certain linguistic features typical of the language of the *Kalevala*.

B. Studies in Folklore, Belief and Culture

Narrative and Belief:
Contemporary Life Histories
and the Grand Narrative of the Vikings

Ulf Palmenfelt

A recurrent theme in John Lindow's scholarly work is the relationship between oral narrative and societies' belief systems or worldviews (see Lindow 1997, 9f; Lindow 2001a, 1f; Lindow 2008, 222ff). Legends help reinforce worldview, he argues in *Swedish Legends and Folktales* (Lindow 1978, 30). I would like to use this claim as my starting point for a discussion about how belief elements are constructed in personal experience narratives—a genre that at first glance might appear to have little in common with the stories usually considered by Lindow: nineteenth century folk legends and Medieval Norse myths. What all narratives have in common, however, is the strong cultural form creating coherent causal and chronological chains of action, thus bringing order and meaning into our lives. Both folk legends and personal experience stories help their users to structure their impressions of the world and both are enacted in the existing everyday world of the narrators.

These stories may tell of local eccentrics, the history of local families, the participation of local men in recent wars, the journey of a local person to the big city, or other unusual or noteworthy events, Lindow writes with local legends in mind (Lindow 1978, 28). The same characteristics might just as well be applied to narrated life histories, one significant difference being that in the latter it is uncommon that persons meet with the supernatural, while legend protagonists often do. Introducing the belief factor, Lindow continues: "Legends detailing encounters with beings of the other world presuppose belief in the existence of these beings, and the possibility of encountering them" (Lindow 1978, 28). In a similar way, I would argue, personal experience narratives also presuppose an acknowledgement of—or belief in, if you will—basic collectively accepted features of local history. You cannot locate your individual life history within the collective framework without taking its inherent cultural demands into consideration.

In early folkloristic scholarship, during the period that according to Lauri Honko was dominated by "the pretext paradigm" (e.g. Honko 2000, 4f), folklore was commonly treated as a source to gain knowledge about early religion or popular belief. The fact that legends and other folklore existed in oral tradition was in a sometimes unproblematized way taken to prove that the contents of the narratives were what people "believed". The belief criterion even constituted part of some definitions of folk legend. The scholarly debate about how to classify folk legends has been long, heated and often concerned with the question of belief. Timothy R. Tangherlini gave an extensive overview of the debate in an article in Western Folklore (Tangherlini 1990). Elliot Oring offered a shorter, updated version, and focused on the belief element in legend definitions in a 2008 Journal of American Folklore article (Oring 2008). Oring exemplifies the two basic meanings of the word "belief" by contrasting belief in supernatural phenomena with belief that the supermarket will provide the items he wants to buy (Oring 2008, 128).

To loosen up the somewhat rigid positions following the legend definition debate, Oring suggests that we should employ the somewhat vaguer term "legendry", which would include also non-narrative elements and "a range of expressions that gravitate around" (Oring 2008, 128) the legends proper. Furthermore, instead of stating anything definitive about the truth or belief status of legend, Oring prefers to say that "legend is concerned with matters of truth" (Oring 2008, 128). In the bulk of the article, Oring then applies elements of classical rhetoric to penetrate what he calls legend's "belief language", "belief vocabulary", and "rhetoric of truth" (Oring 2008, 128).

Following the British folklorists Gillian Bennett and W.F.H. Nicolaisen, our Estonian colleague Ülo Valk states that "personal experience narratives and belief legends share the basic narrative pattern" (Valk 2009, 1) and that both "are told as true stories" (Valk 2009, 1). From a narrative point of view "there is no difference between 'ordinary' and supernatural events" (Valk 2009, 1). Another similarity between legends and personal experience narratives is that to us as culture scholars, both genres provide us with source material concerning "commonly held values and beliefs" in a society (Tangherlini 1990, 379). "Legend and folk belief [...] reinforce each other", adds Tangherlini (1990, 379).

Taking 'belief' in Oring's supermarket sense of the word, I would like to add that personal experience narratives and folk belief reinforce each other, too. When several people continuously repeat similar accounts about a historical event or a social condition, these phenomena may gradually achieve a status of collective acceptance. They come to be regarded as facts; you do not have to prove that they are true every time they are mentioned. They become icons that can be referred to in everyday conversation without retelling the full story. They come to claim recognition within their domains of influence; when a personal experience narrative unfolds in the vicinity of such narrated "facts", the narrator has to relate to them. By being retold often, the narrated facts—or should we call them factoids?—achieve the status of a truth that is possible and culturally accepted for people to believe in.

Material

The material I have used for this article consists of some forty tape-recorded life history narratives. The narrators were all retired citizens of my hometown Visby, Sweden. The recordings were made during a concentrated collection period in the summer and fall of 1995, and the narrators were all living in Visby at the time of the interviews. Thus all these life histories were recounted from the same temporal and geographical standpoint. The material has a clearly defined "here" and "now" (cf. Lindow 2001a, 40ff). Furthermore, the narrators were all born between 1910 and 1930, making them more or less representatives of one and the same generation.

Circular Stories

The orally narrated life history is a cultural form with its own specific genre conventions. Its themes are typically the narrators' chosen memories of their own lived experiences, but the form is seldom a merely chronological enumeration of facts. Structurally the life narrative often moves between descriptive, evaluative, argumentative blocks and epic, dynamic chains of development— always with the same protagonist at the center. The British folklorist Gillian Bennett has notified the existence of "circular stories" that can be described as "clusters of events organized round some central idea" (Bennett 1984, 83) or, in other words, "stories structured in non-final, non-linear forms" (Bennett 1984, 83). These stories are different from "'action narratives'—that is, stories meant to impress, thrill, or entertain an audience" (Bennett 1984, 87). Circular stories, according to Bennett, "focus on detail and description rather than on the unfolding of a plot and they leave the end deliberately open for comment, interpretation and follow-up by the audience" (Bennett 1984, 86).

One of my narrators provides an example of such a circular story when verbally painting a panorama of her childhood neighborhood. Notice how the account starts by mentioning the neighbor Liss Östlund and her beautiful daughter Rosa. The gaze of the narrator then sweeps over houses and blocks, fixing persons and street names to them, mentioning professions and small enterprises. After a full round has been completed, the circular movement is dramatically broken by the beautiful Rosa returning to the story, this time running naked through the streets. The narrative sequence ends by the aged Rosa borrowing a telephone to call the ambulance when her husband dies:

> Our neighbors were Liss Östlund and her daughter
> Rosa in the Klinten. She was so beautiful when she
> was a girl. Madam Pettersson had hired farm hands
> and workmen. She had cows and horses. We
> bought milk from her. We bought milk in a bowl.
> She had horses and cows and chickens. The
> chickens ran about in the square crying. Later they

were not allowed to have chickens inside the city. Outside the city wall she kept pigs. She carried food to them with a yoke.

In the front side of the house Klinttorget number 4 was the entrance to the backyard belonging to Östra Tullgränd. There was a gate leading to the back of the house. The next house belonged to the same yard. That's were the painter Wigström lived. The house was owned by building contractor Hjalmar [last name not audible]. The name of the alley was Östra Tullgränd. Maria Wretberg lived on the first floor at Klinttorget number 1. She worked at horse-dealer Fridgren's office outside the Eastern Gate. There was a horse stable there. Miss Wretberg had a dog that we children were scared of. The Ekengrens lived in the three-story house across the alley. They had several children. Liss Östlund got married to a man from Dalecarlia and they had a daughter who was called Rosa in the Klinten. They said that once when it was cold outside, she came running and yelling along one of the streets downtown. A man had emptied a bucket of water over her and she came running naked as an ice statue. People had to take care of her. I think she is dead now. She had a son and a daughter. When Rosa's husband died, he was suffocated; I remember she came in to us to borrow our telephone (Elsa Pettersson, b. 1915 in Visby).

Narrated Memories

Our memory functions represent limiting factors for what it is possible to recount. We do not remember everything that we have experienced and we are unable to verbalize some of that which we do remember. Only some memories are suitable to convey in narrative form. Classifying a personal experience narrative as a memory is a keying (Goffman 1986, 43 ff) that allows the narrator to make use of certain possibilities and informs the audience of how to interpret it. Well known such keying formulae are: "I can remember...", "I have a strong memory of...", "As far as I remember..." Keyings like these bestow that which is remembered, first with a distinct quality of being something that is selected and thus important, simply by not belonging to the sad category of forgotten experiences. And as we all know there is a constant process of exchange between the two groups: we forget what we once remembered and we come to remember what had been forgotten and we remember vaguely or we forget in part (Ricoeur 2005, 109, 190). Memories presuppose the existence of forgotten experiences.

Second, memories are very personal. We are often astonished at how differently people's minds operate, when comparing what we remember of a certain event with other persons' remembrances of the same situation. This shared experience has led to a cultural agreement that allows every memory narrator to be extremely personal and subjective when deciding what to tell and how to present it.

The Self-Biographical Paradox

The characters in a narrative can be either subjects or objects in relation to the narrated events, answering directly to the grammatical active and passive voice. As active subjects, they will play the role of being agents who initiate changes and push the action forward. As passive objects, on the other hand, they will get the role of being carried away by other agents' actions, as victims in the hands of ruthless villains or an inescapable fate. Handling such moments can sometimes be awkward for a narrator, since the narrating "I" is enacting a social role as the speaking subject in the narrative situation, while the experiencing narrated "I" fulfills a dramaturgical role as an object to exterior influences inside the story. Narrators, who want to be true to their own experiences, cannot easily exclude those episodes of their lives where they for one reason or another were out of control. In instances of this kind, a tension might arise between the narrating "I" who is in control (at least theoretically) of the situation and the narrated "I" who is not in control (at least not all the time). We can call this the self-biographical paradox.

Degrees of Collectivity

From the individual's point of view the source of the external action does not seem to influence greatly the narrative. External is external, passive is passive; if I did not start the action, somebody else did, who, when, and where does not seem to influence the individual's life history in any remarkable way. What does matter, however, is the degree of collectivity of the event in question. The more people involved in or aware of an event, the more likely it is that some kind of folklore will develop around it. We could imagine a sliding scale running from events with a very high degree of collectivity towards totally private experiences.

At a national or regional level we find events that affect many people or are at least known to a substantive part of the population. Here is one example, referred to in a student's essay:

> Kjell had started to study at Uppsala University and was going home to Gotland for summer vacation. On May 7 1945, he had visited a friend in Stockholm and was walking on Kungsgatan on his way to the Central Station. At that very moment, news spread that the German forces had capitulated and peace had been proclaimed. Kungsgatan, at that time one of the leading commercial streets of Stockholm, immediately filled with happy people, walking arm in arm singing and shouting—all in the opposite direction from Kjell striving with his suitcases to catch his train. (Svensson 2002, 10).

Several other events related to World War II recur in my material. Although Sweden did not play an active part in the Second World War, everybody on Gotland, an island in the middle of the Baltic Sea, was affected by it. The consequences of the war echo in nearly every informant's life history. A war as such, however, is too huge and too complicated to be part of an individual life history. To tell the story of a war you need the overview of the historian and the space of a grand narrative.

Individual experiences of the war events concern, for instance, the mobilization, where young men from all over the country were grouped together and shared their worries and their tobacco, as well as their experiences and their stories. At home, women had to use all their creativity to feed themselves and their children in spite of food rationing—if you were not lucky enough to have relatives in the countryside who could send you some potatoes and a pig's leg hidden under the double bottom of a suitcase.

At a lower level of collectivity, action is experienced by a group of people, for instance family, neighbors, friends, workmates, or different kinds of clubs or associations. One woman recounted items of family folklore including an account of her mother who had sailed on the Titanic on the journey prior to the fatal one. One man had memories of how the children in his school class tried to find out the best way of manipulating the teacher into giving them the grades they wanted. One drafted soldier told about how another group of soldiers who were responsible for the distribution of fuel during the war provided extra gas for the military lorries on Saturdays so that they all could go to Slite to dance. Any number of people, from a handful up to several hundred may be included in these kinds of events, and they are likely to appear in similar form in several narrated life histories.

At a private level, the experiencer is alone, although another person or some other outside force initiates the action. Examples from my material include receiving emotionally upsetting phone calls or reading letters that turn out to be decisive for the life paths chosen by the narrators. Dramatic as such experiences may be, they concern only one individual at a time and they are not likely to become the topic of any collective tradition.

Levels of Participation

Just as the experienced events can reflect higher or lower degrees of collectivity, the individual as a participant in the action can be more or less involved. We might talk about higher or lower levels of involvement or participation. In my material I have found examples of at least three different levels of participation. We can speak about **direct participation**, when the narrator has been personally involved in the event. One woman remembered how her mother had scolded her when she had accidentally dropped a bottle of cream, breaking it. One man told about how he, as a boy, was not allowed to visit the other children's homes because he had lice. Another man had, also as a boy, taken part in pushing a railway carriage up a hill and then riding it downhill again and again until a supervisor stopped the boys and the railway company fenced in the whole area.

In cases where the narrator was an eyewitness to an event or in one way or another was affected by the event without participating in it can be labeled **indirect participation.** One man told about how his wife's father died when the Hansa sank. A woman told about the rough swimming instructors of her childhood. One of them had thrown her friend into the water so carelessly that the girl's hip was seriously injured. Another woman had a father who suffered from Parkinson's disease and alcoholism. On his way to a hospital in Stockholm, he jumped off the boat and drowned himself.

At the third level, the narrator has information about the event, often by word of mouth, but was not directly involved in it, nor affected by it. We can label this level **awareness**. Here are some examples from my material:

> Between Visby and Roma, the train went so slowly that people used to step off and walk beside it, picking flowers.

> The workers in the lime stone quarries used dynamite to kill pike in the river.

> There was a saleswoman in the main square who was called "Little Friend". In the mornings, when the rich ladies came shopping, her prices were high,

but in the afternoons, when the working class wives
came downhill to shop, everything was much
cheaper.

To imagine my suggested model graphically, we could picture the
narrated event as sliding along a horizontal scale between the end
poles "private" and "collective". Around the narrated event, we
could imagine a series of concentric circles, running from the
innermost "participant" over the middle "eyewitness" to the
peripheral "word of mouth".

The narrator's level of participation does not necessarily have to
coincide with the event's degree of collectivity, although it often
does. There are purely private experiences where the narrator is an
eyewitness or just aware of the event rather than being a first-hand
participant. Seeing the house cat taking a mouse or finding out that
the paint used last summer has dried in the can are events with a
very low degree of collectivity that can also be experienced at rather
low levels of participation.

Both the quality of the narrative and the credibility of the
narrator are influenced by narrators' classifying the experienced
event as having higher or lower degrees of collectivity and their
positioning of the narrated "I" at higher or lower levels of
participation in relation to the narrated event. An event with a low
degree of collectivity can be narrated with high authenticity and
credibility if the narrator was closely involved in or affected by the
event. Take as an example the sad story about the boy who was
forbidden to play with his friends because he had lice, when it is
told by the boy himself. The story would diminish both in presence
and in directness if told by somebody who had only heard about it.
And imagine what would happen to the story about the sick father
jumping from the boat if it were told not by the daughter but by a
stranger: it would lose much of its strong emotional tension.

Narratives about events with a high degree of collectivity are
subject to qualitatively different rules than more private ones. If you
were on the Estonia when it sank, if you survived the 2004 tsunami,
or if you saw the World Trade Center towers in New York City

collapsing, your narrative would certainly be loaded with authenticity and credibility. Although far from everybody in the world was there, events of this class are known to a substantial part of the world's inhabitants; in a way they belong to all of us and we all have some right to tell our version of them. Equally important, those who actually were there are not totally free to tell memory stories that deviate too radically from the officially accepted ones. In August 2009, at the Nordic conference for ethnology and folklore in Helsinki, I heard my Norwegian colleague Professor Anne Eriksen relate the example about the sole survivor of the 1902 Martinique earthquake (who survived because he was locked in a subterranean prison vault), who constructed ever more fantastic stories about the catastrophe the more times he told about it, since no one could object to them.

My arguments so far can be summed up with some simple cultural principles: (1) a high degree of participation gives you an exclusive right to tell about events with a low degree of collectivity; (2) a low degree of participation does not exclude you from telling about events with a low degree of collectivity (but who would want to hear them?); (3) a high degree of participation gives you a special, but far from exclusive right to tell about events with a high degree of collectivity; (4) a low degree of participation does not exclude you from telling about events with a high degree of collectivity (and again, what interesting aspect could you add?).

Tradition Dominants in Local History

There are also instances were the narrated "I" seems to be in perfect control, acting as a subject; all the same the story line is limited by an external factor from local history that has to be taken into account. In narrated individual life histories it is not surprising to encounter elements of local or regional—or even national and international—history. After all, most narrated events making up individual life histories have actually taken place in physical locations where many other people's lives and many different public events have taken place. Many of these events, more or less external to the individual life history of the narrator, possess an agency of their own making it highly likely that they are referred to in one way or another when a life history touches upon a certain place at a certain time (cf. Tangherlini 1990, 377f; Palmenfelt 2009).

The Swedish folklorist Albert Eskeröd proposed the term tradition dominant to indicate prevailing phenomena (primarily supernatural beings) in local traditions, or in his own words:

> As the concept motif appears to be more appropriate within folk narrative research, it seems proper to identify those various phenomena that dominate a local tradition by the word *tradition dominants*. By tradition dominants thus will be understood such elements that in the common folk tradition dominate different groups within it (Eskeröd 1947, 81. My translation).

As a qualifying criterion, later generations of folklorists have added that tradition dominants, for instance supernatural beings, can be identified through their power to attract features that in other traditions typically belong to other beings, a process usually referred to as motif attraction.

Obviously we can find elements in life histories that possess a similar capacity to dominate local traditions, but these elements are seldom supernatural beings. Instead the dominant units can be points of time, places, events, values, ideas or accepted emotional attitudes that all have become so firmly established in people's minds that they possess an agency to demand dominant positions in all historical narratives.

These dominant units can be regarded as verbal expressions of an ongoing interplay between collective ideas and individually expressed narrative forms. They represent different phases in the process of acquiring solid form. By positioning themselves in relationship to these dominant units, narrators inscribe themselves in the collective body or emphasize that they are rejecting such membership. Dominant units that are repeated often increase in collectivity, gain in volume and importance, which, in turn, makes it ever more difficult for future narrators not to relate to them.

Consequently, this process strengthens the tradition dominants' attractive potential even more.

Narrated History

In the following I will attempt an artificial reconstruction of some physical and mental life conditions in Visby during the twentieth century as I hear the narrators describe them. This is the collectively acknowledged cognitive universe into which the individual narrators' taleworlds are located, making up a frame of reference for their thought, and an arena into which they have to fit their narrated taleworlds. To a certain degree this is actually what life was like in twentieth century Visby. But, on the other hand, the narratives cover a time span of roughly seventy-five years during which substantial social changes took place. Even if the narrators represent different social population strata, they are only forty voices among several tens of thousands of Visby citizens who are not heard in my material. What I can say is that certain facts, formulations and values are repeated so often that they can be considered to be traditional in the sense that they have become part of a collective mind.

Each narrator has to relate to this template which *per se* does not have to be anything else than a mental construct, never formulated verbally and never spoken aloud. Being an insider one develops a sense for what choice of episodes is appropriate, what categories are fitting, which persons, which shops and which streets are proper building stones of the narrative construction, in which modes these elements can be narrated, and— equally important—who and what is never mentioned. When many individuals apply these templates they are successively reinforced and a collectively acknowledged picture gradually emerges. This narrated reality will be regarded as the "true" version.

I will take a closer look at some examples that I have chosen because they show some of these commonly accepted "facts" in detail. Naturally, I will not argue that these stereotypical traits are false and that the narrators are consciously manipulating reality. The narrators certainly had their experiences in the "real" world.

However, pouring the real experiences into the narrative form decontextualizes them (or the memories of them) by re-presenting them in a taleworld (a narrative enclave in the terminology of Young 1987, 33).

Childhood

> Unlike most families we had a father who did not drink. He was orderly, so we really had a good childhood, I guess. There were parents who drank and the children had a hard time.
>
> We had a free life and ran and played in the streets and alleys. We used to pick berries in fall, on Sundays that is, for on Saturdays you had to work. Even if times were scarce, we had a good life. I don't think that we had to go to bed hungry even once.
>
> We had a household pig, as they called it, that was slaughtered in December. My mother didn't have a job, for the wives were always at home, so she sewed clothes and patched and mended. We used to have macaroni with the pork and sometimes a fisherman came and sold herring. We ate a lot of salted herring. In the garden we grew spinach that was stewed. There was a lot of baking at home, round loaves of rye that were dried on a pole. My dentist usually says that I was born in those days when children used to munch on hard bread and that was good for the teeth (Henning Nilsson, born 1922 in Eskilstuna).

This short account contains several stereotypical features. Unmarried men were expected to drink alcohol, play cards and fight (although fighting in those days was honest). When they married, some vague fate seems to have determined whether they would stop drinking or not. Although several women were actually working professionally at the time, the stereotypical picture is that married women were housewives. They were often said to make some extra money for the family by selling eggs, preserved berries or mushrooms, or homemade socks or mittens. There was no communal childcare so, when children were not at school, they were normally outdoors playing. Many homes were small and there simply was not space enough for large groups of children to play indoors.

Family economies were generally strained and it was normal that you picked mushrooms and wild berries in the fall. If you had a garden, you would sooner grow vegetables and berries in it than caring for a lawn and decorative bushes. Cages with chickens were common. Especially during the war years, many kept rabbits in their gardens, and there are many stories about people collecting grass for their rabbits in the fields outside the city wall. Normally you did not keep pigs within the city wall, but outside it there were plenty of inexpensive buildings where people kept horses, cows and pigs. Wandering fishmongers were a common sight, but you could also buy fish at the harbor or the market in the main square. When you were a young father, you would work all day long and chop firewood in the evenings:

> We kept rabbits that we killed and sold. At Hällarna there was a shoemaker living in a cellar. He used to walk down to the harbor in the early mornings to collect shoes for mending. He took bread for salary and we fed our rabbits with his bread. We had a big rabbit that was black and white and he even ate pork. It was a strange rabbit. When I was about to kill it and put it on the chopping block it screamed so loudly that I couldn't kill it. I took it back to the cage and he was fine. Later, I gave it away. Bengt, my son, even took it with him to school. (Nisse Stenström, b. 1916 in Slite).

This story is another example of how families kept rabbits in their gardens as a supplemental food supply. The account makes the point even stronger by telling about an exceptional rabbit that escaped being killed and eaten. Typical is also the categorization of days as consisting of two parts, one when you work as a salaried employee and another when you work with your house, garden or otherwise for the family's direct support or benefit. Just like the fisherman in the former example, there were wandering artisans such as shoemakers and tailors who went door-to-door looking for customers. To me, it is not clear from the narrative why the shoemaker's bread automatically could be used to feed the narrator's rabbits. I take the statement as illustrative of the many existent informal systems of support mentioned in the narratives.

Solidarity

The following story provides a clearer example of friends and workmates helping each other. Even the harsh ship's captain is shown to have a big heart:

> During my years at the Gotlandsbolaget (the local shipping company) I built a house in Järnvägsgatan. They were called "large family homes" and the municipality administered the construction. You were supposed to put in 10 % of the loan in the form of own work, but that was not so easy when you were sailing at sea. I dug the entire foundations by hand; it took me one whole vacation. When the boat lay in harbor, my workmates came and helped me to dig. Once the boat was supposed to leave at 4 pm and I arrived at the harbor a few minutes before 4, but they were already leaving. I yelled and shouted, but they pretended not to hear me. So I was free for another day and a half. The next time I met the captain, he told me to buy an alarm clock. Then I told him to learn how to leave on time. He didn't answer, he just chuckled a little. Afterwards the other guys told me that they had notified the captain that I was not on board, but the captain only said: "We are leaving, he needs the time for his house building. That captain was a bit harsh but still kind (Gösta Österdahl, b. in Bunge).

The Sinking of the Hansa

Although Sweden had proclaimed itself neutral during the Second World War, skirmishes that took place all over the Baltic Sea naturally had a profound impact on everyday life on Gotland. On November 24, 1944 the Swedish passenger ship the Hansa, plying the trade between Visby and the Swedish mainland, sank outside Gotland and eighty-four people died. Hundreds of Gotlanders lost close relatives, but the majority of the inhabitants on Gotland suffered no personal losses. In spite of that, the incident had an overwhelming impact on the Gotland society as a whole. It is not difficult to image how the tragedy could be taken to be a violent and anonymous assault (not until much later was it proven that the ship had been hit by a Soviet torpedo) against all Gotlanders collectively. After six years of tension with belligerent actions constantly taking place in the very vicinity of the island, the sinking of the Hansa became a harsh reminder that wartime brutalities were for real and could hit even civil citizens of a neutral country.

In three fourths of the life narratives I have studied here, the Hansa event is mentioned in one way or another. No other single item comes close to appearing that often. Here is one example of how the news of the disappearance of the ship entered everyday life:

> I had been to school in the morning and I was on my way to work in the afternoon. My friend and I used to go to a café for a cup of hot chocolate and a bun before going to work. After that we made a walk through the streets and outside the newspaper's office we saw the news bill announcing that the ship the Hansa was missing. My friend, well, she had an uncle or whatever who worked on the boat. Then it started. When I arrived at my work, well, one of my workmates, her husband was on the boat. And wherever you went and whomever you met they had somebody onboard, you know. And we found that spooky. Later in the evening we

went down to the harbor to have a look. And there was a raft, a wrecked raft I believe it was that they had found. Somebody had written with a pencil: 'A final greet…' and then it was only a line. Probably several more had been on it. Well, that was unpleasant (Britt Kahn, b. 1930).

This young woman was emotionally troubled for a couple of hours, but she did not lose any relatives or friends in the calamity, and the sinking of the Hansa has no dramaturgical role to play in her life history. Still the potency of the event as a tradition dominant in narrated local history is strong enough to force itself into her life history.

WW2—A Family Trouble

My next example shows another quality in narratives about wartime events. In the life of this Visby family the war interfered rather brutally. One family member actually died and another one suffered a nervous breakdown. The narrator labeled this as "some trouble in the family." I do not believe that the somewhat euphemistic choice of expression should be interpreted as unfeeling or lacking empathy. Rather it could be seen as an example of how it is possible to represent a universal tragedy like a war in one's individual life history. In this short narration, World War II does not function as a tradition dominant. The family in question was in fact affected by the war and in the narrative this is recounted in a low, matter-of-fact voice:

In 1939, we had some trouble in the family, when the war broke out. My grandfather was enrolled and his nerves couldn't take it, so he committed suicide. It's one of those things you do remember. My mother got weak nerves after that. Those things stick. So, from that point of view, war was difficult for us and for many other families. Several of his colleagues did the same thing. Probably they as officers were assigned some hard commitments.

> But they did not have the resources (Siv Jolby, b.
> 1920 in Visby).

Values

Many of the narratives contain an obvious element of
evaluation. It is probably unrealistic to expect anybody to stick to
the role of neutral observer when recounting her or his own life
history. The evaluations normally take the form of generalized
statements in the first person plural: "we had a good time when we
were children"; "we made no great demands on life." The
grammatical form is similar in many of them: my life has been
(hard, poor and full of misfortunes), but still (good, rich, calm, free,
harmonious). A typical example is this:

> Life has been rich, I think. And now you are an old
> woman. And that is all right, too. They come and
> pick me up for lunch and dinner. On Tuesdays we
> do gymnastics. The food is good and the personnel
> are nice. I am grateful for that. And I am grateful
> that my head is still clear. My oldest son is in
> America. I am rich to have children, grandchildren
> and great grandchildren (Fanny Lindström, b. 1911
> in Visby).

The prevalent conclusions resonate with gratitude and satisfaction.
Several declare that they would have chosen a similar life if they
were given a chance to start anew. My overall impression is that
these people have reached a state of reconciliation, where they have
ceased worrying about their own mistakes and pardoned others'
wrongdoings.

All jobs (including the compulsory military service) seem to
have been interesting and enjoyable. All workmates were helpful
and supported each other. In their free time, they organized
barbecues in summer and crayfish parties in fall. Everybody was an
active member and supporter of the trade unions. To a certain
extent the narrators' accounts are definitely representations of
original experiences. But it is also reasonable to consider the

accounts as examples of what in 1995 was possible to narrate about facts and events in earlier twentieth century Visby. These life histories can be regarded as retrospective evaluations made by one generation of Visby inhabitants of their own professional, social, cultural contributions to local history.

Many narrators were eager to emphasize the contrasts between values that they regarded as common to their generation and the morals and ethics that they saw as typical for the younger generations. Within the field of values, the complementary phrases of the imaginary dialogue often appeared in overt form. Here are some examples:

> I feel sorry for the young people today who cannot find any jobs.

> They have no belief in the future and they have nothing to do.

> Young people today never assume any responsibility.

> The respect for other people is gone, especially for older people.

> Today young people are drunk and fight.

> One entire generation will be lost.

> Today's society is no society to grow old in.

> Society today cannot handle the young.

Conclusion

The preceding is (part of) one possible grand narrative about twentieth century Visby. Several others could have been extrapolated from the materials that I have used, and the one recounted here could have been both broader and deeper.

However, there is no doubt that this mental image of twentieth century Visby owns some kind of existence. Many people—both the interviewees and otherwise—refer to fragments of it. In many interactions among Visby citizens it is obvious that you are expected to be familiar with it and relate to it.

From my point of view it is not important to decide whether the facts presented in this grand narrative are historical or not, nor whether the events described have actually happened, nor whether the narrators really "believe" in what they are relating. To me as a folklorist it is enough to be able to show that the fragmentary or embryonic grand narrative does seem to exist and that its mere existence demands that people relate to it. And to my mind, this is also the case with other so-called belief narratives, for instance folk legends. We know that they do exist (or did exist) and we know that people in one way or another had to relate to them. What and how much people actually did believe is more or less impossible for us to decide.

Each individual life history creates its own unique narrated world. In my material the major part of the narrators' lives has been enacted in the same arena during approximately the same period of time: twentieth century Visby. Taken as a whole, the individually recounted narrative worlds (together with several thousand similar narratives not mentioned here) create a fairly consistent image of a universe with static as well as dynamic elements. The static parts, expressed in circular, non-final, non-linear forms, consist of the physical environment with streets, buildings and institutions, but also include a population with specific groups and individuals, among them "local eccentrics" and "local families" (Lindow 1978, 28), recurrent traditions and accepted values. Also among the fixed elements are points of time, dates and years, as well as historical events in a reified form, devoid of their dynamic aspects. It is into this common narrative construction that each individual fits her or his personal narrated world.

While folk legends typically deal with the extraordinary, the deviant and the unexpected, "unusual or noteworthy events" (Lindow 1978, 28), both individual life histories and collective grand narratives are dedicated to normal, everyday, predictable matters. Perhaps one could regard grand narratives as the smallest common denominator of local history, formulating the agreements to which everybody subscribes. Folk legends in contrast explore the boundaries of normality, the almost unknown borderlands facing the backyards of the unbelievable.

Grand narratives lack the legend's focused concentration on one single, dramatically charged chain of events. That may be one reason why they seldom show the elaborate form of the verbally formulated narrative. They have no obvious temporal extension, no clear line of development following a hero's handling of a complication from its introduction to a satisfactory resolution. From the perspective of a single individual it is next to impossible to follow the long and slow developing processes of a society. That is why we perceive of the grand narratives as fragments of an indiscernible whole or as embryos that may once unite into a coherent entity. On the other hand the causal elements appear to be strong. The grand narratives obviously support cause and effect-explanations or function as a common cultural standard with which one can compare one's own experiences and values (Hyvärinen et. al. 2010). Largely, these overarching frameworks consist of non-narrative, descriptive elements and we cannot even say for sure that they have a consistent verbal form. It is in fact likely that they are never narrated. Instead they are ever-present as collective frames of reference for what is considered to be normal and stand as an accepted form governing how to talk about local history. The narrated worlds of the Medieval Norse myths and of nineteenth century folk legends make up similar components of the respective societies' cosmologies. Maybe we could even regard the grandiose epic starting with the creation of the universe out of Ymir's body parts and ending with Ragnarök as the grand narrative of the Vikings?

Our Lady's Maid in Nordic Context

Thomas A. DuBois

John Lindow is justly recognized as a major figure in the study of Nordic folklore. His detailed analyses of Nordic folktales and legends have guided students toward an understanding of worldview and storytelling in preindustrial Scandinavia for more than a generation now. His interest in the linguistic and cultural diversity of the Nordic region has ensured his attention to folklore that cuts across narrow linguistic boundaries, extending west to Iceland, south to the Latin learning of the continent, and east to Finnish and Sámi. He has offered insightful frameworks for understanding the perspectives of tale tellers and their communities within the Nordic region and in their confrontation with ideas or influences coming from abroad. In aiming to pay tribute to John's work, I have chosen to examine three different versions of the tale type ATU 710, "Our Lady's Child." While accepting as useful and enlightening the interpretive frameworks that grow out of the research of Bengt Holbek, I seek here to do something different. I will examine the ways in which these three tales—one Northern Sámi, one Finnish, and one Norwegian—shed light on culturally specific elements of folk justice, especially as related to the conduct of young women. I focus on a question that plays surprisingly little role in deeper psychological readings of the tale type but that seems to have occupied all three narrators of the performances discussed here, i.e., just exactly what the heroine of the tale does wrong and why she deserves her punishment. I believe attention to this issue helps clarify the culturally normative, conscious level of folk narrative that operated in past folktale narration: on a certain level, a story had to pass muster within the value system and concepts of propriety operating within the culture. For the three narrators discussed below, this necessity shaped the ways in which they interpreted both the heroine's transgression and the actions taken by the narrative's villain/donor character to bring her back into proper status within her society.

The set of vaguely similar and possibly originally related tales classified by folklorists under the rubric ATU 710 represents one of the quirkier narrative entities of the European *Märchen* tradition. The tale type—if it is a single tale—generally focuses on the life of a poor girl who is consigned from infancy to work as a servant at the house of a mighty lady, sometimes a crone with a castle in the forest, sometimes no less than the Virgin Mary in Heaven. Whatever the case, the girl grows up in security and luxury, and by adolescence has become a trusted maid to whom the Lady confers the keys of the household before she leaves on errands. The Lady makes only one demand, that the girl refrain from looking inside a particular room (or, of course, a particular set of three rooms). As such tales always have it, curiosity wins out: the girl peeks into the room(s) and sees something momentous: sometimes a harrowing image of people in torment, sometimes a sublime image of the Trinity, sometimes something else of great vividness and/or terror. William Hansen (1996, 272) states that the frightening sight is typical of tales where the Lady is an earthly crone while the sublime sight is typical of versions featuring the Virgin Mary.

No such tendency emerges from the tales discussed in the current paper. When the Lady comes home, she questions the girl about whether she has looked inside the room and, generally, the girl denies having done so. The Lady is not deceived, however, and banishes the girl from the household, leaving her to fend for herself, generally without the use of her voice, and sometimes without any clothes. The girl is found by a prince, who marries her despite her mysterious background and mute condition, sometimes because the Lady has gone to lengths to make the girl as pretty as possible before abandoning her. In time, the heroine gives birth to a child, but the Lady appears on the night of the birth, challenges the girl to admit her wrongdoing and, when the girl refuses, takes the child away. Often, the Lady smears blood around the girl's mouth and on her hands so that the general populace and/or the girl's mother-in-law suspect the new mother of cannibalism. As Ruth Bottigheimer notes (1990, 18), this is a surprisingly commonplace detail in European folktales, "an old, and effective, ploy for disposing of unwanted daughters-in-law." People call for her execution, but the young queen's husband staves off the criticism. The same events recur two more times and, at last, the prince or king is unable to withstand the tide of popular opinion: he consigns his wife to be burned at the stake. On the pyre, however, the heroine does something to redeem herself: either she finally admits her wrongdoing, or she greets her death with resignation. In any case, the Lady returns in the nick of time, restores the queen's children and voice, and leaves her to live happily ever after with the prince/king.

The tale in its Marian redaction (*Marienkind*) figures as number 3 of the Grimms' *Kinder- und Hausmärchen,* based originally on a performance collected from Gretchen Wild in 1807 (Grimm and Grimm 1812-1815). The tale type has received a thorough historical geographic examination by Edeltraud K. Seifert (1952). Seifert's descriptive overview of the type in its geographic spread has been updated in the Amalia *Märchenlexikon,* where the editors suggest that the tale originally featured a saving Madonna figure and a vindictive mother-in-law character responsible for snatching the young mother's children and making her look like a cannibal. The Virgin (particularly in the persona of the Black Madonna) and the mother-in-law characters then somehow fell together, it is suggested, leading either to a redaction in which the Virgin remains recognizable as the religious figure but nonetheless perpetrates cruel tortures, or to a version featuring a dark Lady figure, whose connection with Mary is altogether lost. This view is advanced further in the monograph by Sigrid Früh and Kurt Derungs *Schwartze Madonna im Märchen* (2003).

Because Wilhelm Grimm included the tale in every one of his numerous republications and reworkings of his influential tale collection, Ruth Bottigheimer (1990) uses it as a test case for a computer analysis of Grimm's editorial changes over time. Bottigheimer finds in Grimm's emendations a progressive tendency to highlight the heroine's willful character in refusing to acknowledge her fault and suggests that Grimm wished to make clear that the girl was punished not for her opening the door *per se* but rather for her obstinate refusal to admit her wrongdoing after the fact. As such, the German tale thematizes issues of women's voice and enfranchisment, as Bottigheimer writes: "The relationship between language and power, silence and impotence, is here dealt with explicitly. Those who have the power to speak *(sprechen)* can also make things happen; those who are silenced must bear the consequences of other people's intentions and decisions" (16). William Hansen (1996) provides an overview of the tale type while relating it to the episode of Apollo's rescue of Kroisos from a burning pyre, an ancient narrative which, Hansen suggests, may derive ultimately from the folktale, thus implying the considerable antiquity of the tale, which earlier folklorists tended to view as fairly late and literary.

In a recent examination of female tellings of ATU 480 and ATU 510 in Franco-Newfoundland, Gerald Thomas (2003) has offered a streamlined and useful refinement of Bengt Holbek's masterful *Interpretation of Fairytales* (1987). A key tenet of Holbek's approach to *Märchen* was to see their contents as expressive of the concerns and identity issues of raconteurs or particularly of an adolescent audience. Writes Holbek: "The symbolic elements of fairy tales convey emotional impressions of beings, phenomena and events in the real world, organized in the form of fictional narrative sequences which allow the narrator to speak of the problems, hopes and ideals of the community" (Holbek 1987, 435). Thomas locates the particular stories he studies within Holbek's framework as feminine early-life crisis tales or, in other words, tales that feature an active heroine and a largely passive male counterpart who eventually persevere to become an independent and enfranchised marital unit. In the tales that Thomas analyzes, this low-born young female and high-born young male are guided to social maturity and marital recognition through the agency of a high-born elder female. A "latent...subconscious message to the audience" of such tales is, Thomas suggests, that generational conflict can be avoided and full adult empowerment achieved if a young woman submits dutifully to the instructions and reprimands of her female superiors. For this reason, Thomas suggests, the tale was probably primarily told by women and received its most serious reception from female audiences. Thomas's adaptation of Holbek's theories sheds useful light on the three variants of ATU 710 discussed below, even though the tales were all collected from and by men.

Thomas is careful to point out that, in applying Holbek's analysis to the tales he examines from Newfoundland, he makes no claim of the resulting interpretation having been either conscious or even remotely familiar to the tales' performers and audiences. Rather, these are "latent" meanings that underlie the tales and that encode cultural attitudes toward women, authority, and maturation. A cultural analyst can recognize and discuss these attitudes even if they would have gone unnoticed by performers of the tradition. It is also noteworthy that, in Holbek's framework, *allomotifs* or plot details that vary from version to version of a tale but that fulfill the same function within the tale's underlying symbolic system lose importance as objects of analysis.

In this paper, I suggest that the allomotifs of the heroine's actual transgression and the means by which she recuperates her reputation and status thereafter were significant elements of the story for the raconteurs and audiences discussed below, and that tale tellers spent a good deal of energy trying to make sense of these details in their performances. Their attempts tell us a great deal about cultural values and norms within their own communities, regardless of whether they also contribute to a symbolic exploration of the difficulties of female maturation in the manner described by both Holbek and Thomas. If we bracket allomotifs of this sort as purely of secondary significance to the underlying meaning of a tale, we may lose some of the very foundations that made the tale worth telling for its original performer and audience.

In 1929, the Finnish linguist Paavo Ravila traveled to the Finnish arctic coast at Petsamo to collect samples of the most easterly dialect of Northern Sámi resulting in his study *Ruijanlappalaisia kielennäytteitä Petsamosta ja etelä-Varangista* (1931) two years later. As Marja Leinonen (2007) has shown, the subjects of Ravila's fieldwork were a small population of North Sámi herders who had migrated across the Russian border with their herds during the nineteenth century at a time when adequate reindeer pasturage was growing harder and harder to procure. The herding families, some ten to twenty in number, retained their Lutheran adherence, Mountain Sámi herding customs, and North Sámi language while otherwise mingling and eventually intermarrying with the local Ter and Skolt Sámi populace, most of whom were fishermen and small farmers. Known by local Russians as the *Filmanskoe* or *Finmanskoe*, these herding migrants from Norway and Finland had become largely assimilated into the wider Eastern Sámi culture by the time Ravila arrived to study their language, and he found only two brothers in the Kaakkuri district who still retained the old dialect. One of these was Matti Skore, known as Pankon Matti. Of Matti and his brother, Ravila writes (my translation): "The 'Panko brothers' of Kaakkuri village were originally reindeer herders. They are, however, no longer so themselves, and thus their reindeer-herding heritage has virtually vanished entirely. They cobble together a living from selling hay from their home pastures, fishing, birding, and carpentry"(iv). Matti Skore supplied Ravila with all 41 of the narratives that Ravila included in his text as examples of the Kaakkuri dialect. These Ravila presented in a close phonetic transcription that was intended to allow linguists to recognize the main features of the dialect in comparison with other forms of North Sámi. Skore's version of ATU 710 is number 19 in that collection (125-9).[1]

> Vulggi okta nieida ohcat alccesis biigá-saji. Bođii nisu vuostá. Jearai: "Gosa don nieida vuolggát?"
>
> Nieida celkkii sudnje: "Mun vuolggán ohcat alccesan biigá-saji!"
>
> De dajai dat nisu: "Vuolgge munnje biigán!"
>
> Nieida jearai: "Gii don leat?"
>
> "Mun lean Nieida Márjjá almmis!"
>
> Son vulggii dalle su mielde. Doalvvui su mieldis albmái. Nieida Márjjá čájehii sudnje doppe buot viesusis. Doppe ledje ollu lanjaid ja čábbát. Čuovggái buot golis. Son čájehii juohke lanja. Doppe ledje dain lanjain apostalat illudit. Ja ovtta lanja gilddii:
>
> "Dan it oaččo don geahččat!"
>
> Nieida Márjjá manai reissui ovddas, guttii čoavdagiid su duohkái.

Son jurddašii: Manne son ii leahko dan lanja maid gilddii? Son válddii, ravai dan uvssa ja geahčastii dohko. Doppe lei ruitu duoldamin ja olbmot ledje siste. Son dáppasti fargga uvssa gitta.

Bođii ruoktot Nieida Márjjá, jearai sus: "Leatgo don dan lanja geahččan, maid mun ledjen gieldán?"

Nieida vástidii: "In eisege!"

Son jearai nuppádaššii sus; son ain šiidii, ahde: "in mun geahččan."

Ja nu lávii son vel goalmmádaššii. Nieida ain šiidii.

Dalle son attii losses nahkár niidii ja loittii vuolás ávdin meahccái. Nieida ii dieđe eambbo gosa vuolgit ja šaddai morašii ja gielataga. Beaivvi go badjánii, son čohkká dalle beahcioavsi alde.

Vulggii muhtun gonagas-gánda vuodjit meahccái. Oaidná dat gánda, ahte okta heavuš geahččá čorrui nuppelii luodas. Son orostahtá hehpošiid. Vuolgá geahččat, maid heavuš geahčai čorrui. Son rohttii miehki dohpas ja čuolai daid bestilas lanjaid, mat ledje nieidda birra. Ja bođii su lusa.

De jearai sus: "Maid don dáppe čohkkát?"

Nieida ii veadján maidege sardnot sudnje go lei gielataga. Nieida lei čáppat muođus. Gánda liikui sudnje, dáhtui alccesis gálgun váldit. Nieida ii buktán vástidit sudnje maidege, muhto gulai, maid son sardnui ja vulggii su mielde dalle. Son vulggii vuodjit ruoktot.

Bođii áhčis lusa, máinástii son: "Mun buvttán alccesan gálggu!"

Áhčči dajai sudnje: "Dát lea du duodji: go don leat liikon, anni oaminad!"

Son dalle náitalii suinna.

Jagi geažes son fiidnui gándda ja son lei ain dat nisu gielataga.

Bođii muhtun ija su lusa Nieida Márjjá. Jearai sus: "Leatgo don dan uvssa leahkkun, maid mun ledjen gieldán?"

Son šiidii ain, ahde: "In mun lean leahkkun."

Nieida Márjjá celkkii sudnje dalle, ahde: "jos it sardno, de mun válddán dus dan máná, mii lea šaddan."

Son ii sardnon. Nieida Márjjá váddii dan máná ja
doalvvui mieldis albmái. Šaddai beaivviid máná ohcu.
Olbmot sardnogohte, ahde gonagas-gándda gálgu borrá
iežas dan mánájis.

Gállás celkii, ahde: "Dat ii leat duohta!" ahde "mu
gálgu dan ii bargga."

Šaddai nubbi mánná nuppe jagi.

Nieida Márjjá boðii ohpit ihkku su lusa. Sardnui sudnje
seamma ságaid, ahde: "Leatgo don leahkkun dan uvssa,
maid mun ledjen gieldán almmis?"

Son celkii ahde: "In mun lean leahkkun!"

Nieida Márjjá celkii sudnje: "Jos sardnut, dalle mun
attán ruoktot fas dan máná, maid mun válden dus álggus.
Ja jos it sardno, dalle mun válddán vel dan máná, mii
easka dál lea šaddan."

Son ii dovdástan. Nieida Márjjá váldii vel dalle nuppe
máná maiddái mieldis. Ja olbmot ain eambbo
sardnogohte, gonagas-gándda gálgu borrá iežas daid
mánajis ihkku.

Gállás celkkii, ahde: "ii mu gálgu dan bargga!"

Šaddai goalmmát jahki. Šaddai goalmmát mánná. Boðii
ihkku su lusa Nieida Márjjá ja jearai sus: "Leatgo don
leahkkun dan uvssa, maid mun ledjen gieldán?"

Son šiidii ain, ahde: "In mun lean leahkkun!"

Nieida Márjjá sardnui sudnje: "Jos sardnut, dalle mun
attán dan guovtto máná fas ruoktot, maid mun lean
váldán, ja jos it sardno, dalle mun válddán vel goalmmáda
máná, mii lea dál šaddan!"

Son ain šiidii ja celkkii: "In mun lean leahkkun, inge
geahččan dan uvssa!"

Dalle váldii Nieida Márjjá vel dan goalmmada máná
mieldis ja doalvvui albmái.

Beaivi go lei šaddan, šaddai ohcu máná. Ja olbmot
sardno, ahde son borrá ieš. Su dubmejedje dalle buoldit
vuiggus. Gállás ii veadján bealuštit su eambbo. Dolvvo su,
dan gálggu, olggos ja bidje dola birra su. Son geahččagoðii
birras, oinnii, ahde dál son gal juo boaldá. Son
jurddašašgoðii, beare son buvttašii sardnot, son dál
dovdástivččii, ahde son lea bargan dan, maid su lea
gieldán. Dalle šaddai sudnje jietna. Son dalle sardnui das,

ahde son lea bargan vearre. Olbmot gulle dalle, válde su
eret dolas. Son sardnui buot olbmuide, mot sudnje lea
geavvan. Dalle oažžui buot mánajis ruoktot Nieida
Márjjás ja álggii fas eallit albmáinis.

[A girl set out to look for a servant's position for
herself. She came upon a woman. She asked: "Where, girl,
are you headed?"

The girl answered her: "I am headed off to find a
servant's position for myself!"

At that the woman said: "Come be my servant!"

The girl asked: "Who are you?"

"I am the Virgin Mary of Heaven."

She went along with her. She brought her along with
her to Heaven. The Virgin Mary showed her everything in
her home. There were many rooms and they were
beautiful. Everything glistened of gold. She showed her
each room. There were in the rooms the apostles
rejoicing. And one room she forbade:

"This one you may not look into!"

The Virgin Mary went forth on a journey, left her in
charge of the keys.

She thought, why not open the room that was
forbidden? She took, gripped the door and peaked inside.
There was a pot simmering and people were inside it. She
quickly pulled the door closed.

The Virgin Mary came back and asked her: "Have you
looked into the room which I had forbidden?"

The girl answered: "Certainly not!"

She asked a second time; she continued to deny: "I
didn't look."

And she asked her for a third time; the girl still
denied.

Then she cast a deep sleep upon the girl and lowered
her down to a remote wilderness. The girl doesn't know
anymore where to go, and she became sorrowful and
mute. When daybreak came, she sits on a pine bough.

A certain prince came riding into the wilderness. The
prince notices that one of the horses is looking at
something by the side of the road. He stops the horses.

He goes to see what the horse was looking at by the side of the road. He drew his sword from its sheath and chopped away at the branch cover that surrounded the girl. And he came upon her.

Then he asked her: "Why are you sitting here?"

The girl was not able to say anything to him because she was mute. The girl was pretty of face. The boy liked her and wanted to take her as his wife. The girl was not able to answer anything to him but listened to what he said and went along with him. He headed home driving.

He came to his father and said: "I have got myself a wife."

His father said to him: "That is your affair: if you like her, take her for yourself."

Then he married the girl.

A year later she gave birth to a son and yet that woman was still mute.

One evening, the Virgin Mary came to see her. She asked her: "Have you opened the door that I had forbidden?"

She still denied, saying: "I did not open it."

The Virgin Mary said to her then: "If you do not say, then I will take from you the child that has been born."

She did not say. The Virgin Mary took the child and brought it along with her to Heaven. When the day came, a search for the child began. People began to say that the prince's wife herself had eaten her little child.

Her husband said: "That is not true!" and "My wife does not do such things!"

A second child was born the next year.

The Virgin Mary came to see her again one night. She said the same thing to her: "Have you opened the door that I had forbidden in Heaven?"

She said: "I did not open it!"

The Virgin Mary said to her: "If you say, then I will bring back the child that I took from you in the beginning. And if you do not say, then I will take also this child which has just been born."

She did not confess. The Virgin Mary took the second child also along with her. And the people began to say even more that the prince's wife herself eats her little children at night.

Her husband said: "My wife does not do such things!"

A third year arrived. A third child arrived. The Virgin Mary came to see her at night and asked her: "Have you opened the door which I had forbidden?"

She still denied it, saying: "I did not open it!"

The Virgin Mary said to her: "If you say, then I will give you back the pair of children I have taken; and if you do not say, then I will take this third child that has just been born also."

She still denied and declared: "I didn't open it, nor did I look at the door!"

Then the Virgin Mary took the third child along with her as well and brought it to heaven.

When day arrived, the search for the child began. And people said that she ate the child herself. She was straight away condemned to be burned. Her husband was not able to defend her anymore. They took her, his wife, outside and built a fire around her. She began to look around and saw that now indeed she would burn. She started to think that if she could only say, she would now confess that she had done that which she had been forbidden. And then her voice came back to her. She then said that she had done wrong. The people listened and took her from the fire. She told everyone what had happened to her. Then she got her children back from the Virgin Mary and began to live again with her husband.]

From a linguistic perspective, it is noteworthy how carefully, and apparently consciously, Skore uses different verbs for communicative acts. In this respect, his tale seems to echo the points brought up by Bottigheimer regarding German versions of the story, i.e., it thematizes dramatically the issues of having, losing, and regaining a voice as a female adult. It is difficult to appraise the meaning that the narrator attached to the verb *sardnot* (modern Northern Sámi *sárdnut*), which occurs in the third person some seven times and is also employed in the first and second person as well in speeches by the Virgin. In modern Northern Sámi, the verb refers to speech of marked seriousness, including ordering. In his tale, the narrator generally relies on three different verbs for telling: *sardnui* [she said/declared with gravity], *celkii* [she stated] and *dajai* [she said]. *Celkii* occurs seven times, while *dajai*—the most common such verb in modern Northern Sámi—occurs only twice. The narrator also employs the verb *sardnot* with an inchoative suffix twice, e.g., *sardnogohte,* meaning "they began to say with gravity" when describing the grumblings of the young queen's subjects when she is discovered without a child and with incriminating evidence of infanticide. In addition, the verb *jearai* [he/she asked] occurs six times, describing the speech acts of the Virgin and the prince. The heroine's responses are described with the verbs *šiidii* [she denied], *ii dovdástan* [she did not admit] and *vástidii* [she answered].

Skore's use of the verb *cealkit* poses particular ambiguities for a modern translator. In modern Northern Sámi, the verb is rarely used except in biblical contexts, e.g., to describe Christ's speeches to his apostles. But in Skolt Sámi its cognate form is the common verb for saying, and this linguistic environment may have influenced the narrator's choice. What is most noteworthy is that while the Virgin's speeches are generally described using the weightier verb *sardnot,* the heroine's responses are designated with the apparently more neutral *cealkit.* The Virgin repeatedly invites the heroine to *sardnot,* however, whenever she appears to exhort the young mother to admit her past transgression. It is thus highly significant, I believe, that the heroine finally progresses to *sardnot* at the very end of the story, when she admits her wrongdoing to the whole of the community and then proceeds to relate, or preach, of everything that had happened to her. These two instances of *sardnot* associated with the heroine's speech acts seem to underscore precisely her final finding of a voice in her responsible admission of past mistakes.

Skore is also artful in the terms he uses to describe both the heroine and her husband. These undergo a shift in the story as the characters reach maturity and gain at last the right to live a stable married life with their children. The girl is described as *nieida* [maiden, virgin] until her marriage, after which Skore employs verbs without subject specification or merely with the pronoun *son* [he/she] to refer to the heroine. The prince refers to her as *mu gálgu* [my wife] twice, and eventually the narrator, too, calls her by this title as she is being led to the pyre. For his part, the heroine's husband is described initially as both a *gonagas-gánda* and a *gánda* [king's son" and "young man] and then later as *gállás* [guy] until the very end of the story, when he at last becomes the *álbmáinis* [husband] to match the heroine's status as a *galgu*. These terms, then, reinforce the narrative of gradual empowerment after trials that lies at the heart of the tale as analyzed in Holbek's manner.

The story does not follow Hansen's claim that the Virgin Mary version has a wondrously beautiful sight in her forbidden room, although in this respect it is parallel to the Russian version that Haney translates in his collection (Haney 2001, no. 385, pp. 393-95). Nor does it follow Gerald Thomas's assumption that the tale is told by women, not men. It does follow the pattern of a feminine tale as discussed by Thomas, one with an active heroine and passive hero. Mary is the high-status adult female who instructs the low-status young female on how properly to behave, after which she can assume a full role in her marriage with the high-status young male to whom she has already been married. The linkage between the idea of a forbidden door and the birth of children is fairly emphatic. But crucially, from the point of view of social norms, I believe it is key that the woman saves herself by communicating the truth. Only when she at last relents and admits what she has done can she truly enter into the marriage to which she was unable to assent in words when it first occurred. She finds her voice in admitting her clandestine wrongdoing. In a Sámi village context, where a collective sense of right and wrong was maintained both through storytelling and through more direct means of identifying and chastising wrongdoing, the story's ending seems to make good cultural sense. The Virgin wants her stepchild to understand the importance of admitting her mistakes to her peers and superiors, and she is willing to torment the girl until this lesson is learned. By extension, a Sámi audience could learn the same lesson simply by listening to the tale and taking its implications to heart. When dealing with wrongdoing in a Sámi context, honesty is the best policy, and the tale makes this plain.

A different version of this tale type was collected by Juho Sjöros in Mietoinen, Finland, in 1881, and was printed in the first volume of Pirkko-Liisa Rausmaa's authoritative collection of Finnish folktales *Suomalaiset kansansadut* (1988, 458-462). No informant is noted, and it is clear from the formal, grammatically polished style of the text that Sjöros was committing to writing the story as he had heard or learned it, rather than recording a text verbatim from a single informant's dictation. In the past, Finnish folktales were often collected as story synopses by amateur collectors who were eager to preserve the country's oral tradition and contribute to the great storehouse of collected folklore at the Finnish Literature Society. Consequently, we cannot easily justify an examination of the tale's "oral stylistics" here, although we can certainly make statements about its plot and characterization. The version follows the form that Hansen calls the "Demonic Subtype," one in which the girl comes to the household of a mysterious mortal woman rather than the Virgin Mary.

Oli seppä, joka oli niin erinomaisen suuri juoppo, että hän joi aina vain. Hän joi viimein talonsa ja verstaansa ja pajansa ja pajakalunsa. Hänellä oli vaimokin ollut, mutta kun vaimo näki, että kaikki menee, niin hän otti jotakin heidän tavaroistaan ja osti pienen mökin kaupungin läheltä. Ja vaimo oli raskaana.

Kun seppä oli sitten kaikki juonut, ettei hänellä enää mitään muuta ollut kuin kuusi hopearahaa, hän meni hampunpunojan luo ja osti palan nuoraa, että olisi saanut itsensä hirttää. Hampunpunoja antoi hyvän kappaleen ja sanoi:

"Tuossa on, kyllä pitää!"

Seppä meni metsään ja katseli sopivaa puuta. Silloin ajoi ämmä mustalla hevosella ja huusi:

"Mies, mies! Mitäs meinaat?"

Seppä sanoi: "Meinaan hirttää itseni!"

"No minkä tähden sinä itsesi hirtät?"

"Rahat on loppu. Vanhat on juotu ja uudesta ei ole toivoa," vastasi seppä.

Ämmä sanoi: "Älä itseäsi sen tähden hirtä! Lupaatko minulle sen, jonka vaimosi nyt synnyttää, niin kyllä mina taidan sinua auttaa!"

Seppä funteerasi ensin, mutta lupasi sitten sillä ehdolla, että hän saa sen pitää viisitoista vuotta.

"Saat kyllä," sanoi ämmä, "sen ajan pitää." Ämmä antoi hänelle sitten kukkaron ja sanoi:

"Tässä on sinulle rahaa, että saat itsesi autetuksi."

Seppä meni sitten vaimonsa tölliin ja pyysi lautasen ja kaasi rahaa useamman lautasen täyteen. Sitten hän osti oman pajansa ja omat kalunsa takaisin ja rupesi uudestaan työtä tekemään. Ja eli sitten niin kuin muutkin ihmiset. Vaimo tahtoi kovasti tietoa, mistä hän rahoja sai. Seppä ei meinannut sanoa, mutta täytyi viimein aika voittain sanoa, että hän sen lapsen lupasi.

Se oli tyttö. Kun se oli neljän viikon vanha, se rupesi puhumaan kehdossa ja sanoi, että hänen täytyi nousta ylös tekemään työtä, että hänellä on kiire. Hän nousi ylös ja rupesi tekemään pitsejä ja muita semmoisia, joita ei ennen maailmassa oltu tehtykään. Sitten hänet otettiin yhteen ja toiseen herrasväkeen ompelemaan.

Kerran kun hän oli eräällä kreivillä neulomassa, hän sanoi yht'äkkiä:

"Nyt täytyy mennä kotiin!" Kotona hän sanoi äidillensa:

"Pankaa nyt kaikki kuntoon, nyt tullaan minua ottamaan."

Äiti pelästyi ja sanoi isälle, että tyttö sanoi niin. Isä rupesi laskemaan, ja oli juuri viisitoista vuotta aikaa. Pantiin sitten tytön vaatteet kokoon. Ämmä tuli ja sanoi:

"Eikö niin ole, kuin puhuttu on?" Seppä sanoi:

"On kai."

Tyttö valmistettiin sitten menemään ämmän kanssa. Ämmällä oli mustat hevoset vaunujen edessä niin kuin ennenkin. Ja tyttö istui hänen viereensä. Ämmä otti tytön syliinsä ja sanoi:

"Oletko koskaan pehmeämmällä istunut?"

"Mikä on pehmeämpi kuin oman äidin syli?" vastasi tyttö.

Sitten ämmä antoi tytön maistaa eräästä pullosta ja kysyi:

"Oletko koskaan makeampaa ainetta maistanut?"

"Mikä on makeampaa kuin oman äidin maito?" vastasi tyttö. Tien vieressä oli tuomi, ja ämmä kysyi:

"Tiedätkö, mita varten tuo kuivunut on?"

"Tiedän kyllä, täällä on arkussa hame, jonka minä ompelin sen lehdistä."

Sitten ajettiin isoon metsään ja siellä oli suuri rakennus. Ämmä vie tytön taloon ja käski hänen olla siellä. Hän antoi tytölle paljon avaimia mitkä kuhunkin huoneeseen kuuluivat. Hän sai mennä mihin huoneeseen vain tykkäsi, mutta eteisessä oli yksi huone, josta ämmä sanoi:

"Tuohon huoneeseen et saa mennä!"

Tyttö löysi sieltä semmoisen huoneen, jossa oli kaikenlaisia ruokia, ja semmoisen huoneen, jossa sai nukkua. Hän oleskeli siellä sitten vähän aikaa, ja ämmä tuli hanta sitten katsomaan. Ei ollut vielä mitään tapahtunut. Jätti hänet taas ja meni asiainsa toimitukseen.

Kerran kun tyttö tuli eteiseen, hän ajatteli, mitähän tuossa kamarissa lienee. Ja hän avasi oven. Takaseinästä nosti kuollut ruumis päätään, kun hän oven avasi, kun siinä kävi messinkilanka ovesta siihen ruumiiseen. Kun hän paiskasi oven kiinni, se huusi vielä hänen peräänsä:

"Älä vain tunnusta!"

Ämmä tuli kotiin ja sanoi: "Sinä olet sen eteiskamarin oven avannut!"

Tyttö sanoi: "En mina ole avannut!"

Ämmä vain väitti, että hän oli avannut, ja sanoi sitten:

"Ei se siitä sen paremmaksi tule, sinun pitää saaman rangastuksesi. Tahdotko olla kuuro, mykkä vai sokea?"

Tyttö ajatteli, että jos hän on kuuro, ei hän kuule ihmisten puhetta eikä lintujen laulua, ja jos hän on sokea, ei hän näe Jumalan kaunista maailmaa. Hän vastasi, että hän on mieluummin mykkä.

Oltiin vähän aikaa, ja nainen suuttui ja sanoi, ettei sekään vielä piisaa. Hän vei tytön isolle korkealle vuorelle, ja vuoren alla oli meri. Nainen riisui hänet vallan alastomaksi ja lykkäsi sieltä kalliolta mereen. Mutta siinä oli satainen pohja, ja hän meni jalkaisin toiselle rannalle. Mutta kun hän oli ilki alasti, ei hän voinut mihinkään ihmisiin ruveta yrittämäänkään.

Hän meni suureen ontoon tammeen. Ja siellä olivat kuninkaanpojat linnustamassa metsässä. Koirat, jotka joka paikkaan kurkkailevat, löysivät tytön tammesta. Nuori kuningas meni katsomaan ja kysyi, onko siellä ihminen vai joka peljätys ja käski hänen tulla ulos. Ei tyttö tahtonut tulla, kun hän oli alasti, mutta kun kuningas lupasi ampua, täytyi hänen tulla.

Ja se oli niin erinomaisen kaunis ihminen, ja nuori kuningas otti hänet vaimoksensa, vaikkei hän mitään puhua osannut. Mitäs tästä, hän sai tavalliseen tapaan lapsen. Ja se ämmä tuli ja kysyi:

"Tunnustatko?" Hän vastasi:

"En!" Ämmälle hän sai vastatuksi, ja kuka tahansa olisi kysynyt, että tunnustatko, niin siihen hän sai vastatuksi.

Ämmä otti hänen lapsensa ja pani luita hänen viereensä. Sitten luultiin, että hän on lapsensa syönyt.

"Metsästä se on tullut," meinattiin, "se taitaa joku villieläin ollakin."

Mutta nuori kuningas puolusti häntä, vaikka hänkin kovin suri, että hän sillä tavalla lapsensa menetti. Mutta kun hän oli tavattoman kaunis ja kovin erinomainen kaikissa toimissaan.

Sitten hän sai lapsen toisen kerran. Ämmä tuli ja sanoi:

"Tunnustatko sitä muinaista kamarin oven avaamista?"

Hän sanoi: "En!"

Ämmä vei jälleen hänen lapsensa ja pani luita viereen. Eikä sittenkään vielä nuori kuningas antanut, vaikka hänet olisi tuomittu lavalla poltettavaksi. Nuori kuningas oli nähnyt sen ämmän, joka häneltä kysyi, ja sanoi:

"Kuinka sinä vastaat semmoisille haamuille etkä vastaa, kun minä puhun?"

Kolme kertaa kävi niin. Kolmannella kerralla hänen ylitseen kävi tuomio, että hänet pitää lavalla poltettamaan. Sitten lava oli valmistettu ja paljon väkeä koossa. Ei kuningas olisi sittenkään vielä antanut, mutta se oli lain asia. Siinä oli kolme veräjää, ja joka veräjä piti semmoista ääntä että:

"Tunnustatko?"

Ja hän vastasi: "En!" Ja kuningas ihmetteli:

"Kuinka sinä vastaat veräjille, mutta et vastaa minulle?"

Sitten hänet pantiin jo lavalle, ja valkea oli sytytetty ja
juuri tarttumassa hänen vaatteisiinsa. Ämmä tuli ja kysyi:
"Tunnustatko?"
Hän vastasi: "En!"
Ämmä puhalsi valkean sammuksiin ja sanoi:
"Sinä olet ollut uskollinen, ja tässä ovat lapsesi!"
Ne olivat kaksi niin kovin kaunista poikaa ja yksi tyttö.
Sitten hän sai ruvetuksi puhumaan.
Kuningas vei hänet iloiten kotiin. Ja hän pyysi
katsomaan vanhempiaan. Kyllä ämmä hänet sitten jo
rauhaan jätti, kun hän oli osannut pitää puolensa eikä ollut
tunnustanut.

[There was a smith who was such an enormous
drunkard that he was always drinking. At length, he drank
away his house and his workshop and his smithy and his
smithy tools. He had a wife as well, but when that wife
saw that everything was going, she took a little of their
goods and bought a small cottage near the city. And the
wife was pregnant.

When the smith had drunk everything away, so that he
had but six silver coins left, he went to a hemp twister's
and bought a piece of rope so that he could hang himself.
The hemp twister gave him a good piece and said:
"There you go, that will bear it!"
The man went into the woods and looked about for a
suitable tree. Then an old crone came riding by on a black
horse and shouted:
"Man, man, what do you mean to do?"
The smith said: "I mean to hang myself!"
"Well what do you want to hang yourself for?"
"My money is gone. The old has all been drunk and
there is no hope for new," said the smith.
The crone said: "Don't hang yourself on that account!
If you promise me that which you wife is giving birth to
now, then indeed I can help you!"
The smith thought it over for a bit, but then promised
on the condition that he could keep the child for fifteen
years.

"You can indeed keep the child for that time," said the crone. The old woman gave him a purse and said:

"Here is some money for you, that you can get yourself some help."

Then the smith went to his wife's place and asked for a plate and poured money out until it covered several plates. Then he bought back his own smithy and tools and started to work as before. And he lived like other folk. His wife wanted terribly to find out where he had gotten the money. The smith didn't wish to tell, but finally he had to admit that he had promised the child.

The child was a girl. When she was four weeks old, she began to speak in the cradle and said that she had to get up and start working—she was in a hurry. She got up and started to make lace and other such things that had never before been made in this world. Then she was invited to go sew at a nobleman's house.

One time when she was sewing at a count's home she suddenly said: "Now I have to go home!" At home she said to her mother:

"Put everything in order, they're coming now to take me."

The mother took fright and told the father what the daughter had said. The father started to count and it had been exactly fifteen years. Then they got the girl's clothes together. The crone came and said:

"Is it not so as we discussed?"

The smith answered: "It is indeed."

The girl was made ready to go with the crone. The crone had black horses pulling her carriage just as before. And the girl sat down beside her. The crone took the girl onto her lap and said:

"Have you ever sat on anything softer?"

"What is softer than one's own mother's lap?" answered the girl.

Then the crone gave the girl something to drink from a bottle and asked:

"Have you ever tasted anything sweeter?"

"What is sweeter than one's own mother's milk?" answered the girl.

Beside the road there was a bird-cherry, and the crone asked:

"Do you know why that is dried out?"

"I know indeed. In the trunk here is a skirt that I sewed from its leaves."

Then they drove into a great forest and there was a big building. The crone took the girl into the house and bade her stay there. She gave the girl many keys that corresponded to each of the rooms. She was allowed to go into any room she liked, but off the front room there was a room about which the crone said:

"Into that room you may not go!"

The girl found a room in which there was all sorts of food, and another where she could sleep. She stayed there for a little while and the crone came to see her. Nothing had happened yet. She left her again and went about her business.

Once when the girl came into the front room, she wondered what might be in that room. And she opened the door. From beside the back wall a dead body raised its head when she opened the door because there was a brass wire that led from the door to the body. When she slammed the door shut, the body called after her:

"Just don't admit it!"

The crone came home and said: "You have opened the front room door!"

The girl said: "I have not!"

The crone just claimed that she had opened the door and then said: "There's nothing for it but that you receive your punishment. Do you want to be deaf, mute, or blind?"

The girl thought that if she were deaf she would not hear the talking of people or the songs of birds, and if she were blind, she would not see God's beautiful world. She answered that she would rather be mute.

After some time, the woman grew angry and said that that would not be enough. She took the girl to a high mountain by the edge of the sea. The woman stripped her of all her clothes and kicked her off the cliff into the sea. But the sea had a sandy bottom there and she went by foot to the other shore. But because she was completely nude, she couldn't turn to anyone for help.

She crept into a hollow oak. And there came some princes bird-hunting in the forest. The dogs that were poking their noses in everywhere found the girl in the oak. The young king went to see and asked whether there was a person or some spook there, ordering her to come out. The girl didn't want to come out because she was nude, but the king threatened to shoot otherwise, and so she had to.

And she was such an exceptionally beautiful person that the young king took her as his wife, although she could not say anything. And in time she had a child by the usual process. And that crone came and asked: "Do you admit it?"

She answered: "No!" That crone got her answer, and if anyone in the world had asked, "Do you admit it?" they would have gotten that answer too.

The crone took her child away and put bones beside her. Then they thought that she had eaten her child.

"She came from the forest," they said, "she seemed to be a wild beast of some sort."

But the young king defended her, although he grieved sorely to have lost his child in this way. But she was incomparably beautiful and exceptional in every manner.

Then she had a child for a second time. The crone came and said:

"Do you admit opening the door to that room back then?"

She said: "No!"

The crone took away her child again and placed bones beside her. The young king still did not give her up although she would have been burned at the stake. The young king had seen that crone who questioned her and said:

"Why is it that you answer an old ghost like that but don't answer when I talk to you?"

A third time it happened in this way. On the third time the judgment came down upon her that she should be burned at the stake. Then the pyre was prepared and

many people gathered. The king himself went to bring
her there, as he loved her greatly. The king still wouldn't
have given her up but it was a legal necessity. There were
three gates and at each gate a voice asked:
"Do you admit it?"
And she answered: "No!"
And the king wondered: "How is it that you answer the
gates but you do not answer me?"
Then she was placed on the pyre and the fire was lit and
was just reaching up to her clothes. The crone came and
asked:
"Do you admit?"
She answered: "No!"
The crone blew out the fire and said: "You have been
faithful, and here are your children!"
They were two wonderfully handsome boys and one
girl. Then she began to be able to speak.
The king brought her home rejoicing. And she asked to
visit her parents. Indeed the crone left her now in peace,
for she had known how to stand her ground and had not
admitted (1881).]

As noted above, it is pointless to examine Sjöros's version in
terms of its oral stylistics, as the tale as we have it has passed
through a thorough literary reworking. Nonetheless, certain
tendencies remain which may have existed in oral versions of the
tale and which certainly find parallels in Skore's Sámi version. For
instance, a similar shift occurs in the words used to refer to the
heroine after she enters her marriage. Throughout her childhood in
the castle of the crone, the heroine is described as *tyttö* [a girl]. And
she is still referred to as *tyttö* right up until the time that the prince
compels her to come away with him: "Ei tyttö tahtonut tulla, kun
hän oli alasti, mutta kun kuningas lupasi ampua, täytyi hänen tulla"
[The girl didn't want to come out because she was nude, but the
king threatened to shoot otherwise, and so she had to]. From this
point onward in the text, the heroine is referred to only as *hän*
[he/she]. As in the Sámi version, then, the narrator seems unwilling
to accord the heroine any of the linguistic designations we might
expect given her changed status. She is not yet the wife, queen, or
mother that she seems. Interestingly, in the line quoted above, we

see that the prince has already been elevated to the status of *kuningas* [king], although the narrator often modifies the designation by referring to him as *nuori kuningas* [young king]. In comparison with the *gánda* of the Sámi text, this young king seems fully in control of the situation throughout the story, although he is compelled at last by law to let his wife be burned: "Ei kuningas olisi sittenkään vielä antanut, mutta se oli lain asia" [The king still wouldn't have given her up but it was a legal necessity]. The pronoun usage in the text thus clearly supports the psychosocial interpretation of the tale as a search for acceptance of one's status as an adult and a finding of one's voice as a woman. The male character, on the other hand, does not seem to need the agency of the crone to achieve this status shift.

Sjöros's 1881 version of the tale accords well with the characterization of the type 710 included in Antti Aarne's 1911 study *Finnische Märchenvarianten* (no. 713). As is typical in these Finnish versions, the tale opens with the deplorable life of the girl's alcoholic and suicidal father. A mysterious crone, who insists on taking the couple's baby in exchange for her help, finances the man's economic recovery. In Sjöros's version, the girl seems affected by her father's bargain even from birth. Immediately aware of her limited time with her parents, she starts to do housework as an infant and soon becomes an expert seamstress. She is hired out to fine houses to do their sewing, a task she dutifully performs until the day that has been appointed for her journey to the crone's. At that point, she seems to have foreknowledge of the crone's approach and doughtily prepares for her new life with the mysterious woman. At the crone's home she lives a comfortable life, and is entrusted with the keys of the household. She succumbs to the temptation of the forbidden door, however, and finds there a frightening corpse that nonetheless warns her not to admit anything, a detail typical of all the versions Aarne discusses. Through her subsequent harrowing adventures, the girl heeds the corpse's warning and refuses to admit her wrongdoing at every turn. Eventually, she is rewarded for her persistence, as the crone appears for a final time at the pyre, restores the heroine's children and voice, and leaves her to live happily ever after.

Sjöros includes details that seem to depart from the tale as narrowly conceived but that help to characterize the figures in the story. The crone asks the girl a set of questions that the girl answers without difficulty, displaying in her answers her greater esteem for her home and mother than for anything associated with the crone. When taking the girl into her arms for the first time, the mysterious crone asks if she has ever felt an embrace so tender. "Mikä on pehmeämpi kuin oman äidin syli?" [What is softer than one's own mother's embrace?] the girl replies with defiance if not also a certain mournfulness. So, too, the crone's drink cannot equal the sweetness of the girl's mother's milk, and the local tree pointed out by the crone is recognized as the source of the girl's material for a dress. The heroine's pointed replies, when coupled with her miraculously precocious speech and seeming complete foreknowledge of her future, create an image of a far more out-spoken and confident heroine than one finds in either the Sámi or Norwegian versions considered here. This girl knows her mind and she speaks it, although she is also careful to heed the corpse's advice in never admitting to having looked in the room when the question is asked. Given her talkative nature, one can imagine that it was quite a hardship to choose to be mute, and the young king, her husband, also comments with some irritation when he observes the girl speaking to the crone when she has never used her voice with him. The heroine makes no answer to his questions, however, and he does not seem to harbor any grudge, as they eventually live happily ever after.

What is most striking about this Finnish version, of course, is the fact the heroine is rewarded for precisely the opposite reason for which she is rewarded in the Sámi version of the tale. Where the Sámi heroine is saved and receives her children back once she tells the truth, the Finnish heroine wins the day through her steadfast denial of the truth. The Finnish woman knows how to keep a secret, and is not afraid to do so even though her life is threatened as a result. It is apparent in fact that, were it not for the reappearance of the crone just in the nick of time, the woman would have gone to her death before admitting her disobedience. As the narrator summarizes at the end of the tale: "Kyllä ämmä hänet sitten jo rauhaan jätti, kun hän oli osannut pitää puolensa eikä ollut tunnustanut" [Indeed the crone left her now in peace, for she had known how to stand her ground and had not admitted].

It is hard not to see this difference as having a cultural resonance of some sort: whereas the Sámi girl gains her happy ending only by swallowing her pride and admitting her misdeed to the entire community, her Finnish counterpart earns her reward by keeping her mouth tightly shut. In a context in which farm girls were frequently sent to manor houses as servants, the virtue of keeping a household's secrets could be seen to loom large. The same went for daughters-in-law, as Leea Virtanen (1994, 338) has pointed out: brides were exhorted to keep the secrets of their new households, taking any disappointments, frustrations, or frightening secrets they might come upon in their new lives out into the seclusion of a forest to confide to the trees alone, and not to neighbor women. As one informant of the 1880s put it: "People kept all their sorrows within their own four walls" (338). The secrets of the household must be kept come what may, and the daughter-in-law represented a major threat to this conspiracy of silence. It is sometimes difficult for a modern American reading audience to understand the value agrarian Finns placed on a culture of denial and suppression of open communication. American psychotherapy would easily label such tendencies seriously dysfunctional, and counsel instead a household culture of open communication. Households that keep their skeletons deeply buried in their closets are regarded as corrosive and detrimental. Nevertheless, this same guardedness was a valued trait in subordinate women in agrarian Finland, at least to judge from the reports of informants from the nineteenth century and various items of recorded folklore like songs, legends, or the tale at hand. Thus, the narrative inscribes for its audience an ideal of young female behavior, just as surely as does the Sámi tale. And it is probable that a knowing Finnish audience member would see the tale as making sense, even if the girl's refusal to tell the truth can seem anything but logical or heroic by modern American standards.

We may also note that the fact that the tormenter here is no longer the Virgin helps remove the narrative situation from a straight choice between truthfulness and lying. Instead, the tale seems to erect a set of challenges that the girl needs to surmount in order to free herself (and indirectly, her family) from the original dilemma created by her father's drinking problem and suicidal tendencies. On the psychological level, perhaps this version of the tale is still about the same thing as the Sámi one, i.e., the low-born heroine's finding of an adult voice and successful marital status through the agency of a high-born adult female. But on a much more concrete level of daily life and female responsibilities, this tale paints a very different picture, one consonant with the life of a Finnish girl of the servant class in the late nineteenth century. In her annotation of the tale, Pirkko-Liisa Rausmaa (1988, 502) notes that Finnish versions of ATU 710 never feature the Virgin Mary, nor does the heroine ever admit her wrongdoing, no matter what threats she faces. Denial can be seen as a powerfully heroic act in some cultural contexts.

A third story completes our examination. Jørgen Moe recorded the tale in 1838 from Lars Svendserud of Ringerike, Norway. Like the other two stories described above, then, it is a tale told by a man, even if the plot features a heroine and can be classified as a "feminine" tale. The tale was reprinted as no. 12 in the collection *Ridder Skau og Jomfru Dame: Eventyr frå Ringerike*, published by Det Norske Samlaget in Oslo in 1969 (Alver et al 1969). As such, it became part of a multi-volume collection entitled *Norsk Eventyrbibliotek*, selected because of its apparent typicality for the Ringerike region and because of the quality of the narration as recorded and presented by Moe as part of his grand tale-collecting project. It is certain that Moe found the tale printable and indeed, representative of Norwegian oral tradition:

> Langt, langt borti en stor skau budde en gang et par fattigfolk. Kona kom i barselseng og fødte et barn, ei vakker datter. Men de var så fattige at de visste ikke hvordan de skulle få barnet til dåpen.
>
> Mannen måtte da en dag ut for å se å få faddere som sjøl kunne ofre. Han gikk hele dagen bade til den eine og til den andre. Men alle sa de at de nok ville være fadder, men ingen syntes de hadde råd til å ofre sjøl.

Da han gikk heim om kvelden, møtte han ei vakker frue, som var så prektig kledd og såg så inderlig snill og god ut. Hun baud seg til å skaffe barnet til dåpen, men sia ville hun ha det. Mannen svarte at han først matte spore kona si hva hun ville. Men da han kom heim of fortalte det, sa kona beint ut nei.

Andre dagen gikk mannen ut att, men ingen ville være faddere når de skulle ofre sjøl, og alt han bad, så hjalp det ikke. Da han gikk heim att mot kvelden, møtte han på nytt den vakre frua som såg så blid ut, og hun gjorde det same tilbudet igjen.

Han fortalte kona det som hadde hendt'n, og hun sade att dersom han ikke neste dag kunne få faddere til barnet, så fikk de vel la frua få det, sia hun såg så god og snill ut.

Den tredje dagen mannen gikk ut, fikk han heller ingen faddere, og da han møtte frua igjen om kvelden, lovte han å la henne få barnet når hun ville skaffe det dåp og kristendom.

Om morgenen kom hun så dit mannen budde, i følgje med to mannfolk, tok barnet og reiste til kirka med det, og der var det døpt. Så tok hun det heim med seg, og der levde den vesle jenta hos henne i flere år, og fostermora var alltid snill og god mot henne.

Da jenta var blitt så stor at hun lærte å skjønne, laga fostermora seg til å reise bort.

"Du skal få lov å gå hvor du vil," sa hun til jenta, "bare ikke i de tre kammersa jeg nå viser deg." Og så reiste hun.

Men jentungen kunne likevel ikke la være å gløtte litt på den eine kammersdøra, og husj! Så flaug det ut ei stjerne.

Da fostermora kom tilbake, vart hun vond og truga fosterdattera med å jage henne bort. Men barnet gråt og bad for seg, og så fikk hun til slutt lov å bli.

Om ei tid skulle fostermora reise bort att, og så forbaud hun jenta å gå inn de to kammersa hun ikke hadde vært i. Hun lovte å ta seg i vare.

Men da hun hadde gått aleine ei stund og tenkt og grunna på hva som vel kunne være inne i det andre kammerset, kunne hun ikke holde seg fra å gløtte litt på døra og kikke inn, og husj! så flaug månen ut.

Da fostermora kom at, og såg att månen hadde sloppet ut, vart hun sørgmodig, og sa at nå kunne hun slett ikke ha henne hos seg lenger, nå matte hun bort. Men jenta gråt så hjertelig og bad så vakkert for seg, og så fikk hun da lov til å bli denne gangen også.

Ei tid etter skulle fostermora reise igjen—jenta var alt halvvoksen den gangen—og da la hun henne alvorlig på hjerte at hun slett ikke matte prøve å gå inn i eller se inn i det tredje kammerset.

Men da fostermora hadde vært borte ei stund, og jenta hadde gått aleine i langsommelig tid og var blitt bade kei og lei, så tenkte hun: "Nei, så morsomt det skulle være å se litt inn i det tredje kammerset!" Hun tenkte først at hun ikke ville gjøre det like fullt, for fostermora si skyld. Men da hun andre gangen kom på det, kunne hun ikke berge seg lenger, hun syntes hun skulle og matte se inn in kammerset. Hun gløtta litt på døra, og husj! så flaug sola ut.

Da fostermora nå kom tilbake, og såg at sola hadde fløyet ut, vart hun reint ill ved, og sa at nå kunne hun slett ikke få lov å være hos henne lenger. Fosterdattera gråt og bad enda vakrere enn før, men det hjalp ikke.

"Nei, nå må jeg strafe deg," sa mora, "men du kan ha valget: enten du vil bli den aller vakreste av alle og ikke kunne snakke, eller du vil bli den aller styggeste og kunne snakke. Men bort fra meg må du."

"Så vil jeg helst bli vakker," sa jente. Og det vart hun au, men fra den tid var hun mållaus.

Da hun var kommet bort fra fostermora, gikk hun og vandra gjennom en stor, stor skau. Men alt hun gikk, vart det aldri ende på den.

Da det lei mot kvelden, klauv hun opp i et høgt tre som stod like over ei olle, og satte seg til å sove om natta.

Tett ved låg et slot, og fra det kom ei terne tidlig om morgenen. Hun skulle hente tevann fra olla til prinsen. Terna såg det vakre ansiktet i olla, og trudde at det var henne sjøl. Så kasta hu vassbøtta, sprang heim og slo på nakken og sa: "Er jeg så vakker, så er jeg for god til å gå og bære vann."

Så skulle ei anna i vei etter vann, men det gikk like ens
med henne; hun kom også tilbake og sa at hun var for
vakker og for god til å gå etter vann til prinsen.

Så gikk prinsen sjøl, for han hadde lyst til å se hvordan
dette hang i hop. Da han kom til olla, fikk han au se
bildet, og straks såg han opp. Der ble han da vár den
vakre jomfrua som satt oppe i treet. Han lokka henne ned
og tok henne heim med seg, og ville endelig ha henne til
dronning, fordi hun var så vakker. Men mor hans, som
levde ennå, ville ikke. "Hun kan jo ikke snakke," sa hun,
"og det kan gjerne være et troll-menneske." Men prinsen
gav seg ikke før han fikk henne.

Da de hadde levd sammen ei tid, vart hun med barn, og
da hun skulle føde, lot prinsen sette sterk vakt omkring
henne.

Men i fødselstimen sovna alle sammen, og da hun
hadde født, kom fostermor hennes, skar barnet i
veslefingeren og smurte dronninga om munnen og på
fingeren med blodet, og sa til henne: "Nå ska du bli så
sørgmodig som jeg var da du hadde sloppet ut stjerna."
Så vart hun borte med barnet.

Da de vakna, de som var satt til vakt, trudde de at
dronninga hadde ett sitt eie barn, og den gamle dronninga
ville ha henne brent, men prinsen holdt slik av henne, og
til slutt fikk han bedt henne fri fra straffa, men det var
med nød og neppe.

Andre gangen den unge dronninga skulle i barselseng,
vart det satt dobbelt så sterk vakt som gangen før. Men
det gikk nettopp like ens, bare at fostermora sa: "Nå skal
du bli så sørgmodig som jeg var da du hadde sloppet ut
månen." Dronninga gråt og bad—for når fostermora var
der, kunne hun snakke, men det hjalp ikke.

Nå ville den gamle dronninga endelig ha henne brent,
men prinsen fikk da bedt henne fri den gangen au.

Da dronninga skulle i den tredje barselsenga, vart det
satt tredobbelt vakt omkring henne. Men det gikk like
ens: Fostermora kom mens vakta sov, tok barnet og skar
det i veslefingeren og smurte dronninga om munnen med
blodet. Og så sa hun at nå skull dronninga bli så

sørgmodig som hun sjøl hadde vært da sola var sloppet ut.

Nå kunne ikke prinsen på noen måte få frelst henne. Hun måtte og skulle brennes. Men nettopp i det samme de leidde henne opp på bålet, fikk de se fostermora, som kom med alle tre barna. De to leidde hun ved handa, og det tredje bar hun på armen.

Hun gikk bort til den unge dronninga og sa: "Her er barna dine, nå skal du få dem att. Jeg er jomfru Maria, og så bedrøvet som du nå har vært, var jeg, da du hadde sloppet ut sola, månen og stjerna. Nå har du lidd straff for det du gjorde, og fra nå av skal du igjen kunne snakke."

Så glade dronninga og prinsen vart, kan alle lett tenke seg, men ingen kan si det. Sia var de lykkelige støtt, og mor til prinsen holt også av den unge dronninga fra den tid av.

[Far, far away in a great forest there once lived a poor couple. The woman was expecting and gave birth to a child, a pretty daughter. But they were so poor that they did not know how they would bring the child to be baptized.

The man had to go out to see if he could find godparents who would themselves pay the offering for the baptism. He went about from one to the next all day long. But although everyone said they'd gladly be godparents, no one felt they had the money to pay the offering themselves.

As he was going home in the evening, he met a pretty woman, who was so finely dressed and looked so wonderfully kind and good. She proposed that she could bring the child to be baptized, but said she wanted to keep the child herself. The man replied that he would first have to ask his wife what she wanted. But when he came home and told her of it, the wife said no straightaway.

For a second day the man headed out again, but no one wanted to be the godparents if they had to pay the offering themselves, and no matter how many he asked, it was of no use. When he was coming home again in the evening, he met the pretty woman again who looked so gentle and she made the same offer again.

He told his wife what had happened, and she said that if he could not find godparents for the child on the following day, they should let the woman take her, since she looked so good and kind.

On the third day, the man went out but still found no godparents, and meeting the woman again in the evening, he promised her the child if she would provide it with baptism and Christianity.

The next morning she came to where the man had instructed her along with two attendants. She took the child and traveled to the church with it, where it was baptized. Then she took it home with her and there the little girl lived for some years, and her foster-mother was always kind and good to her.

When the girl was old enough that she had learned to reason, her foster-mother prepared to travel away. "You have permission to go where you wish," she said to the girl, "just not in the three rooms I will show you now." And then she left.

But the young girl could not let well enough alone and peeped through the door of the first room. And whoosh! Out flew a star.

When the foster-mother came back, she was cross and angry and nearly ran the girl off. But the child cried and pleaded and so at length she received permission to stay.

After some time, the foster-mother needed to travel again, and so she forbade the girl to enter the two rooms that she hadn't been in yet. She promised to be on guard.

But when she had been by herself a while, and thought and imagined what might be inside the second room, she couldn't keep from opening the door a crack and peering in. And whoosh! The moon flew out.

When the foster-mother came again, and saw that the moon had slipped out, she was sorrowful and said that now she absolutely could not let her stay there any longer but must go away. But the girl cried in so heartfelt a manner, and pleaded for herself so prettily, that finally she received permission to stay there this time as well.

Some time thereafter, the foster-mother needed to travel again—the girl was half-grown up by this time—and then she let it be known with all her heart that she absolutely could not try to enter or look inside the third room.

But when the foster-mother had been gone for a while, and the girl had been alone and become bored and was sick and tired of it all, she thought to herself:

"Well, how fun it would be to look inside that third room!" At first she thought that she would not do it after all on account of her foster-mother. But when she came upon it a second time, she could not stand it any longer: she felt that she should and must see inside that room. She opened the door a crack. And whoosh! The sun flew out.

Now when the foster-mother came back and saw that the sun had flown out, she was quite beside herself and said that now she could absolutely not stay there any longer. The foster-daughter cried and pleaded even more prettily than before, but it was of no use.

"No, now I must punish you," said the mother. "But you can have a choice: either you can be the prettiest of all but not be able to speak, or you can be the ugliest of all but be able to speak. But in any case, you must be away from me."

"I would at least like to be pretty," said the girl. And she was so already, but from that moment on she was rudderless/voiceless.[2]

When she had left her foster-mother, she went about and wandered in a great, great forest. But everywhere she went she was always alone.

When evening came, she climbed up a tall tree that stood above a spring. She settled down there and went to sleep for the night.

Nearby there stood a castle, and from there came a servant girl in the morning. She was supposed to draw some water for tea for the prince from the spring. The servant girl saw the beautiful face reflected in the spring and thought it was her own. So she threw down her water pail, ran home, and tossed her head, saying: "I am so pretty that I am too good to go about hauling water."

So a second servant girl had to go after the water, but the same thing happened with her. She came back and said that she was too pretty and too good to fetch water for the prince.

So the prince went himself, because he wanted to see what was going on. When he came to the spring, he also saw the reflection and immediately looked up. Then he spied the pretty maiden who sat up in the tree. He called her down and took her home with him and wished at last to make her his queen, for she was so pretty. But his mother, who was still alive, did not want it so.

"She cannot even speak," she said, "and she may be one of the troll folk." But the prince did not give up until he got her.

When they had lived together for some time, she became with child, and when it was time for her to give birth, the prince ordered a strong guard around her.

But at the hour of the birth, when everyone was asleep, and after she had given birth, her foster-mother came, cut the child on the pinky and smeared the blood around the queen's mouth and on her fingers, saying to her: "Now you shall feel as sad as I was went you let out the star." And then she was gone with the child.

When they awoke, those that had been set to guard her believed that the queen had eaten her own child, and the old queen wanted her burned. But the prince stood up for her, and finally he was able to get her freed from punishment but just by the skin of his teeth.

A second time the young queen was about to give birth, and a watch of double the strength was set to guard her. But it happened just as before, except that the foster-mother said: "Now you shall feel as sad as I was when you let out the moon." The queen cried and pleaded—for while the foster-mother was there she could speak—but it was of no use.

Now the old queen wanted her burned at last, but the prince was able to get her freed this time as well.

When the queen was set to give birth for a third time, they set a watch three times as strong around her. But it happened just as before: the foster-mother came while the watch slept, took the child and cut it on the pinky and smeared the queen around the mouth with the blood. And she said that now the queen should feel as sad as she herself had been when the sun was let out.

Now the prince could in no way save her. She must and should be burned. But just at the moment that they led her up to the pyre, the foster-mother appeared with all three children. Two of them she led by the hand and the third she carried in her arms.

She went over to the young queen and said: "Here are your children, now you shall have them back. I am the Virgin Mary, and as miserable as you have been now, just so was I when you let out the sun, moon, and star. Now you have suffered punishment for what you did, and from now on, you shall be able to speak."

The prince and queen were so glad, as anyone can imagine, but few can say. They had come to a happy ending, and the prince's mother was fond of the young queen from that time onward.]

As a transcribed rendering of a single narrator's performance, taken down by hand and reworked to one degree or another in the process of creating a fair copy of the text, this story can be seen as occupying a medial position between the exact phonetic transcription produced by Ravila in his fieldwork on the Kola Peninsula, and the clearly reworked, grammatically regularized rendering produced from unidentified informant(s) by Sjöros. The tale is full of pithy turns of phrase and dialect constructions that lend it a much more local feel than what one finds in the Finnish story. At the same time, it is hard to know exactly how many of such details are attributable to Svendserud the narrator and which are more likely attributable to Moe the collector/editor. As numerous folklorists working on the tales of the Brothers Grimm have shown, truly "verbatim transcription" only became a reality with the invention of mechanical recording equipment. Nonetheless, there are linguistic details that are certainly evocative in the text, such as the narrator's switch from calling the Virgin *fostermora* [foster-mother] to simply *mora* [mother], precisely at the moment in which the Virgin is compelled by justice to punish and banish the girl after her third transgression: "'Nei, nå må jeg strafe deg,' sa mora" ['No, now I must punish you,' said the mother]. Thereafter, the narrator returns to calling her *fostermora* for the remainder of the story, until the very end when the foster-mother identifies herself as the Virgin Mary and restores the heroine's children and status.

As with the other two texts, an examination of the terms used to describe the heroine can provide interesting evidence regarding the text's meaning and the narrator's attitudes toward its characters. The heroine begins as *barnet* [the child] and progresses to *jenta* [maiden] once the mysterious lady has adopted her. Yet, in contrast to the other two stories, her elevation to the adult status of queen is not diminished in any way in the text: from the moment of her marriage she becomes *dronninga* [queen], or at very least *unga dronninga* [the young queen] so as to distinguish her from the dowager queen. Thus, we find none of the strategy of linguistic avoidance of status designation noticeable in the other two versions. The prince, on the other hand remains *prinsen* from first to last, apparently obliged to wait for his mother's death or retirement before assuming his status as king.

Of course, this difference in how the heroine is referred to in the Norwegian text as compared with the Sámi and Finnish versions correlates well with the shift in the way in which the heroine's transgression is interpreted. For, if Wilhelm Grimm was certain that Marienkind was not being punished for her disobedience in opening the door but rather, for her willful refusal to admit her error thereafter, Lars Svendserud does not seem to have shared this opinion. In his version, the heroine is clearly and emphatically punished for her misdeed (trebled in this case). The Virgin says so at every opportunity, and although the girl begs for forgiveness on each occasion that she breaks her lady's rules, she never denies her actions in words. Indeed, if the German tale underscores the importance of truth-telling for subservient women, there seems to be no such lesson here. Instead, as Kathy Stokker (2009) has noted in other connections, there seems to be a kind of folk attenuation of Catholic theology at work, in which the girl needs to requite her wrongdoings with penance before receiving forgiveness. Once the girl has suffered as much as Our Lady suffered from having her star, moon, and sun released, she is forgiven and restored to her happy married existence. Indeed, the heroine never seems to have much trouble finding her voice to plead or argue with her foster-mother, although she is willing to give it up rather than become ugly: "'Så vil jeg helst bli vakker', sa jente" ['I would at least like to be pretty,' said the girl]. From the standpoint of the Norwegian narrator, this choice is clearly the right one, for, although she temporarily loses her ability to speak, she nonetheless gains a prince for a husband by doing so, and will live the rest of her life in happy wedlock, the recognized queen of the land who in the end is valued even by her mother-in-law: "og mor til prinsen holt også av den unge dronninga fra den tid av" [and the prince's mother was fond of the young queen from that time onward].

In this Norwegian tale, the Virgin seems a good deal kinder than her counterparts in either the Sámi or Finnish tales. She first appears in the story as an answer to the poor couple's need: without her monetary assistance, they cannot bring the child to church for baptism. In exchange for this favor, the Virgin—described only as a "fine lady"—insists on adopting the child, an act which the child's mother at first vehemently resists. Nonetheless, once the lady has become the child's foster mother, she treats her with great kindness, even when the girl repeatedly breaks the household's only stated taboo. Once the girl has released the sun, the Virgin is compelled to banish the girl, but she does not seem to take any joy in doing so. So, too, when she comes to visit the heroine after the birth of each of her children, the Virgin does not challenge the new mother to admit her wrongdoing. Rather, she simply informs the new mother that she is now experiencing an equivalent sorrow to the one that the Virgin had endured through the girl's acts of disobedience. The girl *is* punished for her acts, but it is a punishment that seems to have an intended ending all along: once the girl has been made to experience comparable sorrow, the Virgin reappears to restore her to all her wealth, social standing, and marital bliss. When the Virgin returns at the end of the story, lovingly cradling the youngest child and leading the other two by the hand, it is evident that she never intended to see the girl burned at all. Rather, she has planned a tough-love punishment that will hopefully teach the Norwegian heroine the ramifications of her acts of disobedience.

In this sense, the Norwegian version of the tale does not lend as much support to the psychosocial readings one can make on the basis of German, Sámi, or Finnish versions. The girl does not come into her voice through the offices of the high status woman. Instead, she learns a lesson of value to girls in nineteenth-century Norway: obedience. She learns to heed her superiors' commands, understanding that when she does not do so, she causes pain to her superiors. And further, she learns that disobedience cannot always be avoided by pleading: at some point, transgressions will be punished, and then they will be punished to the full extent that a sense of justice requires. Once the heroine has broken the taboo for the third time, she is destined to be punished for all three transgressions, despite all her blandishments and tears.

Comparison of these three versions of ATU 710 can teach us much about folktales, their allomorphs, and their interpretation. Whereas analysis of folktales along the lines described by Holbek and Thomas can help uncover latent psychosocial meanings within at least some versions or renderings of the tale, a focus on the cultural significance within a tale's array of distinct plot or character variations (i.e., its allomorphs) can help us recover the more proximal, conscious logic of individual storytellers in trying to make sense of their tales within the own culture's value system and notions of behavioral propriety. Tale tellers encoded cultural ideals in their tales for the benefit of young listeners, although these could vary from narrator to narrator or from culture to culture. While Skore's tale underscores the importance of humble honesty after wrongdoing, Sjöros's version idealizes a gritty determination to keep secrets buried. And Svendserud's version warns listeners of the importance of heeding rules in the first place. On this level of individual culturally-embedded performances, the three tales examined no longer become variants of a single tale-type; instead, they are revealed as what they no doubt were to their original performers: unique and meaningful tales performed within an ambient system of values. In all three cases, the men who told these tales expressed their understandings of the behaviors that a young woman should display if she wanted to live happily ever after.

Notes

[1] For the ease of modern readers of Northern Sámi, I present the text here in regularized orthography. For the ease of readers unfamiliar with the language, I include a translation.

[2] The term used here, *mållaus,* can mean "without voice," but also "without direction." Since both meanings seem in play here, I have employed them both, suggesting that the narrator was making a play on words. Thanks to Scott Mellor for this and other advice concerning the Norwegian translation.

Waking the Dead: Folk Legends Concerning Magicians and Walking Corpses in Iceland[1]

Terry Gunnell

Quite understandably, much of the emphasis in folk tale research in recent years has come to focus on the performances and repertoires of individual storytellers,[2] their contextual relationship within their social or geographical surroundings (see, for example, Holbek 1998; Tangherlini 1994; Lindow 2008), or the socio-linguistics involved in the individual storytelling "event" (see, for example, Bauman 1986; Siikala 1990). Less interest is paid to the nature of the local beliefs, the process of change involved in legends as they are passed on, or the "repertoires" of legends told within particular areas (see, for example, Júlíana Magnúsdóttir 2008). This is, in part, the result of the awareness of the pointlessness of searching for an ancient *ur*-legend or *ur*-fairy tale, and our understanding of the political agendas originally involved in the creation of "national" folk tale collections which distorted the image of the "tradition" and beliefs reflected in these narratives (see, for example, Gunnell 2010a). One might say that the investigation of "national spirit" has given way to the investigation of "individual art".

Nonetheless, as we are all aware, the individual storyteller and the stories they tell still inhabit a historical, cultural, geographical, moral and social surrounding. They also use a language and set of cultural vocabulary that they have acquired from those around them, and their narratives need the interest and understanding of their audiences if they are to receive a hearing (and then, perhaps, get transmitted to others). As Elliott Oring has recently stressed, there is thus still good reason to consider the nature of the

235

"tradition" involved, even though it may have had very little "national" about it (Oring forthcoming). Most storytellers, even today, will see themselves first and foremost as people with roots in a particular area rather than a particular nation (as Bostonians, Brightonians, Berkeleyans or Balestrandinger), and the same applies to the past. To some degree, it might be argued that research into this "local" identity got lost in the mix when "local" narratives found themselves transformed into "national" materials. It deserves more attention than it has previously received. Indeed, there is still good reason for undertaking studies into these local beliefs and "traditions", using comparative materials from other areas (and even other nations) to pinpoint ecotypical features (differences or particular emphases). These have a great deal to tell us about the local societies, local networks and senses of local identity in both the past and the present. Databases of legends like those at present being compiled in both Iceland and California (of Danish legends) have a great deal of potential in this regard.[3]

The paper that follows deals with a particular Icelandic narrative tradition that is not only comparatively unique in comparison to most mainland Nordic, British and Irish traditions, but also comparatively limited in area within Iceland itself. On the surface, there would be nothing particularly strange about this were it not for the fact that most of the other Icelandic folk beliefs reflected in the Icelandic legend tradition seem to have obvious roots in the more southerly Nordic mainland and especially in Norway (Gunnell 1998, 2001 and 2004). Others occasionally point to connections with Celtic tradition.[4] Both features are, of course, quite natural considering the fact that recent genetic research supports the inference of early historical records that suggest that the Icelanders had roots in both the Nordic countries and Scotland and Ireland.[5] It is likely that up to one half of the first Icelandic female settlers and one fifth of the men were Gaelic, that is to say, they came from Scotland or Ireland, probably as slaves (Agnar Helgason 2000a, 2000b, 2001). A large percentage of these people must have survived and had children. Of course, the slaves were often involved in rearing the children, even if their own language seems to have been banned (Gísli Sigurðsson 1988a, 33). Most of the rest of the Icelandic settlers came from Norway, and especially western

Norway. All of this is echoed in the nature of Icelandic legends and folk beliefs, past and present: The legends about the so-called *álfar* [elves] (Gunnell 2007) or *huldufólk* [hidden people] have forms well known in Norway. The beings themselves, though, are rather different to those described in Norwegian folk legends: Icelandic *álfar* do not have tails, they are not pagan, they do not eat manure, they do not look like Johnny Rotten, and they do not live beneath our feet.[6] Even though the expression "*huldufólk*" is also found in Norway in the local form *huldre* (probably a *noa* expression like the Irish "good people" or "little people"), the hidden Icelandic *álfar* are no *underjordiske* beings: they tend to live "up" in rocks and hillsides (very much like the Irish *sídh*: see, for example, Ó hÓgáin 2006, 206-12); they might also have connections with the dead (like the Irish *sídh*); they look just like us, and they have never had much trouble with Christianity. Over and above this, Iceland has similar changeling beliefs to those found in both the Gaelic and the Nordic countries;[7] it has both Gaelic and Nordic forms of waterhorse legends;[8] it has selkie tales like those found in Scotland and Northern Norway;[9] both Nordic and Gælic variants of "The Death of Pan" legends;[10] and tales of laughing *marbendlar* (Nordic mermen) that echo the tales of laughing leprechauns in Ireland (Chesnutt 1999). In general, along with Shetland, Orkney, and, to a lesser degree, the Faroe Islands, Iceland forms part of the high arch of the North Atlantic cultural bridge which offers connections between the Gaelic and Nordic cultures. In general, the same thing is reflected in most Icelandic ghost tales, except for those that I will be discussing in the following article: in other words, the tales of the wakened or raised dead. In this case the Icelandic tradition seems to be closer to that of Haiti than Hardanger or County Clare.

Before preceding any further, it should be stressed immediately that the Icelandic concept of the walking dead in the past was somewhat different to the way most of us understand ghosts. The dead that return in Icelandic legends—and indeed those talked about in accounts of *reimleikar* [hauntings] in the Old Icelandic sagas going back to the twelfth century (see, for example, the account of Fróðárundrið [the Fróðá River wonder] in *Eyrbyggja saga* 1935, 139-52) were seen as being essentially corporeal, and would have had enormous trouble walking through walls without losing important

parts of their anatomy. It was possible (if not common) in both
sagas and legends that people sometimes physically wrestled with
ghosts when they encountered them.[11] Some later folk legends tell
of them visiting young women (usually ex-lovers or women who
had spurned them) at night in their beds, and even producing
children with them (something that sounds particularly kinky and
more than slightly problematic).[12] When out walking, it is
sometimes noted that their graves lie open, and they can be
prevented from returning by someone rolling a ball of wool into
their open coffins (see, for example, Jón Árnason 1954-1961, I, 255
and 274-6).

The background of such beliefs is, of course, a mixture of
Catholic Christian and pre-Christian Norse ideas. It appears that the
pre-Christian people did not conceive of people as having souls in
the same way that Christians did (Strömbäck 2000a; Alver 1989).
Furthermore, the first Icelandic settlers were buried in graves with
weapons, clothes, food, rowing boats and even a slave or two
(Kristján Eldjárn 2000)—all of which seems to have been expected
to be of use in the next world (whatever that was conceived of as
being). The Christian dead, meanwhile, were believed to be waiting
in their graves for Doomsday, at which time they were expected to
sit up, re-flesh themselves, and marvel at the sight of Jesus coming
over the eastern horizon (*Revelation* 21.13; Parker Pearson 2003, 6).
It comes as no surprise that the Icelandic *Landnámabók* (Book of
Settlements) and the later sagas tell of deceased heroes being heard
singing in their graves, complaining about the company they have
been given (see, for example, *Landnámabók* 1968, 105; *Brennu-Njáls
saga* 1954, 193-4), or physically beating up any interlopers planning
on robbing their graves (*Grettis saga* 1936: 108-19; and *Hrómundar
saga Gripssonar* 1944, 276-8). In the thirteenth-century *Eyrbyggja saga*,
a house is taken over one Christmas, first of all by a dead woman
who is discovered doing some cooking naked in the kitchen, and
then by two groups of dead people from the local graveyard and the
bottom of the sea who move into the main room of the hall and
end up engaging each other in the old Nordic equivalent of a food
fight, showering each other with mud and water (*Eyrbyggja saga*
1935: 145-52; see also Gunnell 2004).

In short, the idea for many Icelanders prior to the advent of spiritualism in the late nineteenth century was that the dead were essentially not dead but sleeping, and could be "woken" or made to "rise" (cf. *Luke* 8.52; *Matthew* 9.24); in other words, they had the potential of coming back to life if they had good—or bad—cause to do so.[13] The idea of "waking the dead" in Iceland and some of the other Nordic countries (both in pre-Christian times and at the time at which the folk legends were collected) was thus very different to the process of "raising spirits" at a séance.[14] In spite of this, accounts of people physically raising the dead and not only asking news of them but dispatching them to attack other people or carry out errands seem to have been both relatively popular and common in the Icelandic folk legends collected in the nineteenth and twentieth centuries (and in earlier legal accounts), and most particularly in legends from the north and west of Iceland. The Icelandic *sagnagrunnur* database of printed legends[15] contains references to over 150 such legends.[16] What is even more intriguing about such accounts is that in their extant form, they have hardly any direct parallels in Iceland's neighboring countries.

A natural beginning is to outline exactly what was believed to be involved in raising—or, as the Icelanders say, "waking"—the dead (*að vekja upp draug*)? Jón Árnason, the librarian who organized the collection of material for the first and main national collection of folk legends published in 1862-4, writes the following detailed summary of techniques said to have been used for waking the dead in Iceland. It includes some useful information about how people imagined the appearance and behavior of the raised dead. Jón's account appears to be drawn largely drawn from material contained in two or three of the accounts he was sent, in addition to his knowledge of Old Norse literature. It is worth quoting at length, not least because it reflects a growing conflict in the understanding of the walking dead and beliefs about whether they were spiritual or corporeal. Jón writes:

Uppvakningar eða sendingar

Sumir segja að taka skuli dauðs manns bein eitthvert og magna það með fjölkynngi, svo að það fái mannsmynd,

og senda síðan þeim, er maður vill mein gjöra. Ef sá er
sendingin er send er svo fróður, að hann geti hitt einmitt
á það beinið í uppvakningnum er tekið var úr hinum
dauða eða og að nefna hann með réttu nafni, orkar
draugurinn ekkert á manninn að vinna, og verður að
hverfa svo búinn frá honum [...] segja þó aðrir að meir
þurfa við að hafa ef menn vilji vekja upp drauga. Fyrst er
þess að gæta að það sé gjört á nóttu, sem sé milli
föstudags og laugardags og jafnframt sé hún annaðhvort
milli hins 18. og 19. eða 28. og 29. einhvers mánaðar; en
einu gildir hver mánuðurinn er og vikan. Skal
særingamaður sá er vekja vill upp draug kvöldinu áður
snúa "faðirvor" öfugt og rita það á blað eða bjór með
keldusvínsfjöður úr blóði sinu, er hann vekur sér á vinstra
handlegg; einnig skal hann rista rúnir á kefli og fara síðan
með hvorttveggja út í kirkjugarð um miðnætti, ganga þar
að einhverju leiði því er honum sjálfum lízt; en þó þykir
varlegra að ráðast heldur að hinum minni. Skal svo leggja
keflið á leiðið og velta því fram og aftur um það, en þylja
á meðan öfugt "faðirvor" upp af blaðinu og auk þess
ýmsa töfraformála sem fáir munu kunna. Fer þá leiðið
smásaman að ókyrrast og ýmsar ofsjónir að bera fyrir
særingamanninn, meðan draugurinn er að mjakast upp; en
það gengur seint því draugar eru sárnauðugir að hreyfa sig
og segja því: "Láttu mig vera (eða liggja) kyrran." En
hvorki má galdramaðurinn gefa sig við þá bæn né láta sér
bregða við ofsjónirnar, heldur þylja þulur sínar í ákafa og
velta keflinu þangað til draugurinn er hálfur kominn upp.
Jafnframt skal hann þó vandlega gæta þess að eigi hrynji
moldin úr leiðinu þegar það fer að ypptast því þeirri mold
verður ekki komið ofan í aftur. Þegar draugurinn er
kominn hálfur upp úr skal spyrja hann að tveimur
spurningum, en eigi þremur því ella mundi hann hverfa
niður aftur fyrir þrenningunni og eru spurningarnar vanar
að vera: 1. hver hann hafi verið í lífinu, og 2. hversu mikill
maður fyrir sér. Aðrir segja, að spurningin hafi verið að
eins þessi eina: "Hvað ertu gamall." Ef draugurinn segist
hafa verið meðalmaður eða meir til burða þykir eigi
ráðlegt að halda lengra áfram með því það liggur fyrir
særingamanni að takast á við hann á eftir, því draugar er

ákaflega sterkir [...], og er það sagt að þeir hafi hálfu meira afl en þeir höfðu í lífinu að tiltölu við aldur sinn. Þetta er því ástæðan til þess, að særingamenn velja helzt til uppvakninga börn, tólf til fjortán ára gömul, en annars kostar menn sem ekki eru komnir yfir þrítugt og alls ekki þá sem eldri eru en þeir sjálfir.

Þegar draugurinn segir til sín og aldur síns, kominn upp úr gröfinni til hálfs, kemur særingamaður honum niður aftur ef honum sýnist svo eða hann heldur áfram særingunni unz hann er kominn alveg upp. Þegar draugar koma fyrir upp úr gröfum sínum vella öll vit þeirra, munnir og nasir, í fróðuslefju og saur til samans og heitir það náfroða; hana á galdramaður að karra af þeim með tungu sinni [...]. Þar með skal hann vökva sér blóð undir litlu tánni á hægra fæti og vökva með því tungu draugsins. Þegar særingamaður er búinn að þessu segja sumir að draugurinn ráðist á hann og verður þá særingamaður að neyta allrar orku til að koma honum undir; ef það tekst og draugurinn fellur er hann úr því skyldur til allrar þjónkunar við galdamanninn, en verði draugurinn manninum yfirsterkari dregur hann manninn með sér í gröf sína og hafa þeir engir aftur komið sem þangað hafa komizt á vald drauga. En aðrir segja svo frá að særingamenn ráðist á drauginn þegar hann er aðeins kominn upp til hálfs og brjóta hann þannig á bak aftur fastan á fótum og fatlaðan eins og þeir eru meðan ekki er búið að sleikja upp á þeim vitin og vökva þá á volgu mannsblóði. En lítist nú særingamanni einhverra hluta vegna að láta drauginn ekki koma lengra upp en til hálfs og vilji reyna að koma honum niður aftur dugar oftast til þess að nefna þrenninguna eða lesa faðirvor rétt; [...] En komi særingamaður draugnum ekki niður fylgir hann honum og niðjum hans í níunda lið. Slíkt hið sama gjöra og draugar þeir er framkvæmt hafa það er höfundar þeirra hafa lagt upphaflega fyrir þá nema þeir þurfi að hafa þeirra not til fleiri sendiferða eða fái þeim fyrir komið og mega þá galdramenn eiga nokkuð hjá sér ef þeir eiga laglega að geta það prettalaust; því aðrar sagnir segja að

draugar séu æ að magnast hin fyrstu fjörutíu ár sem þeir
eru ofanjarðar, standa í stað hin næstu fjörutíu ár, en fella
af hin þriðju fjörutíu ár; lengri aldur er þeim ekki ætlaður,
nema áhrínsorð eða ummæli valdi (Jón Árnason 1954-61,
I, 304-6).[17]

[Some say that to do this, one must take one bone from a
dead man and put magic strength into it so that it takes
on human shape, and then send it to attack those one
wants to harm. If the man against whom such a *sending* is
sent is clever enough to strike precisely the bone inside it
which had been taken from the dead body, or to name it
by its right name, the ghost will not be able to do
anything to him and others will have to leave him alone.
[...] But others say that more than this is needed to raise
a ghost. First one must see that it is done on the night
between a Friday and a Saturday, and preferably between
either the 18 and 19 or the 28 and the 29 of a month; but
which month or week it is does not matter. The sorcerer
who means to raise the ghost must, on the previous
evening, write the Our Father backwards on paper or
parchment with a water-rail's quill, using his own blood,
drawn from his left arm. He must also carve certain runes
on a stick, and take both of these to the graveyard at
around midnight, and there go to whichever grave he
chooses—but it is though prudent to pick out one of the
smaller ones. He must lay the stick on the grave and roll it
too and fro, meanwhile chanting the Our Father
backwards from his paper, and also certain formulas that
few people know.

Then little by little the grave begins to stir, and various
strange sights appear to the sorcerer while the dead man
is being very gradually raised: but it goes very slowly, as
the dead are most unwilling to move, and say, "Let me be
quiet!" But the wizard must not give in to their pleading,
nor yet let himself be dismayed by the sights, but mutter
his incantations faster than ever and roll the stick until the
dead man is half out of the ground. He must also take

care that none of the earth falls beside the grave when it starts rising, because that earth will never be got back in. When the dead man has risen half way out, he must ask him two questions (not three, or he will sink down again out of fear of the Trinity); the usual ones are who he was in his lifetime, and how powerful a man he then was. Others say there was one question only, namely: "How old are you?" If the ghost says he died as a middle-aged man or older, it is not thought safe to proceed any further, because at a later stage the sorcerer will have to wrestle with the ghost, and ghosts can be extremely strong, […] their strength being said to be half as great again as it was in life, and so proportionate to their age. That is why sorcerers prefer to raise children of about twelve to fourteen, or at any rate people who are not over thirty, and never on any account those older than themselves.

When the dead man has said who he is and is half way out of the grave, the sorcerer can either drive him down again if he chooses, or can continue the spells till he is quite out. When the dead first emerge from their graves, their mouths and nostrils are all bubbling with a frothy mixture of mucus and mud known as "corpse froth"; this the wizard must lick off with his own tongue. […] Then he must draw blood from the little toe of his right foot, and moisten the ghost's tongue with it. Some say that as soon as he has done so the ghost will attack him, and he will need all of his strength to get him under; if he succeeds and the ghost falls, then the latter is henceforth bound to serve the wizard in every way; but if the ghost is the stronger, he will drag the man down into the grave with him—and those who thus come into a ghost's power never return again. But others say that it is the sorcerer who attacks the ghost when he is only halfway up, forcing him onto his back while his legs are still caught fast and keeping him there until he is ready to lick his mouth and nostrils and moisten his tongue in warm human blood.

Now if for any reason the sorcerer chooses not to let the ghost come more than half way, and prefers to send him down again, it is usually enough to speak the name of the Trinity or to say the Our Father the right way round [...]. If the sorcerer does not send the ghost down again, it will follow him and his descendants for nine generations. So too do ghosts that have finished the tasks their raisers first gave them, unless the sorcerers send them on other errands or manage to get rid of them—and he is a good wizard who can do this without danger! For some say ghosts get stronger and stronger for the first forty years they are above ground, stay unchanged for the next forty, and dwindle away during the third forty; they do not normally remain active any longer unless some spell or word of power causes them to do so (translation based on Simpson 2004, 164-6).]

Of course, there is nothing original about the magical liminal setting of the churchyard at midnight. The same applies to the elements of saying the Lord's Prayer backwards and forwards, and the use of blood and runes. The key difference here is the sheer physical detail, which is underlined in a number of Icelandic legends about people waking the dead: the elements of froth cleansing, the tongue licking and the need to wrestle physically with the infuriated being. These were problems that Faust never encountered with Helen of Troy. Indeed, the differences in approach between classical accounts of raising the dead and those known in Iceland are made very apparent in an Icelandic parody of the Faust story which tells of a young student called Bjarni who apparently summoned up Helen (here called Elín Stjarna [the star] from Greece). According to the legend, Bjarni and his friends were not overly impressed by Helen's famed beauty when she made her (physical) appearance: she was somewhat bloated and had a spot on her forehead. The story also notes that she stank so much when she left that those present completely lost their sense of smell from that time onwards (Jón Árnason 1954-61, I, 528).[18] Physicality of this kind tends to be very much to the fore in most Icelandic ghost legends.

Something else worth noting from Jón Árnason's introductory account given above is his statement that the person raised should be young (ideally a child). The reason given here is that, as noted, the magician is going to have to wrestle the bad-tempered revenant once it gets its feet free of the earth. As noted above, wrestling with supernatural beings is another common feature of Icelandic legends. If the male hero of a legend meets an outlaw in the landscape, the odds are that he will have to wrestle with him. The same applies to ghosts (from Grettir and Glámur onwards, see above), and any dead body that you are trying to raise. As Jón Hnefill Aðalsteinsson once suggested (Jón Hnefill Aðalsteinsson 1998, 163-74), the motif provided drunkards with a very useful alibi when they eventually reached home with their clothes covered in mud. In a wider sense, the wrestling motif in Icelandic legends seems to be a kind of rite of passage involved in moving between worlds, something that underlines you have won your way into the next world. The idea of magicians physically having to wrestle the raised dead into submission is thus no surprise: tt is essentially a visualization of the implied mental struggle involved. More troubling though (and worth bearing in mind) is the aforementioned suggestion (reflected in many legends) that it is best to raise a child, and ideally one that has only been dead for a short while, and has thus not fully attained the supernatural strength that accompanies complete "deadness". Considering the corpus of Icelandic raised-dead legends, the ideal candidate would seem to have been a young homeless girl who had died of exposure when walking across the moors,[19] or someone who had been drowned and washed up:[20] in both cases, we are dealing with social (and geographical) outsiders, the "dead without status" (Pentakäinen 1989), who have not achieved a secure position within the civilized world that might prevent them being used by the magician for his evil machinations. This says a great deal about the earlier Icelandic view of local community (Gunnell 2005): such social outsiders ("them" as opposed to "us") were regarded as nameless "objects" which could go on being used as objects. Indeed, it is noteworthy that in the awoken-dead legends in which they often figure, these people are rarely given personal names or genealogical relations (something very important for Icelanders, past and present).

The preference for raising dead outsiders could nonetheless have its own complications if taken too far. One of my favorite Icelandic legends of this type deals with an inexperienced (and uneducated) youth who made a central error of judgment when setting out to raise a supernatural servant: set in the south of Iceland where a number of shipwrecks used to take place, this legend tells of two young men who, in the early eighteenth or nineteenth century, apparently decided to raise one of the dead in a churchyard at Villingarhólt in Árnessýsla.[21] The two lads apparently went into the churchyard at night and went through the usual motions over a grave. A muddy, and probably scantily dressed figure started rising from the ground. Unfortunately it was a Dutchman in the account collected by Ólafur Davíðsson or a Dane in the account recorded by Guðni Jónsson. They managed to wrestle the corpse to the ground, but, according to Ólafur Davíðsson, when they tried to give it instructions as to what it should do for them, it simply looked puzzled, not understanding a word of what they said. It could not even be sent back to where it came from. The local priest (in Ólafur's account said to be Tómas Guðmundsson who served as a priest there in 1821-55) was little more help when it came to Dutch or the Danish dialect, and the dead man had no Latin and even less Greek. The apparent upshot was that the dead foreigner plodded around after the boys and their relations for several generations. (According to Ólafur Davíðsson, the whole event was witnessed by a local traveller, and remembered by the son of the befuddled priest).[22]

Being a tramp (or foreign sailor), dying of exposure or drowning, and then getting raised from the graveyard they had at last attained, before being interrogated, licked in the face and wrestled to the ground are good reasons for any self-respecting ghost to be riled. Worse still was that some accounts suggest that chanting, questioning, licking and wrestling were not an ultimate guarantee of success: One legend which exists in two versions from Skagafjörður in the north of Iceland tells of a man who was taking a stroll past a graveyard one evening when he encountered his local priest (named Þorvarður Bárðarson in one account) wrestling with a female corpse that he had just raised from her grave. The priest seemed to be on the verge of losing the battle, so the watcher, peering over the wall, casually advised the priest that it might help if he bit the corpse on the left breast. While this seemed to do the trick, it apparently had a negative effect on the relations between the priest and the man in question, who soon found himself under supernatural attack from the priest (with the aid of the dead woman whom he had summoned).[23]

Another feature of Icelandic raised-dead legends is that they commonly follow up the description of the raising with another episode (which makes these accounts even more unique). When the second episode is not related to magicians attempting to gain magical books hidden in the graves of other magicians,[24] it tends to deal (more often) with how the raised revenant is sent to attack other people in the form of a so-called *sending*, sometimes in the form of a cloud or a fly,[25] but most often physically and on foot, like a form of slow-motion snail-mail virus.[26] In the case of the cloud- or fly-*sending* legends (which conflict with the idea that a physical body has been raised), the *sending* often ends up being stopped up in a bottle or a hollow horse-bone by the person under attack.[27] Such legends are, of course, local variants of the accounts of Pandora's box; of Nordic legends telling how the Devil is enticed into a nut (cf. ATU 1164; and Asbjørnsen and Moe 1995, I 184); or other Nordic legends telling of how the personified Black Death is trapped in a utensil or some meat (Kvideland and Sehmsdorf 1988, 346-7; Tangherlini 1988; and af Klintberg 2010, 338 [Legend type 516]). Typically, these legends tend to involve a final episode in which someone else opens the bottle or takes the stopper out of the end of the bone, releasing the spirit.

Of more interest here is the other type of *sending* legend in which the raised figure finds itself having to walk through the countryside (sometimes right across Iceland) to attack the person the magician wishes to harm. The identity of those on the receiving end of such attacks varies. They might be another priest, an ex-lover, or someone who owns some land that the magician wants. In one or two cases, it is simply the magician's wife, who has been irritating him (see, for example, Ólafur Davíðsson 1978-80, II 237-44). In many examples, however, the attack fails because the recipient shares the same skills as the first magician and knows how to send the *sending* back.

The following legend telling of the "ghost" Skinnpilsa (Ólafur Davíðsson 1978-80, I 355-7) is somewhat typical of the *sending* genre. Set in Skagafjörður in the north of Iceland, like many such legends, it tells of a man named Hallur who lived on a farm called Geldingaholt in the nineteenth century. Hallur was a famed wrestler, and on one trip to take part in the fishing in the south of the country, he happened to defeat one of the best wrestlers in those parts. His opponent, a particularly bad loser, swore that he would get revenge. The story now cuts to another farm not far from Geldingaholt where a magician happened to be living (indeed, if we trust the legend tradition, magicians seem to have been living on every other farm in the north and west of Iceland: see further Simpson 1975; and Ólafur Davíðsson, 1940-3). The account describes how one winter's day, the magician was watching his flocks, and spied a strange girl dressed in skins walking northwards down the canyon. The magician asked her where she was going, and she honestly informed him that she was on her way to murder Hallur. The magician promptly locked her in a shed, and ordered her to stay there until he opened the door again (a parallel to the bottle/ bone motif noted earlier). He also banned everyone else from opening the door until he had had a good sleep and worked out what to do next. His wife, in need of some wool, naturally opened the door, meaning that the *sending* set off for Geldingaholt with the magician in hot pursuit. The story now changes perspective once again, jumping to Geldingaholt where Hallur, who, according to the account, was heading out to scratch his pony, discovered that its neck had been broken. The magician then arrived in the nick of time, and the two of them joined forces, fought the *sending* and sent her back to attack her former master. The master then sent her off again, but now allowed her to go wherever she liked. She ended up at a farm in the Skagi district where she apparently caused no end of trouble. This continued until one night, when she was discovered sitting on a bed by one of Iceland's so-called "power poets" (Almqvist 1961). He attacked her with some of his poetry, and eventually forced her into a marsh, where she has supposedly remained ever since.

The concept of dead Icelandic *sendingar* having to walk endlessly back and forth across the country between their masters was bound to have long-term consequences for the figures in question (according to the legend tradition). One wide-ranging revenant, a young boy who had apparently died of exposure before being raised and later came to be called "Írafellsmóri" [Írafell Red] seems to have attracted sympathy from those who told legends about him.[28] According to one account, a priest from the Mývatn area called Jón once encountered him walking north. The priest realized that he and his family were the boy's likely targets. He also noted that the poor corpse had worn out his shoes and socks, and was walking on bare and bloody feet. He had apparently also dispensed with his trousers (the story stressing that he was "berr upp í rass" [lit. "bare-arsed"]), clearly not the most attractive figure to find standing beside your bed in the night. Taking pity on him, the priest offered the boy a pair of boots and an overcoat (some say a hat as well)— on condition that he kept away from the priest's house until his new footwear wore out (Jón Árnason 1954-61, I 369-70). This particular being, who later seems to turn into a kind of family *brownie* or *nisse*,[29] even being given regular offerings of food by householders to keep him at bay, was clearly one of the lucky ones. Another *sending* is said to have walked his legs down to his knees for his masters.[30]

The Icelandic legend tradition suggests that most *sendingar* were apparently used by Icelandic magicians to attack other people or their livestock. Some, however, were used for more mundane purposes (whereby they appear to take the role of witches' familiars or other figures like Puck or Caliban in *A Midsummer Night's Dream* and *The Tempest*). One legend tells of a famed magician from the West Fjords, Jóhannes á Kirkjubóli, who apparently invited an ex-enemy to a dinner party, and then sent a young drowned girl that he had raised across the mountains to a local merchant's shop in order to steal tobacco and alcohol for him and his guest. The account tells how some hours later (an interesting time lapse underlining that these beings did not move as fast as Puck), the merchant became aware of someone entering his shop. The next thing he knew was when he awoke to find himself lying on a floor awash in alcohol. The girl returned home later that evening only to be rewarded by being sent off to Hell to await further instructions (Ólafur

Davíðsson 1978-80, II 260-2 [Vestur Ísafjarðarsýsla]). Another account tells of two magicians (one a priest, the other a farmer) who had their *sendingar* fight each other as a form of entertainment (*Huld* 1935-6, I 82 [North Iceland]). Yet another legend tells of a farmer who dispatched his *sending* to attack another farmer with a bag full of dog feces (Torfhildur Hólm 1962, 27 [Mývatn; Þingeyjasýsla]).

Many *sendingar* legends end by stating that the being (or spirit) in question later went on to haunt the family and relations of either its sender or its receiver for centuries to come in the form of what is often termed a *fylgja* (lit. "follower") spirit. Family *fylgjur* of this kind are also very Icelandic, and they are still known today.[31] Until very recently, Icelanders have rarely talked of ghosts haunting buildings, largely because their concept of a building involved an element of temporality: buildings constructed of turf and stone did not tend to last long, and they had to be rebuilt comparatively regularly. Thus, in the Iceland of the past, instead of the haunted house, legends tended more often to tell of semi-corporeal beings like those noted above haunting families. Known as *mórar* (lit. "earth-reds") or *skottar* (lit. "tassled hats"), these beings (usually in human form, but sometimes in the shape of an animal, like the famous half-flayed-bull *fylgja*, *Þorgeirsboli*[32]) are said to have caused various kinds of bad luck for the families in question, killing livestock, driving family members insane, and causing prolonged illness. They are also commonly said to precede family members whenever they travel, making themselves known at the prospective host's establishment by appearing before the arrival of their owners, or causing damage. In all likelihood, many of these beings are probably sometimes personifications of a certain maleficent family gene. In other cases, though, as with *Írafellsmóri* (noted above), these beings seem to take over the role of semi-humorous house-spirits like the aforementioned *brownie*, *nisse* or *tomte* (two types of spirit that, interestingly enough, were never imported to Iceland from Scandinavia or the Gaelic area)[33] or the witch familiars known in both Nordic and British folk lore: they can occasionally be sent on errands to harm local opponents. Like the house spirits, they are hard to get rid of, and some, like *Írafellsmóri*, even get given regular bowls of food to keep them friendly.

So much for the archetypical formats of the Icelandic "waking the dead" stories. Of the approximately 150 examples noted in the *Sagnagrunnur* database, it is noteworthy that a large percentage of them are set (or told in) the magician-ridden north-western fjords of Iceland. The next most frequent areas are other northern areas such as Skagafjörður and Þingeyjasýsla.[34] Interestingly enough, many of these accounts (like other Icelandic legends of magicians: see Simpson 1975) center around the activities of Lutheran priests. Equally noteworthy is that the database of recorded legends from the second half of the last century kept in the ÍSMÚS sound archive of the Árni Magnússon Institute in Iceland (another 11,000 narratives) contains only one *sending* account of this kind (http://ismus.musik.is/, accessed April 25, 2011). This underlines that the *sendingar* beliefs (and the narratives associated with them) are clearly a thing of the past.

Even more intriguing is why legends of this kind should be found in parts of Iceland but not in those other parts of the world that Iceland has had most contact with throughout the centuries (mainland southern Scandinavia and the British Isles). Furthermore, what do these legends say about the people that told them, their beliefs, their attitudes and their world view, and in particular the apparent natures and pastimes of Icelandic Lutheran priests (as opposed to those of their counterparts in neighboring countries who seem to have been less occupied with raising and wrestling corpses)?

In answer to these questions, it should first of all be noted that the concept that the dead could be woken in order to asked for information about the future (which apparently resided with the dead) was comparatively deeply rooted in the Old Norse culture consciousness. The medieval monologic and dialogic Eddic poems, *Völuspá* (The Song of the Seeress: *Eddadigte* 1961-71, I, 1-15) and *Baldrsdraumar* (The Dreams of Baldur: *Eddadigte* 1961-71, II, 69-71) show the god Óðinn being engaged in such activities when trying to deduce the date and nature of *ragnarök*.[35] However, this motif was clearly more than merely mythological. It seems to reflect a recognized practice: at least one Old Norse law contains an article banning people from undertaking so-called *útiseta*, that is literally "sitting over" graves, probably for the same purpose as that behind Óðinn's trip to Hel (in other words to learn about the future), and the same is implied by various Icelandic sagas, and even the seventh-century Eggja rune stone from Sogn in Norway.[36] All the same, none of these sources describes the practitioners of such magic ever raising the dead from their graves, licking their faces, and then sending them off on evil errands. The earliest potential parallel occurs in a short *páttr* contained in a late fourteenth-century manuscript about a poet called Þorleifr Ásgeirsson. The account in question, *Þorleifs þáttr jarlsskálds* (*The Tale of Þorleifur the Earl's Poet*) tells of how Þorleifr apparently irritated an earl of Norway in no small degree by gate-crashing his Christmas party and then using magical poetry to make the earl's thighs itch, his beard fall out, and then cause the hair to drop off one side of his head. The earl, based in the area around Níðarós (modern Trondheim), gained his revenge with the help of two local goddesses. They advised him to have a man killed and then have his heart placed in a washed-up log. The log then came to life and was given the name of Þorgarðr and a magic halberd. The account then tells how Þorgarðr set off by sea for Iceland and how, on meeting Þorleifr at the next parliament meeting, he thrust the halberd deep into him before diving into the earth (*Þorleifs þáttr jarlsskálds* 1956).

As the Icelandic scholar Einar Ólafur Sveinsson has noted (Einar Ólafur Sveinsson 2003, 194-5; see also Simpson 2004, 166-7), this unique account offers obvious parallels with the later *sendingar* stories, but it seems unlikely that a single account of this kind would have sparked off an entire genre of legends in Iceland. In all likelihood, the account had roots in an already-existing tradition known in Iceland. Bearing this in mind, it is worth remembering that the earl in question is said to have been based in Þrandheimur (Trondheim/ Trondelag in Norway) and that Trondheim at this time, was deep in Sámi (Lapp) territory. This was an area where West Germanic and the Sámi people lived together. It is also noteworthy that unlike the other Nordic peoples, the Sámi do have a legendary tradition which offers many close parallels to the Icelandic *sendingar* legends, enough parallels to make one wonder whether the Icelandic *sendingar* legends might actually be at root Sámi rather than Nordic.

Snorri Sturluson's thirteenth-century Icelandic description of the magical skills of the god Óðinn given in *Ynglinga saga* (in *Heimskringla*: see Snorri Sturluson 1941-51, I, 18) certainly implies that Snorri (who had been to Trondheim) was well aware of the nature of Sámi magic and the Sámi magicians known as *noaidit* (pl.). The same awareness of Sámi practice is apparent from the Latin *Historia Norwegiae* from the twelfth to the thirteenth century (*A History of Norway* 2001, 5-7). The nature of *noaidit* practices in slightly more recent times has been succinctly reviewed in, among other works, Neil Price's *The Viking Way* (2002). As Price notes, one form of Sámi magic referred to as *noaidevuohta* centres around "causing injury to people, animals and property"; "fighting/ killing a hostile *noaidi*"; "communicating/ mediating with the dead"; and "providing protection from a hostile *noaidi*" (Price 2002, 275; see also other sources referred to here). Elsewhere these activities are divided more specifically. Among others, Price (2002, 253) quotes a Sámi called Johan Fannki who states that the worst kind of *noadi* (sing.) in the past was the so-called "*piedjē-nåitē*" (lit. a "sender-*noaidi*"), who was believed to have the skill of negotiating with buried dead, and sending their "spirits" to attack his enemies by driving them insane. Apparently protection from such evil beings could be gained by calling on other *noaidit* called "*tivvô-nåitē*" (lit. *noaidit* who put things right and can protect).

The nature of the dead spirits that such Sámi *noaidit* sent at people (sometimes referred to as *gandar*) and the methods by which they were controlled are elucidated still further by the Sámi Johan and Per Turi in their *Lappish Texts* (1918-9: 108-15, and 133-43 [tales about *noaidit*]). The Turis describe a particular *noaidi* "trick" whereby:

> When some one who has died recently who was of your kin, or who was an especially good friend of yours while he lived—then he is still your friend. And then you must buy a silken band, three times six inches long; and when you come to the dead person, then you must uncover him and then draw the silken band back and forth over the mouth [i.e. between the lips]; and then you must take him in your arms and turn three times around against the sun

(counter-clock-wise) and say: "Thou shalt help me whenever I call thy name!" And then you must place him exactly as he was placed before. And then he has got that employment [to be the helping spirit of the *noaide*]. But you must do that work right at midnight—that which here is described (Turi 1918-9, 108).

A page later, the Turis describe "another performance". This runs as follows:

When you wish to put evil on somebody, then you must go to the churchyard and say: "I am in need, be of help to me now!" And then you must take sand from the churchyard in a white cloth. And then you must say what you want to be done and what he [whom you will harm] has done against you, and then you must say that person's name. And after this you must give something [i.e. a sacrifice] to the churchyard. And then you must go and proceed to that person [whom you want to harm]. And then you have to say [silently] what you want to have done [whether the ghosts shall kill the person or only torment him a while] just at the moment when you pour [the churchyard sand] on that person. But you must take care that you do not perchance pour some of the sand on yourself. And when you have done that, then you have put ghosts on a person (Turi 1918-9: 109).

The Turis then add:

When such a noaide who has learning and still has his teeth: Then he still has his full power. And when he needs to take to witchcraft, then he goes to the churchyard and then he calls out: "Arise, all sinful souls since the times of Adam, and fair mother too!" And then they begin to bang the coffins open, and they rise as many as a fog. And then he tells [them] to whom he wishes [them to go] and what he [i.e. the enemy] has done. And then he says whether he wants them to torment him only, or to kill him. And then

they rush forward and do what has been commanded
(Turi 1918-9: 109-10).

Apparently skilled *noaidi* magicians can see who is attacking them by
looking into a glass of brandy (Turi 1918-9: 111). And once the
magician can see how the being has been sent, he can deal with
them in the following way:

> [H]e begins [to exorcise the ghosts] and if he sees how it
> has been put on, then he can surely lay them once: But if
> he [who sent them] is much stronger [than the noaide],
> then he will send them again; but in that case they will
> often attack a member of the family of that person [who
> was first possessed]. And if they are again exorcised, then
> they will again attack someone of the same family. But if
> he [who exorcises them] is much stronger [than he who
> has sent them], then they will attack the same person who
> sent them out or who had them sent out. And if he is
> even stronger, then he will send them right back to the
> church-yard; but in order to be able to do that, it must be
> such a one as is noaide of God, or who works by the
> power of God (Turi 1918-9: 111-2).[37]

The parallels between the Sámi and the Icelandic belief
traditions are obvious, and especially with regard to how these
malevolent beings are raised and sent back and forth by magicians
who are sometimes at war with each other (Bø et al 1981, 64 and
250-1); and how such spirits can occasionally attach themselves to
families. Certainly, the *noaidi* tradition seems to be more
"shamanistic", and the *noaidi sendingar*, while they originate in the
churchyard, tend to be spirits and to fly rather than walking across
the countryside without any trousers on, but otherwise the essential
features are strikingly similar. How, though, could such a tradition
have reached the northwestern part of Iceland where the Sámi
language would have been incomprehensible?

If there are links between the Sámi and the Icelandic tradition
(as there seem to be), they must go back to before the time of the
outbreak of the Black Death in the early fifteenth century when

direct contacts between Iceland and Norway came to break down to be replaced by Danish rulership of Iceland (Björn Þorsteinsson and Guðrún Ása Grímsdóttir 1989, 117, 177-9, 235 and 247). Certainly, as Hermann Pálsson has underlined several times (Hermann Pálsson 1996a, 14-26; 1997), not only had the early Icelanders come into contact with the Sámi (referred to as Finns in both saga and folk legend tradition) before that time but also a number of the first Icelandic settlers had in fact actually come from the northern parts of Norway and clearly had Sámi genes. *Landnámabók* (from the start of the twelfth century) tells, for example, of one female settler, Þuríðr *sundafyllir* (the Sound Filler), who came to be based in the west fjords and was known for her magical skills at attracting fish (*Landnámabók* 1968, 186).[38] Bearing all of the above in mind, it would seem that if the Icelandic "raised dead" legends and beliefs have connections to Sámi practice and beliefs, they must have roots in the medieval times. If this is so, these legends would once add further weight to the idea that the comparatively isolated immigrant island community of Iceland preserved some very old beliefs and traditions over several centuries.[39]

The original nature of the settlement pattern in Iceland is one vague suggestion for why Sámi beliefs about magic may have come to Iceland. Another question is why they should have persisted, and why, of all places, in the western fjords, and the areas of Skagafjörður and Þingeyjasýsla in the north. There are several possible reasons for this. The real heart of the belief about magicians and *sendingar* appears to be in the western fjords which were—and are—very isolated indeed and still quite difficult to get to. The mountains and fjords of the area (not encountered anywhere else in Iceland to the same degree except in the east) also resulted in the evolution of some very close, insular communities and, as a result, a stronger sense of "insiders" and "outsiders", both in the sense of "insiders" living inside the valley and "outsiders" living elsewhere and also "insiders" within the immediate community and "outsiders" living on the edge or coming in from outside of the community. The latter group would have included odd farmers living outside the central community and priests who were sent into the community from outside (bringing with them Latin books and "foreign" ways of talking).

In their overview of Iceland and its people, *Travels in Iceland 1752-1757*, the visiting naturalists, Eggert Pálsson and Bjarni Pálsson note how (compared to other Icelanders) the people of the western fjords are somewhat "ancient in their ways" and not terribly friendly. They write that:

> The inhabitants of the northern part of Arnarfjörður are large and ruddy. They are well-made, courageous, and much disposed to fight when irritated or offended. They have retained in their costume the ancient fashion of the country, namely wide clothes in the antique style; those of Önundarfjörður, situated to the north of the port of Dýrafjörður, let the beard grow and also adopt the old mode of dressing. The people in the vicinity of Breiðafjörður and Arnarfjörður, are much attached to the study of natural history, and are well skilled in botany and mineralogy (Eggert Pálsson and Bjarni Pálsson 1975, 106-7).

In other words, these people came across as somewhat old fashioned, easily offended and interested in botany and geology. Furthermore, they were not terribly healthy. As Eggert and Bjarni add: "At a certain age, the people in this part of Iceland are particularly subject to diseases of the chest, which terminate in consumption" (Eggert Pálsson and Bjarni Pálsson 1975, 107). The authors later add that "everything that was bad, whether melancholy, vapours, epilepsy, convulsions, palsy, or apoplexy, was attributed to the manoeuvres of the evil spirit" (Eggert Pálsson and Bjarni Pálsson 1975, 113).

In short, it is not so surprising that people of this kind should have picked up popular associations with magic and witchcraft, something that gained firmer foundations at the time of Iceland's comparatively limited witchcraft craze in the seventeenth century when a number of men, mainly from the west fjords, came to be burnt at the stake, largely at the instigation of two officials from the area (Ólafur Davíðsson 1940-3; and Ólína Þorvarðardóttir 2000). The fact that in Iceland it was almost only men that were burnt is also worth bearing in mind, not least because it reflects the later legendary tradition in which those magicians who send dead corpses to attack others also tend to be males. Indeed, the same applied to the Sámi *noaidit* (Price 2002, 249-65). Furthermore, it is also noteworthy that four witchcraft cases from 1625, 1631, 1671 (2) include suggestions that the accused had actually awakened the dead and sent them to attack others causing sickness (Ólafur Davíðsson 1940-3, 71 and 109). One man was accused of digging up a dead body, possibly to collect belly fat for magical purposes in 1686 (Ólafur Davíðsson 1940-3, 314, 345 and 491). Obviously the later legends discussed in this article were not merely a narrative tradition: they were based on a living belief that people could and did raise the dead for magical purposes in these parts, a belief which clearly also existed in the seventeenth century. The same idea can be seen in the extant Icelandic "Black Books" from the same period that contain protective runes said to be designed to protect people from outside attacks by evil spirits.[40]

A feature of earlier rural Icelandic society which played a key part in the transmission of legends and beliefs across the country, especially between the north and south and the north and north-west, was the comparatively unique nature of migratory work on the island which gave rise to closer links between some areas than others. The best areas for fishing in the winter (when farm workers were freed from work in the fields) were the south of Iceland and the western fjords. This meant that the farmers in the north would send their male workers away for the winter to work on fishing stations in the south, the south-west, and the north-west (the western fjords) (Gunnar Karlsson 2000, 109). This explains why very similar legends are often found in the north and south (but less direct similarities in the fjord communities of the east and west), and then in the north and the northwest, the latter areas also maintaining comparatively close trading connections throughout the rest of the year. It is thus not surprising that we find similar accounts and beliefs running across the north of Iceland; nor is it surprising that people from the north should associate the western fjords with winter darkness, mystery and isolation (something perpetuated when they passed on their legends to the even more distant people in more widely distributed farming settlements of the south). Furthermore, it is of little surprise that the volcanically active area in the north around Mývatn with its hot springs, volcanoes and lava should have come to be associated with devilish activities in the minds of visiting outsiders (even though the same associations never appear to have grown up around the more active volcanoes of the south, such as Hekla or Katla).

In short, the idea that the north and northwest should have been associated with magical activities and that ancient Sámi-like concepts of magic might have been perpetuated there is comparatively understandable. However, why should Lutheran priests have come to be connected with such stories? Iceland shares the folk narrative tradition of Lutheran magician-priests with Norway, Denmark and Sweden (Gunnell 1998), and one can quite easily understand why priests might have been connected with the Devil in the minds of the general populace. After all, they were themselves outsiders in the local community, and many of them seemed to see the Devil wherever they went, even if no one else did (Lindow 1978, 155-8). They also possessed large black books written in a foreign tongue that told them all they needed to know about the Devil and were well aware of what hellfire was going to be like. Over and above this, they lived next door to the churchyard and had close contacts with the dead at funerals. In fact, in some places they could sometimes be seen talking to the dead after they had been buried: when the weather was bad in Iceland, priests sometimes would have had difficulties in getting to isolated farms in Iceland to carry out burials. This meant that sometimes bodies had to be buried without the priest being present, and when that occurred, a pole was hammered down into the grave over the top of the heart. This could then be withdrawn when the priest eventually arrived, allowing him to pour consecrated earth down onto the buried coffin as he carried out the official burial service (Árni Björnsson 1996, 412-3). It is not surprising that priests also became associated with the local concepts of magic.

Legends like those discussed above thus say a great deal about the Nordic people's attitudes to their Lutheran priests, whom they seem to have been viewed with a kind of nervous respect. This applied especially in Iceland. Some of the magically-associated parsons told about in Icelandic legendary tradition seem to have seen as protectors of the downtrodden against the authorities, foreign outsiders and the Devil, legends about them often showing a touch of humor but simultaneously warning against the dangers of laziness, vanity, selfishness and recklessness. These priests, like Sæmundur *fróði* [the wise], Eiríkur á Vogsósi and Hálfdán á Felli are light-hearted trickster figures. Certain other priests, however, seem to have been viewed as a downright menace: this applies particularly to those who are said to have been engaged in raising the dead in order to threaten their neighbors.

In this connection, it is worth considering the element of sympathy or empathy in the legends in question (Palmenfelt 1993). Here it is clear that while some of these legends involve an element of respect for the activities described or even humor, hardly any sympathy is ever shown for the magician who raises the dead for negative purposes,[41] whether it be a priest or a farmer. More sympathy is given for the footsore innocent outsider that is raised, licked, wrestled and overworked or for the person who is attacked—if, that is, they have done little or nothing to deserve being attacked, perhaps nothing more than rejecting the advances of the love-sick magician or nagging him too much. Knowledge is always respected in Icelandic legends (Hastrup 1990, 197-243), but the activities in question reflect misused, selfish knowledge which runs against the spirit of communal cooperation and hospitality that were so central for survival in the rural societies of the past, be they in Scotland, Norway or Iceland. Waking the dead appears to have been a particularly Icelandic form of selfish Black Magic, the nation's own particular form of maleficent witchcraft. The legends underline that people believed in it, were afraid of it, and had little respect for those who used it against others.

As with the witchcraft legends of Scotland and mainland Scandinavia, when it comes down to it, what we see in the Icelandic raised dead legends reflects, first and foremost, a rural community trying to explain—and personify—the recurrence of illness and bad luck. The same thing applies to legends of changelings (Lindow

2008); to farm spirits like the *nisse* or *tomte* or the witches' familiars stealing milk and hay;[42] to legends of the personified Black Death,[43] and legends dealing with the "evil" eye (Dundes 1981). Indeed, it might be said that the *sending* revenant that causes illness is itself a kind of personified "evil eye", something that is traced back to a particular person whom the community has some reason to be wary or afraid of. I have personally heard legends of this kind told (accompanied by certain belief) in Kenya. They echo in many ways an account contained in one of the aforementioned seventeenth-century Icelandic court records from the trial of a man called Jón Rögnvaldsson, from Svarfaðardal in Northern Iceland in 1625. Jón was burnt at the stake after having apparently raised a dead corpse and sent it to attack another man at a nearby farm who was suffering repeated illness. Apparently the only proof to support this hearsay was the discovery of some runes in Jón's house (Ólafur Davíðsson 1940-3, 109).

In short, folk legends of this kind tell us a great deal about the communities in which they were told and passed on to others. They represent a very special kind of historical record: while they might not provide us with historical facts, they pass on a great deal about cultural connections, inherited views, cultural concepts and the cultural vocabulary adopted to explain things that rural people in the past did not understand. They are thus invaluable source materials on the worldviews of people of the past and how they tried to understand the seemingly incomprehensible events that were taking place around them in their daily lives.

Notes

[1] This article is based on the Alan Bruford Lecture presented for the School of Scottish Studies, University of Edinburgh in conjunction with the Scottish Storytelling Festival, in Edinburgh, October 27, 2008.

[2] See, for example, Dégh 1995; Pentakäinen 1998; Kaivola-Bregenhøj 1996; Siikala 1990.

[3] See Gunnell 2010b; and
http://notendur.hi.is/terry/database/sagnagrunnur.htm and
http://dev.cdh.ucla.edu/~newmedia/DFL2/index.html (last accessed
April 25, 2011).

[4] See, for example, Almqvist 1991b: 1-29 and 155-65; Christiansen 1959;
Gísli Sigurðsson 1988a, 60-1.)

[5] See *Landnámabók* 1968; Gísli Sigurðsson 1988a; Hermann Pálsson 1996a.

[6] For a quick comparison in English, see the Nordic legends of "hidden
people" recorded in Kvideland and Sehmsdorf 1988, 144-238; Lindow
1978, 88-104; and the Icelandic legends contained in Simpson 2004, 27-
76. With regard to the tourist image of the Norwegian troll, see Conrad,
this volume.

[7] Kvideland and Sehmsdorf 1988, 207-13; Lindow 2008; Mac Philib 1991;
Christiansen 1992, 109-13 (ML 5085).

[8] See further *Landnámabók* 1968, 120-1; Simpson 2004, 110-4; and
Almqvist 1991a.

[9] See further Christiansen 1992, 75 [ML 4080]); Thomson 2001; and
Simpson 2004, 114-6.

[10] See further Kvideland and Sehmsdorf 1988: 229-30; Christiansen 1992,
183-8 (ML 6070A and 6070B); Jón Árnason 1954-61, I 610.

[11] See, for example, *Grettis saga* 1936: 108-19; Jón Hnefill Aðalsteinsson
1998, 143-74; Gunnell 2004.

[12] See, for example, Jón Árnason 1954-1961, I 274-7; trans. in Simpson
150-3.

[13] See, for example, Jón Árnason 1954-1961, I 270-72: the famous legend
of the "Djáknin á Myrká" (the Deacon of Myrká).

[14] On the idea of *útiseta* (lit. "sitting out" on graves or at other liminal sites
like crossroads), see further Jón Árnason 1954-61, 422-5.

[15] http://notendur.hi.is/terry/database/sagnagrunnur.htm; last accessed
April 25, 2011; see also Gunnell 2010.

[16] See Arngrímur Fr. Bjarnason 1954-9, II.1, 33-4, 44-6, 80-3, III.1, 94-5, 87, III.2, 37-8, 64-5; Guðni Jónsson 1940-1957, I 87, II 6-8, 106, 124, 140, 142-8, 150-1; Helgi Guðmundsson and Árngrímur Fr. Bjarnason 1933-49, I 91, II 199-202, 223-9, II 159-61, 223-9, III 144-9, 181-2, 265-8, 350-2; *Huld* 1935-1936, I 55-6, 79-84, 89-94, 96-7, 99-105; Jón Árnason 1954-61, I 304-8, 310-3, 320-2, 333-4, 338-9, 353-4, 355-7, 361-2, 364-73, 378, 386-7, 528, 545-6, 591-592, III 339, 370, 381-2, 389, 391-5, 397-8, 403-4, 407-8, 411, 413-4, 547-9, 620, V, 461; Jón Thorarensen 1971, I 15-16, 225-228, II 176; Jón Þorláksson 1956, 302-5, 323-4; Magnús Bjarnason 1950, 142; Oddur Björnsson and Jónas Jónasson 1977, 196-8; Ólafur Davíðsson 1978-80, I 340-9, 355-65, 359-61, 370-5, 382-3, II 28-9, 167-8, 211-2, 222-4, 226-8, 231-2, 237-44, 254-8, 260-4, 277-8, III 82-5, 127-36; Sigfús Sigfússon 1982-93, II 199, 203, 211, 220, 298, V, 402, 429-430, 434-435; Sigurður Nordal and Þorbergur Þórðarson 1962, I 40-41, 44, II.5, 32, 37, 114, II.7, 287, 292, 296, 300; Torfhildur Hólm 1962, 1-2, 27, 40, 65-6, 195-196; Þorsteinn Erlingsson 1954, 310; Þorsteinn M. Jónsson 1964-1965, I 172-3, IV, 325, 327-8, III 275, 291-2, 294, 339.

[17] For other accounts describing the methodology, see Arngrímur Fr. Bjarnason 1954-9, II.1, 80-83 (Ísafjörður); Jón Árnason 1954-1961, III 370 (Barðaströnd and Skaftafellssýsla); and 547-9 (Strandasýsla).

[18] For other accounts of Icelandic students in Copenhagen raising the dead, see Ólafur Davíðsson 1978-80, I 340-2 and III 127-36; and Magnús Bjarnason 1950, 142. See also Jón Þorláksson, 1956, 323-4 for an account of how two learned men, Oddur the lawyer and Páll Vídalín, attacked each other with raised figures. The dead met up on the way, and ended up fighting until they disappeared.

[19] See, for example, Jón Árnason 1954-61, I 353-4; III 411; Ólafur Davíðsson 1978-80, I 355-7, and II 260-2; Arngrímur Fr. Bjarnason 1954-9, III.2, 37-8; Helgi Guðmundsson and Árngrímur Fr. Bjarnason 1933-49, III 144-9; and Sigfús Sigfússon 1982-93, V, 402.

[20] See, for example, Jón Árnason 1954-61, III 381-2, 413-4; Ólafur Davíðsson 1978-1980, II 211-2; 222-4; Helgi Guðmundsson and Árngrímur Fr. Bjarnason 1933-49, III 350-2; *Huld* 1935-6, I 89-91, Guðni Jónsson 1940-57, II 140; and Torfhildur Hólm 1962, 1-2.

[21] See Guðni Jónsson, 1940-57, II 140; and Ólafur Davíðsson 1978-80, I 342. Similar problems are encountered in an account about the priest, Snorri Bjarnason, who lived in the late eighteenth century, told by Helgi

Guðmundsson and Árngrímur Fr. Bjarnason 1933-49, II 223-9 (set in Aðalvík in Vestur Ísafjörður).

22 For other amusing accounts of "apprentices" having trouble with waking the dead, see Jón Árnason 1954-61, I 546, III 403-4; and Þorsteinn M. Jónsson 1964-5, III 339.

23 *Huld* 1935-6, I 79-82 (collected by Gísli Konráðsson) and Jón Árnason 1954-61, I 360-1 (collected by Jón Borgfirðingur Jónsson).

24 See Jón Árnason 1954-61, I 310-3 (Eyjafjarðarsýsla), 545 (Árnessýsla), 572-5 (Rangárvallasýsla); and III 620 (Árnessýsla). As the references indicate, most of these legends seem to come from the south of Iceland.

25 Cloud: see, for example, Ólafur Davíðsson 1978-80, I 344-5; II 260-2; and *Huld* 1935-6, I 102-3. Fly: see, for example, *Huld* 1935-6, I 79-82; and Jón Árnason 1954-61, I 360-1; cf. Jón Árnason 1954-61, I 308-10. It should be noted, though, that not all *sendingar* were seen as being raised bodies. In a number of cases (accounts from different parts of Iceland), they seem to be spirits that centre around a single bone: see, for example, Jón Árnason 1954-61, I 308; and III 389; Helgi Guðmundsson and Árngrímur Fr. Bjarnason 1933-49, I 91; Ólafur Davíðsson 1978-80, I 343-5; and Þorsteinn M. Jónsson 1964-1965, I 173.

26 See, for example, Jón Árnason 1954-61, III 411, where the *sending* is said to have walked his legs down to his knees; it is noteworthy that there is never any talk of *sendingar* riding horses.

27 Jón Árnason 1954-61, I 320-1; I 321-2; *Huld* 1935-6, I 83-4, 99-103; Ólafur Davíðsson 1978-80, I 345-6; II 237-44; II 260-2.

28 On Írafellsmóri, see further Jón Árnason 1954-61, III 407-8, I 364-73 (Gullbringu- og Kjósasýsla); and Guðni Jónsson 1940-57, I 87 (Gullbringusýsla), and II 106 (Snæfellssýsla).

29 On the Nordic farm guardian spirits known as *nisse, tomte, gardvord, rudningskarl, haugbonde* and other names, see for example, Kvideland and Sehmsdorf 1988, 238-47 and Lindow 1978: 138-44; regarding the Scottish brownie, which has a similar role, see further McNeill 2001, 128-30.

[30] See Jón Árnason 1954-61, III 411 (Húnavatnssýsla); and Ólafur Davíðsson 1978-80, I 355-7 (Skagafjarðarsýsla) for another example of a long-distance-walking *sending*.

[31] See Jón Árnason 1954-61, III 407-8; Simpson 2004, 157-62; Ásdís A. Arnalds et al, 2008.

[32] On *Þorgeirsboli*, see further Ólafur Davíðsson 1978-80, II 277-8; Sigurður Nordal and Þorbergur Þórðarson 1962, II.7, 287, 292, 296, 300; and Guðni Jónsson 1940-57, II 124.

[33] The reason for why these spirits did not come to Iceland from Scandinavia with other types of folk belief was because these spirits seem to have been originally connected to farm grave mounds (and imagined farm forefathers) going back to the Iron or Bronze age. Unlike Shetland and Orkney (where the farm-spirit beliefs continued in the shape of the more Gaelic brownie), Iceland (and the Faroes) did not contain such ancient grave mounds when the settlers arrived, and thus provided no physical foundation for such family spirits. All the same, Iceland is still dotted with numerous so called *álagablettir* or "power points" which, like the old farm grave mounds in the Nordic countries in the past and the fairy *raths* in western Ireland even today, are supposed to be left undisturbed: see further the recent folk belief survey carried out in Iceland: Ásdís A. Arnalds et al. 2008.

[34] Of those "raised dead" legends in the database that are clearly associated with a particular area, 53 come from the north of Iceland (20 from Þingeyjasýsla; 14 from Skagafjörður; 6 from Eyjafjörður; 5 from Húnavatnssýsla; and 8 from Norður Múlasýsla); and 32 from the northwest (19 from "Vestfirðir", 8 from Strandasýsla; and 5 from Barðarströnd). Only 10 come from the west of Iceland (4 from Breiðafjörður; 4 from Dalasýsla; and 2 from Borgarfjörður), and 18 from the south of Iceland.

[35] The concept of "að sitja úti" is directly referred to in *Völuspá*, st. 28 ("ein sat hón úti").

[36] Grønvik 1985, 162-7. For references to the concept of "að sitja úti", see *Þorleifs þáttr jarlsskálds* 1956, 227-9; *Orkneyinga saga* 1965, 145; and the west Norwegian older Gulaþingslög (from the eleventh / twelfth century): MS DonVar 137 4o [c.1250] and MS NRA 1 B [1200-1250]): where, in a twelfth-century addition, a ban is placed on "utisetu at vekía troll upp. at fremía

heiðrní með því" [sitting outside to awaken trolls, and thus carry out pagan activity] (DonVar 137 4o)/ "utiseto menn. er troll veckia" (NRA 1 B [people sitting outside who awaken trolls]): *Den eldre Gulatingslova* 1994, 53 (article 32). On *útiseta*, see also Hermann Pálsson 1997; Strömbäck 2000b, 127-36; and Price 2002, 168-9.

[37] For another account of *noaidit* and the dead, see Qvigstad and Sandberg 1887, 189-94: "Lappen i noaideskolen" (the Sámi in the *noaidi* school).

[38] It is worth noting that *Landnámabók* tells of at least ten settlers who, like Þuriðr, come from "Hálogaland" (Hålogaland) in northern Norway, where people lived in close contact with the Sámi people.

[39] To the best of my knowledge, there are no sources suggesting any close contacts existed between the Sámi and the Icelanders in more recent times which might have given rise to such a belief tradition being passed on at a later stage.

[40] See Ögmundar Helgason 2004, 158-60: Lbs 143 8vo from the seventeenth century (10r-12v); and Magnús Rafnsson 2008, 154-5, 198-201, 244-5 and 254-5: Lbs 2413 8vo (written c. 1800) and Lbs 764 8vo (written c. 1820).

[41] The attitudes reflected in legends about raising the dead as a means of gaining access to a particular book are more complicated. While the activity may be frowned on, all the legends in question suggest the activity was worthy of some grudging respect, if only because of the risks it entailed, and the learning it needed.

[42] Kvideland and Sehmsdorf 1988, 171-9, 238-41; Lindow 1978, 140 and 170-2; Simpson 2004, 185-8.

[43] Lindow 1978, 71-5; Tangherlini 1988; Gunnell 2001.

"To market! To market!":
Markets and the Märchen in
Nineteenth Century Denmark[1]

Timothy R. Tangherlini

> *Bønderne skulle føre deris Vare til Kiøbstæderne, og dem paa*
> *offentlig Axeltorve og Markeder fal holde, og ej dem til Høkkere og*
> *Forprangere, som Landet omløbe, sælge. Giøre de herimod, have*
> *forbrut Varenis Værd til Kongen, og Varene, om de af Kongens*
> *Foged antreffis kunde, iligemaade være Kongen hiemfaldne*
> (Danske Lov 1683, Book 3, Chapter13, Paragraph 26).[2]

Concerns about markets and their regulation have crept into
everyday conversations in no small part due to the recent collapse
of global financial markets. The disintegration of the largely
unregulated Icelandic banking system in late 2008 and the ensuing
tsunami of financial devastation that swept over the country stands
as a noteworthy example of the domino-like cascade of financial
failures that has shaken the world during the past five years.
Subsequent events such as the monumental fraud of Bernard
Madoff's Ponzi scheme have added fuel to that narrative fire. There
can be little doubt that the economic integrity of communities large
and small alike has been threatened by these events. Not
surprisingly, stories that address the underlying causes of the crisis,
detail its impact on individuals and families, and explore possible
reactions from the reasonable to the extreme have become not only
a mainstay of the popular mediascape, but also an important part of
peoples' informal storytelling (Appadurai 1996).

Michel de Certeau reminds us that stories, particularly informal
narratives about events from everyday life, act as "repertoires of
schemes of action," affording people an opportunity to evaluate
collectively a range of possible reactions to the situations presented

in these stories (de Certeau 1984; Labov and Waletzky 1967). The
complications presented in these stories mirror events that people
confront in their daily lives and often revolve around the
codification of threat. As such, the stories reflect an ongoing
realistic engagement of storytellers and their audiences through
storytelling with their social, political and physical environments
(Tangherlini 1994). Examining how storytellers represent these
threats, the various strategies they propose to repel these threats,
and the success or failure of those strategies offers a fruitful avenue
of investigation into the role storytelling plays in the ongoing social
negotiation among community members of the shifting values
governing economic and social behavior. The manifestation of
economic threat in traditional storytelling is usually highly
personalized and focuses more on individuals than institutions. In
this manner, systemic threats such as wide scale financial crises or
underlying changes in economic organization that challenge existing
ways of "doing things" are brought down to the level of micro-
economics. Nevertheless, these individual crises are often cast as
arising from macro-economic currents far beyond the control of
individuals and small communities. Sometimes storytellers attribute
these threats to the machinations of the ruling classes and other
times they attribute them to the incomprehensible actions and
unstoppable efforts of supernatural or magical beings.

The strategies to deal with these threats and the outcomes of
these strategies contribute to the ongoing negotiation of social
ideology where the rules governing economic behavior comprise a
key component of that ideology (Tangherlini 2008a, 2008b, and
2010). These stories offer insight into economic questions such as
what to trade, where to trade, when to trade, with whom to trade,
and further comment on the role of money in trade and
institutional rules governing trade. In short, the stories comment on
economic behavior, markets and their regulation. Stories that
explore economic threats and the strategies to countermand these
threats are by no means recent phenomena and can be found in
most archives of traditional narratives. At the same time, many of
these stories have been overlooked as potential sources for
understanding normal peoples' responses both to gradual changes

and catastrophic shifts in the economic landscape since their subject matter is not overtly linked to these economic events.

In a now classic article from 1982, John Lindow explored the role that stories of buried treasure play in addressing the rapidly changing rules of economic behavior in eighteenth and nineteenth century Sweden. Lindow considers George Foster's notion of "limited good," a concept Foster developed to describe economic behavior in peasant societies, and offers a critical exploration of the motivations storytellers may have had for telling these tales. Ultimately, Lindow rejects the discussions of limited and unlimited good that have swirled around tales of buried treasure since Foster's seminal article as overly normative (Foster 1965; Kaplan and Saler 1966; Foster 1966; Dundes 1971; Mullen 1978). Rather than attempting to align the ambiguous aspects of Swedish tradition with one economic model or another, he proposes to read the stories according to their relevance to the storytellers' lived experiences, noting, "Rather than seek limited or unlimited good, I would look first to the realistic background of the traditions" (Lindow 1982, 272). In so doing, he provides an analysis that reveals how these stories created meaning for their largely rural narrators and audiences even as the attitudes expressed in these stories toward treasure and its acquisition remained ambivalent.

Most recent studies of traditional Scandinavian narrative as a window onto the changing economic conditions of nineteenth century farming communities have followed Lindow's lead and focused primarily on legend tradition. Legend, given its close connection to the everyday life of the storytellers, is well suited for addressing issues such as economic threat and economic opportunity (Tangherlini 1995, 1998a, 1998b, 2008b, 2010; Lindow 2010). By way of contrast, the *Märchen* has rarely been explored in the context of economic behavior. One exception to this may be Bengt Holbek's monumental study of the nineteenth century Danish *Märchen* (Holbek 1987). In this largely psychoanalytical exploration of the *Märchen*, Holbek recognizes that the tension between the actors on the high level and the actors on the low level recapitulates class divisions in eighteenth and nineteenth century Scandinavia (Holbek 1987, 525). The resolution of the tale with a low level actor marrying a high level actor expresses a form of economic wishful thinking. In a time when economic mobility was severely limited, the characteristic *Märchen* move of the poor young boy to rich royal was one of pure fantasy, but one redolent of the economic longings of the largely peasant class who told *Märchen* (Holbek 1987).

Holbek's observations not withstanding, studies of the *Märchen* rarely explore the economic dimension of these tales and, if they do, address it *inter alia*. Since the inception of the field of folklore, the main focus of *Märchen* studies has been on discovering narrative structures; classifying tales according to motifs and types; the historical development of the tales; the geographical distribution of tale types and motifs; source criticism; the psychological dimensions of tales and tale telling; and storytellers and their communities (Propp 1928; Röhrich 1964; Lüthi 1968; Dégh 1962; Dundes 1964; Holbek 1987; Uther 2004; Bottigheimer 2009; Ziolkowski 2010). Lindow's work broadens this state of affairs, as his article includes a consideration of *Märchen* alongside legends in his discussion of the buried treasure tales (Lindow 1982). If one takes a cue from Lindow and considers the realistic background of certain *Märchen*, it becomes clear that these tales, in a manner similar to the legend, also offer narrators an opportunity to interrogate aspects of economic organization and to suggest solutions to problems such as poverty that confronted many *Märchen* narrators and their audiences.

Not surprisingly, the solutions to economic problems proposed in *Märchen* are usually more extreme than the solutions offered in legend. Economic features of the *Märchen* tend to be exaggerated— poor people are destitute, the wealthy are kings, queens, princes and princesses, money is heaped up in giant piles, and treasures are so immense or so valuable that they exist far beyond the realm of human experience. Exaggeration and the representation of quality by quantity are, of course, well-known characteristics of the European *Märchen* (Holbek 1987, 442-444). Although common wisdom proposes that *Märchen* take place in an imagined world— one that follows its own internal logic and can be at a great physical and historical remove from the external reality of the tale tellers—

studies such as Holbek's propose anchoring the *Märchen* world in a reality much closer to that of the storytellers (Galloway Young 1987; Holbek 1987). The fictive world of the *Märchen* is not foreign to the world in which the storytellers lived their daily lives and the intersection between these two worlds—the fictive world of the *Märchen* on the one hand and the real world of daily life on the other hand—can for some tales be much greater than usually acknowledged. While legends quite clearly rely on a fictive model of the narrator's daily world, that same fictive model informs numerous *Märchen* as well. Since it is far beyond the scope of this brief study to explore the generic differences between legend and *Märchen*, a more productive route will be to posit that the boundary between these genres in the repertoires of many nineteenth century Nordic storytellers is fuzzy, and that the stark division between the fictive world of the *Märchen* and the realistic world of the legend is not a productive division (Grimm 1816; Pentikäinen 1968). Breaking this immutable boundary between the legend and *Märchen* allows for a consideration of economic concerns and behavior in the *Märchen* as closely related to the external reality of the tale tellers and recognizes that etic categories such as *Märchen* and legend often have little relevance to the storytellers themselves (Dundes 1962).

A common opening for many *Märchen* in Danish tradition takes the form of Vladimir Propp's well-known eighth function, lack (Propp 1928). A poor family teeters precariously on the brink of financial ruin and decides to sell their last valuable possession—a cow for example—at the local market. In a tale told by Margrete Jensdatter, the situation is presented as follows:[3]

> Der var en Mand og en Kone, de sad ved en bitte Næring og kunde ikke vel begaa dem. Saa Længe Konen havde noget Lærred at sælge, saa flyede hun Manden et Stykke efter et andet, for at han kunde faa en Skilling til at faa Udgifterne dækket, men til sidst var det forbi med det, og saa gik det dem til sidst saa nær, at de havde ikke uden deres Ko at gjøre i Penge. Saa siger Manden om han skulde ikke trække til Marked og sælge den. Jo, det tykte Konen nok; der var jo ikke andet at gjøre, og det var da bedst at blive ved Husværselet saa længe de kunde. Han

trækker altsaa med den og paa Vejen kommer han saa til
en Mand, der gik i forunderlig Klædedragt. Han gik i en
stor lang Kappe, der naaede ham rent ned til Halene, og
saa var det endda en Sommerdag. De kommer saa i Følge
med hinanden, og Manden spørger ham, om han skulde
til Marked. Ja han skulde, nu var det gaaet ham saa nær, at
han havde ikke andet end den Ko at sælge. "Vil du sælge
den til mig?" siger den fremmede. "Jo, det vil a jo nok,
hvis du vil give nok for den."

[There was a husband and wife, they had a tiny little
holding and couldn't make ends meet. As long as the wife
had some canvas to sell, she would giver her husband one
piece after another, so that he could get a shilling to cover
their expenses, but finally it was over with that, and finally
it got so bad that they didn't have anything left that they
could convert to money but their cow. Then the husband
asks if he shouldn't pull it off to market and sell it. Yes,
the wife thought that he should do that; there was
nothing else to do and it was best to have a roof over
their heads as long as possible. He pulls it along and along
the road he meets a man who was walking along in a
strange outfit. He was wearing a big long cape that
reached all the way to his heels even though it was still
summer. They follow along with each other, and the man
asks him if he was headed to market. Yes he was, now
things had gotten so bad that he had nothing but his cow
to sell. "Will you sell it to me?" asks the stranger. "Yes, I
certainly will, if you'll give me enough for it."]

The opening of this tale sets the action firmly in late nineteenth
century rural Denmark, with all of the economic challenges
confronting the rural poor. Here, the couple subsists on a tiny plot
of land and worries about the specter of homelessness at a time of
decreasing government investments in poverty assistance
(Jørgensen 1940; Tangherlini 2010). Margrete Jensdatter had a great
deal of personal experience with situations like this, having spent
much of her adult life flirting with life in the Danish poor houses.
Perched on the edge of homelessness, she too worked at last ditch

enterprises that had little chance of staving off the inexorable march of poverty. By situating her tale in a fictive world reminiscent of her own environment, the wishful thinking of the *Märchen* becomes intensified—the story is not a pure flight of fantasy but rather the exploration of a more grounded "what if" scenario.

The opening of the tale also defines a lack that is historically conditioned. As the Danish economy moved fitfully toward a relatively open-market system replacing the inefficient yet relatively low-risk manorial system, many small holders, day-laborers, single mothers and elderly *aftægtsfolk* [pensioners] found themselves in increasingly difficult economic situations (Tangherlini 2010; Dybdahl 1982, 9). While the late nineteenth century saw an explosion in the number of small holdings, the land these small holders acquired was often the worst possible land: it was too rocky, too small or too nutrient-poor to produce enough food to support a family let alone farm animals (Hvidt 1990; Bjørn et. al. 1988). Consequently, many small holders had to rely on secondary sources of income such as weaving, clog making, bread distribution, or knitting. In many cases, small holders simply hired themselves out to more prosperous farmers as day laborers. These endeavors often lead to an unsustainable economic cycle: too much time spent earning money to support the farm meant not enough time spent farming. When the farm faltered, people were forced to work harder in their secondary employment, leaving even less time for their own farming. Ultimately, many of these smallholdings proved to be unsustainable and were acquired by larger farms or simply abandoned.[4]

The opening situation of Margrete's tale, then, refracts many of the economic concerns of her peers: with the dissolution of the manorial system starting in the late eighteenth century, farmers, small holders and day laborers became, willingly and unwillingly, individual players in the greater market-based economy. They could no longer rely on the *fælleskab* [collective] that characterized social organization during the manorial period for support (Christiansen 1996). At the same time, the promise of economic stability that came with private ownership proved to be illusory for the majority of the new small holders. Their economic situation was no more stable than the recently drained heath on which many of their houses were built (Dybdahl 1982, 93-104). Margrete's audience would have recognized their own economic concerns from the very opening lines of the story.

The couple's decision to "liquidate" their economic lack appears perfectly rational: given the choice between homelessness and the sale of a capital investment (the cow) they choose to sell the cow. They seem to be well aware of the risk they are taking by selling their only cow: they will no longer be able to produce milk or butter and consequently will have limited opportunities for economic survival. In short, the sale amounts to an act of desperation that will only stave off the seemingly inevitable descent into poverty by a few months. Yet they understandably find this preferable to leaving their house and throwing themselves on the mercy of the deeply troubled poverty assistance system (Jørgensen 1940).

What is left unsaid in this tale, since Margrete and her audience easily understood it, was that the possibility of having a choice of this sort was a relatively new phenomenon. Prior to the changes of the late eighteenth century that included the elimination of adscription and villeinage, the partitioning of the large manors, the sale of the Royal estates, as well as the reapportionment of the fields, most of the rural population had few marketable assets that were theirs to sell (Hvidt 1990 242-243). If they were in a position to sell assets, they would usually sell to the manor or other members of the closely circumscribed *fælleskab*. It was not until the Constitutional reforms of the late 1840s and subsequent legislative implementation of those reforms in the ensuing decades that small holders and day laborers became meaningfully integrated into the monetized market economy (Hvidt 1990, 243). Seen in this light, Margrete's tale foregrounds these new rules of economic behavior for small holders and day laborers, the ones on the lowest rungs of the economic ladder who had previously been denied meaningful access to the markets. These people were far less experienced with markets and their vicissitudes and found themselves at a distinct disadvantage in many economic transactions. The markets, of course, were far from being "free," and commercial interests, such as the market towns, the larger land holders, the craftsmen and other guilds used their political clout to structure these new markets in such a manner that preserved as many of their earlier advantages as possible. So, not only were small holders new to the markets, a disadvantage in and of itself, the markets were skewed against them. Despite these clear disadvantages, the new social organization forced the rural lower classes into an economic position where they had to contend with the capricious nature of these allegedly open and increasingly global markets. Consequently, storytelling offered a productive forum for exploring the markets and proposing possible strategies for making the markets work in one's own interest. It could also be used to exact narrative revenge on the people who had mastered the new economy and exploited this position of economic ascendancy to take advantage of those on lower rungs of the economic ladder (Tangherlini 2008b, 360).

While Margrete's story has her couple turning toward the open markets as a last ditch effort to forestall the march of economic change, the decision to sell goods at market does not accrue only to those in dire financial straits in Danish *Märchen*. The anonymous monetized market was quite distant from the earlier highly localized barter dominated system of exchange that was well understood and the rules of which were greatly influenced by the likelihood of repeated transactions.[5] Peder Johansen tells a story where the opening situation describes a single mother who sends her seemingly dim-witted son to market. In this case the item to be sold at market is homespun—a product that would have previously been used in barter or traded locally. While one can infer that the family's economic situation is not as drastic as in the previous tale (selling the loom, for instance, would be analogous to selling one's cow), the capital risk associated with weaving homespun "on spec" lingers just below the surface and contributes to the tension of the opening situation:

> Der ude paa Dover Hede laa et lille Hus, og i det boede ikke andre end en gammel Kone og hendes Søn. En Dag, som Konen var ved at væve, blev hun lige færdig med et kjønt Stykke Vadmel, og aaa siger hun til Knægten: "Hør, Jens, nu kan du tage det Stykke Vadmel og gaa til Aarhus

med og sælge for mig. Det kan ikke hjælpe, du gaar til
Skanderborg, for der kan du ikke blive af med det, og du
skal have en Mark for Alen. Men lad mig nu se, du bærer
dig lidt ordentlig ad."—"Ja, det skal a nok," siger han, og
han tager Tøjet og gaar med. Saa gaar han nu om ad
Hemstok. Der staar de Henstok Mænd uden for og
Snakker. "Hvor skal du hen med det Tøj?" siger de, "du
farer saa stærkt."—"Ja, a skal til Aarhus med det for min
Moder."—"Naa, det skal du, hvad skal det da koste?"—
"Det skal koste en Mark."—"Ja, saa er det da ikke værd,
du gaar længere for den Sags Skyld, saa vil vi tage det."
Det var Knægten saa meget glad til, og han faar hans
Mark, og de faar Vadmelet.

[There was a tiny little house out there on Dover heath,
and no one lived there but an old woman and her son.
One day as the woman was weaving, she finished up a
very nice piece of homespun and so she says to the boy:
"Listen Jens, now you can take this piece of homespun
and go to Aarhus with it and sell it for me. It won't help
going to Skanderborg, because you won't be able to get
rid of it there, and you're to get 1 mark for each two-foot
length. But please let me see that you can do this
properly."—"I certainly will," he says, and he takes the
cloth and goes off. Now he goes past Hemstok. The
Hemstok men are standing outside there talking. "Where
are you going with that cloth?" they say, "You're going so
fast."—"Yes, I'm bringing it to Aarhus for my
mother."—"Oh, are you now? How much does it
cost?"—"It costs one Mark."—"Well, then it's not worth
your trouble going any further for that, we'll take it." The
boy was quite happy about that and he gets his Mark and
they get the homespun.]

The young man circumvents the market and its vagaries by
selling local, a resolution to the initial situation reminiscent of the
local sale of the cow in Margrete's story. The boy does not have
nearly the same success as Margrete's couple: in their case, avoiding
the market (and thus avoiding at least momentarily the intrusion of

market economics in their daily lives) leads, after some difficulty, to great and lasting fortune. In this case, the boy discovers he has been cheated, having sold the entire bolt of homespun for the much lower unit price.

In another tale, an impoverished couple decides on a different strategy for staving off the collapse of their personal economy.[6] Rather than selling assets, they decide to hire a young man to make one last attempt at reaching sustainability: if they can produce enough to feed themselves and a worker, they will be able to hold onto their farm, sell their surplus at market and use this new capital to reinvest in their operation. Again, from the repertoire of Peder Johansen:

En Aften omkring ved Novembers Tide sad Manden i Hellede og Snakkede med hans Kone om, at de ikke kunde Svare, hvad de kunde, og at de blev nødt til at opgive det, dersom der ikke blev andet Raad. Saa gav hun ham det Raad, at han skulde se at faa sig en stærk Karl, og saa skulde de arbejde dygtig paa Jorden, saa maatte de nok kunne saa Føden ud af saadan en Mark. Han befandt, at Raadet var godt, og gik saa til Ry Marked, hvor der var Folkemarked den Gang. Da han kommer ned til Glentholm, som den Gang kaldtes Ry Mølle, saa kom han i Følge med en stor Karl, og de gik og snakkede med hinanden. Saa viste det sig, at de gik efter det samme, og kom ogsaa til Rette paa halvvejs. De gik da hjem igjen, og Lønnen blev saadan, at Karlen skulde gaa for, hvad Manden kunde give, og siden, naar Manden faldt fra, skulde han have Støtterne (hus og det hele).

[One evening, around November, the farmer in Hell sat and talked to his wife and said they couldn't pay what they owed and they'd be forced to give up, unless they figured something out. She told him that he should find a good strong farmhand and work hard on the land, and then they should be able to get food from such a field. He thought the advice was sound and he went to Ry market, where in those days there was a general market. When he

gets down here to Glentholm, they called it Ry Mill in
those days, he catches up with a big farmhand, and they
went along and talked together. It turned out that they
were headed to find the same thing and they reach an
agreement about half way there. They went back home
and the pay was going to be that the farmhand was to get
what the farmer could afford, and when the farmer later
gave up farming, he was to get the property (the house
and everything).]

The agreement that the man makes with the farmhand is not
unusual as it mimics the standard outlines of an *aftægt* agreement, a
form of pension guarantee that allowed for the relatively stable
transfer of real property while insuring that elderly people would
not live out their last days in utter poverty. In each of these cases, a
brief transaction on the way to the market concludes the opening
situation and sets up the ensuing action. Each tale leads in its own
fashion to a positive outcome for the initially poor farmers. Just as
importantly, the resolutions of the tales have devastating
consequences for the poor farmers' wealthy antagonists.

All of these tales are marked by considerable violence
subsequent to the initial transaction. This violence gestures
metaphorically to the underlying violence wrought by the market
system itself. In the first tale, the bottle the man receives turns out
to contain a magical genie that provides the couple with food and
riches. A jealous and wealthy neighbor tricks the man into selling
him the bottle, and the next bottle the man acquires contains
violent gremlins that beat him senseless. Ultimately the man
manages to swap bottles with his now even wealthier neighbor,
recovers the first bottle and the wealth that flows from it, and his
wealthy neighbor is forced into poverty. In the second story, the
young man is tricked by the Hemstok men several times before he
finally turns the tables on them, first tricking them out of their
money, then tricking them into destroying their own livestock, and
finally tricking them into killing their wives and drowning
themselves. In the third story, a variant of the widely attested Big
Claus Little Claus story, the farmhand is able to guarantee wealth

for himself and his employer, while laying utter ruin to the wealthy neighbor, the neighbor's family and farm.

All of these initial transactions seem quite innocuous: in the first tale, the farmer trades his wreck of a cow for a magical bottle, in the second tale, the young man agrees to sell the homespun locally for what he thinks is a good price and, in the third tale, the farmer and the farmhand reach an agreement before they reach the marketplace. What goes unsaid is that all of these transactions are illegal and would be immediately recognized as such by a contemporary audience. Because of these early transgressive transactions, the ensuing almost spasmodic violence that characterizes these tales is likely not as unexpected for the contemporaneous audiences as it is for the modern reader. A fourth tale told by Villads Skov highlights the transgressive nature of these initial transactions:

Det var gaaet den fattige saa nær, at han havde ikke uden én Ko, og den skulde han nødsages til at sælge for at faa Brød i Huset. Saa trækker han til Marked med den en Dag, men da han kom til en Korsvej, kom der i det samme en Vogn kjørende med den anden Vej, og der sad en tre Karle paa. De spurgte ham, hvor han vilde hen, og han vilde saa ogsaa vide, hvor de skulde hen. Ja, de skulde da hen at hænge det Menneske, der sad imellem dem, for det var en Mestertyv,

"Jeg synes, at det er en stor Synd at hænge ham", siger den fattige, "for det er jo et Menneske, der er frisk og rask."

Ja, det kunde ikke hjælpe, hænges skulde han. "Men maaske du kunde have Lyst til at at bytte og have en Karl for en Ko, saa kan vi blive fri for at hænge ham, og du faar din Vilje."

Ja. det var ogsaa det samme, siger han, og saa bliver han resolveret paa at gjøre den Handel med dem, og de

beslutter dem til at sige, naar de kom tilbage, at Tyven var
rendt fra dem.

[Things had gone so bad for the poor one that he had
nothing but a single cow left, and it looked like he was
going to have to sell it to get some food. So one day he
drags it off to market, but when he gets to an intersection,
a wagon all of a sudden comes driving up in the other
direction, and there were three farmhands sitting in it.
They asked him where he was going, and he wanted to
know where they were going. Well, they were going to
hang the person sitting in between them, because he was
a master thief.

"I think it is quite a sin to hang him," says the poor man,
"because he is a strong, healthy person."

Well, that didn't matter, he was to be hung. "But maybe
you want to trade and get a farmhand in exchange for a
cow, and then we won't have to hang him, and you'll get
your way."

Well, that's all the same to me, he says, and then he
decides to make that deal with them, and they decide to
say when they get back that the thief had escaped from
them.]

That the farmhand is a thief on his way to being executed is an
interesting element of this tale and emphasizes its transgressive
nature. The farmhand is to be punished for violating the rules of
market behavior, a seeming recognition of the necessary and
inviolate nature of the regulation of the market place. But all of the
men who are party to this trade care little for these rules. Here,
everyone is made better off from the trade, offering an amusing
gloss on Pareto efficient solutions to any given market problem.[7] If
one disregards the rule of law that has for the most part not served
any of these people particularly well, the solution is surprisingly
efficient: the men get a valuable cow, the farmer gets a strong
farmhand, and the farmhand gets his life. The amusingly subversive

nature of this transgressive deal—exchanging a cow for a thief—is actually present in the other stories as well, albeit not as overtly. All of the stories, then, begin in a transgressive realm that fundamentally challenges the existing laws governing commerce and then proceed to pile transgression on top of transgression until finally a new and inverted economic order emerges.

As in most of Europe, the laws governing markets and the concessions made toward market towns were quite strict in nineteenth century Denmark. Well up into the nineteenth century, market towns were given privileged status in Denmark as a form of protection for the town-centered trades, but also as a means for preventing the development of a black market not easily subject to taxation. A one and a half *mil* (11.25 km or 7 mile) buffer zone existed around all market towns, preventing any small shops from opening inside this zone. In 1857, a new commerce law codified many of the emerging rules governing trade and was supposed to implement the guarantees of the 1849 Constitution concerning free trade since, prior to then, most trade in the provinces had been governed by the rules set forward in the Danish Law of 1683 (Johansen 1979 35-36). Importantly, the commerce law of 1857 maintained the buffer zone around market towns (Næringslov Section 1, paragraph 14). Even with the adoption of the 1857 law, it took several years for these reforms to be implemented; implementation was inconsistent, and the law generally favored the market towns and other established commercial enterprises. By the mid 1880s, the economic landscape was changing so rapidly that urgent calls for reform of the commerce law finally resulted in a legislative proposal in 1893; even those proposed reforms were never able to gain majority support in parliament (Dybdahl 1982, 228-233). Consequently, most small holders and rural poor found themselves subjected to conflicting and inconsistently enforced rules governing trade and were forced to contend with markets that were not structured to support low level trade.

One of the fundamental rules governing trade up through most of the nineteenth century was the strict prohibition of engaging in transactions on the way to or from markets, practices that were referred to in the earlier Danish laws as *forprang* and *landprang*. The prohibition was motivated by many factors. Market towns wanted to protect their important role in the surrounding area as centers for trade and all of the direct and indirect economic benefits that accrued to being the center of trade. Similarly, the Crown wanted to make sure that they could exert control on markets through taxation and keep close tabs on the development of commerce throughout the realm. Not all of the rules were entirely skewed toward the Crown and the established merchant class. There was a clear incentive for people to trade at market, where competition could help avert the most obvious abuses in setting prices that occur when one party to the transaction has more information about the current market value of goods than the other. Indeed, this type of abuse lies at the very root of the problem in the second story, where the Hemstok men take advantage of the boy by purchasing his goods at prices far below fair market value. In the other stories, the value of the goods is more difficult to discern—a cow should be more valuable than a bottle, for instance, but it depends a bit on the cow and it depends a bit on the bottle.

Given that strong prohibitions existed against trade on the way to or from markets, and that these prohibitions and the proposed risks attendant breaking these prohibitions were well known among the rural population, the opening situations of these tales signal the narrators' intention to challenge the existing economic order. From the very start the narrators point their protagonists down a road that diverges substantially from the one that hews to the rules governing social and economic interaction—even though they intend initially to follow that road to market, they all seem to decide that their financial well-being might lie well off this standard route; their economic journey on the straight and narrow has not, after all, been smooth. A rural Danish audience would be immediately attuned to the transgressive nature of the transaction that initiates the remaining part of these tales. Alerted to the transgressive nature of the story, the audience would be eager to discover how the poor farmers ultimately turn the tables on the economically oppressive system that dangles the free market in front of them, but erects almost insurmountable barriers to making it work for them.

Since the divergence from the rules governing normal economic behavior happens so early in each of the stories, it seems clear that the narrators present their accounts as challenges to the emerging market system, a system that was clearly skewed in favor of the wealthy. Three of the stories open with a description of the tense relationships between a wealthy farm and a poor farm and, in his introduction to his story, Villads Skov goes so far to mention that his story is about how the poor and rich eventually end up trading places. The reasoning that each of the tales follows is fairly clear: the law forbids one from engaging in transactions outside of the highly regulated market place. These protections are in place largely to preserve the wealth of a few at the expense of many and only offer marginal protection to the small market player. Out of bounds transactions, by contrast, have the potential for remarkably large pay-offs, pay-offs so large that they completely invert the existing economic order. Perhaps the danger of these transactions, then, is more to the existing order than to the poor who, in these tales, realize that they have little to lose and quite a bit to gain. Returning to Lindow's plea for a "realistic" interpretation of the tales, one can imagine that the storytellers and their audiences could find justification for their resistance to the rules of trade that severely limited their options through the telling of these tales—in each one of them, a willingness to skirt the prohibition on trade outside of the markets results in significant positive gains.

Interestingly, the tales align well with the tales of buried treasure considered by Lindow (1982). The bottle that guarantees the ultimate wealth of the poor famer and his wife is a gift from a mound dweller, a class of supernatural beings closely related both to economic transactions and to buried treasure in Danish legend tradition (Tangherlini 1998b):

Da han nu kommer hjem, saa spørger Maren: "Naa hvad fik du saa for Koen?" "A fik en Flaske!" "En Flaske!" siger hun helt forundet, og saa fortalte han det hele om den Mand, og hvordan han saa ud. Ja, ham kjendte Konen godt nok, det var én af Højfolkene. Nu skulde de til at prøve Flasken, og saa skulde de til at ønske. Manden tykte, an vilde have Gaasesteg, og saa stod den paa

Bordet. Han skar saa Hul paa den, og da var Kroppen
udstoppet med ene Penge, og de trillede ud paa Gulvet.
Nu kan det nok være, de blev glade, nu havde de jo rigelig
Erstatning for deres Ko, og havde Penge nok til
Udgifterne. "Ja, vi kan jo ønske os nogle flere en anden
Gang," siger Manden, og de satte dem saa til at spise.

[When he gets home, Maren asks: "Well, what did you get
for the cow?"—"I got a bottle!"—"A bottle?" she says,
utterly dismayed, and then he told her the whole thing
about the man and how he looked. Yes, the wife knew
him well, that was one of the mound dwellers. Now they
were going to try the bottle, and they were going to wish.
The man thought that he wanted roast goose and there it
was on the table. He cut into it and the body was stuffed
with coins, and they spilled out onto the floor. Now they
were happy, now they'd gotten plenty for their cow and
had lots of money for their expenses. "Well, we can wish
for more another time," says the husband and they sat
down to eat.]

Importantly, the access to the treasure represented by the bottle
derives from a willingness to break the laws governing fair trade.
But the underlying evaluation that the concept of "fair trade" was
hardly apt for the highly regulated market structure that existed in
rural Denmark: the shift toward a more broadly based market
economy forced small holders to act as market players even when
the market was rigged against them. It was not a question so much
of limited or unlimited good, but rather a question of whether to
play by rules that put one at a significant disadvantage. By stepping
outside the bounds of the regular market system and engaging in an
illegal transaction with a completely new market segment (here, the
"outgroup" of the mound dwellers), the poor farmer is able to
secure his well-being and punish the wealthy farmer to boot.

It was not until the rise of the cooperative movement in the
final decades of the nineteenth century that many Danish small
holders were able to participate in the markets on a more even
footing with the farmers and large landholders for whom the new

markets worked well. The cow as a symbol of access to the market was well known to all of the rural population: if one had a cow, one had milk. If one had milk, one could produce butter and possibly cheese. All of these were valuable commodities in high demand that could be sold or bartered. With the prohibition on non-market sales, however, opportunities to develop a sound financial basis even with a very small herd were essentially nonexistent. That two of the stories mention trading cows should come as no surprise. In both of these cases, trading the cow is the last resort—signaling that the farmer and his wife do not expect to remain in the marketplace. If selling a cow is transgressive in its rejection of the emerging market economy, then selling the cow on the way to market is all the more transgressive bordering, in fact, on the subversive. What makes these sales even more intriguing is that they are barter transactions—thus eschewing the last aspect of the emerging market system, the monetized transaction.

In two of the stories, the cow is traded for a farmhand—one of these farmhands is a thief on the way to his execution, while the other one turns out to be a psychopath. In both cases, the farmhand's subsequent actions reject all of the underlying rules of the marketplace and, quite frankly, all of the rules of civil society. An intriguing episode occurs in Villads Skov's tale, where the farmhand uses a seemingly market based negotiation over price to steal butter:

> Han faar Bæsterne for og kjører saa af Sted med nogle tomme Fjerdinger. Da han kommer til Sandbakken, fylder han dem med Sand og lægger hvert Laag nok saa kjønt paa. Derefter kjører han til Byen og ind ad en Kjøbmands Gaard, hvor han strax giver sig i Færd med at bære Fjerdingerne ind ad Pakhuset og sætter dem der lige Side med en Del andre Smørfjerdinger. Saa gaar han ind i Butikken og siger, at han er her med et Læs Smør, om de vilde sige ham, hvad Pris de gav for det. Ja, de gav saa og saa meget. Nej, den Pris vilde han ikke sælge Smør for, det var saa og saa godt, han kunde sagtens faa mere for det et andet Sted, og hvad han kunde nu rimle op. Ja, de gav ikke mere, sagde de, og saa rejste han af ud til

Pakhuset og skulde nu have Smørret læsset paa Vognen igjen, men passede naturligvis paa at faa nogle andre Fjerdinger, der var virkeligt Smør i, og saa kjørte han lige hjem til den fattige Mand med det.

[He gets the horses harnessed up and drives off with some of the empty forms. When he gets to the sand pit, he fills them with sand and puts each cover on nicely. Then he drives to the town and into a grocer's farm, where he immediately begins carrying the forms into the warehouse and puts them down next to the other butter forms. Then he goes into the store and says that he has come with a load of butter, and he wanted to know what they would pay for it. Well, they paid so and so much. No, he wouldn't sell butter for that price, it was so and so good the butter, he could certainly get more for it another place, and whatever, he just made something up. Well, they wouldn't pay any more, they said, and so he went out to the warehouse and was going to load the butter back into the wagon, but made sure of course that he took some other forms, which really had butter in them, and then he drove straight home to the poor man with it.]

As noted, the trade of the cow for the farmhand that initiates the story is well outside the bounds of legal behavior, violating not only market rules but also freeing a dangerous criminal (whose crime was theft, the antithesis of proper market behavior). Here, the theft of butter relies on the idea of a market for its success—by expressing his disgust at the low price offered for his fictitious butter, the farmhand is able to make off with the dairy's butter. Indeed, much of the story, from the trade at the beginning of the story, to the theft of grain to this theft of butter rely either on the violation of the rules that govern trade or a deliberate manipulation of the transaction setting, such as the substitution of sand for butter. Through these manipulations, the narrator exacts at least narrative revenge on the wealthy who, in the view of many poor small holders, had unfairly structured the market in their favor. In their stories, the storytellers repay systemic theft with actual theft and systemic violence with actual violence.

The labor market was equally regulated as the market for goods. Although the *stævnsbånd*, a system of registration that guaranteed the manor farms a steady and essentially captive labor supply, had been abolished at the end of the eighteenth century, the movement of young men and women between farms was still highly regulated. Consequently, opportunities for employment were limited, and the chances of finding an exceptional farmhand for reasonable wages were similarly limited. In the ATU 1535 tales, the poor farmer is able to find such a worker whose uncouth methods help him attain significant wealth. The attainment of wealth always comes at the expense of others—but this should not be interpreted as a case of the zero sum game of limited good. Rather, those who are punished are the wealthy—people who have taken unfair advantage of others to advance their own fortunes. As such they are worthy of punishment.

Throughout these stories a profound critique of the structure of the emerging free market system bubbles just beneath the surface. The rules governing trade were skewed against the small holders, at the same time as those small holders were being increasingly forced to act as regular actors in the market. To most small holders, many of the rules must have seemed both capricious and unfair—why should a person not trade on the way to and from market, when the market offered little opportunity for participation as an equal? In legends of buried treasure, breaking the rules usually results in punishment of one form or another. Treasure hunts fail when the hunters see their village in flames, or when they violate the interdiction on talking—resolutions that suggest that community takes precedence over individual gain. The premise, of course, is that the community is strong and mutually supportive, and that the distribution of wealth is fair and equitable, despite its irregularity. These tales reject that suggestion. Instead, the emergence of the free market economy forces people into untenable situations where they have to sell their last productive possessions to unscrupulous traders. Their only hope is to step outside the bounds of this highly regulated market and play by a different set of rules.

Lindow's proposal to read the tales in a "realistic" context proves to be a productive one. The shifting terrain of economic production and trade placed many small holders in dire straits. The playing field was tilted against them, and strategies for overcoming the obstacles to sustainability were hard to come by. The what-if scenarios of stepping outside the boundaries of that economic playing field explored in these narratives must have been liberating. Using the market against the very ones who had structured the market must also have been appealing. Generally, people do not consider *Märchen* to be subversive. But in these cases, the rural audience would have recognized early on in the tale that these were stories about crossing boundaries, breaking the law and upending the emerging economic order. Interestingly, it did not take long for the small holders to upend the market system that put them at a competitive disadvantage. They did not do it by eschewing the rules of trade, but rather by cleverly making the market work for them. By banding together in cooperatives in the waning decades of the nineteenth century, the Danish small holder, once unable to compete in the free market, all of a sudden found himself part of a global economy supplying butter and cheese to kings and queens. The buried treasure turned out not to be buried at all. It was in the cow being dragged off to market.

Notes

1 For the sake of this study, the German term *Märchen* is used to refer to any tale cataloged in the index of Danish Fairy Tales in the Evald Tang Kristensen collection (Brandt 1974).

2 Peasants are to bring their wares to the market towns, and keep to the plazas and markets, and shall not sell their wares to the hucksters and deal makers who wander about the countryside. If they violate this rule, and thereby infringe the value of the wares to the Crown, and the wares, if recovered by the Royal bailiff, shall be confiscated by the Crown.

3 The full texts of all four of the stories considered in this study are available at http://www.purl.org/lindow/tales.html. These stories can be categorized as falling into three categories. Two of the tales involve acquiring the services of a farmhand who turns out to be ruthless in his murderous efficiency in gaining wealth for the family who hires him. These tales have many similarities to tales classified as ATU 1535. One of

the tales involves trading a cow for a magical bottle that in turn becomes the object of the wealthy farmer's jealousy, and is similar to ATU 564, 595a, 331 and 332. The fourth story involves the young man who is repeatedly cheated out of his goods on his way to market, before violently turning the tables on his antagonists.

[4] This process offers a strange echo to the American housing market in the last years of the first decade of the twenty-first century.

[5] Strategies for transactions when one has a high expectation of future transactions are considerably different than situations where the likelihood for future transactions is small or non-existent. In the first situation, one would more likely pursue a strategy of "tit-for-tat," recognizing that one should not try to cheat a potential future trading partner. In the latter situation, one may be more likely to pursue a "winner-take-all" strategy, where one has no consideration for potential retaliation. A discussion of these strategies and an overview of the shift from a barter economy to a monetized economy can be found in Tangherlini 1998b.

[6] This tale is similar to ATU 1535.

[7] A "Pareto Efficient" solution to a problem is one in which no solution exists that would make parties any better off without making someone worse off.

"This is what trolls really look like": The Folklore that is Norway

JoAnn Conrad

If Norway were to show the world a single work of art which would most truly express the Norwegian character, perhaps the best choice would be the folk tales [of Asbjørnsen and Moe], published for the first time more than a hundred years ago and later illustrated by Erik Werenskiold and Theodor Kittelsen (Shaw 1960, 5).

In my own childhood those collections by Asbjørnsen and Moe were important and I have memories of my father reading them to me... the illustrations [of Werenskiold and Kittelsen] are very well known for Norwegians and I would guess conceived of as an integrated part of the collections. It is hard to think about these stories without the illustrations. The fairytale "kvitebjørn kong Valemon" (variant of the beauty and the beast) is strongly connected to Kittelsen's wonderful picture of the princess riding on the white bear, and probably more known to most people than the story itself (Selberg, Personal Correspondence).

Asbjørnsen and Moe's folktales have established our impression of what a Norwegian folktale is like, a picture which comes close to the real thing. The large number of new editions and new selections from Asbjørnsen and Moe's collections have become the classic expression of the Norwegian folktale tradition. With the brilliant illustrations they were to receive later, they have become representative of Norwegian folktales, both in Norway and abroad (Johnsen 2010).

> Together with Jørgen Moe, P. Chr. Asbjørnsen played
> an important role [in constructing] the Norwegian
> identity in the 1800s... he should be seen as a
> storyteller who was instrumental in consolidating
> Norwegian culture and Norwegian identity
> (Kvideland 1999).

Introduction—Dusting off the Canon

The story of folklore in Norway is interestingly unique in that
there is such long-standing uniformity and convergence of the
material and the analysis into the general story of Norway itself.[1] As
is reflected in the quotes that initiate this article, the story follows a
now well-rehearsed line: Norway, after independence from
Denmark (1814), fully embraced the tenets of Romantic
Nationalism (read: Herder and the Grimms), and in doing so sought
to return to the "hidden Norway" of the past by retrieving the lore
from the peasants in the countryside as a national heritage. This
endeavor was almost single-handedly carried out by the team of
Asbjørnsen and Moe, whose collections shaped not only
generations of Norwegians, but also defined the distinct folklore of
Norway to the international scene. This folklore was typified by its
rural characters, its droll humor, its trolls, and its plucky, clever
hero—Askeladden. It was further manifested in the illustrations
that accompanied the texts, most often those of Erik Werenskiold
and Theodor Kittelsen.

What is remarkable in the case of Norway is the consistency
among the public imagination, the canon, and the analysis of that
material, both within Norway and within the international folklore
community, and its persistence over such a long time span—to the
point that it has attained a kind of "doctrinal unassailability"
(Joerges 1999). The works of Asbjørnsen and Moe have been
transformed into a cultural artifact. This artifactualization of
collected texts into a standardized corpus follows what Roland
Barthes has termed *Mythologization*—those processes through which
the contested spheres of multiple narratives are made singular and
thus absolute, and in which stories and actors are dehistoricized and
resignified to conform to the larger narrative. Importantly, these

processes conceal themselves and consequently their ideological motivation (Barthes 1972). In the case of the Norway, not only the folklore but also the "forefathers" of Norwegian folklore—Asbjørnsen and Moe themselves along with a select group of illustrators—have also become cultural artifacts, transformed into mythic personages emptied of their historical specifics (although the reiteration of their biographies is part of the mythologizing process) and filled with new significance.

These processes of artifactualization are illustrated by the introductory quotes, each of which contains an important, unexamined assertion: (1) the folklore collections of Asbjørnsen and Moe are (direct) expressions of the Norwegian character; (2) the tales and illustrations are texts of enculturation and pedagogy, creating a national imagination; (3) the collections of Asbjørnsen and Moe are classic (real) examples of Norwegian folklore (and, by implication, others are spurious); and (4) the tales are constitutive of Norwegian culture and identity. Of course, all of these beg the question of *a* Norwegian identity, which is prior to and exemplified by rather than constituted in the collections. Furthermore, a fundamental question arises here: Does the material, in the case of Norway, drive the theory, or is it the other way around? The aim of this article is to revisit some of these "origin stories," to "dust off" (Haugan 1991, 50; quoted in Hult 2003, 12) the Asbjørnsen and Moe franchise, and to show that the uniqueness of Norwegian identity is in part a historical, *literary* construction that exists despite the data, or, more to the point, *a priori* to it. Specifically, rather than focus on the folklore of Norway through the tales, this article looks at the standard narratives about Asbjørnsen and Moe, arguing that these unexamined "background stories" play a fundamental role in the construction of Norwegian-ness (*Norskhet*).

"The work known as 'Asbjørnsen and Moe' is a corporate body"

The first great collectors of Norwegian folktales were Peter Christen Asbjørnsen and Jørgen Ingebreksten Moe. Asbjørnsen was a forester and lived, much as an American forest ranger would, in all parts of Norway. He was an extraordinarily good collector and had the help of a scholar in Moe. Together they published the first edition of Norwegian folktales in the 1840's (Thompson 1961, 317).

[In] the first collection of *Norske folkeeventyr*, both writers are fully and completely equal, both have the same part" (Moe 1927, 86).

The first of the collections was (sic) published in booklet form from 1841 to 1844. These were followed by other collections, edited partly by Asbjørnsen and Moe together, and partially by Asbjørnsen alone. However it is fully justifiable to view all these collections as one work (Hoel 1948, 98; quoted in Hult 2003, 23).

Publications of Asbjørnsen and Moe, jointly and individually, began in earnest in 1841, and continue to the present. It is critical to remember that while Asbjørnsen and Moe were collaborating and consolidating their separately field-collected narratives into their joint work *Norske Folkeeventyr* [*NF*] 1841-1844, Asbjørnsen himself was working on a very different body of material, both in content and presentation: *Norske Huldreeventyr og Folkesagn* [*NHFS*] [Norwegian Huldre Tales and Folk Legends] volumes one (1845) and two (1848).[2] Subsequent editions and collections mixed and matched narratives from these two very different works, reducing them and recontextualizing them into collections that were further framed by theoretical and analytical introductions, notably by Jørgen Moe and later by his son, Moltke.[3]

Although the bulk of the collection and editing was finished by the 1850s, the recombination and the runaway publication of subsequent collections and children's books derived from these collections eventuated in the dominance of particular tales across several generations. This combination of standardized tales, analysis, and interpretive illustrations have become, in effect, a corporate entity. Moreover, in the narrative of Norwegian Folklore, Asbjørnsen and Moe themselves have been consolidated and transformed into a corporate entity as well. Convention holds that it was Moe who contribute the aesthetic and stylistic aspects, whereas

Asbjørnsen, the rugged type, was the collector (see Thompson, above). Consolidating the lives and works of Asbjørnsen and Moe requires the selective retrieval and recontextualization of biographical and historical information that then is merged with the edited and re-collected stories to construct a unified text of Norwegian folklore.

Asbjørnsen was born in 1812, the year of publication of the first volume of the first edition of the Grimms' *Kinder- und Hausmärchen* [*KHM*] and two years before Norway's independence from Denmark (Grimm and Grimm, 1812-1815). Jørgen Moe was born one year later in 1813. The story of the two collaborators inevitably focuses on their initial meeting in school, and their shared love of nature and lore. What is deemphasized is that their collaboration in creating the collections really only spanned the decade of 1840 to 1850, after which Moe gave over his work to Asbjørnsen completely, while Asbjørnsen turned his attention more towards his work in science, nationally and internationally. Their educations, and their main collaborative effort occurred in a specific moment in time. This effort was historically, politically, and socially distinct not only from the context in which the Grimms issued their *KHM*, but also distinct from the conditions during which the *illustrated and edited* collections appeared in the second half of the nineteenth century and the beginning of the twentieth century. In the rush to associate the pair with the Brothers Grimm, two important differences are obfuscated. First, both Asbjørnesen and Moe had careers in civil service, locating them in the intellectual milieu of the Christiania elite. Second, the historical conditions of Norway in the first half of the nineteenth century were radically different from the conditions in which the Grimms developed their *Kinder- und Hausmärchen.*

"Asbjørnsen and Moe were driven by Romantic Nationalism"

Of the various folklore collections from the Asbjørnsen and Moe corpus, the first appears in the 1837 *Nor, en Billedbog for den norske Ungdom*, a collection ofstories published as a solo effort by Asbnørnsen in an illustrated magazine for children. This early collection included at least three standards that would reappear in subsequent collections: "Somme Kjærringer ere Slige" (Why wives are so); "Kari Træstak" (a version of ATU510); and "Gutten, som gik til Norden Vinden" (The Boy who went to the North Wind—a version of ATU 563) (Jæger 1896, 305). This initial foray into publishing is important because it clearly aligns folklore with children's literature and with a nationalizing/pedagogic enterprise, both of which are clearly part of a modernizing project aimed at the creation of a new generation with not only nationalistic but bourgeois sensibilities despite the tiny size of the middle class in Norway during that period. Additionally, *Nor* is written in Dano-Norwegian, and the linguistic changes of later editions—rendering dialectic, spoken Norwegian into written Norwegian—are as yet absent. The stories are an amalgam of what could be identified as international tale types and migratory legends, speaking, perhaps, to the impossibility of such generic categories, especially cross-culturally. More to the point, the inclusion of widely distributed fairy tales, tales that are not specifically from a Norwegian context, suggests that at this moment in Norwegian history (the mid-nineteenth century) the impulses of nationalism and education had not as yet consolidated fully.

Norske Folkeeventyr (1841-1843), the truly collaborative effort of Asbjørnsen and Moe based on their fieldwork experience, is an expanded collection of these wonder tales. Each of the tales stands alone and is not related to the adjacent tales—that is, the context *is* the collection. The characters are rather generic, many from royalty (ironic from a country with no native monarchy). Despite this, and partly because of it, descriptions and analyses of the work starting with the 1852 "Introduction" to the second expanded edition to the *NF*, have tied it to the quintessential folklore text of Romantic Nationalism—the Grimms' *Kinder- und Hausmärchen* (Grimm and Grimm 1812-1815).[4] That link is made because Asbjørnsen and Moe were clearly influenced by the work of the Grimms' *KHM* as a model for the organization of *Norske Folkeeventyr*, and because the ideological assumptions driving the Grimms in their endeavor are unquestioningly assumed to be the same in the case of Norway.

The Herderian legacy in the Grimms' *KHM* is well-documented, as are the role of folklore in the German nationalist enterprise and the processes by which literary tales were rendered "oral" through "distressing" to conform to the imperatives of that enterprise (Abrahams, 1993; Stewart, 1991; Harries, 2001; Bendix, 1997; Warner, 1996). All of these have been transferred to the understanding of the ideology at work in "Asbjørnsen and Moe". But folkloristic over-generalizations claiming that the collaborative efforts of Asbjørnsen and Moe were motivated by Romantic Nationalism miss an important and obvious fact: the conditions out of which Romantic Nationalism emerged did not exist in Norway. In other words, Norway was not Germany, nor were the back stories of the Brothers Grimm equivalent to those of Asbjørnsen and Moe.

In the first half of the nineteenth century, Norway's population was roughly ninety percent rural. Even by 1855, well past the foundational work of Asbjørnsen and Moe, the population was only thirteen percent urban; sixteen percent in 1865; and twenty-eight percent in 1900 (*Statistiske oversikter* 1948, 31). By contrast, Germany in 1871 was twenty-four percent urban, and, by 1910 was fifty percent urban (Kollmann 1969, 62). A look at the growth of large cities is likewise instructive in comparison: Oslo, had a population of 57,000 in 1865, whereas Berlin had a population of 828,000 in 1870 (Mitchell, B.R. 1992, 72). In the last quarter of the nineteenth century, the growth rate of large cities in Germany was a staggering +442% (Kollmann 1969, 62). Industrial development in Norway, if it did exist, was still in the primary industries of timber harvesting, fishing, mining, and later in the 1850s and 1860s, textile-related industry or, in other words, those industries that did not require or constitute urbanization. It was only in the period after 1865 that more rapid urban-industrialization occurred, but even at the turn of the century, only one third of the Norwegian population was urban (Moe, T. 1977, 37). Furthermore, industrial workers in Norway did not make up large portions of the population throughout the nineteenth century: ten percent of the total workforce in 1850, and thirteen percent in 1865 (Grigg, 225). All this to suggest that the motivating condition for the Romantic reaction—the loss of traditional, rural life—was not manifest in Norway, which until the very end of the nineteenth century was in fact pre-industrial, particularly in the period in which Asbjørnsen and Moe collected and published their *Norske Folkeeventyr.* This critique of urbanization, and the notion that the countryside had been "lost" to the pressures of modern industrialism is contradicted by population studies done in Germany where it was found that the movement to the cities was spurred on by instability in the countryside due to overpopulation and unemployment, which exacerbated the poverty among the mostly unpropertied peasant class. The great irony of urbanization in Germany was that, along with emigration, the internal migration of large portions of the rural populations into the industrializing cities stabilized rural life, so that urbanization and industrialization effectively revivified "traditional" rural life (Bahrdt 1961, 17).

There are further complications in the direct translation of the German *Volk*—which became associated with rural peasantry—as equivalent to the Norwegian *bonde.* Again, the conditions for radical social change in Germany at the time of the industrial revolution were related to the class relations in which peasants for the most part were living in near-feudal conditions, did not own land, and were part of a structural underclass. The Norwegian *bonde* in contrast were historically landed farmers, who as early as the 1830s were incorporated into the Norwegian parliament—a move which in turn effected education reform (Coe 1999, 34). In arguing *against* the analogy of German Romanticism and the Norwegian situation, Moltke Moe stressed that historically the Norwegian *bonde* had long familiarity with both written and oral folk traditions (Moe, M. 1927, 49).

In Germany, Romanticism was a reaction to what was perceived of as the ravages of industrialism, urbanism and modernity and the loss and alienation that resulted from these. Romanticism sought in the anti-modern a palliative to these perceived runaway forces, and found its expression in an aesthetic located most dramatically in Nature and in the voice of the natural Folk, the non-urban peasantry. The Folk—*das Volk*—in Herder's usage as well as that of the Grimms, referred to a pre-industrial simplicity of the un-educated, rural peasant who would be the bearer of all things pure, uncontaminated, and authentic. The lore, the poetry of this Folk, was thus the medium of their un-self-conscious expressions. As Stewart has indicated, the folk had to be invented before the folklore, and thus the category of the folk is one that is imagined by the bourgeoisie (1991). Emergent nationalism, in this context, easily configured this Folk as that which was distinct and unique in contradistinction to others. The direct appropriation of the word "Folk," and the assumption that its invocation in German works such as the *KHM* is equivalent in its meaning to *Norske Folkeeventyr* not only disregards the polysemous nature of the word in German, it also generalizes the specific Herderian gloss, and extrapolates it to conditions in Norway that do not match those in Germany. In the German context, the Folk were a literary construct that first necessitated an absence, a nostalgia for the Folk, the loss of innocence in the face of industrial modernization, and was also the legacy of a historically class-based society. In Norway, the Folk might more be said to refer to the collective group that is Norwegian (who are unified in their place, lore, and language) in contrast to *Danish* more than to an idealized type that calls upon a pre-modern past.

Literary rendition of this "unmediated" language of the folk was configured as the direct collection and transcription of the "poetry of the folk" or folklore from the illiterate Folk by the Folklorists. In the case of the Grimms' collections, a literary heritage was occulted, and elaborate attempts to stage orality were incorporated into the texts and into their own mythologization (Warner 1996, 188-193). This was to be achieved through a series of devices that rendered the language of the oral-folklore bearers transparent. That is, literary standards were adopted that mimicked what met expectations of "folksy speech"— the insertion of proverbs, short sentences, dialog, colloquial/dialogic lexical items–all of which masqueraded as a seamless translation of an oral form to the written. Based on this circular reasoning, "distressed," written collections of folklore bore the tell-tale verifying and authenticating marks of orality and authenticity: we knew from the form of the written text that the tales were "oral." The Grimms constructed a literary form in accordance with their ideological expectations of the Folk, and achieved this at physical and intellectual distance from actual rural inhabitants. By contrast, Asbjørnsen and Moe both engaged in collection in the field. Here it is important to note that Asbjørnsen the biologist/forester and Moe the cleric—both civil servants—

would have had occasion to enter into the day-to-day affairs in the countryside as part of their jobs, in addition to their specific fieldwork endeavors. With Oslo a rather minor urban center, the country life was not an imaginary realm nor was it in danger of disappearing. The motivating impulse of salvage, so clearly driving the work of the Grimms and effected only through distance, was thus absent for Asbjørnsen and Moe, who mirrored the form and organization of the *KHM* for their *NF*, but not the ideological motivation or the collection methods. It is from this perspective that we need to see such validating and apparently authenticating statements about the work of Asbjørnsen and Moe by the Grimms, such as the one found in a letter from Jacob Grimm to Jørgen Moe, dated May 9, 1852: "The Norwegian fairy tales are the best fairy tales... In your collection both story and representation are excellent" (Grimm 1916, 180).[5] Rather than evidence of the superiority (read: authentic by virtue of their apparent "orality,") or of the philosophical identity of the work of the Grimms with *NF*, we should see this in the context of the many metanarratives and metadiscursive ways in which the Grimms sought to legitimate their literary conventions and delegitimize other forms, such as Jacob Grimm's praise for the simple language of Charles Perrault and criticism of the work of the other French salon writers as overly long and flowery, evidence of their literary nature. The Grimms were seeking to establish their vision of what folklore was, and *Norske Folkeeventyr*, in addition to being modeled on the *KHM*, conveniently was used to validate its claim on authenticity.

If *Norske Folkeeventyr* was the scion of *KHM* in a format that fulfilled the conventions and expectations of "authentic folklore," then Asbjørnsen's solo work, *Norske Huldreeventyr og Folksagn* was quite another matter. A collection of twenty-seven clusters of legends contextualized by the locale, the tellers, and the local lore, the collection is also contextualized for the readers through the device of the outer frame narrative recounted by an urban narrator. Each cluster mimics a legend-telling context that is explicitly local, and in which the stories, the underlying beliefs and discussions, the frames of reference, and the narrators are also local. It is into this local setting that the outer frame narrator has stepped. Hult has defined the "dialectic between narrator of the frame story and the created folk storytellers and their tales [a]s the dialectic between the urban and rural, the refined and unrefined" (Hult 2003, 44). But, as Oring has shown us, legends, by their very nature are also discourses on the nature of "truth," open-ended, suggesting possibilities but never achieving closure (Oring 1990). More recent work on frame narratives themselves, such as the work of Stephen Benson, situates frames as intermediaries—liminal texts—between the oral and the written, in their mimicry of an oral tale-telling encounter. Frames are full of unrealized and untold potentialities of all the actors in each embedded narrative and can thus be seen as generative models of narrative itself. Benson continues: "... while the standard collections of folktales are ostensibly authentic but implicitly literary, the various cycles of unashamedly literary tales are structured both implicitly and explicitly, around a staged orality: they mimic orality by staging the event of their narration" (Benson 2003, 46).

In subsequent redactions to the Asbjørnsen and Moe corpus in which stories from *NF* and *NHFS* are indiscriminately combined, the context of the frames (the original discursive premise in NHFS) is rendered irrelevant and disposed of. In fact, much of the folkloristic metadiscourse on their work discounts *NHFS* because of its putative literary nature—a nebulous and circular set of criteria clearly hinging on the authenticity so critical to *KHM*. The "taming" and recontextualizing of the rambling frames of *NHFS* within the more formulaic *NF* can be seen as the ideological work required to maintain a national narrative of unity, based on the idealized rural story teller.

"Asbjørnsen and Moe were radical linguistic innovators"

[Danish] was...poorly suited for retelling fairy tales, which stemmed from a uniquely Norwegian tradition, and had its sources in local dialects that were even more distinctive than they are today. Asbjørnsen and Moe solved the problem by applying the principles of the Brothers Grimm: using a simple linguistic style in place of dialects, while maintaining the original form of the stories. At the same time the language in the tales also contained many words from Norwegian dialect, and helped create an autonomous Norwegian written language, distinct from Danish (*Wikipedia*).

Conventional wisdom firmly establishes Asbjørnsen and Moe as following in the footsteps of the Grimms both in blazing new folklore collection methods and linguistic reform through the use of a standardized peasant speech in their folklore collections. But parallels between the methods of the Grimms to "convey the language of the folk," and those of Asbjørnsen and Moe have conflated and obscured the multiple, and often conflicting strands of Romanticism, processes of self-promotion and mythologization, linguistic reform, and educational reforms. This process can be seen in the marginalization of works of other Norwegian collectors and the elevation of the corporate works of Asbjørnsen and Moe. The collections of the likes of Andris Vang (1850 *Gamla Reglo aa Rispo ifraa Valdris*) written in dialect; Just Qvigstad (1887 *Lappiske eventyr og Folksagn*, with G. Sandberg); and, most dramatically Andreas Faye (*Norske [folke]sagn* (1833 [1844])) written in Danish, are not as well known, and certainly do not claim to be representing *the* folklore of Norway, but rather work against the narrative of national, linguistic, and cultural unity in their regional emphasis. Although Faye's work preceded *NF* by a full decade, it has been denigrated as not fulfilling the goals of a "true" representative folklore collection and as being hampered by cumbersome (Danish) academic language. Amundsen (2010-11) has suggested that this dismissal was an opportunistic maneuver on the part of Faye's competitor, Jørgen Moe, to cast himself as the real bearer of the words of the folk. This self-mythologization was self-interestedly also perpetuated in the editorial work of Moe's son, Moltke. More importantly it continues to this day in the dismissive and non-specific assessment of Faye's work as "dry," while reiterating the now unquestioned logic that Asbjørnsen and Moe used "a simple linguistic style... while maintaining the original form" (Kaplan 496; Dorson 1968: vi; Aschehougs Norgeshistorie, 1997; Wikipedia). Although the language of *NF* is praised as exemplary, its construction was quite different from that of *KHM*.

The enterprise of the Grimms, as we have seen, was that of a reclamation project. In contrast, Asbjørnsen and Moe sought in *NF* to insert aspects of regional spoken Norwegian into the form of international tales and into the written language of the realm, Dano-Norwegian. Both were premised on the notion of the value of traditional narratives of the folk, but the method of collection and presentation are quite distinct. Mette Rudvin and Popp have analyzed the changes in *NF* over subsequent editions, and have shown a gradual process by which an overall gentle modification of the existing Dano-Norwegian written form, introducing lexical, pronunciation and orthographic differences, was the basis of their *fornorsking* [Norwegianization]. Accordingly, the process of *fornorsking* in *NF* represents a shift but not a departure: "For the tales to become a truly national symbol that could be understood and accepted by the urban bourgeoisie, they had to be transmitted in a literary form and in the (quasi-)Danish language—precisely that language form from which Norway was struggling to free herself... [thus] the explicit and fundamental prerequisite, authenticity, was false, and, equally important...had it not been false (i.e. bourgeois, and not rural) the folk tales would not have gained acceptance as canonized literature" (Rudvin 1999, 37). Consequently *NF* can be seen as a transitional work – allowing for and anticipating the major language reforms of the late 1800s and early 1900s, but neither a radical nor an anti-establishment one.

Far from developing a radical new Norwegian language, Asbjørnsen and Moe used Dano-Norwegian as the base onto which to gradually superimpose regional differences. The language that eventually emerged from this kind of gradual approach was *bokmål*, one of the two officially recognized Norwegian languages in Norway today. However, Asbjørnsen and Moe collected their material from the Southeast region of Norway, and did not include material from the Northern and Central regions, thereby effecting a dominance of the southern dialects. As with the use of the extant, albeit modified, Dano-Norwegian written language, this southern tilt realigns their work with the status quo: "One of the reasons the Asbjørnsen and Moe corpus received such national acclaim and consensus was precisely that it embodied both the myth of a national identity and of a national language in a relatively conservative (i.e. Danish) form, and therefore functioned as a compromise between an emerging national identity and the maintenance of an (elite) conservative linguistic and literary form" (Rudvin 1999, 30; citing Elviken 1931). *Fornorsking* itself is problematic, for the *idea* of a Norwegian that is distinct from Danish not only stands in contradiction to the effective use of Danish in writing and the overarching similarities between spoken Norwegian and Danish, but also against the *reality* that Norway to this day maintains three official languages and revels in the close-to-incomprehensibility of some regional speech. The story behind this language policy and its integration through education reform is also part of the context from which to understand the role and meaning of the work of Asbjørnsen and Moe.

Although it is now axiomatic that Asbjørnsen's Romantic agenda shaped his language adaptations in *NF* and that these were key elements in the eventual dominance of *bokmål*, there were other scholars in this period who advocated more radical language reform. Ivar Aasen is at the forefront of these reformers. Himself from Western Norway, he sought to combine aspects of most spoken dialects, assuming a common underlying structure of Old Norse. Thus Aasen incorporated the language of the folk *landsmål*—with the remote past in a unified, romantic solution to the language of the new Norway; Aasen's suggestion was one of the only real challenges posed to Dano-Norwegian. But although the elite theoretically embraced the principles of *Nynorsk* (*landsmål*), in practice, they and the *bonde* themselves were more apt to prefer *bokmål*. This position reflects the state of compulsory education, literacy, and children's books, which also involve Aasen, Moe and others.

Elementary education became compulsory for rural children relatively early in Norway, in 1839 (cf. 1763 in Prussia, but between 1870 and 1880 in England, and 1882 in France.) At this point Norwegian universal education and the entry of educated peasants into political life put national unity at odds with the Romantic valorization of the illiterate peasant. This situation was mitigated somewhat in curriculum reforms that focused on orality, folklore, "mother tongue" etc., while still shaping students into civic responsibility. But folklorists and educational reformers were split on the manner in which folklore was to be configured and incorporated into the curriculum. Teachers, such as Ivar Aasen, and Knud Knudsen militated for instruction to be in *landsmål*, and for it to stimulate national feelings based on the circulation of folksongs, mythology, and folktales. But as compulsory education really began to take effect after the 1860 Primary School Law, and as the practical needs for standardized and universal writing skills rose in response to the new economic demands, the rhetoric of nationalism (and the use of *landsmål*) was replaced by the pragmatics of *bokmål* (Wiggen 2009, 1536). At this very moment, the new, illustrated *NF* was put into widespread circulation. At the same time, the romantic context of the folktales of the countryside was absorbed into the educational project through mass produced textbooks and mass, standardized education.

Shortly after the collaborative efforts of Asbjørnsen and Moe resulted in *NF,* Moe produced a solo effort, *I brønden og i tjernet* (1851), referred to as Norway's first children's book. It was a sweet, didactic, and moralizing storybook based on the lives of two young children and their rather muted adventures, revealing as much about Moe the pastor/educator as it does about Moe the folklorist. Moe was a member of the first generation of Christiania-trained pastors who went out into the countryside to preach a unified message. They were often on the front lines of implementing and forming education reform. Arguably Moe's fame from *NF* enhanced the standing of his children's book, and, beginning in 1892, portions of this book were included in Nordahl Rolfsen's *Lesebok for Folkeskolen*, a textbook which was in print until 1950 and for which the total print run was eight million volumes.[6] These schoolbooks, based on the ideas first advanced with the promotion of the Folk Peasant Schools, shaped the reality of generations of Norwegians in the late nineteenth century and throughout the twentieth century. Standard chapter headings served to construct a normalized re-presentation of Norway for its youngest citizens: "Rundt Norge" was full of regional landscapes and people (with archetypal fishermen of Lofoton and reindeer herders of Finnmark); Norwegian Heroes with Nansen, Amundsen and Thor Heyerdahl; Norwegian History that included the Vikings; and literary classics including Ibsen along with folksongs and folktales from the collected works of Asbjørnsen and Moe. It is through these texts and their illustration—the visualization of these imaginary realms—that the various collected works that had once been local and regionally specific became the common national text for subsequent generations.

Interestingly, in the collapsing and incorporation of the works of Asbjørnsen and Moe along with the reconfiguration and recontextualization of selected stories out of *NHFS* into this corporate work, the most linguistically discursive of Asbjørnsen's works is diminished. Subsumed now into the general narrative of Norwegian folklore, this work was originally structured as framed story-telling vignettes in which an urban outsider enters into a local realm and engages with local stories and their tellers, described by Hult as a "dialogue between *riksmål* [Dano-Norwegian] and *landsmål* ...creat[ing] an open-ended work of multi-layered discourse subject to diverse interpretation"(Hult 2003,174). Through this framing technique, Asbjørnsen was able to effect a contextualized and localized story-telling situation, with competing voices, languages, and interpretations within the frame itself. In the *NHFS*, the legends are amorphous, the tellers are more "real" and therefore sometimes rough and mean-spirited, and the dialects and sensibilities are regional, hardly presenting an image of a unified Norway.

Asbjørnsen's frame narrator, situated at the intersection between the urban and rural, not only facilitated and translated the world of the folk to the urban audience, he appropriated the landscape of the countryside for them. As Hult notes, "This ability to engage the reader in the physical topography enabled Asbjørnsen's work to serve as a guide for the appropriation of the Norwegian natural world for his contemporary readers, the urban elite whose task it was to build a Norwegian national identity" (Hult 2003, 72-73). Asbjørnsen's role here, in the larger narrative, is itself "natural" – he is the forester, the robust man who knows nature, and in this role he is again reconfigured, in a revisionist historical mode, as a pioneer, with implications beyond the realm of the natural sciences. He has been referred to as the man who introduced Darwin to Norway. Richard Dorson goes so far as to claim that he translated *Origin of Species* into Norwegian (Dorson 1968, vi). In fact, Asbjørnsen's minor and obscure reference to Darwin was unremarkable: "Darwin's new theory of creation" was published in 1861 in the newspaper *Budstikken* under a pseudonym. At the time, Asbjørnsen, the biologist, was much more involved in animal husbandry, and science and technology were seen as tools to enhance the then-growing economy. It was not until 1889 that the *Origin of Species* was finally translated in Norway, a significant lag in terms of the intellectual firestorm it created in most of Europe and the flurry of translations that immediately followed its release (compare Germany 1860, Sweden 1871, and Denmark 1872). This lag has been attributed to a generally "anti-empiricist" and "Hegelian" stance among Norwegian academics. This stance, along with religious opposition, posed a "formidable barrier" to the reception of the theory of natural selection and the new natural order it proposed (Glick 1974, xx; Lie 1985 and 2000). Ironically, the (erroneous) reference to the reception of Darwin in Norway as evidence of radical reform tendencies is revealed to be an indication of academic conservatism. Here Asbjørnsen the academic, language reformer, and folklorist must be seen in the context of his work with Moe, the state-employed, state-trained Lutheran pastor (later bishop). Once again, we see the dehistoricization of Asbjørnsen in the myth making of Norway. Only in hindsight could his linguistic work be reshaped as radical, and it is arguable that the popular reception of *NF* is due to the fact that it was conventional in form and in language.

"Th. Kittelsen established...what a Norwegian troll really looks like"[7]

Similar to the processes of canon formation with Norwegian folktales and the subsuming of the story of Asbjørnsen and Moe into that enterprise, certain accompanying illustrations and their illustrators, through generations of reprinting, have become not only canonical, but have emerged themselves as markers of Norwegianness. It is not an exaggeration to claim that popular perception of Norwegian tales (and trolls) is now determined by the visual imagery of Erik Werenskiold and Theodor Kittelsen.[8] They are at once irrevocably linked with the narrative of Norway's folklore and with the works of Asbjørnsen and Moe, as well as circulating as fragments, decoupled from their original context and yet serving to reinforce that vague, recognizable sense of *Norskhet* that is now the larger context.[9] These two illustrators provided the now-iconic illustrations to the tales; their paintings hang in the National Gallery in Oslo and flow freely through the commercial sphere, reproduced as postcards, souvenirs and in hundreds of picture books. Yet the scientific orientation of the *non-illustrated* collections of Asbjørnsen and Moe of the 1840s can be historically and ideologically differentiated from the illustrated children's books of the late 1870s and 1880s, and this shift can be seen as a shift in the role of these stories in the national narrative itself.

Werenskiold and Kittelsen were not the first or the only illustrators of the work of Asbjørnsen and Moe. The first was Johan Fredrik Eckersberg (b.1822; d. 1870) who was a contemporary of Asbjørnsen and Moe. Eckersberg's place in the art milieu was dictated by the then powerful and conservative Christiania Art Association, a group of "wealthy dilettantes whose taste was often conspicuously reactionary," who sponsored German-influenced works (Lindwall 1982, 37). Known more generally for his Romantic landscape paintings, Eckersberg was trained in the Düsseldorf School. It is his illustrations that feature in Asbjørnsen's first foray into illustrated books, both Christmas story collections, aimed specifically at children—1850 *Juletræt* and 1851 *Juletrold*. Partial and widely eclectic in scope, these early children's books reflect the conflicting aims of pedagogy, nation building, nostalgia and progress. The 1851 *Juletrold* includes translated (imaginary) stories from Arabia, Persia, and the like in an Orientalist vein, alongside translations of the stories of the Grimms.[10] The 1850 *Juletræt*, of which twenty-three thousand copies were printed, includes some of the stories out of *Norske Folkeeventyr*, illustrated for the first time. This volume represents one of the first instances of the widespread distribution of materialized imaginaries of fantasy characters, trolls in particular. Two of the stories included are common in subsequent collections: "Smaagutterne some traft trodene paa Hedals skogen" and "Guldfuglen." A comparison of Eckersberg's early renditions of the trolls of these stories with their parallels by Werenskiold and Kittelsen provides an opening into a more nuanced and historically informed analysis of the relationship between these illustrations and what ultimately became linked to Norwegian identity.

Fig. 1: Eckersberg's 1851 rendition of trolls in "Smaagutterne some traft trodene paa Hedalsskogen"

Fig. 2: Eckersberg's 1850 illustration of the trolls in "Gullfulgen" from 1850 Juletræt.

Similarly, striking is a comparison of Eckersberg's 1850 trolls with Kittelsen's illustration of the same story 30 years later.

Fig. 3: Småguttene som traff trollene på Hedalsskogen by Erik Werenskiold ca. 1878-79.

Fig. 4: "Gullfuglen" illustrated by Th. Kittelsen in P. Chr. Asbjørnsen og J. Moe (1883).[11]

Clearly what a troll has come to *really look like* is the result of editorial decisions shaped by the political and cultural changes that occurred in the second half of the nineteenth century. Those images in their repetition and distribution have in turn become naturalized in the popular imagination over generations.[12]

When Werenskiold was introduced to Asbjørnsen in 1878, he was given a list of stories to illustrate. Back in Munich, in communication with Asbjørnsen, he produced nearly a quarter of the illustrations for the 1879 illustrated *Norske folke og huldreeventyr* (Marit Werenskiold, *NSL* online), a compilation of both *Norske Folkeeventyr* and *Norske Huldreeventyr og Folkesagn*. According to Marit Werenskiold, his trolls in "Smågutterne som traff trollene på Hedalsskogen" were adapted by Kittelsen when he later joined in illustrating *Eventyrbog for Børn* in 1883. Kittelsen began his association with Asbjørnsen at the end of the collector's life, a time in which the emphasis in publishing the stories had taken a new turn towards children's books, which, now edited by Moltke Moe, were primarily illustrated by Kittelsen and would inform generations, through textbooks and children's books, what trolls really looked like.

Werenskiold (b. 1855) and Kittelsen (b. 1857) were not only contemporaries who worked in the same artistic milieu both internationally and within Norway, but they were a full generation younger than Asbjørnsen, Moe, and Eckersberg. Despite the fact that Werenskiold and Kittelsen have been so emphatically linked with *Norske Folkeeventyr* and with Asbjørnsen and Moe, in the thirty years between the first collections and their most famous illustrated collections, Norway had become a different place. The *bonde* were now in Parliament in part because of the educational reforms put in place earlier. In academia the gentlemen folklorists had given way to radicalized left-leaning nationalists (Amundsen 2010-11, 10). Rather than being tied to the social and political milieu of Asbjørnsen and Moe and the Norway of the mid-nineteenth century, Werenskiold and Kittelsen should be seen in the context of the intellectual and artistic radicals of the 1880s and 1890s, members of the Christiania Bohemians and others who carved out a particular type of Norwegian modernism in *fin de siècle* Norway. This movement is linked to disruptions and developments in the natural sciences, as well as to investigations into the nature and limits of the self, the emergence of spiritualism, psychoanalysis, and the new technologies of revealing (and projecting) the inner self including X-rays, microbiology, photography, film.

Werenskiold and Kittelsen, like other Norwegian artists of the nineteenth century, trained abroad and were involved with (or at least aware of) international art movements and innovations. In 1875 Werenskiold, and year later Kittelsen were sponsored by the Christiania Art Association to study in Munich, where the art scene was under the sway of French realists, turning away from the conservatism of the Düsseldorf School-trained generation of Eckersberg, and away from the overblown sentimentality of Romanticism. This generation of Norwegian artists shared in this reorientation. In rejecting Romanticism and turning to a new "realism," a showdown with the Christiania art establishment was inevitable. In 1882 Werenskiold led the strike that forced the dissolution of the conservative art association (Lindwall 1982, 38). Thereafter artists organized themselves according to their own artistic ideas, rather than being controlled by forces outside of the art community. In this manner, the Munich and Paris-inspired artists of the 1880s in Norway were politically radicalized. Ironically, crediting Kittelsen with *fixing* the image of the troll is to miss the recurrent challenges within his broad body of work to any fixity or singular version of reality.

"Det rusler og tusler rasler og tasler": Illustrating Liminality

Kittelsen was born in 1856, one year before Freud, and six years before his countryman Edvard Munch. Rebelling against the German-influenced establishment in Christiania, he and others of his generation would soon radically break from their conservative patrons, and gravitate towards Paris. Impressionism (roughly spanning 1870-1880), influenced by Hemholtz's (1850s) groundbreaking discoveries in optics, interrogated the very ways of seeing, and redirected artists towards an emphasis on the constitutive qualities of light itself. But Realism and positivism would fall prey to growing disillusionment about modernization in the face of economic crises and socio-economic polarization. This development intersected with work very late in the century and in a variety of fields that focused on investigating an interiorized self, questioning the limits of the self and of space, time, and vision-based empiricism. So, for example, one has Charcot's experiments in hypnosis beginning in 1882; Röntgen's discovery of the X-ray in

1895; Freud's "Studies on Hysteria" in 1893; Muybridge's introduction of the zoetrope in 1893; 1882 Tesla's discovery of the magnetic field. In addition, spirit photography, séances, spiritual revivals, and magic lantern phantasmagoria were both popular forms of entertainment and alternatives to institutional science and religion. All these combined in an artistic turn to symbolism and subjectivity: "This fusion of inward-turning psychology and collectivizing political spirituality in the 1890s in Northern Symbolism is not a peripheral aberration but a juncture of tendencies that were in constant tension within the general reaction against modernization that swept Europe" (Varnedoe 1982b, 19). Whereas the Paris Symbolists sought meaning away from their "over-civilized" city life in "Primitive" realms, as Gauguin did in Tahiti, or in the realm of the symbolic and the imagination, Norwegian artists turned home to their roots: "Nordic artists turned away from the evolutionary optimism and from the bright light of the Impressionists. The new trend paved the way for an individualistic, often gloomy philosophy of life" (Sarajas-Korte, Salme 1986, 40). Never apparently comfortable in the documentary aspect of realism, Kittlesen was beginning to explore in his work the margins between perceived nature and inner feelings through the ambiguous and phantasmagoric landscapes of the North.

Leaving aside the suitability and limitations of cross-cultural applications of such specific movements as Impressionism, Realism, Symbolism, and Expressionism, it is clear that this generation of foreign-trained artists were influenced by the experiments in artistic expression, were politically radicalized, and synthesized this in a particularly Norwegian context with Norwegian subject matter to effect changes not only the in meaning of art but in the visualization of Norwegian-ness itself. Along with other artists in this cohort such as Eilif Peterssen, Harriet Backer, Kitty Kielland, Christian Krogh, some of whom also contributed to the illustrated works of Asbjørnsen and Moe, Kittelsen emerged as a transitional figure. Situated at the moment between the romantic landscape painters and the expressionist work of Munch and others, his work challenges the boundary of nature and culture, and in this ambiguous nature interrogates the boundary between reality and fantasy. Light itself was to become a theme for Nordic artists, and the long twilight of summer was a distinctive aspect of much of Kittelsen's work. Focusing on nature's effect, on the perception of the encounter, and on the ambiguity and variability of perception, Kittelsen also presents his work intersubjectively, in a manner not unlike Asbjørnsen's as he guides the reader through the frames of the *huldre* and folk legends in *NHFS*. His landscapes are immediately accessible to the viewer who is drawn into this subjective experience. Each landscape asks, "is this real, or imagined?" His 1900 "Det rusler og tusler, rasler og tasler," from his collection *Tirilil-Tove*, destabilizes the viewer and provokes a subjective, immediate response—a hesitation. Kittelsen seems to be visualizing the terrain of the legend, painting a discourse on the nature of reality(ies).

Fig. 5: Det rusler og tusler rasler og tasler (1900).

Fig. 6: Kornstaur i måndskinn, ca. 1900

One can imagine oneself walking along a forest path, dimly lit, and encountering this form, and momentarily experiencing a hesitation, that split second in which reality as we know it shifts slightly. Similarly, in Kittelsen's "Kornstaur i måndskinn," the viewer is drawn into a visual experience that mimics a *memorate*. Honko's classic description of the combined effects of a long summer work day fading into a long disorienting twilight alone in the pastures, sleep-deprivation, and perhaps a little alcoholic enhancement playing tricks on one's perception is easily read into these straw men/haystacks (Honko 1964, 11). In describing his own time in Lofoten, Kittelsen writes: "Men når man er alene, ser man gjerne mer, blikket blir skarpere, det blikk som vender innad" [but when one is alone, one really sees more, your eyes are brighter, the gaze turns inward](Kittelsen 1957, 4).

Kittelsen was a prolific artist and writer, producing many works in addition to his illustrations for the children's books of Asbjørnsen and Moe, and in many of these he plays with boundaries, perceptions, permeability. He explores life and death in his chilling, anthropomorphic series on the fourteenth century Black Death; and plays with his own legends and accompanying illustrations in *Trollskap* (1892) and *Tirilil-Tove* (1902). Underlying this work is a blurred, unsettling uncertainty, an ambiguity, a liminality that allows for multiple reactions and perceptions, for subjectivity. In this sense Kittelsen is clearly of his time, paralleling much of the great Gothic works of the *fin de siècle*, but his work does not that easily lend itself to the certainty of the nationalist narrative. Only in the conflating of Kittelsen's story with that of Asbjørnsen and Moe and deploying it in the service of Norwegian identity formation can we say what a troll *really* looks like, and that it was Kittelsen who gave us this vision.

Notes

[1] John Lindow was my advisor and my mentor for my Ph.D. in folklore. I'm thankful to him for his guidance and friendship over these years, and I'm happy to begin to revisit this issue of trolls in Norway in this festschrift piece.

[2] My translations are based on the primary content.

[3] At the time when Asbjørnsen and Moe were actively working on the collections in the 1840s, the Scandinavianist movement was quite strong in the capital, and did not abate until the 1860s, long after their work together had stopped. It is arguable that rather than being initiated as a nation-building text, their work was rehabilitated as one in later periods of high nationalism. A look at other publications by Asbjørnsen individually suggest a much more cosmopolitan attitude towards quite clearly literary folktales. See, for example 1851 *Juletrold*, in which two tales are translations from the Grimms' *KHM*, one a translation from Th. Croften Croker, whose Irish tales were translated into German by the Grimms. It also includes "Arabian" and "Persian" tales, situating Asbjørnsen's book in the context of the larger "orientalist vogue" that began in eighteenth century French Literary Tales (Zipes, 1999) and quickly spread to Germany and England. Asbjørnsen also collaborated with Johann G.T. Grässe on the 1858 *Nord und Süd: ein Märchen-Strauss* which includes translations of European tales, literary fairy tales, legends (including one from *Norske Huldreenentyr og Folkesagn*), as well as ones from Scotland, Germany, and France (Arabian).

[4] Hansen writes, "...the importance of German romanticism on the Norwegian is overwhelming as it concerns the greatest source of all romanticism in the various countries: folk poetry...For Asbjørnsen and Moe the German influence is completely determinative...[t]his influence comes first and foremost from the Grimm brothers' *Kinder- und Hausmärchen...*" (1932: 137). Similarly Dorson notes, "Norway [after 1814]...immediately embarked on a quest for her national identity through history, folklore, and language...According to the romanticist ideas of the mid-nineteenth century, the true character of the old, pure Norway, unsullied by foreign invasions, was to be discovered in the conservative peasant" (1966:289). Kaplan, writing of the debt that Asbjørnsen and Moe had to the Grimms' *KHM*, and how both were indebted to Herder's concept of *folkness*, states: "In folkness resided a romantic notion of authenticity, which was rural, ancient, original, natural, and unmediated ... the folk poetry of the peasantry" (2003:492).

[5] Repeated by Hansen, 1932: 149. Dorson, makes a strange reference to it, saying the "end product" of Asbjørnsen and Moe (again, the corporate product) "so appealed to Jacob Grimm that he described them as the best Märchen in print," (1968:ix); and the uncited reference shows up in fairy tale websites and in the "Scandinavian Tales" section of the *Greenwood*

Encyclopedia of Folktales and Fairy Tales, pg. 839: "Jacob Grimm himself declared that the Norwegian Folktales were superior to all other folktale collections." This illustrates the ways in which the metanarratives attendant to folklore circulate freely and are quite protean in nature, offering up a variety of meanings from the same originary statement.

[6] For examples of these schoolbooks, see online: www.bymuseet.no

[7] "Th. Kittelsen," at www.lokalhistoriewiki.no

[8] Erik Werenskiold's contribution to the illustrations of Asbjørnsen and Moe was larger and began earlier, and his contribution to the direction of art in Norway is much more significant. In the extraction of a minimal set of images now circulating, the trolls of Kittelsen are dominant, and popular references to *the* significant folktale illustrator tend to overwhelmingly be to Kittelsen.

[9] In an interesting case of reappropriation, several Folk Metal, and in particular Black Metal bands use Kittelsen's images on their cover art (See the band Buzrum's *Hvis lyset tar oss* (1994), and *Filosofem* (1996) as examples). Fans continue with tattoos and other body adornments. The nostalgic return to a more pure imagined time clearly here has seriously different meanings in today's context.

[10] www.nb.no

[11] In a self-referencing move, Kittelsen's 1887 oil painting "Kristian Hjerteknuser" (kittelsen.efenstor.net), shows a young boy reading a book in which this picture of the trolls is visible on the opened page. This again points to the ways in which these books, in the 1880s were directed towards children, and how they were rather commonplace. But this picture is reprinted without the story, with the caption "Da slo trolla opp latterdøra" in the 1955 *Videre fram I. Lesebok for framhalsskoler og andre ungdomsskoler* (Rolfsen). Also in this reader are stories about Ibsen, and the Kon-Tiki.

[12] Anecdotally, as I was preparing this article, I showed these images to my now-grown son, who spent some of his childhood in Norwegian schools. His response to my scrolling down to the trolls of Werenskiold and Kittelsen: "Now *these* look like trolls" (Conrad, 2000).

Thomas Kinkade's "Solvang": Painting, Performativity and the Third Gaze

Hanne Pico Larsen

First you take Thomas Kinkade, *"The Painter of Light,"* known for his otherworldly universe of impressionistic *plein air* paintings of cottage scenes, serene pastoral motifs, lighthouses, and lit paths. Then you take Solvang, a quaint little tourist destination in California that markets itself as "The Danish Capital of America." You ask the American painter to paint the quaint little town, and then you look at the result: a painting of a reproduction of an idea of a nation. The painting stands as an idealized image of an already idealized environment.

In this article I examine how a particular painting of Solvang came into being, and how the painter, Thomas Kinkade, subsequently presented it. In addition, I investigate how the image created in the painting fits tourists' perceptions of the town. Interwoven in the discussion are two concepts of "the tourist gaze," introduced first by John Urry and subsequently challenged by Dean MacCannell with his concept of "the second tourist gaze" (Urry 1990; MacCannell 2001). In order to understand the totality of tourist gazes I propose the inclusion of a "third gaze." This gaze is one produced by the tourists themselves and thereby reveals what the tourists actually see. This "third gaze" is not a phenomenology of the tourist gaze, nor of the tourist experience (Cohen 1979; Redfood 1984; Wang 1999). Instead this notion of "the third gaze" is influenced by the notion of "tourist shame" proposed by John Frow and the "third person effect" proposed by W. Phillip Davidson (Frow 1991; Davidson 1983). To illustrate what the tourist actually sees and to support the idea of the "third gaze," I explore the thoughts of three tourists whom I asked to comment on both Solvang the tourist place and "Solvang," the painting.

Solvang

   Danish immigrants founded the small town of Solvang in 1911. Back then it looked quite different from how it looks today. In regards to architecture, there was nothing to see in pre-picturesque Solvang, nothing of visual interest that separated Solvang from other rural sites nearby. In 1947 Solvang was discovered by the "The Saturday Evening Post," and soon after tourists arrived on the scene (Larsen 2006). Today Solvang has been molded to fit the contours of a picturesque old time American town, even if it really is a modern American city combining nostalgia for the past, theming and commodification. Like so many other California themed environments Solvang attracts a wide rage of tourists but the place is most often considered an inauthentic "tourist trap" in spite of its "real" Danish history (Howser 2002).

   Solvang with its distinguishing built environment has long been the subject of various reproductions including posters and postcards, billions of tourist photographs, and several professional depictions. Symbols which refer back to Solvang, which again in turn refer back to Denmark—for example the ubiquitous red wooden shoes that litter the Solvang shops, images of the little mermaid, and windmills of all sizes—have been endlessly reproduced and sold as souvenirs to visitors. Of course, these emblematic items are sold alongside other trinkets with little relevance to Solvang or to Denmark for that matter. Consequently, through these reproduced emblems of ethnicity and nostalgia, Solvang sells ethnicity and heritage even if not necessarily Danish ethnicity or heritage. The Thomas Kinkade painting of Solvang is a fantastic, colorful example of both a visual representation of Solvang the tourist town, but it is also case in point of Kinkade's own production. Whereas Solvang might not sell "real" Danish heritage it sells the "feel" of Old time Europe. Similarly, Kinkade does not paint "real" places, rather he creates a "desire to feel" a particular place (Boylan 2011, 13).

"Solvang" and its Creator

The main visual axis of Kinkade's "Solvang" painting is defined by the easily recognizable main street of the town. Parked along the curb sits an antique Mercedes even though the painting is supposed to depict a recent scene. Green trees and yellow half-timbered houses with thatched roofs line both sides of the street. One of the buildings is clearly an inn seemingly inviting the viewer to stay. On the other side of the street, there is an old-fashioned light post that is lit, even though the painting depicts a daytime scene. Flowers and Danish and American flags vie for attention while people stroll along the walkways under a light blue sky punctuated with white, fluffy clouds. The sunlight sends its rays through the painting and the trees within it, and there is an abundance of Kinkade's signature light/shade effect. The painting is colorful yet calm, and the peace and quiet in the painting borders on the therapeutic.[1]

According to the Kinkade Company, the painting "Solvang" was created on May 14th 2004 between 11 am and 4 pm, "in order to get the most light."[2] A somewhat conflicting account related by a sales associate in the Solvang Kinkade Gallery has it that Kinkade began to paint early one morning in June, 2004 while his four daughters waited in the lobby of the Petersen Inn. Kinkade had commissioned in advance a photograph of the location he wanted to paint and had prepared a preliminary painting. With professional expediency he filled in the gaps, finished up around 10:00 a.m., and then set off for Morro Bay, another nearby tourist attraction, to complete a painting of Morro Rock.[3] It would appear that the act of the painting of "Solvang" was a speedy, routine composition shoe-horned into a tour of Southern California tourist attractions that he had planned to paint for his Central Coast Galleries at Pismo Beach, Solvang and Morro Bay.

Apparently after the gallery owner saw the painting, he asked Kinkade to add some details including six human figures, one dog, three Danish banners (including one on which the name Solvang was printed) and one American banner.[4] A photograph of Kinkade with his easel and the painting was taken on Mission Drive at the spot where he had painted, and the photo was then displayed in the gallery. If one looks closely, one can see that the added details do not appear in the photograph.[5] Whereas Kinkade's paintings often lack people in order to underscore the peace and solitude of the scene, and to allow viewers an opportunity to project themselves into the imaginary harmonious landscape, Solvang is about people. Without people, there would be no Solvang.

The disjuncture between the two accounts may be due to faulty memories, but whatever the account, Kinkade did in fact erect his easel on the main drive of Solvang across the street from the Petersen Inn Village and did in fact paint "Solvang." The painting process cannot be seen as a holistic one, since both the lighting effects and the identifying local details are detachable, layers or façades easily added to the base. The limited edition *"Solvang plein air,"* listed by the gallery as "a collector's piece," was released in July 2004. One thousand nine hundred prints of the "Solvang" painting were made available for sale for prices ranging from six hundred dollars to eleven hundred and forty-five dollars, depending on size and framing. For an additional one hundred dollars, one could get the painting signed and remarqued by Kinkade.[6] In addition, with each purchase, one would receive a discount of twenty percent off a one night stay at the Petersen Inn, the inn depicted in the painting.[7]

The story behind the decision for Kinkade to paint Solvang is interesting. Considered along with the account of the painting process, the decision was not nearly as devotional an act as the promotional materials suggest. It turns out that a manager at the Kinkade Company has Danish roots and had always wanted the painter to go to Denmark to paint. The manager was also on friendly terms with the owner of the Thomas Kinkade Gallery in the Solvang Petersen Village Inn, who was the son of one of Solvang's pioneering entrepreneurs who, in turn, was the man behind the architectural transformation of Solvang from southern Californian town to European fairy tale. The two friends joined forces and persuaded Kinkade to go to Solvang and paint, which he eventually did. This Solvang/Kinkade connection might explain why the painter chose to paint this hotel rather than one of Solvang's many windmills, which are among Solvang's most recognizable icons.

Painting and Performance

Painting is a performance; it is the execution of an action, a fulfillment of a claim, promise or request, and its exhibition of its end products makes it part of a public presentation. The painting "Solvang" was created in response to a request, and it is now exhibited in Solvang among other places. Kinkade did not choose to make the painting of "Solvang" a public performance though, as he does not normally paint publicly. There was nothing in the local press announcing the painting of the painting, and the actual event was ostensibly done in the wee hours, before the sun came out and brought people who potentially could have observed the performance. What could have been a great public event as well as a fresh input into the prevalent experience economy both in Solvang and for Thomas Kinkade, was instead executed in silence. One can imagine that an onlooker would have been a bit disappointed when discovering that the painting was almost done before it was even started, and that the (religious) light was not applied until much later. An onlooker might also have felt deceived when seeing what was over the painter's shoulder was not necessarily reflected on the canvas. The viewer is encouraged to imagine a different process and would find this imagined process at odds with how the painting was actually produced. That might be the reason why the painting was not a performance in the public shared-space sense of the word.

One can decode a different type of performance by examining the promotional materials that introduce the painting. Instead of the deconstruction of an illusion, which would have followed from actually witnessing the creation of the painting, the promotional materials offer the construction of an illusion for the prospective buyer: a series of pictures of the painter painting on location.[8] The promotional material supposedly offers an opportunity to look over Kinkade's shoulder and see the real thing, here Solvang, at the same time as one can see the glossy, impressionistic counterpart created by Kinkade. The prospective buyer also glimpses the almost-finished painting, and finally the end product hanging on the gallery wall itself. It is a staged performance, one that attempts to provide the painting with a legitimate stamp of authenticity.

The verbal impression Kinkade gives of his engagement with the painting process in the promotional material is also contrived and holds little authority especially in light of the different accounts about the painting's genesis. One flyer describes the paintings coming into being as follows:

> After a restful night's sleep in the famed Petersen Village Inn with my family, I set out to paint the idyllic village of Solvang. The lush blooming streets, thatched rooftops and half-timbered buildings transported us back in time to Europe when life seemed more simple and unhurried. Old World charm. Romance. Tranquility. I invite you to enjoy SOLVANG with us![9]

The tranquility of Kinkade's alleged experience contrasts sharply with the "hit and run" performance described by the gallery staff. On a second flyer Kinkade makes it sound as if a spontaneous act of painting took place. The narrative itself is a short, sensory one:

> Danish flags fly proudly on the streets of SOLVANG...some five thousand miles west of Copenhagen. When the Kinkade family visited "The Danish Capital of America" right here in Santa Barbara County, we found ourselves transported in the spirit to the enchanting land of Denmark.
>
> We strolled the lush, blooming streets of SOLVANG, past thatch-roofed inns and quaint half-timbered houses, savored the rich perfume of Danish pastry shops, sampled old-world cuisine, and admired the little wooden trolls and other Danish crafts in the gift shops. I was enthralled by what I saw, and, as so often happens, was moved to set up my easel and paint the town. It was a lovely, sunny day, and shadows dappled the tree-lined streets as I worked. The old-world flavor of the town struck me as deeply romantic, so I made my SOLVANG into a

tribute to my lovely wife, Nanette. If you look closely, you'll discover a sign bearing my wife's name, as well as a number of hidden "N's" scattered among the houses. My family has enjoyed the chance to travel together in Europe on occasions; what a pleasure it has been to discover this bit of the old country right here in my beloved California. I invite you to enjoy SOLVANG with us.[10]

Kinkade proposes that he was transported in spirit to Denmark, a faraway country where he has never been. This romantic transportation inspires him to dedicate the painting to his wife, as is the case with many of his other paintings. The hidden N's are not unique to this particular painting, but instead form part of an elaborate and idiosyncratic system of symbols that he applies to all of his paintings, something that is expected from his audience.[11] That Kinkade has to sell his paintings using images of himself painting as if to prove that he was really there attempts to magnify the idea that the project is based on untainted reality and the presence of pure love, dedication and real emotional investment. This position contrasts with the actual motivation for the project as one based on commercialization, mass-production, and money. The paradox of this painting is that it commercializes his love for his wife while denying its very commercialization. Ultimately, what is sold in the painting is a landscape of the present upon which the moral order of the past is carefully and lovingly grafted. Solvang, with its quaintness, simplicity, and nostalgia, like the Kinkade painting, sells itself as an icon of this past where peace and proper moral order still reign.

"Solvang" and the Tourist Gazes

The dialectics of tourism revolves around the gaze. John Urry suggests that a component of the tourist experience "is to gaze upon or view a set of different scenes, of landscapes or townscapes which are out of the ordinary" (Urry 1990, 3). Some of the distinguishing characteristics of the tourist gaze that Urry identifies reveal a great deal of the Solvang/"Solvang" dialectic writ large:

The tourist gaze is directed to features of landscapes and townscapes which separate them off from everyday experience. Such aspects are viewed because they are taken to be in some sense out of the ordinary. The viewing of such tourist sights often involves different forms of social patterning, with a much greater sensitivity to visual elements of landscape or townscape than is normally found in everyday life. People linger over such a gaze which is then normally visually objectified or captured through photographs, postcards, films, models and so on. These enable the gaze to be endlessly reproduced and recaptured (Urry 1990, 7).

What Kinkade did with Solvang is not mere hocus-pocus. Instead he follows the gaze of the tourist, capturing it through painting. Consequently, he enables this particular gaze as something that can be endlessly reproduced and recaptured. The painting and Solvang itself are about the deception of time and the speed of life. They are about the idyllic holiday filled with leisure, sun, and light. This idyllic deception is encapsulated in the stationary antique car. A contemporary view of the same scene shows the street filled with moving cars, emphasizing that life is actually lived at full speed. Whereas Urry uses the notion of the "tourist gaze" to explore the history of tourism, the changing economics of the tourist industry, and the tourist workforce, he averts his gaze and not only avoids the question of what tourists actually see, but also fails to reveal how the tourists perceive what they see.[12]

Dean MacCannell disputes Urry's idea of the tourist gaze because of its lack of agency writing, and proposes the "second gaze".[13]

The second gaze is always aware that something is being concealed from it; that there is something missing from every picture, from every look or glance. This is no less true on tour than it is in everyday life. The second gaze knows that seeing is not believing. Some things will remain hidden from it, even things with which it is intimately familiar. It cannot be satisfied simply by taking leave of the ordinary (MacCannell 2001, 36).

Jonathan Culler goes further, treating tourists as semioticians who travel from site to site, decoding tourist attractions:

> The tourist is interested in everything as a sign of itself, an instance of a typical cultural practice... All over the world the unsung armies of semioticians, the tourists, are fanning out in search of signs of French ness, typical Italian behavior, exemplary Oriental scenes, typical American thruways, traditional English pubs; and, deaf to the natives' explanations that thruways just are the most efficient way to get from one place to another... (Culler 1988, 155).

Urry seconds this idea, calling the tourist gaze "signposted." Since the gaze is signposted by the tourist industry, it requires little skill for the tourist to decode it. Kinkade can be seen as maybe not a master of light, but of semiotic coding, placing signs (and not only the aforementioned N's) all over the recaptured tourist gaze.

Scholarly engagements with the tourist gaze hence propose a gaze that is partially satisfied with visuals provided by the entertainment industry. The ones who gaze are always aware that something is missing and try to see through, past and beyond the provided images. Interestingly, audiences not only decode these images for whatever signs have been placed there, but go even further in their imaginary game, reinforcing the signaled markers and strengthening the illusion.

Paul Fussell had evokes the notion of the "anti-tourist," suggesting that the "anti-tourist deludes only himself. We are all tourists, now, and there is no escape" (Fussell 1980, 49). In the same vein, Donald Redfoot begins his discussion of tourist authenticity, angst, and modern reality by asserting: "The tourist has become the symbol of a peculiar modern type of inauthenticity"

(Redfoot 1984, 291). The "Post-Tourist," as proposed by Feifer, is a product of postmodernism and exhibits three main features: (1) the playful post tourist does not have to leave the house to experience many of the most typical objects for the tourist gaze; (2) the post tourist is like a chameleon who is aware of the changes and the various of choices offered, allowing the post tourist to freely pick and choose from the different options. The post tourist's gaze is adapted to sacred, informative, educational, or simply beautiful objects; (3) the post tourist is not bound by class, moving freely between high culture and low brow pleasure-seeking tourism, discovering amusing contrasts and delight in both (Feifer 1985).

Tourist Shame, the Third Person Effect and the Third Gaze

When asked, many people would not admit to being a tourist, but see others as tourists. Being a tourist enjoying tourism and the visual consumption of sights is not considered negative *per se*, but the term tourist has a slightly derogatory ring to it, an attitude promulgated by intellectuals, tourists themselves, as well as the tourist industry. John Frow describes this as "the phenomenon of tourist shame" (Frow 1991, 146). This shame "accompanies both the most snobbish and the most politically radical critique of tourism" (Frow 1991, 146). MacCannell describes it as follows:

> Touristic shame is not based on being a tourist but on not being tourist enough, on a failure to see everything the way it "ought" to be seen. The touristic critique of tourism is based on the desire to go beyond the other "mere" tourists to a more profound appreciation of society and culture... (MacCannell 1999, 10).

This structural moment of tourism, the overt disappointment, has been recognized but has not been given the necessary attention in the vast body of literature devoted to the tourist experience. Despite this potential for shame, lots of tourists enjoy what they do and see while on tour. This same conflict between enjoyment and shame happens with Kinkade and his paintings. People do buy his paintings. They spend lots of money on his art and enjoy it. Still, it is not very "artsy" to like Kinkade (Boylan 2011). Scholars, professional art critics, and connoisseurs have ignored Kinkade and in so doing let the non-experts know that they consider Kinkade to be bad art, if they consider it art at all. This functions in the very same way that travel writers often let us know that Solvang is in bad taste, a tourist trap to be avoided. Kinkade sells art by the carloads, and Solvang has lots of visitors (Boylan 2011; Larsen 2006). Somewhere they must exist: those people who appreciate tourism, reproductions of various kinds, and Kinkade paintings. However, in my search for this presumably large group of people who go to Solvang, enjoy it, and who can look at the Kinkade painting of Solvang and admit liking it, I have come up empty handed. Tourists are notoriously difficult to interview, and I did not have the chance to linger in a Kinkade gallery for long periods of time.

A partial solution to this problem of people expressing distaste for experiences they clearly enjoy may be found in W. Phillip Davidson's idea of the "third person effect":

> A person exposed to a persuasive communication in the mass media sees this as having a greater effect on others than on himself or herself. Each individual reasons: "I will not be influenced, but they (the third persons) may well be persuaded." In some cases, a communication leads to action not because of its impact on those to whom it is ostensibly directed, but because others (third persons) think that it will have an impact on its audience. (Davidson 1983, 1)

For Solvang, this means that nearly every tourist will claim that he or she is not terribly fond of Solvang, admitting that it was interesting to visit, but suggesting that others probably like it more. Versions of this statement proved to be more or less standard when I questioned tourists at random on the streets of Solvang. Referring to a third person seems to make the enjoyment of Solvang safer for the first person tourist. People asked to look at and evaluate the Kinkade painting reacted in a similar way. Indeed, almost everyone I asked about either Solvang or the painting exhibited the "third person effect" in some form or another in his or her responses.

The Third Gaze at Solvang

A combination of Kinkade's painting of Solvang and a visit to the town inspired a San Francisco journalist to write:

> Solvang, Santa Barbara County. On Solvang's main street there's a Thomas Kinkade gallery with a cute little green awning, and in its window is a Thomas Kinkade painting – of Solvang's main street, with the Thomas Kinkade gallery and its little green awning. This hall-of-mirrors drives home the point that the Danish-style village, with its cheery flower boxes and faux-thatch roofs, is a Thomas Kinkade painting come to life. How you react to the place will depend largely on how you feel about the self-proclaimed Painter of Light (Flinn 2005, F7).

In this brief comment, one can easily trace the "third person effect": if you like the Kinkade Solvang painting you like the place, he does not but some people, "they" do. To explore this phenomenon in greater detail, I asked three Solvang tourists to look at Kinkade's painting and write down their impressions about the painting, their experience of Solvang and their imaginings of Denmark. All three of my subjects (one woman and two men) had been to both Denmark and Solvang, and were curious to see how Denmark was interpreted. They are not Danish citizens, although one has a Danish parent and another has Danish ancestors. All of them are well educated, one is a high school teacher, one is post-graduate student of architecture, and one is a practicing psychologist. They are all engaged observers and their analyses are fairly sophisticated. They might not be typical Solvang visitors, but of course it is hard to label any visitor "typical." They are however, part of the large group of tourists who visit out of curiosity because they have an interest in all things Danish. They were asked if they knew the painter, if they liked his painting of Solvang, and what it told them about Solvang. They were also asked if they would buy the painting.

First Account

"I actually think I do know the painter...he is not my favorite. I think the painting is fairly banal; I wouldn't personally want to own it. However, the impression it gives me of Solvang is in point of fact fairly close to the impression I had of the town when I visited. The painting thematizes three things, which remind me strongly of my visit. First, there's the blending of a form of *Americana* with a form of *Denmarkana*. *Denmarkana:* We have the Danish flag, the depiction of the *bindingsværk*[14] façade of the Petersen Inn, and the *Ye olde village* feeling of, for instance, the script on the flag which reads Solvang and the script on the sign which reads Nanette. *Americana:* the old-timer car, the American flag, the Main Street feeling. This fusing of an interpretation of Denmark as quaint, old-fashioned, clean and small, and an interpretation of the American small town as it was fifty years ago fits nicely with my impression of what Solvang itself is trying to convey to its tourists. Second, the painter focuses on touristy things: the people in the picture (all white) stroll slowly about in casual clothing, apparently enjoying the town, the inn in the foreground speaks to the issue of lodging, and the weather is perfect for an outing. Here again, I think the painting is addressing a key theme of Solvang, namely tourism, Solvang as a safe excursion for middle of the road (white) Americans looking to relax, eat, sleep in pleasant surroundings. Third, the painter has striven for a kind of Light Impressionism, or blurry, light-filled Realism, a genre which works well with Solvang's depiction of itself as a Denmark away from Denmark: impressionistic, sunny, and (maybe?) better than the *genuine* article. The grimy canals of inner Copenhagen is not what Solvang is about, rather a light fantasy or blurry reality is being sold to the public. I am unmoved by the painting; it is a piece of kitsch in my opinion which I don't want to look at for long. I don't want to visit Solvang again seeing it, perhaps because it does give me a fairly good idea of what Solvang is like, or at least the image Solvang wants to portray: unreflective Denmark blended with unreflective America.[15]

Second Account

I remember Solvang as an amalgam of images: the windmill, the bakery, the parking lot where I left my car, somewhat surprised that there was no charge for parking. But I remember the feeling of Solvang well; it was one of those warm, windy California days when everything moves slowly and it feels like you're inside an oven. I didn't have sunglasses with me so I squinted through the strong afternoon sunlight. I wish the real Solvang were as shady as the one depicted in Kinkade's image; for a painter of light, there's an awful lot of shade. I stumbled around, disoriented. Solvang is the kind of place where it's hard to get your bearings and you later realize that someone has designed the environment to be disorienting. Hungry, I found myself at a bakery. I don't remember what I ate, but I do remember that it was stale. Heat and *wienerbrød* do not mix.[16] Solvang, I decided, was not for me. And that would explain my reaction to the painting, which sends all sorts of signals about for whom Solvang is actually intended.

The painting is loaded with symbols, mostly obvious ones, like the three variations of Danish flags, the green awning of a Thomas Kinkade store (just in case you missed the prominent signature in the bottom right corner), and the most obvious symbol of all, the one sitting on top of the sole car's hood: the aspirational 3-pointed star of the Mercedes logo. That logo is the effective focal point of the painting. If only it were a newer model, it would be the perfect trope, for the automotive equivalent to a Kinkade painting would be a modern Mercedes-Benz. Both are mass-produced products of questionable quality, but status symbols for the status conscious. But, unfortunately for my rhetorical purpose, the car isn't new; it's an old model with patrician curves. One does not drive this kind of car; rather, it is the style of car in which one is driven. I imagine that this one is poised by the curb, the handsome chauffeur waiting to take the idle and fashionably bored Bunny and Beauchamp back to Santa Barbara for another horrendously common five-course dinner with Mummy.

But the idle rich are not the target market for Solvang, just as they are not the target market for this Kinkade. The fact that this painting exists indicates that there is a market far, far larger than the idle rich; Kinkade is too ruthless of a businessman to make a product for such a limited market. The people that would buy this image are the same people who would buy other Kinkades. They value art that is direct, approachable, and understandable, art that is decorative in the sense that it matches the sofa. They've heard of Monet's ubiquitous haystacks and bridges (whose technique Kinkade seems to ape) but they probably haven't had the privilege of an education in art. That's not saying they are uneducated, for they may have gone to college or business school. Like a Mercedes-Benz, Kinkade's paintings may be mass-produced, but they are not inexpensive. They are, put another way, solidly middle class. According to the schema laid out in his chatty book *Class*, Paul Fusell would categorize Kinkade consumers as the middle middle.[17] (Middle refers to their relative social position, which exists independently of income). They are, I take from my visit, the same people whom the planners of Solvang hope to attract. Judging from the image, Solvang is a place for a genteel stroll, a sleepy weekend at the Petersen Village Inn, and a cup of tea at Nanette's.[18] It's a place for the conspicuous consumption of leisure. When I visited Solvang on that baking spring day, I was expecting a cultural experience of some degree; instead, I found shops.

The curious part about it is that this collection of standardized tourist activities and the stage set of related places, universally present in all western countries, is sold to the tourist as an authentic Danish experience. There's a strange sense in Solvang that, at any given moment, the facades of the buildings, the Danish flags, the blond shopkeepers will, at some silent signal, roll back like those revolving ad placards at the mall. Whoosh! The entire fake set is replaced with a different style of architecture, a different national symbol, and shopkeepers of different pigmentation lording over the same shops full of different *heritage* goods. One moment you're in Solvang; then— bang!—it's Disneyland.

The earnest fakeness of it all seems to be summed up by the windmill, which is intended to communicate Danishness, but instead just comes across as foreign (and by foreign, I mean out of place, rather than exotic). Holland, as any American school child can tell you, is famous for windmills. Dutch and Danish both start with "d." Is Solvang secretly intended to support the stereotypical American confusion of Europe? Upon learning that I had attended school in Switzerland, a friend once asked me if I had to learn Swedish. All those little countries up north, it seems, are just too confusing. Thus, Americans invented the concept of Scandinavia. But even that reduction seems too confusing for the denizens of Solvang; it's not Denmark, not even Scandinavia, but an imagined Europe of *Olde Tymes.*[19]

Third Account

The first time that I was in Solvang I was returning from Los Angeles and arrived there after dark. The streets were deserted and the restaurants fairly empty. It felt like everyone had left for the day and there were just a few stragglers around finishing up their work before they left also. It was quite different than what one might feel in a downtown of a typical city at night, where there may be empty streets but the residue of life is all around you in the smells, the trash, and even the occasional person who seems more part of the day's leftovers or a nighttime denizen, than a foreign entity on its way out. Although I love walking around cities at night, even late at night, I did not feel comfortable walking around there. But not out of fear for safety. To do so would have felt like I was being rude, acting in poor taste.

I was up early the next morning and walked around as people began to appear. Like in any city people began to appear in shops and opening up their businesses. I again felt a bit like an intruder who had snuck in and was peeking behind the scenes at activities that were not meant to be observed, let alone by outsiders. The people themselves, however, seemed no different than people in any American town.

When looking at Kinkade's painting the first thing that caught my eye was the car. It is pretentious and immediately I think of a cheap painting being hawked at Fisherman's Wharf for the mid-western vacationer who will think that they have bought a real painting when they return home with it. The car is also very un-Danish. My experience of Danes in general is that they don't 'show-off,' whereas a majority of Americans seem to know little else in the way of interpersonal interactions.

The picture is artificially bright in a way which seems more appropriate for Main Street at Disneyland. This same quality is continued in the "clean" streets and groomed shrubs. It looks sterile, cold, and not at all inviting. My experience of Danes is quite the opposite. I find them to be warm, generous, and perhaps more concerned with the other person's comfort than their own.

The flags in the painting are quite prominent. I find that Danes love their flag and display it much more frequently than Americans display their flag. But the flags in the painting seem artificially placed more to draw attention to themselves. They do not convey a sense of pride, but rather an absence of pride and treating one's self image (as a nation) as trivial. They are more appropriate in nature to a modern day Fourth of July parade.

The style of the left main building is reminiscent of what I might expect to run across in the Danish countryside but not in a city building. The placement of the buildings is spread out which contrasts with my image of Denmark where buildings feel closer to one another and often connected to one another. So there is a disconnectedness rather than an interconnectedness which would be more of the feel of Denmark.

Except for the car, the painting does capture some of the feel that I remember of Solvang. It is an odd town in that it is a real city where people live and work, while at the same it is a "set" and doesn't have the organic feeling that a city which has grown over many years has. Again, it looks like Main Street at Disneyland, but it is filled with real people who have real lives within the buildings and on the streets. This is not portrayed in the painting which only conveys the Disneyland quality and is thereby deceptive even of this deception. The people of Solvang are not actors on a stage even if the buildings in the town and the painting create the sense of a stage. This creates an odd feeling when there. One is tempted to relate to everyone as if they were props, but as soon as you interact with them they are normal people not pretending to be something which they are not. It is difficult to imagine feeling any of this in characters in the painting.

I don't know what Solvang is trying to project as an image, but the one which it does project while there is shallow. To this extent it demeans the people who live and work there, treating them as something other than working people who struggle with the same things with which all of us struggle. The only things Danish about Solvang for me are the superficial facades of some of the buildings, and the stereotypical food which captures none of the diversity and complexity of the Danish diet. Although individuals in the shops are cordial and even friendly verging on warm, the lust for life of Danes is absent. Whether it is someone on the train, in a shop, drinking beer late in the evening beside the canal in Nyhavn, or in a crowd bicycling through the streets, there is an almost sensual infusion into the activity which you do not see in America and not in Solvang.

It seems like most Californians know of Solvang, but almost none have ever been there. I do not think that it is uncool, but more that it is of only passing interest and not worth a side trip instead of something more exciting like the Madonna Inn. Last year my cousin and his wife visited from Denmark and stopped in Solvang on a return from Southern California. They were polite, but had little to say of it. I felt that they did not want to embarrass us by divulging their experience of the town.[20]

All three informants notice the impressionistic polished image, which shows Solvang as an "Unreflective Denmark blended with unreflective America."[21] Their accounts confirm that the painting reflects the impressions they have of the place suggesting that the Kinkade painting can be counted as rather successful in capturing Solvang. Yet in all of these accounts, the authenticity of Solvang along with the authenticity of Solvang as depicted in the painting, is rejected. At the same time, these informants let us know that maybe the authenticity might not be that important. As one informant says the painting depicts a "… Denmark away from Denmark: impressionistic, sunny, and (maybe?) better than the 'genuine' article."[22] The painting of Solvang and Solvang itself lure their audiences into nostalgic thinking, with an altered perception of time where the speed of life slows down to a standstill. Here one can go and hide if one can afford it. As my informants note, it is not for the poor and it is predominantly white. All three informants are themselves from the white upper middleclass, so they can easily decode the signs in both the painting and in Solvang, the tourist place, recognizing it as a location targeted exactly at them. It is perhaps even more interesting to note how they distance themselves from the both the painting and its subject. This distancing is a perfect example of "tourist shame," that "rhetoric of moral superiority" that MacCannell so aptly describes (MacCannell 1999, 9). As predicted by Culler, all of my informants had no trouble decoding the semiotics of the painting and the place, revealing in their analyses the "third person effect." That they reject the two representations of Solvang—one the painting and one the town—going out of their way to comment on the vulgarity of both underscores how the critique of tourism belongs to the tourists themselves (Enzensberger 1996). Simultaneous with the act of rejecting Solvang, the three informants trust that others might find it appealing. One of the informants points out that the kind of customer who would buy Kinkade's art is the same kind of tourist who comes to Solvang. And all three draw attention to what one calls *Danamarkana*: the old car, the flags, and the Main Street feeling.[23] Here the phenomemon is a fusion of something old and European but hard to place: "Dutch and Danish both start with 'd'. Is Solvang secretly intended to support the stereotypical American confusion of Europe?"[24] one of the informants asks rhetorically. All of my informants agree that Solvang is ultimately an American place for the American tourist.

The informants retell their first encounters with Solvang and, in analyzing the painting and the place, distance themselves from both rejecting the notion of authenticity and deferring the appeal of the place to that of the third person. There is nothing wrong with that, the reasoning goes, since there must be tourists who like both the town of Solvang and Thomas Kinkade. Each of these narrators of tourist experience comes close what has been labeled "the tourist moment" (Hom Cary 2004). This moment is one where the tourist, through the narration of his or her experiences as a tourist, erases the tourist-as-subject and thus goes beyond being a tourist. Rather than detailing an "authentic experience," the three narrators all engage with the positionality of the "post tourist."

They playfully juggle their experiences and analyze the multitude of layers that emerge in both Solvang the place and "Solvang" the painting. In Kinkade's painting, Denmark and Europe become iconic of a world long lost, one that is transfixed by the nostalgic white, middleclass tourist gaze where peace, tranquility and, above all, family values reign. As the first informant aptly states, Solvang attracts a very particular type of tourist with very particular types of desires and very particular values. Kinkade's paintings—as mirrored in Solvang (or is it vice-versa?)—embody, sell, and produce the US white middle-class tourist gaze that seeks refuge in a world where things are "still alright." As such, Solvang can be seen as a counter-image of the society that the tourist is trying to escape for a day or two. In Kinkade's picture, this nostalgic world is crucially and centrally made up of family values. Implicit in the need for the painting is the unspoken fear that these values are crumbling. It is not accidental that the Kinkade painting is accompanied by a very particular narrative, one that endorses values of heterosexual love and dedication. The painting—and by implication Solvang—become pure instantiations of "real love" and "the proper family" as performed by Kinkade and his wife and those nostalgically desired values of family, time, simplicity, tranquility, stability that are seamlessly transposed onto a faux European landscape of the past defined by white people, small towns, and small inns.

Conclusion

Kinkade paradoxically does an excellent job of painting a "first tourist gaze" painting, one that corresponds with the image of the town and its tourist dialectics. But as MacCannell points out, people do not stop with this first gaze; rather, they move on to the second gaze, looking beyond the surface image. Even if the tourist has fantastic critical skills coupled to a sophisticated ability to decode the semiotic signs of a tourist image, it does not necessarily mean that anything is lacking. These two first tourists gazes, fully ideological in their construction, can very well supplement each other, and do not necessarily conflict. To move beyond this situation, I propose the importance of a "third gaze," that of the actual tourist as verbalized by tourists themselves. This third gaze is aptly illustrated by the construction of Solvang the town and "Solvang" the Kinkade painting. Both painting and place are rejected by the first and second person tourist gaze, and the appeal of both are ultimately deferred to the appreciation of the other(s), the third person(s).

Notes

[1] http://www.purl.org/lindow/solvang.html Accessed November 18, 2011.

[2] J. B. Manager of Corporate Events, The Thomas Kinkade Company (3-23-05, Morgan Hill).

[3] D. M. Sales Associate, Thomas Kinkade Gallery (6-17-05, Solvang).

[4] D. M. Sales Associate, Thomas Kinkade Gallery (6-17-05, Solvang).

[5] http://www.purl.org/lindow/pleinair.jpf

[6] A drawn, etched, or incised scribble or sketch done on the margin of a plate or stone and removed before the regular printing. To "remarque" refers to a process used by French painters to authenticate a work by drawing an original sketch.

[7] http://www.purl.org/lindow/sales.jpf

[8] http://www.purl.org/lindow/pleinair.jpf

[9] http://www.purl.org/lindow/advert.jpf

[10] http://www.purl.org/lindow/solvang.html Accessed November 18, 2011.

[11] J. B. Manager of Corporate Events, The Thomas Kinkade Company (3-23-05, Morgan Hill).

[12] Later in his career Urry did analyze the tourist perception of photographs (Crawshaw & Urry 2005).

[13] In 2005 MacCannell pointed out the dissolution of front and back in such arenas as landscape, architecture, and personal taste, thus gesturing toward the inapplicability of Goffman's categories toward contemporary tourism theory. D. MacCannell, *Staged Authenticity Today*, keynote speech, *On Voyage: New Directions in Tourism Theory* Conference, UC Berkeley, 7 October, 2005.

[14] Half-timber.

[15] K. L. June 10th 2005.

[16] Danish pastry.

[17] The book referred to is *Class: A Guide Through the American Status System* (Fussell 1983).

[18] Nanette is the name of Kinkade's wife, it is not a teashop.

[19] J. B. April 14th 2006.

[20] R. T. April 10th 2006.

[21] K. L. June 10th 2005.

[22] K. L. June 10th 2005.

[23] K. L. June 10th 2005.

[24] J. B. April 14th 2006.

Fieldwork material, quoted interviews (in the author's possession):

J. B. Manager of Corporate Events, The Thomas Kinkade Company (3-23-05, Morgan Hill).

D. M. Sales Associate, Thomas Kinkade Gallery (6-17-05, Solvang).

K. L. (6-10-05, Solvang).

R.T. (4-10-06, Oakland).

J.B. (4-14-06, Berkeley).

The Spiritual Life of the *Seite*

Tok Thompson

The *seite* (spelled variously) is an important component of the cosmological world of the traditional Sámi.[1] The *seite* appear in many forms: man-made or natural, made from various materials, with sizes ranging from pocket-sized to large gathering areas. The *seite* are used by individuals, families, or whole communities, and played an integral role in traditional Sámi religious life. They are also tied to other areas of this religious life, such as shamanism and animism, through the idea of sacrifice. This paper reviews the scholarly discussions of *seite*, and attempts to arrive at an explanation of the traditional Sámi *seite* that can account for all its appearances and known aspects. In doing so, I find it necessary to examine the context in which the *seite* exists—that of traditional Sámi animism.[2] Using this framework, I suggest that analysis of the *seite* complex may be able to provide us with a glimpse into the cosmological views of the traditional Sámi, particularly in the role of spirit forces in the physical world.

Seite is a term that resists easy translation into English, perhaps in part due to radically different cultural traditions in the ways of conceiving the spiritual world. Like all sacred traditions, discussing the *seite* entails an investigation of the spiritual traditions surrounding the topic. A large focus of this paper is to arrive at a coherent explanation and understanding of the term *seite* and the history of *seite* sites in Sámiland. At its most basic definition, the *seite* may be said to be a particular form of material (usually stone, and often associated with particular sites) where there is a concentration of spiritual power. These concentrations of power are neither fully natural nor fully man-made in the Sámi view: rather, *seite* reveal a cosmological view of interplay between human and spiritual agents, and the complex traditions linking matter and spirituality.

Very often, a Sámi *seite* was a site of sacrificial worship, but it could also be a small object or "portable site." It would seem to be a distinctly Sámi oicotype of the worship of inanimate nature, a worship that is shared to some degree with other Finno-Ugric speakers such as the Ostyaks, Vogules and Samoyeds (Castren 1955, 21; Lehtisalo 1955). Items of sacrifice at the *seite* were usually animals, although there are archaeological and folk records of money or other valuable goods that were also used as sacrifices (Turi 1918-19, 8; Backman 1985, 92; see also Lahelma 2006 and Broadbent 2004). The animal to be sacrificed was usually related with the expected return. For example, a sacrifice of fish was generally held near a fishing stream and was performed to guarantee a bountiful harvest of fish. The *seite* were held to be cognizant entities that could help community members acquire resources that were scarce at times, particularly resources such as game.

Spiritual Life of the Seite.

The notion of a spirit supposes something characterized by having will, volition, awareness, and susceptibility. Like a shaman breathing life into a sending, a Sámi could muster various spiritual forces in a particular geographic area into a particular manifestation, and then communicate with this entity. This outlook would work equally well whether viewing a large mountain *seite* or a small hand-carved wooden post. The idea of a site seems crucial to the *seite*: even if the article to be worshiped was a small hand-crafted item, it was not kept inside a house or niche, but put outside in a site where it was in touch with the earth. A chthonic connection may have been prevalent: the *seite* always appears on the ground. This location may well have to do with the notions of the dead as being contained in the underworld: the spirit world was contained in, or at least related to, the *terra firma*. This connection between the earth and the spirit world may also explain why the *seite* seem to have had limited geographical reach in their abilities. In addition, there may be a connection between the site and a chthonic notion of fertility. In general *seite* were located in an area of lush growth (especially grass), or if not, and during wintertime, green fir branches were strewn about them (and when these withered, they were replaced with fresh green ones) (Holmberg 1915, 100). In short, there are connections between the sites chosen and their chthonic roles as dwellings of the dead, and as producers of new life.

We can view the *seite* as having been sites that were accumulations of spirit power. This accumulation, while often existing "naturally," could be augmented by the layperson by using the ritual of sacrifice to transfer spirit power from one object or groups of objects (i.e., a reindeer skeleton) to the *seite*, creating also a link between himself and that spirit power. Noting that the *seite* would also have had will, volition, awareness, and susceptibility, they could have then been entreated, bribed, or cajoled to expend their power for the good of the worshiper.

Theoretically, according to this view, nearly any object could have been made into a *seite*. Of course, choosing an object nearly devoid of spirit power makes a poor start for the accumulation necessary for a *seite*. The lack of initial spirit power may have also suggested that such an object would have been a poor receptacle for spirit forces, unable to keep them localized. Certainly it is obvious that striking physical manifestations of earth and stone were held as having spirit power, and making particularly appropriate *seite*.

There are numerous scholarly considerations of the *seite*. Many of the writers, however, investigate only one manifestation, often focusing on rock formations, rock paintings, or mountains as *seite*. Some studies focus only on *seite* made of stone rings that are often found at fishing sites (see Vorren, in Ahlbäck 1987, 94). Yet smaller man-made manifestations also seem to have been common among the traditional Sámi. I believe that any theory attempting to describe the *seite* should strive to describe all of these manifestations equally well. Early scholars naturally ascribe much of the *seite* as having developed along unilinear evolutionary stages from pre-animism (or "naturism" as Clodd refers to it) to animism and then to polytheism (Clodd 1905, 26). Reuterskiold, for example, hypothesized that originally every strikingly shaped tree or stone was thought to have a spirit inside (quoted in Karsten 1955, 21). These later became divinities shaped by the Sámi into anthropomorphic forms—a process that does seem to occur in many, but not all, *seite*. According to Reuterskiold's theory, the worship of mountains was a later development than the worship of unfashioned stones, and the worship of anthropomorphized shapes was an even later development, one leading towards the stage of polytheism. Karsten states, and I agree, that Reuterskiold's theory is limited by his imposed notion of strict evolutionary stages, yet his views correctly acknowledge the spirit the power in the *seite*.

While these early scholars often focused on making the *seite* fit the theory of cultural stage development, later scholars often took divergent paths in describing the *seite*. Holmberg generally refers to the *seite* as "gods" (Holmberg 1915, 101) and more specifically as tutelary deities of a lineage, connected with ancestor worship (Holmberg 1915, 104). Hultkrantz has written a great deal on Sámi religion and sees the *seite* as a general adaptation to pastoral nomadism: "(T)he cult of seite was common in all Lapp regions, and it is therefore important to know its ideological background. Probably the seite-cult was basically a relic from the ancient hunting and fishing culture, functionally adapted to reindeer nomadism in later times" (Hultkrantz 1955: 88).

Manker, in contrast, proposed that the *seite* was a synthesis of an incarnation of a divine ruler of the region, and the center of power for that region. As others have noted, Manker endorses the notion that ancestor worship was also involved in the *seite*, pointing out that the *seite* is frequently found in the *saivo* region, described by many as the realm of the dead. While the notion of a "divine ruler" may seem a bit of a poor fit for traditional Sámi society with its stress on egalitarianism and canon-less cosmological views, Manker is doubtless correct that there was an important connection between the *seite* and the *saivo*.

Saivo and Ancestor Worship

Saivo denotes a spiritual realm, consisting both of a physical place in this world (most usually mountains and lakes) and the spirits that inhabit that physical place. Hultkrantz agrees with Blackman that the term *saivo* "should primarily refer to the Saami guardian and helping spirits living in a sacred mountain"

(Hultkrantz 1985, 111). However, *saivo* were also closely connected with the dead, who play a major role in Sámi religion. Indeed, the spirits of the dead were understood to be in the realm of the *saivo*. It is interesting to note that Harva asserts that the worship of *seite* originated in this ancestor cult, while both Karsten and Hultkrantz note that this view is unsupported by any specific evidence (Harva 1955, 18).

Although some scholars see a definite connection—nearly an equivalence—between the *saivo* and the *seite*, it is important to note that distinctions were made by the traditional Sámi, and thus should be maintained by the interpreter. One important difference is that the *seite* was never a man's personal guardian spirit. The *seite* was a physical manifestation of a concentration of spiritual power, especially useful for producing bounteous harvests. Also, a *seite* was never a lake, but always some manifestation in wood or stone. Part of the confusion may arise since a *saivo* could be referred to as residing in a mountain, and the same mountain could be referred to as a *seite*. Still, not all *seite* are described as having *saivo*, and vice-versa. This view may also stem from attempts, such as Varian's (Varian 1987, 94) at defining the *seite* using just one or two of its possible manifestations. There is clearly some sort of connection between the *saivo* and the *seite*. In Turi's tales, ghosts are often seen at the old, abandoned *seite* (Turi 1918-19, 10). This appearance of ghosts at the *seite* take together with the Sámi belief in ghost spirits lingering around their gravesite, as well as the dead's connection to the *saivo* realm of the dead, suggest that sacrificed animals might link the *seite* and the *saivo*. This assumed link falls far short of the definite and intimate connection that several authors have proposed.

Society and Seite

One of the apparent anomalies in the study of the Sámi is that although they are often classified as pastoral nomads, their religious structure has much more in common with the animism usually associated with hunting and gathering societies. One way to resolve this paradox is to note that many of the traditional Sámi have never been pastoral nomads, and yet by and large share the same religious outlook (as Hultkrantz notes, there is a more detectable Scandinavian influence in the contact zones). The switch from a hunting and gathering society to reindeer herding is generally held to be a relatively late phenomenon among the Sámi, quite possibly well after 1500 CE (Hultkrantz 1985, 20). It is thus not surprising that the essential elements of traditional Sámi religion remained essentially that of a hunter-gatherer society (Hultkrantz 1985, 23). Reindeer herding may have influenced the *seite* complex in the pastoral nomad groups making it more focused on the reindeer and territorial usufruct rights. Parpola (2004) and Shumkin (1996) have argued from an archaeological standpoint that the *seite* derives from the most archaic aspects of Sámi pre-Christian religion with truly ancient roots as far back as the early Neolithic. Ultimately, *seite* worship seems to have been formed in a hunter-gatherer society. We should bear this in mind while examining social and social-structural approaches to the issue.

Animism

One of the most fundamental beliefs of animism is a belief in various spirit forces underlying the natural world. These spirit forces are seen as malleable, and, ultimately, controllable forces. In addition, these spirit forces are generally conceived of as cognizant or otherwise "alive." Such spirit forces included, but were not limited to, the Western idea of "souls," or spirit forces underlying humans. While Western cosmology usually limits souls as belonging to humans, it is obviously a gray area, with some people assigning animals some form of soul as well. The Sámi concept, then, was elaborate, including all sorts of spirit forces underlying most objects in the world, and even some processes and diseases. In addition, many spirit forces were present in the spirit world without being directly reflected in the natural world so that the physical world is an incomplete reflection of the spiritual world.

While animism is usually classed as a religion, it may be more useful to note that animism is also (and perhaps even more so) a particular worldview (see, for example, Pentikäinen 1997, 52). Whereas modern Americans often view religion only as dealing with the divine, most animists would not draw such a fine distinction between the profane and the sacred. "Religion" would thus be a bit of a misnomer in the worldview of animism. "Spirituality" perhaps comes closer, but is still limited by our own modern definition. Hence I prefer the term "worldview," noting that the view implied by the term includes in this case the spiritual and often cosmological as well.

All scholars agree that the Sámi are animistic. Manker states of the traditional Sámi: "Forces of nature were regarded by them as divinities, and all things—animals, plants, or lifeless object—had a soul. The dead continued to live in a world not much unlike that of the living. The [Sámi] lived in a spiritual world that was for them as real as the material world. This was pure animism."[3] More recently, Mulk agrees on the centrality of animism: "Everything was regarded as living, as a part of the cosmos" (1994, 130). Thus, we can thus safely speak of the *seite* complex as existing within a framework of animism. Shamanism, the craft specialization often found in an animistic framework, is also usually credited to the Sámi, albeit sometimes with provisos. Shumkin, for example, sees shamanism as a more recent influence from the east (albeit still ancient: two thousand BCE or so), adding to the animistic framework already focused on the *seite* (Shumkin 128). Other authors (Hagen) have noted the degree to which the *noaide*, sometimes instead translated as "wizard," seems distinct from his shaman contemporaries of their circumpolar neighbors to the east.

Looking at animism as a "deficient religion," an approach that is an artifact of colonialism, has tainted much of the work done on the topic. The view almost certainly stems from the implicit acceptance of the teleological view of cultural stage development. Rather than an "evolution" of cosmology, in fact, the changes in religion may have much more to do with changes in economic, social, or political systems undertaken by the societies deeming themselves "developed." Hultkrantz suggests that one can see the shift from the hunting and gathering society of the traditional Sámi to pastoral nomadism as producing an ancestral "Spirit of the Reindeer" (Backman 1985, 24). Ostensibly this can be attributed to changes in the economic base, but it also seems to hearken back to stage evolution theories, with the "Spirit of the Reindeer" representing the change to polytheism accorded those of the higher cultural stage. While it is possible to generalize the "spirits of the reindeer" (animistic ancestor worship) to "Spirit of the Reindeer" (polytheism) and even, theoretically, to the Great Spirit (monotheism), it should be noted that these distinctions are made by scholars, and not by the animists themselves. It may be that in the animistic worldview of the cosmos there would be no need to differentiate between all three such labeling of things, or that such a labeling might be more arbitrary than real. In this case the Sámi may have shifted the frame of reference towards reindeer concerns, more than undergoing a complete shift in worldview, as is implied by any notion of "moving toward polytheism." In other words, the emphasis simply shifted according to the needs of the community—in this case, in securing more reindeer fecundity and general welfare—just as it normally would at various seasonal sites, such as the fish *seite* at the fish camp.

The Dead

Among the most important spirit forces for the Sámi are the spirits of the dead, often identified closely with the *saivo*. The Sámi, like most people in the world, believe in some sort of spiritual existence after death. They also believe that one could communicate with the dead. It is generally agreed that ancestor worship was important to the Sámi, and Krohn and Harva go so far as to say that it was the most important religious form for the traditional Sámi (Karsten 1955, 106). Yet the label "worship" may be misleading. Various accounts tell of the dead being feared as malignant entities, and other accounts tell of the dead being held in servitude by the living (Turi 1918-19, 15). It seems that the relationship between the attitudes of worship and servitude may have been a fluid one, and the dead may have been variously entreated, bribed, or cajoled according to local tradition or even individual circumstances. Certainly, the dead were never thought of as unreachable, and instead often had the characteristic of being far too present (Karsten 1955, 110).

In spite of the danger inherent in dealing with the dead, it was often considered worthwhile. The dead were considered to have knowledge otherwise unavailable to the living. Communicating with these, and other similarly dangerous spirits, was the shaman's specialty. The *seite* was connected with the idea of spirits of the dead primarily through sacrificial acts. It may well be that the some of the same cultural principles applied to the human realm of the dead may be applied to the non-human realm. If this is the case, then it may prove interesting to note similarities and differences between these two traditions—ancestor worship and the interconnectedness of the sacrificial animal to the rest of the animal species or ancestral spirit force. It is also interesting to note the Sámi's chthonic notion of the proper placing of the human dead—in general, these were held to be properly buried as near as possible to the place of death (Karsten 1955, 110). This proximity suggests a link between the spirit and the ground. If this Sámi view were also true of their view of animal souls as well, the merging of them into the *seite* through sacrifice would be an inherently natural act, albeit one magnified by human agency.

Localizing Spirits

Karsten states that the ancient Sámi had "a general vague idea about the nether regions also being inhabited by mysterious spiritual beings, but this idea did not become localized in the proper sense of the word until they found an obvious testimony of their existence through some remarkable concrete phenomenon above ground. Then they were at once ready to personify and to deify it" (1955, 19). Karsten's theory is attractive in that assumes a background of belief in spiritual forces. Still, he does not allow the ancient Sámi to have a fully animistic viewpoint, instead limiting them to a "vague idea" about the nether regions. Also, he limits the origins of the *seite* to be in the Sámi 's recognition of something remarkable in a natural object. This stance may be hard to reconcile with the other more unremarkable *seite*, and the also-prevalent construction of *seite*, often from wood poles, unless one is prepared to argue that these are a later development.

The creation of *seite* versus the "discovery" of *seite* is a thorny issue: to what degree is the *seite* a natural process, and to what degree is it influenced by human agency? In this regard the *seite* has analogies to other supernatural entities, one group of which is the spirits of the dead. These spirits were often "trapped" in grave tokens or other fetishes, to become slaves to the living, particularly the shaman. Another would be the Sámi *stallo*, which could either be made by a shaman, or be encountered in a "natural" state. In looking at the *stallo* (and other shamanic spirit traditions), it is important to note that the shaman forms the substance quite naturally and mechanically, and then ritually brings the spirit into the form. There is a question, then, whether the shaman "creates" the spirit, or merely localizes an already existing spirit from the spirit world into a particular manifestation. An example of this would be the creation of the *tupilak* by Eskimo shamans, as reported by Merkur (Ahlbäck 1987, 287). It is the second explanation that I believe may serve as a model for the "creation" of a *seite*.

Once a notion of localizing spirit forces is in place in a cosmology, the pathway for the *seite* becomes clear, whether this notion was originally because of striking natural shapes becoming personified (as per the view of Lahelma), or because of some other practice, such as the shamanic creation of a *stallo* or the custom of the carved burial totem. A striking natural phenomenon might be have been recognized as an exceptional manifestation of spirit power. Still, it seems unlikely that these would have been considered as "of themselves" fully *seite*, for, as Karsten himself notes, the power of the *seite* "appears to have been wholly dependent on the sacrifices offered to it" (1955, 23). Even if Karsten overstates the point, it is clear that there is a close relationship between human action and the existence of the *seite*. Per Hogstrom notes that that the power of the *seite* was usually proportional to the number of worshipers and the amount of sacrifices. He also observes that, "if it happens that the offerings are suspended, they at the same time lose their power and then are not able to do good nor ill" (Karsten 1955, 92). As such, a *seite* could be threatened, punished, abandoned, and even destroyed. All this suggests that *seite* were to some degree made, and that people worked to bring the spirit power into them.

Still it would be a mistake to say that the *seite* were never viewed as outward manifestations of spiritual forces inherent in natural features. Fellman, for instance, says that in general all stones and mountains that were strikingly shaped were seen as sacred (Karsten 1955 13). In a society that accepts the localization of spirit forces, this might in fact make for a proper start for a *seite*. The less striking *seite* manifestations, or the man-made ones, would then be, according this hypothesis, more (and perhaps even wholly) the results of human action in localizing the spirit forces, a position borne out by Hogstrom (Holmberg 1915, 109), who reports that the Sámi regarded the *seite* of stone to be much more holy than those of wood. The line between the two concepts might have been very fluid. A particular site might have been chosen as a *seite* because of a belief in some resident spirit power, which could then have been further augmented by worship and sacrifice. Huggert perhaps puts it best: "The divine or sacred was something that the Saami perceived in nature. An unusual geographical formation could indicate the presence of the divinity. When a formation was interpreted in that way, it soon stood out as having a distinctive character and had the capacity to be a holy place" (Huggert 2000, 63). The *seite* is a nexus between the human realm and the spirit realm.

Proprietary Rights, Gender, and other Social Roles

Seite sites anchored usufruct traditions of territory, inscribing the landscape with spiritual as well as political ties to individuals, families, and villages. Recent reviews have emphasized the ideas of territorial rights and local *seite*, particularly in the historic age of early Norse colonization and territorial expansion (*e.g.* Broadbent 2004, Huggert 2000). The worshipers of the *seite* could be few or many. There were village *seite* of differing rank, importance, and number of worshipers, and there were individually worshiped—or "owned" depending on one's view—*seite* as well (Tornaeus, in Karsten 1955, 19). Accordingly, the *seite* has a great deal in common with owned spirits found in many animistic worldviews.

Among the Sámi, the shaman would frequently own *saivo*. Backman asserts that this ownership was formerly common among other Sámi as well (Ahlbäck 1987, 118). These *saivo* spirits could be handed down along family lines, and there is some evidence to suggest that they were even bought and sold, and used as dowry (Ahlbäck 1987,115). Yet one difference between the *saivo* and the *seite* is that the *seite* were not particularly associated with shamanism or with shamans. An explanation for this might be that the notion of *seite*, that is the localization of spirit forces in a physical manifestation maintained by sacrifice, is itself already a craft, a known narrative, and thus achievable by laymen. *Saivo* spirits, while ownable by laymen, were usually "captured" by the shaman. Indeed it was the shaman who were the usual owners of *saivo* (Ahlbäck 1987,113), although they could sell these spirits to others.

Like the *saivo*, however, some proprietary rights of the *seite* are apparent (Karsten 1955, 19). Colinder quotes Jessen as saying that one man was known to have owned thirteen sacred places, his wife six, and their daughter six as well (Colinder 1949, 167). Although women could own *seite*, the *seite* conceptually remained in the domain of men: women were not normally allowed to sacrifice at them, or even to be near them. There were many taboos and prescribed avoidances for women regarding the *seite*, a phenomenon consistent with the taboos on women regarding much of the spiritual world. Yet these taboos seem particularly salient in the *seite* case, since the *seite* were usually used for the increase in the masculine realm of game.

These proprietary rights, as well as the actual belief and worship of *seite*, point to multiple functions for the *seite* in the Sámi society. The ability to communicate with spirits to acquire food must have been a valuable resource to a society relying on the fickle hand of nature. Similarly, the proprietary rights of worship must have acted as a homeostatic device for the society: those in charge were able to plead for sustenance for the whole group. If the *seite* failed, and game was not forthcoming, the site could be deemed powerless and destroyed in a scapegoating act venting community anxieties.

Spiritual Role of the Seite and Their Sacrificial Offerings

One way to approach this underlying belief system is to inquire into the spiritual role of the sacrificial worship given to the *seite*. Several writers speak of the sacrifice as "gifts" or bribes to the recipient (Holmberg 1915, 111). In the case of the Sámi blood-sacrifice system, the sacrifices are described as "gifts of food" for the gods. Some theorists have been led by this idea to comment on the poor nutritional value of some of the items left (horns, bone, etc.) as being related to "traditional Sámi stinginess" (revealing the racism inherent in much of the early Nordic scholarly views of Sámi), or to be puzzled by smaller *seite*-like unique natural objects left as sacrifices.

In trying to avoid these pitfalls, I think it is important to take the view shared by Karsten and others, that what was "consumed" by the *seite* was the spirit power localized within the sacrificial item. The horns were no more important to the sacrifice than rock was to the *seite* itself. What was undertaken was on the spiritual plane, and what was transferred was spirit power. This power was considered to be connected to the physical object. Karsten notes that "by blood-sacrifices or other offerings they tried to transfer to the god or *seite* the power he needed to be enabled, in his turn, to help man in his struggle for existence" (1955, 21). Importantly, Karsten includes "other offerings" besides blood-sacrifices, although the blood-sacrifices do seem to have been the most salient feature of their worship. In the animistic worldview of the traditional Sámi, there may have been no difference on the spiritual plane between an offering of blood and of something else, for everything is aware. The Sámi Johan Turi says: "The animals, the trees, the stones and other inanimate things have lost the power of speech, but they still retain hearing and intellect. Therefore it is necessary to treat the animals well and to regard all things as if they were living beings who hear and understand" (Karsten 1955 22).

The spirit world was a constant companion to the Sámi who considered there to be connections between many, if not all, beings in the spirit world. This spirit world was a more or less differentiated but interwoven mesh of spirit forces, some localized in one direction, some in others, but all ultimately a part of the same spirit world. Nothing, it seems, could be truly removed from the spirit world. Spirit forces could, however, be localized differently—the shamans could control spirits or bind them to a particular locality, person, or grave site (Backman 1985, 206). Similarly, the sacrifice of an animal to a *seite* was ultimately a transfer of the spirit power of the animal. Here again spirit power, while not removable from the spirit world, could be localized, and accumulated at a particular physical manifestation. In doing so, the Sámi ultimately attempted to build a localization of spirit power that could effect fortuitous change.

Worship itself seems to have had the potential to influence the spirit world. Blood-sacrifice certainly seems to have been able to form a link between the ancestral forces of the sacrificed while non-blood sacrifices and worship created links to the officiator. Perhaps worship is best viewed as the officiator creating a link between his spirit force and the *seite*'s. In other words, the officiator allows a part of his self to be consumed, in order to be bonded with the *seite*'s spirit force. This interpretation of worship is deliberately reminiscent of Mauss' theory of the gift in which he articulates an elemental notion of reciprocity. Writing about the exchange of material items, he says, "everything is stuff to be given away and repaid. In perpetual interchange of what we may call spiritual matter, these elements pass and re-pass between clans, and individuals, ranks, sexes, and generations" (Mauss 1954, 11-12). Once given, the gift has not merely passed on, but rather has created a bond between the giver and the receiver. The very act alters the both of them, and in some sense joins them. Some theorists of the *seite* believe that this elemental notion of reciprocity accounts for the very origin of the *seite*. Colinder states: "It seems natural to the nomad that he should now and then give a reindeer to the habitual calving place, or to the glacier where his reindeer used to cool and find refuge from the midges on hot summer days" (Colinder 1949, 165). This notion of creating a link with the Otherworld may be in important one. Turi writes of a sacrificer: "And the Devil it was who received his offering and protected his seite, and it were the angels of the Devil who should protect him in all affairs and be of help whenever it was necessary. And when he died, then he became an angel of the Devil, and that he must be now" (Turi 1918-19, 13).[4] Compare this with E. O. James' statement in his classic *Sacrifice and Sacrament*, where he states that: "...the primary purpose of the sacrificial gift is to establish and maintain a vital bond of union between the worshipper and the object of worship..." (James 1962, 26). While Jan de Vries asserts that "it appears impossible to find a positive sense in slaying humans and animals, as an offering to the gods," and continues by noting that "[t]he question is whether we are able to point to any culture within which such sacrifices are meaningful" (de Vries 1967, 203), such sacrifices make perfect sense given the cosmological worldview of the traditional Sámi. It is precisely our separation of the death of animals from the divine world that obstructs Western apprehension of the potential spiritual meaning of such actions.

Conclusion

Since souls in this worldview are not wholly differentiated from their ancestral spirit force, we can speak of an amorphous spirit force, comprised of different spirit forces, subsuming some spirit forces, and being subsumed by others in turn. It is ultimately the same structure as life itself, albeit on a spiritual plane: Eating, growing stronger, being eaten by others. The Sámi included human souls with the other spirit forces—using the same metaphor, we can see that the traditional Sámi placed themselves, their very souls, within the food chain, in the circle of life itself, rather than outside of it or above it. With this view, it becomes easier to understand the functioning of the *seite* within Sámi cosmology. In describing, as many do, the *seite* as divine, it raises improbable notions that the Sámi actually believed that interestingly shaped rocks were gods, even though the *seite* manifesting great power were treated with the respect normally accorded the divine. It also raises questions as to the Sámi's sacrilegious behavior when the gods did not perform as expected. If we view the *seite* as living organisms, then when the *seite* does not produce the required results, it is interpreted as no longer channeling the spirit force requisite of that respect—not very "lively". At that point, there is nothing there to consider very religious.

The move towards viewing the *seite* as "alive" is surely an improvement. The *seite* has, like many objects in an animistic worldview, a dual meaning: that of the profane object, and that of the spirit power localized in (or through) that object. The spirit power of the *seite* was inherently an entity, which became more powerful the more spirit force it subsumed. It was localized in a particular object that was in turn localized in a particular place. It had ties to various ancestral spirits and it had deep bonds with the spirit forces in a given geographic area. Viewed in this manner, the *seite* can be seen as a portal to the chthonic realm itself, out of which life emerges and to which it returns.

Notes

1 In this chapter, I use "traditional" to mean those Sámi following the practices and cosmologies that were lodged with the Sámi communities before the cultural encroachment of colonization.

2 Several recent works have explored both Sámi shamanism's uniqueness and its ties to wider Northern Eurasian shamanism. See, for example, Hagen (2006).

3 Eliade asserts that shamanism is preeminently a religious phenomenon of Siberia and Central Asia, although he includes "arctic" peoples as well in other places. Even Eliade, however, does not limit the accounts of shamanism to these areas.

Celebrating Difference, Enforcing Conformity[1]

Valdimar Tr. Hafstein

El Condor Pasa

The Intangible Heritage Convention was a long time coming. It is customary within UNESCO to speak of three decades of negotiation. A letter dated 24 April 1973 is thought to mark the beginning of these concerns in the UN. The letter is addressed to the Director-General of UNESCO from the Minister of Foreign Affairs and Religion of the Republic of Bolivia. "My ministry has made a careful survey of existing documentation on the international protection of the cultural heritage of mankind," the letter begins, and it has found that all existing instruments

> ... are aimed at the protection of tangible objects, and not forms of expression such as music and dance, which are at present undergoing the most intensive clandestine commercialization and export, in a process of commercially oriented transculturation destructive of the traditional cultures... (Republic of Bolivia, Ministry of Foreign Affairs and Religion 1973)

In his letter, the Bolivian minister makes three suggestions: first, that a new protocol be added to the Universal Copyright Convention from 1952 "declaring all rights in cultural expressions of collective or anonymous origin which have been elaborated or [have] acquired traditional character in the territory of particular Member States to be the property of such States;" second, that a convention be signed "to regulate the aspects of folklore preservation, promotion and diffusion" and an "International

Register of Folkloristic Cultural Property" established alongside it; and, third, that the Intergovernmental Committee of the Universal Copyright Convention adjudicate any disputes concerning the "assignation of paternity between two or more States in respect of common forms of expression" (Republic of Bolivia, Ministry of Foreign Affairs and Religion 1973).

I'll come back to the suggestions, but first I would like to tell you a story about this letter. It is an account that UNESCO sometimes gives about how it came to concern itself with folklore. It begins three years before this letter was delivered by diplomatic courier; it begins with the release in 1970 of the album *Bridge over Troubled Water* by Paul Simon and Art Garfunkel (Albro 2005, 4; Honko 2001; Sherkin 2001, 54 note 13). On one of the tracks, Simon and Garfunkel perform "El Condor Pasa," accompanied by the Peruvian group Los Incas, whom they had heard perform this song at a concert in Paris. "El Condor Pasa" is an indigenous folksong from the Andes, arranged and incorporated into a larger composition in 1913 by the Peruvian composer and folksong collector Daniel Alomía Robles. In Robles' version, the song commemorates an indigenous revolt against white oppressors who abuse the native population while the condor soars above, ruler of the skies and spirit of the Incas. *Bridge over Troubled Water* won the Grammy award for the record of the year and instantly reached the number one spot on Billboard's pop album chart, where it sat for six weeks. It is still one of the highest-selling albums of all time.

Perhaps the American artists were showing solidarity with poor, oppressed peoples in performing "El Condor Pasa." Whether or not that was their intention, there was no jubilation in the Andes. On the contrary, as seen from the Andes this must have looked less like a celebration of indigenous music and more like exploitation. Rich Americans had ransacked the musical tradition of poor people in the Andes and made a lot of money, not a dime of which was returned to the rightful "owners"—a pattern not unfamiliar from colonial expropriation, though this time around even the condor itself was siphoned off, a symbol of native pride. The whole affair left a bad taste in many mouths and, according to this etiology, the Bolivian letter to UNESCO's Director General in 1973 is a political expression of this bad taste (López 2004; Moreno; Sherkin 2001, 54 note 13).

The story is more intricate, however, if we read against the grain. Consider its political backdrop. The government that sent this letter was a military dictatorship, led by General Hugo Banzer who came to power by coup in 1971. He banned opposition parties, suspended trade unions, and shut down universities. Not surprisingly, Banzer's regime also had strained relations with the country's indigenous groups. The Aymara and the Quechua lived in abject poverty in the highlands and towns of Bolivia, their lands confiscated and their identities suppressed. Meanwhile, the military regime celebrated their expressive culture and appropriated it as the national-popular culture of Bolivia. Banzer was in power during the golden age of the folkloric spectacle, which celebrates traditional costume and music and dance in colorful performances of national pride and harmony; indeed, the folkloric spectacle was a favorite form of entertainment under dictators, from Franco's Spain and Salazar's Portugal to Pinochet's Chile and Banzer's Bolivia (cf. DaCosta Holton 2005; Ortiz 1999).

It is important to understand, then, that the Bolivian government's efforts to protect an indigenous Andean folksong hide the real oppression of indigenous peoples within Bolivia in this period. This is especially insidious because "El Condor Pasa" is a song of resistance. As a matter of fact, the South American dictators of the 1970s also appropriated the condor, converting a symbol of defiance to a symbol of compliance enforced at gunpoint: along with Pinochet and others, Banzer was one of the ringleaders in "Operation Condor", a transnational murder ring coordinated by intelligence agencies to quash dissent (McSherry 2005). The lesson of "El Condor Pasa" thus extends beyond the transnational flows of culture. This story explains how folklore came to be inscribed on the international agenda, but it also sheds light on the uses of folklore in hegemonic strategies within states, how folklore is instrumentalized in subject formation under conditions of internal colonialism. What's more, these are difficult to disentangle; invoking a threat from the outside (e.g., "the most intensive clandestine commercialization and export"), the government's measures for protection may in effect serve as means of dispossession.

Filching and Clandestine Transfer of Another People's Culture

The 1973 request from the government of Bolivia was a major catalyst for the inscription of folklore on the international agenda. After more than three decades of deliberations, it is extraordinary to consult the letter from 1973 and to find how closely the work still being conducted follows its formulation and how little the problems seem to have changed, despite dozens upon dozens of expert meetings, workshops, roundtables, consultations, committees, and fact-finding missions over the course of these decades (Hafstein 2004b).

Questions of property, sovereignty, and the role of the state still rank high among concerns to be addressed, and they are all still very contentious. The need for registers and lists is still a divisive question (Hafstein 2008). Moreover, the transnational circulation of folklore remains a source of considerable dispute concerning the so-called "paternity" of particular traditions. As evidenced by the Bolivian minister's misgivings about "the most intensive clandestine commercialization and export" of Bolivian traditions, patrimonial pride is often intertwined with an aggrieved sense of ownership or entitlement that demands recognition. This is perhaps most obvious in repatriation claims and cases (Brown and Bruchac 2006, Greenfield 1996, Skrydstrup n.d.). Driven, seemingly, by just such a sense of aggrieved ownership, several local councils responsible for safeguarding designated UNESCO masterpieces have sought to trademark "their" practices or have threatened to launch copyright proceedings to suppress what they claim are unauthorized copies of their heritage by outsiders, in some cases neighboring towns. Among the UNESCO masterpieces involved are the carnival in Binche in Belgium (Tauschek 2007), the Patum festival in Berga, Spain (Noyes 2006), and the Oruro carnival in Bolivia (Oruro Carnival).

Such legal actions blatantly ignore the actual workings of traditional culture and make unwarranted assumptions about the uniqueness of the practices they seek to protect (cf. Noyes 2006). Indeed, I would argue that copying is the condition of culture. If copulation is the central act on which humanity's biological continuity depends, reproduction is at the heart of the cultural condition. We are born into culture, it precedes and constitutes us. Human beings become cultured—become human—through mimesis: allowing themselves, by means of imitation, to become possessed.

Under certain conditions, however, the relationship is reversed: people possess culture. In a private property regime, culture is appropriated and defined as an asset, much in the same way that land is translated into real estate; it enters the system of property relations and acquires exchange-value. Through this reversal, culture suddenly becomes subject to theft. Imitation has to be regulated and unlimited proliferation of copies becomes inappropriate. The institution of authorship is one of the central tools developed to contain this proliferation and regulate imitation (Foucault 1977). Authorship, in the modern sense, arises as a product of possessive individualism in Western societies, as a complement to the individual subject who gains substance through its possessions and creations. The legal counterpart to authorship is the institution of copyright. Together these institutions seek to "authorize" and thus restrict copying as a form of exchange. Hence, culture is parceled up into "works" and reified as "intellectual property" or "cultural property" (Hafstein 2004a; Hesse 1991; Jaszi 1994; Rose 1993; Woodmansee 1994a and 1994b; Woodmansee and Jaszi 1994).

Returning once more to the Bolivian letter from 1973, the minister expresses grave concern about the foreign appropriation of Bolivian traditions. In particular, he seems concerned that his neighbors are ripping off Bolivian songs, dances, and costumes:

> In the sphere of the dance, folk dances . . . are being appropriated by other countries wholly unconnected with their genesis to be passed off by them, even in international competitions, as folk dances of their own. In the particular case of Bolivia which, owing to its geographical situation, suffers greatly from

> depredations of this kind, certain organizations from
> neigbouring countries go so far as to send here
> complete sets of costumes for the main Bolivian folk
> dances, and engage "embroiderers," "mask makers"
> and even choreographers (of peasant "folk" origin) to
> organize this switching or deliberate non-spontaneous
> transculturation process which amounts to the
> filching and clandestine transfer of another people's
> culture. (Republic of Bolivia, Ministry of Foreign
> Affairs and Religion 1973)

And then there is of course the story of Simon and Garfunkel
and "El Condor Pasa." Since national laws are unable to contain
unlicensed appropriation by non-nationals, the Bolivian minister
suggests adding a special protocol to international copyright law
that would enable governments to control the circulation of
folklore by making it state property: "declaring all rights in cultural
expressions of collective or anonymous origin which have been
elaborated or [have] acquired traditional character in the territory of
particular Member States to be the property of such States" (ibid.).

Mercifully, the minister's suggestions have not been
implemented. While a few states—notably Ghana (Kuruk 1999,
799; cf. Expert Criticises Copyright Bill 2005), but others as well—
have gone ahead and claimed all folklore in their territory, the last
thing anybody needs is for the international community to declare
all vernacular culture state property. If this has not happened,
however, it has not been for lack of trying. Indeed, UNESCO
collaborated in the 1970s and early 80s with the World Intellectual
Property Organization (WIPO) to create an international copyright
instrument that would have done just that. The fruits of this
collaboration were two in number: in 1982 the organizations
adopted the so-called "Model Provisions for National Laws on the
Protection of Expressions of Folklore against Illicit Exploitation
and Other Prejudicial Actions". These were not widely used to
develop national legislation, however, and their effect on the
international circulation of folklore has been very limited. Two
years later, in 1984, the same organizations proposed a "Draft
Treaty for the Protection of Expressions of Folklore" that dealt

with intellectual property protection at the international level. Due to strenuous objections from richer states, however, the Draft Treaty was never adopted.

After the treaty was rejected in the mid-1980s, UNESCO and WIPO parted ways. The work on folklore protection at the international level has since been on two separate tracks. WIPO has dealt with questions of ownership and exchange, whereas UNESCO has dealt with safeguarding and listing. After a bad run of unsuccessful attempts, the new Intangible Heritage Convention is looking promising, at least by political measures: a binding instrument entered into force in April 2006 and three years later 112 states were already parties to it.

Meanwhile, in Geneva, the World Intellectual Property Organization operates a special body that emerges out of this same history: The Intergovernmental Committee on Intellectual Property and Genetic Resources, Traditional Knowledge and Folklore. Founded in 2000, the committee owes its existence to dissatisfaction among poorer countries with the global imbalance of the intellectual property system, and to pressure from indigenous peoples worldwide. Its mandate is to discuss and negotiate local and international measures to protect folklore and traditional knowledge using the intellectual property regime (Wendland 2004; cf. Hafstein 2004a).

Folklore is the Anti-Authored

The system of intellectual property protection, which is supposed to encourage creativity and innovation, systematically excludes the knowledge and creativity of a large portion of humanity—the same people, in fact, who are denied medicine because of intellectual property. Thus, in order to qualify for copyright protection, a work of art, a design, or a piece of music, must be an original creation of a particular author. Likewise, in order to be granted patent protection, technology and know-how need to pass the test of novelty and involve an inventive step. By means of such criteria, traditional knowledge and expressions are ruled out on principle.

The concept of the creative process that underpins regimes of intellectual property is based on the ideal of the solitary genius; this Romantic notion, canonized in international law, has no patience with cultural processes or with products that are developed in a more diffuse, cumulative, and collective manner, where it is impossible to fix specific steps like invention or authorship at any given point in time.

The Romantic authorship ideal is intimately associated with the rise of capitalism. Its historical emergence coincides with the liberalization of the book trade in Europe and the invention of copyright. Thus in England, for example, a monopoly system was put in place when the printing press first arrived; the king licensed only a handful of printers to use the printing press, printers who belonged to the Stationer's Company. After a run of three centuries or so, this licensing system was replaced in the 18th century by a market system; instead of total monopoly being invested in a few publishers, any publisher could now claim a limited monopoly right in a particular book for a restricted period of time: invoking this "copyright", the printer could prevent others from copying the book for a given number of years. At the end of that period, the protection expires and the work enters the public domain, which means anyone is free to copy it, distribute it, and use it at will (Rose 1993; Patterson 1968).

However, the public domain did not predate copyright—it came into being with copyright and through copyright. Before copyright was invented, the right to copy any and all books in Britain belonged exclusively to printers in the Stationer's Company: There was no public domain. Moreover, when the law of copyright was formulated, first in Britain, then in France, Germany, and the United States, legislators also imposed limits on the kind of work eligible for protection. These limits were measured by the criterion of originality, and they were entangled with an ideal of authorship that was beginning to emerge in this era. Therefore, the law of copyright also placed in the public domain all works that did not fit the individual author-concept of the time and did not measure up to the criterion of originality: this included tales and ballads that people had begun to collect from popular tradition in this same period—for after all this is also when Percy's *Reliques of Ancient English Poetry* and Macpherson's *Works of Ossian* first saw the light of day and Herder's *Stimmen der Völker in Liedern* swept across the continent (Stewart 1994; Woodmansee 1994b). The invention of the public domain relates directly to the invention of folklore as a category and concept. In other words, folklore and the public domain have been related from the outset.

Folklore, in fact, came to be defined as such only with reference to norms of originality and ownership intrinsic to authorship and the intellectual property regime. A critical genealogy allows us to understand folklore as a constitutive outside of authorship. Folklore is the non-authored, or better yet, it is the anti-authored.

The Universal Mimicry of the Subaltern

The formation of folklore as a discursive category is thus to be sought in the rise of possessive individualism in the expressive sphere. More precisely, popular tradition is the remainder of the author concept. It stands in precisely the same relation to the author as the popular masses do to the individual bourgeois subject, by which they are remaindered. These are, if you like, residual concepts. They are brought into being through the invention of authorship and subjectivity, in much the same way as the public domain was brought into being through the creation of intellectual property. To cite a parallel, with the ascendancy of psychoanalysis in the early twentieth century, normalcy came to be defined through its remainders, neurosis and insanity (Baudrillard 1994, 145). I would suggest that the collection and study of folklore circumscribed the author concept in a similar fashion.

The distinction between authorship and folklore, and the distinction between intellectual property and the public domain, go hand in hand, of course, with the division of wealth, within society and between societies. The author came into his own as a hegemonic reflex of the rise of the European bourgeoisie and the ascendance of the bourgeois subject. While Romantics elevated bourgeois authors to the rank of original geniuses and ratified their private ownership over their own works, they also coined concepts like "folktales" and "folksongs" to refer to texts circulating among common people, which, in contrast to novels and books of poetry, were supposedly recycled, unauthored, and not owned by anyone. Thus, creativity and originality were the privilege of the bourgeoisie, while the masses were unoriginal and could only transmit the songs and tales of earlier generations. The art of the common people consisted only of copies. It took bourgeois authors to create original works of art out of these artless texts of popular tradition. Their originality entitled them to property rights in their art, whereas the recycled poetry of the commoners belonged to no one in particular and was there for anyone's taking.

In fact, folklorists went so far as to posit aristocratic origins for popular tradition: that folksongs and the like had been composed by men of refined taste and good breeding before sliding down the social ladder to commoners who preserved them in bastardized versions, as in Hans Naumann's theory of folklore as "gesunkene Kulturgut" (see esp. Bendix 1997, 113-118; Dundes 1969, 5-7). Such theories rationalized bourgeois claims to folk culture, as well as the scholarly task of reconstruction.

The theory of gesunkene Kulturgut was one side in a debate vociferously fought out in the early twentieth century, a debate that is in essence political (Vaz da Silva 2010). The other side, which ultimately won out, dismissed the search for absolute origins in favor of a theory of gradual adaptation through imperfect imitation, captured in Phillipps Barry's succinct formula of "individual origins and communal re-creation" (Barry 1914, 1934, and 1961; see Hafstein 2004a, 308-309).

Barry's formula reworks that of Swiss folklorist Eduard Hoffmann-Krayer, who, in 1903, wrote, "Die Volksseele produziert nicht, sie reproduziert" ("The 'soul of the folk' does not produce, it reproduces"). If we cross Hoffmann-Krayer with Italian marxist Antonio Gramsci, and substitute the notion of subalternity for the Romantic "Volksseele", we have, I think, a rather accurate representation of the hegemonic view of cultural production among subordinated groups: *The subaltern do not produce, they reproduce.*

This applies not only to European peasants, of course, but to other categories of subalterns, such as, for example, African-Americans in the United States. Thus, it was a commonplace well into the twentieth century that African-American expression was based on mimesis, that it was unoriginal—reproductive rather than creative (this was supposedly not the case with white artists). In a treatise from 1933 titled "Characteristics of Negro Expression", folklorist Zora Neale Hurston even made a point of discussing "[t]he Negro's universal mimicry" (Hurston 1999, 293). She notes that "[i]t has been said so often that the Negro is lacking in originality that is has almost become a gospel" (Hurston 1999, 300). Hurston objects to this common wisdom, "because", she remarks with characteristic acuity, "[w]hat we really mean by originality is the modification of ideas" (Hurston 1999, 300).

Subalterns in Western societies were not alone in being sentenced to perpetual redundancy. Note that Zora Neale Hurston spoke of the "the Negro's *universal* mimicry", and indeed "African Africans" were sentenced to endless repetition and mimicry in much the same way as African-Americans. It was the same with other colonized populations; their artistry was conceived of as mere reproduction. Their arts and culture consisted entirely of copies: the repetition of traditional songs, dances, legends, rituals, and visual patterns. Indeed, these traditions were recorded by ethnographers and held up as a mirror to the colonizing gaze.

Colonial subjects stood outside the dominant regime of property relations. They were not measured by the model of possessive individualism and the bourgeois subject. Their expressions and their know-how were thus never eligible for copyright or patent protection. Instead, these belonged categorically to the public domain and were there for the picking. That much is clear from countless examples of exploitation of indigenous music, design, and medicinal knowledge by corporations whose products, on the other hand, are all copyrighted, patented, or trademarked (Brown 2003; Feld 2000; Hafstein 2004a; Shand 2002). As may be recalled from the story of "El Condor Pasa," this is also a grounds for the appropriation of indigenous culture by a hostile state through the representation of indigenous expressions as a national-popular culture, patronized by the same state that disinherits and silences the indigenous populations.

If we cross Zora Neale Hurston with a postcolonial Gramsci, we come up with "the universal mimicry of the subaltern." Colonial populations didn't "have" culture, culture had them. They did not produce it, they were produced by it—possessed by means of mimesis. The ethnographic genre documented such culture and helped to produce colonial subjects, not least by cultural instruments.

Meanwhile, in the West, cultural production was a matter of individual artistry and subject to individual ownership. In a couple of centuries, the eighteenth and the nineteenth, an anti-Copernican revolution occurred in the cultural field, a Copernican revolution in reverse: one that returned man to the center of his universe, crafting his existence and creating his own world. A fundamental shift took place, after which man was not so much creature as creative; no longer was the stress on man as creature, but on man as creator. Until the eighteenth century, the verb to create was only used in conjunction with the divine: "In the beginning, God created heaven and earth." Creativity, in other words, was a divine attribute. It is only in modern times that humans seize this divine spark for their own use—a feat worthy of Prometheus himself (Abrams 1971, 272-282; cf. Oxford English Dictionary 1989 "create", "creation", "creative").

The spark seems not to have been divided equally among humankind, however. Under what James Clifford describes as the "art-culture system", "we" have art, whereas "they" only have a culture (much like we have the wealth whereas they have, again, a culture). Clifford's art-culture system echoes the West-and-the-rest divide between originality and reproduction, or between creativity and tradition (Clifford 2002). On both sides of this divide, however, we are talking about powerful tools to produce subjects: whether it's self-sufficient individuals (on the model of the creative artist-author), dependent colonial populations, independent nations, or semi-autonomous cultural communities.

Intangible Heritage is Community

Intangible heritage is such a tool. Like other heritage interventions, references to intangible heritage stake a claim to culture and they organize the social field around that claim. Intangible heritage is many things, but not the least of them is an instrument for constituting collectivities. It constitutes collectivities around residual culture: craftsmanship, storytelling, rituals, dramas, and festivals (Hafstein 2004b; Kirshenblatt-Gimblett 2004).

Historically, as we know, the monuments, landscapes, and folklore, which later came to be organized under the common rubric of heritage, all played a significant role in the creation of modern nation-states. Indeed, heritage continues to be an important instrument for representing the nation, focusing the political imagination on particular representations of the national community. Often, this is achieved by glossing over difference, demanding allegiance to a uniform national culture and history through selective oblivion, at the expense of alternative loyalties (see, e.g., Anderson 1991; Bendix 2000; Klein 2006; Poulot 2006).

It has become increasingly difficult, however, to imagine such national monocultures, what with the multiplication of diasporic and cross-border communities, and with the resurgence of indigenous groups and regional identities. Under these circumstances, many governments have come to acknowledge and even promote "communities" as cultural and administrative units. Although such communities represent a perennial source of slippage for the project of the nation-state, a new form of governmental rationality is nonetheless emerging that focuses on "the organization of self-regulating communities that are, in some respects, disconnected from the larger wholes of nationally defined societies" (Bennett 2000, 1421).

According to sociologist Nikolas Rose, governing through community is part of an important turn in liberal government. It represents a shift in focus away from the individual in society towards communities as mediating entities, to which individuals owe allegiance and through which they reform and manage themselves. At various levels of government, from the local to the international, we observe this new emphasis on communities as an innovative way to make sense of collective existence, but also to make it calculable and administrable. Over the last twenty-five to fifty years (beginning at different times in different places), but especially in the last decade, "a whole array of little devices and techniques have been invented to make communities real" (Rose 1999, 189). There has been a phenomenal upsurge of new kinds of expertise through which "community" has been "transformed into an expert discourse and a professional vocation". As Nikolas Rose points out, "community is now something to be programmed by Community Development Programmes, developed by Community Development Officers, policed by Community Police, guarded by Community Safety Programmes and rendered knowable by . . . [scholars of] 'community studies'. Communities [have become] zones to be investigated, mapped, classified, and documented" (Rose 1999, 175). We can add to this enumeration the many institutions of community heritage.

Every claim of community refers to something that already exists and to which we owe allegiance; and yet our allegiance to these communities is something we need to be made aware of; it requires the work of educators, campaigns, activists, and professional manipulators of symbols (Rose 1999, 177). As cultural studies scholar, Tony Bennett, has remarked, "at the same time that it is central to this new conception of governing...community has constantly to be rescued from its imminent disappearance or, because the perceived need for community often precedes its existence, [it has] to be organized into being" (Bennett 2000, 1422-1423).

The communalization of heritage and cultural policy helps to form and to reform population groups—local, indigenous, and diasporic communities—and thus to orchestrate differences within the state. In other words, it's a strategy for coping with difference. Population groups are subjectified as "communities" and their practices and expressions are objectified as "intangible heritage". Government can then act on the social field through communities and by means of, among other things, heritage policies.

The World Heritage Convention from 1972 defined heritage in spatial terms, as monuments, groups of buildings, and sites, as well as natural reserves and parks. This heritage is by definition expressed as territory; territory that can be delimited, measured, and mapped (Pressouyre 2001, 57). In fact, territory is so central a defining characteristic of this heritage that it is fair to say that in certain respects *heritage is territory*. It is other things besides, but whatever else it may be, in terms of the 1972 convention, heritage is territory.

The *in*tangible heritage, on the other hand, represents a shift away from territorial definition. The relationship of intangible heritage to its practitioners is not mediated through land or territory. Instead, intangible heritage objectifies the practices and expressions of human communities. It is defined ethnographically rather than topographically. Intangible heritage emerges out of an intervention in community practices, and this intervention defines and delimits the community. If then, tangible heritage is territory in some sense, then by the same token it stands to reason that *intangible heritage is community*. Ultimately, this shift makes community itself subject to conservation in the face of its purportedly steady decline in the modern world.

Empowering Communities, Amplifying Hegemony

Community is a moral principle that metanarratives of modernity always used to figure as a lost cause, a virtue no longer viable except perhaps in premodern enclaves on the peripheries of the modern world: grains of salt falling through the hourglass. If that sounds familiar, it is perhaps because community shares this gloomy prognosis with folklore and with heritage itself. Endangered and in the eleventh hour, community is a worthy object of contemplation for the patrimonial conscience.

In fact, community is the most fundamental intangible heritage that UNESCO's new convention sets out to safeguard. It is an important objective of the convention to build communities with which their members identify, even if many states are careful to define the terms of such empowerment. This desire to empower communities is already apparent in the convention's definition of intangible heritage:

> The "intangible cultural heritage" means the practices, representations, expressions, knowledge, skills… that communities, groups and, in some cases, individuals recognize as part of their cultural heritage. (Article 2, paragraph 1)

This is perhaps better described as an indefinition. The convention's circular formula begs the question of what the term "community" denotes. In fact, it requires the definition of the communities with which states are supposed to consult and cooperate. In order to involve communities in safeguarding it is necessary first to delimit them, to define membership in them, and to designate an authority with which to consult and cooperate.

As Dorothy Noyes has noted part of the political attraction of communities lies in their apparent naturalness (Noyes 2003). Despite appearances, however, communities need to be made up. Boundaries and distinctions have to put in place. These spaces have to be visualized, surveyed, and mobilized. Intangible cultural heritage does just that: it converts cultural practices into resources for administering populations.

In this way, empowerment ultimately depends on subjection. This is the classical paradox of subjectification for, as Foucault argues, subject formation takes place in the element of power. The moment at which we attain status as subjects in our relations with ourselves and others is also the moment of subjection in which we become subject to a set of rules and norms of behavior; subject to definitions, boundaries, and exclusions already imposed on the discourse in which we assume a subject position. Thus the communities to which UNESCO's concept of intangible heritage refers itself are all positioned squarely as collective subjects within states and subject to states. Indeed, their empowerment cements their administrative bonds to central government, even as it loosens their cultural bonds.

By defining community, providing it with outside expertise, and translating its marginalized practices and expressions into the official order of representation, this process demonstrates how residual and alternative culture—like craftsmanship, oral tradition, or ritual—is incorporated into official culture (cf. Williams 1977, 122). Traditional practices are converted to heritage and, in the words of Barbara Kirshenblatt-Gimblett, given a "second life as exhibits of themselves" (Kirshenblatt-Gimblett 1998, 150). In addition to performing themselves, however, they also perform affective relationships and identities. They perform the subject position of the community.

The intangible cultural heritage, as conceived of by UNESCO, is appointed, assembled, and interpreted in part by or in consultation with the communities that it represents. To the extent that community members are integrated into the work of representation and made responsible for it, the intangible heritage enfranchises communities and gives them a voice. In so doing, however, an attempt is also made to fix particular sets of relations and authority as relatively stable units—communities—that speak with one voice. The danger, of course, is that the patrimonial regime will wind up suppressing multivocality, amplifying internal hegemony—the one voice—and thus drown out dissent.

With its programs of preservation and promotion and with its specialist knowledge and outside expertise, intangible heritage offers tools that communities can use to organize themselves as spaces of identification. In principle, the intangible heritage convention offers a vision of "unity-in-diversity", a celebration of difference and harmony. In practice, it runs the risk of enforcing conformity within the diverse communities it designates.

Proliferation of the Social

Like intangible heritage, intellectual property also creates subjects. I referred above to the invention of the authorial subject, the ultimate in bourgeois possessive individualism; but intellectual property in traditional culture constitutes collective subjects, and it constitutes them around communally owned expressions and local knowledge. In this sense, when we deal with collectively copyrighted folklore, patented traditional knowledge, or trademarked traditional patterns and images, we are always dealing with incorporated culture. Intellectual property requires organized collective subjects to hold and manage the property rights, to negotiate with outsiders, and to benefit from any remuneration. If such subjects are not in place—and usually they are not—then the intellectual property regime will bring them into being. Like intangible heritage, intellectual property thus contributes to what, in another context, Michel Callon calls the proliferation of the social (Callon, Barry, and Slater 2002).

Such traditional culture is "incorporated", then, in the sense that it brings into being collective corporate entities: fixed communities vested with administrative powers. Moreover, it also incorporates those communities and their expressions into hegemonic modes of representation and exchange—the patrimonial regime and regimes of intellectual property. That is not necessarily a cause for alarm: In so far as intangible heritage and intellectual property contribute to a proliferation of the social, they have at least some potential to help create a more multivocal world with a greater variety of subject positions to adopt. They help to forge new ways to stake claims and to make oneself heard.

Don't let the traditionalist rhetoric fool you. Although the cultural practices in question may be residual, the collectives organizing around them are emergent. Local and indigenous groups, though they may have an old history, are inventing new forms of social agency and implementing new institutional configurations. The communities involved with intangible heritage and the various collective rights holders in intellectual property are heterogenizing what were once homogenous fields. Or I should say not homogeneous but homogenizing, for copyright and patent law structure creativity through their individualist model in much the same way as heritage helps organize nation-states as individuals-writ-large (as Plato would have them be): heritage has been to the nation what the work of authorship is to the individual (see, e.g., Dumont 1986 and Handler 1988; cf. Poulot 2006).

These models are still in place, of course; they are even expanding at an unprecedented rate. Even so, they are no longer so solid or as singular as they once were. Their rapid swelling has opened up cracks and crevasses, and through these new social formations are emerging, new identities, actors, and collectivities. As Michel Callon has observed, modernity was a constant battle against such overflowings and overlaps, against mixes and hybrids and multiplicities (Callon, Barry, and Slater 2002). The institutions that were created to fight this battle are no longer equal to the task; while they work hard to bring the emergent groups into their fold, to shape them to fit into modern regimes, their success can only be partial. With one foot inside regimes of patrimony and intellectual property, the new subjects have a leg to stand on and a little room for maneuver, and new unexpected social groups are constantly emerging. For them, heritage is a tool of change.

Notes

[1] This paper is an extension of my dissertation research on UNESCO and its intangible heritage convention, which John Lindow supervised. John brought me to Berkeley where I completed first an MA in folklore with Alan Dundes and him and then a PhD in Scandinavian, again with the two of them as my advisers and mentors. John chaired my dissertation committee at Berkeley and I (and this paper) owe much to his invaluable guidance at all stages of my research and writing.

As an anonymous reader pointed out to the editors, the paper is, in his or her words, orthogonal to the other chapters and the overall theme of the book. That remark sums up my relationship to the field of Scandinavian studies during my Berkeley years. My involvement in the department and in the field of Scandinavian was always primarily an extension of my relationship to John as my adviser, and John advised me in his capacity as a brilliant folklorist, not so much as a medievalist or a scholar of Norse philology (though he trained me in those fields too). For all of this, and for all his encouragement, his example, his help, and the countless letters he wrote for me, I owe him big time.

I'm grateful to the editors, Merrill Kaplan and Tim Tangherlini, for putting together this festschrift for John and for seeing it through, and for their generosity and patience, which I tested and found to be great. I would also like to thank: Guðný Helgadóttir and Sveinn Einarsson, former secretary-general and chairpersons of the Icelandic UNESCO Commission, for allowing me to tag along to UNESCO meetings as part of the Icelandic delegation; Rieks Smeets and other members of UNESCO's Intangible Heritage Section for their time and generous assistance; Mahmoud Ghander who helped me excavate the UNESCO archives; Regina Bendix and the SIEF board for appointing me as SIEF's observer meetings of WIPO's committee; Wend Wendland of WIPO for all his goodwill and insights into the process; Alan Dundes, Regina Bendix, Barbro Klein, and Barbara Kirshenblatt-Gimblett for their invaluable guidance at various stages of my research; and Martin Skrydstrup, Marteinn Helgi Sigurðsson, Ólafur Rastrick, and Chiara Bortolotto for reading parts of this text in manuscript—the article would be better if I had heeded all their suggestions. Part of the research for this article was conducted with the help of grants generously provided by Rannís—the Icelandic Centre for Research, the International Center for Advanced Studies at New York University, and HERA (Humanities in the European Research Area).

"A New Start For Greenland": *Julie AllStars* and the Act on Greenland Self-Government

Kirsten Thisted

What do the wording of a legislative act, a piece of popular culture and the negotiation of national identity have to do with each other? In fact quite a bit! In the Arctic regions, politics and collective/social identities are being negotiated in everyday life, including the world of modern media, where popular culture not only reflects so-called "reality" but is also deeply involved in creating it. This article discusses how, in spring 2010, a piece of popular culture became a symbol of the renewed relationship between Denmark and Greenland, a renewed relationship that had been instituted with the Act on Greenland Self-Government in 2009. The case also demonstrates that, although many studies of popular and commercial media show how these media reproduce stereotypes and inequality in majority-minority relations, these media can in fact be used actively by minorities to negotiate power relations and challenge stereotypes.

"AllStars," which is produced by Danish TV2, is a talent show in the same vein as "Pop Stars" and "The X Factor" ("American Idol")—but for choirs instead of individual performers. The choirmasters are professional musicians who assemble their choirs based on open auditions held in selected cities around the country. Thus, the show has an emphasis on place and local character. The show aims to represent all of Denmark, including the so-called "fringe areas", which are not widely exposed on national television. The first season, 2008, was actually won by a choir from the small island of Bornholm, while Denmark's second-largest city, Århus, won in 2009.

In 2010, the competition was between four choirs led by four young musicians: Niarn (born 1972), a rapper from Aalborg; Rasmus Nøhr (born 1979), a singer and guitarist from Nørrebro, a district in Copenhagen that is sometimes referred to as "Nørre Bronx"; Johnson (born 1979), a rapper from Århus; and Julie (born 1979) a singer from Nuuk, Greenland's largest city and the seat of the Greenland Government.[1]

In "AllStars" there are no judges. The competition is based exclusively on audience votes via SMS. The prize is a relatively modest 250,000 Danish kroner (approximately 50,000 US dollars), which is donated to a charity previously selected by each choirmaster. The choirs compete for the honor and the pleasure of being able to pass on the prize money to their chosen charity. Compared with other television contests, the show has a very relaxed tone. The emphasis is not on the contestants' flaws or awkward moments, and there is neither tough critique nor intrigue. As might be expected, the show does not receive nearly the same ratings as The X Factor, which is quite popular in Denmark (2.2 million viewers watched the X Factor final in 2010 out of a total population of 5.5 million).

Nevertheless, more than 950,000 people watched when the Greenlandic choir was named the winner of "AllStars" 2010 and, on average, 750,000 people watched the show each week. Not bad, considering that the competition took place in late spring, coinciding with good weather and the spring break. "AllStars" 2010 also collided with the large-scale Eurovision Song Contest, held in Oslo, which drew some 1.6 million Danish viewers. Still, "AllStars" 2010 was one of the most watched television programs in Denmark during those weeks. Likewise, the program's website and the clips on YouTube have had impressive click-through numbers.

As expected, the program drew considerable interest in Greenland. But the overwhelming scale of the interest surprised both the choir and the organizers. Considering the historical background of Greenland-Denmark relations, it was almost inevitable that the choir and the choirmaster would be seen as representing not only Nuuk but all of Greenland. The official final was between the cities of Nuuk and Aalborg, but by that point, the contest had clearly turned into something resembling an international soccer final, as many Greenlanders put it. The contest became a platform for playing out a basic narrative in the Greenlandic narrative tradition: The poor little Kaassassuk, the underdog who finally steps up to prove his worth.[2] The word "proud" was used time and again in the television show, in news coverage, on talk shows that addressed the contest and, not least, in the final episode, when the entire choir went to Greenland to hand over the prize money. Powerful emotions were at play and openly expressed. Naturally, there were proud parents and friends, but more than anything, all of Greenland was proud on behalf of the nation. Some even went so far as to call the final victory "a new start for Greenland."

The forcefulness of the response says a great deal about the current temperature of the relationship between Denmark and Greenland and the highly asymmetric balance of power that has characterized post-colonial relations. Internally in Greenland, the program developed into a powerful element in *nation building*, while externally, in relation to the outside world, it served a similarly effective role for *nation branding*.

Post-Colonial Relations Between Denmark and Greenland

The briefest possible version of recent Greenlandic history begins with colonization in 1721. Until then, whalers had visited Greenland's west coast, but these visits were seasonal and occasional, and the visitors had no intentions of reshaping and reforming the country's inhabitants. Colonization and the arrival of missionaries changed this situation dramatically. Greenland now became a Danish colony, a status that was maintained until 1953, when a constitutional referendum in Denmark instated Greenland as an equal part of the Danish realm. Greenland became Denmark's northernmost county, and every effort was made to bring Greenland more on par with Denmark with regard to material living conditions and education levels. Danish teachers, builders, administrators etc. arrived in Greenland in great numbers. All the while, the local population felt increasingly held in contempt and reduced to spectators to these events. Danes seized the leading positions, and a controversial "birthplace criterion" meant that Greenlanders were not paid the same as Danes for the same work.[3] In other words, colonial relations were far from eliminated. The situation was a prototype case for "almost but not quite" policies, embedded in an implicit, race-related concept of "almost but not white" (cf. Bhabha 1994). This state of affairs eventually led to the demand for Home Rule, which was instituted in 1979. With the Home Rule Act, Greenland gained jurisdiction over most of its internal affairs. The Act on Greenland Self-Government from 2009 is an expansion of the Home Rule Act, with Greenlanders gaining some input into foreign policy matters.[4] The key point here is the altered discourse when the Self-Government Act refers to the relationship between Denmark and Greenland in comparison with the discourse in the Home Rule Act. The Greenlandic Home Rule Act opened with these words:

> We, Margrethe the Second, by the Grace of God Queen of Denmark make it known: Recognizing the exceptional position which Greenland occupies within the Realm nationally, culturally and geographically, the Folketing has in conformity with the decision of the Greenland Provincial Council passed and We by Our Royal Assent confirmed the following Act about the constitutional position of Greenland within the Realm:

> Chapter 1: Greenland is a distinct community within the Kingdom of Denmark. Within the framework of the unity of the Realm, the Greenland home rule authorities shall conduct Greenland affairs in accordance with the provisions laid down in this Act.

By contrast, the Act on Greenland Self-Government opens with the following wording:

> We, Margrethe the Second, by God's Grace Queen of Denmark, hereby announce that: The Danish

> Parliament has passed the following Act, which We have ratified by giving Our assent:

> Recognising that the people of Greenland is a people pursuant to international law with the right of self-determination, the Act is based on a wish to foster equality and mutual respect in the partnership between Denmark and Greenland. Accordingly, the Act is based on an agreement between Naalakkersuisut [Greenland Government] and the Danish Government as equal partners.

With phrases such as "exceptional position" and "a distinct community within the Kingdom of Denmark," the Home Rule Act clearly expresses a sort of minority status, a deviation from the norm of the majority; the Self-Government Act, by contrast, finally openly acknowledges the Greenlandic people as "a people pursuant to international law." Furthermore, with coded terms such as "partnership," "equality" and "mutual respect," the Act strives to eliminate the old relationship of subservience. It is also surely no coincidence that the Greenlandic word for Greenland's government, *Naalakkersuisut*, appears in the Self-Government Act instead of the Danish term that was used in the Home Rule Act: "The Landsstyre." To claim the untranslatability of a particular word or concept lends it special weight and importance, and hence, this is a widely used strategy by regimes seeking to state the cultural supremacy of the empire (Venuti 1992). The inclusion of a Greenlandic word in the Danish version of the Act sends the opposite signal, as the former colonial power expresses its respect for the Greenlandic language and culture and acknowledges the Greenlandic political system as an equal negotiating partner.[5] The Act was passed with overwhelming majority in a referendum in Greenland and was enacted on 21 June 2009, the thirtieth anniversary of the introduction of Home Rule. The date marks the longest and brightest day of the year, and since 1983 it has also been Greenland's national day.

Even though Nuuk (and all other towns in Greenland) are integrated into the Danish postal system, with Nuuk assigned the zip code 3900, it still might seem somewhat paradoxical that Nuuk was suddenly manifested as a Danish city, precisely at a time when Greenland had acquired self-government. At first glance, that sort of thing might have seemed much more natural in the past. As the analysis will show, however, it is quite logical that a phenomenon such as *Julie AllStars* occurs precisely in the self-government context.

Julie and her Choir

Julie (Julie Berthelsen) is a hot name in contemporary pop music, both in Greenland and in Denmark. For the two countries to even have a shared idol is in itself a novel phenomenon. Granted, the 1980s had Rasmus Lyberth (born 1951). In fact, he was almost more popular in Denmark, where he virtually epitomized Greenlandic culture, associated with the traditional life of the hunters and fishermen and the grandiose Arctic nature. Traditional Drum Song, the Greenlandic harmony choirs and Rasmus Lyberth—*that* was regarded as the essential Greenlandic sound, at least in Denmark. In Greenland, of course, the spectrum was much wider, from whaler-inspired folk dancing and "Hawaiian music" to electric rock, which gained widespread popularity from the 1970s and on. Interestingly, the Danes actually preferred Rasmus Lyberth when he did Greenlandic lyrics compared to when he performed in Danish. They were much less interested in what he was singing than in experiencing this exciting touch of an exotic and alien world that was evoked so vividly by his powerful and strangely vibrato voice.

Julie, on the other hand, sings mostly in English but also in Danish and Greenlandic. As such, she is a member of a globalized elite that navigates effortlessly between not only two but in fact a whole range of languages and cultures. Julie Berthelsen became a household name in both Denmark and Greenland in 2002 when she came second in the television talent show *Popstars*. By 2010 she had released four albums.

In connection with "AllStars" Julie held two auditions: one at the culture center Katuaq in Nuuk and one at the culture center *Nordatlantens Brygge*, home to the Icelandic embassy and the Faroese and Greenlandic representations in Copenhagen. With this move, she highlighted the fact that many Greenlanders reside in Denmark, either permanently or on stays of varying duration—just as she herself originally went to the Danish city of Århus to study medicine but now lives permanently in Copenhagen. Thus, she voiced the feelings of many when she said the following words about her dual sense of belonging in the first episode of the show:

> Grønland er jo mit hjem, det er jo der, jeg har mine minder, det er jo der, jeg har mine rødder, og det er jo der, min familie er. Men der er jo ingen tvivl om, at nu har jeg også boet i Denmark i rigtig mange år efterhånden, og som jeg altid har sagt lidt til venner og bekendte, så er det lidt som at leve med hjertet delt. Men Grønland, det *er* hjemme!

> [Greenland's my home, after all, that's where I have my memories, it's where I have my roots, and it's where my family is. But there is no doubt that I have also lived in Denmark for many years now, and I've always said to friends and acquaintances, it's a bit like living with a heart divided. But Greenland, that's *home!*][6]

Julie picked her first nine choir members in Nuuk and the last thirteen in Denmark, although some of the latter actually lived in Nuuk and were only in Copenhagen on brief visits.

Another significant aspect was that in advertising her auditions she did *not* call for "Greenlanders" but for people "with an attachment to Greenland." This meant that in Denmark, at least initially, there was quite some talk about the fact that the choir did not "look Greenlandic." However, determining who is Greenlandic is no simple and straightforward matter. The image that most people outside Greenland have of a Greenlander revolves mainly around appearance and language. A Greenlander looks like an "Eskimo" and speaks Danish with a Greenlandic accent, because *kalaallisut* (part of the language group *inupiaq*) is the person's native language. That is indeed true for some people but, over the years, the Greenlandic population has mixed with many other peoples. One would have to look far and wide to find a Greenlander who does not number one or more Danes among their closest relatives. A fairly large number of Greenlanders have Danish as their first language. Throughout the 1960s and 1970s it was common to place Greenlandic children in Danish classrooms in order to maximize their opportunities in modern society. Throughout the first half of the 1900s there was a pronounced desire among many Greenlanders to improve their Danish skills, as Danish was the gateway to the modern world. The Greenlanders wanted increased emphasis on Danish in schools, but for a long time the Danish administration was reluctant to do so because they worried that the Greenlanders might become estranged from their background of hunting and fishing, which was the main occupation at the time and considered the "natural" occupation. After 1953, when Greenland was formally recognized as an equal part of the Danish realm, and Danish workers and professionals poured into Greenland to boost the development, the situation was virtually turned upside down, so that Danish now became the dominant language of education (Langgård 1992, Jensen 2001). The Danish children attended strictly Danish-speaking classes, and so did most of the children of mixed parentage as well as some children of parents who both had Greenlandic as their first language. The latter group had Greenlandic as their oral language but never learned to read and write Greenlandic. This means that Greenlandic language skills exist on very different levels for different parts of the population (Langgård 2003).

Naturally, like Julie, many of the Danish children who grew up in Greenland came to consider Greenland *home*. The same is true, of course, of many of the immigrants who came to Greenland as adults and chose to settle and work there. Some of these immigrants speak Greenlandic, others do not.

During the Home Rule period, as in the colonial era, strict distinctions were drawn between who was Greenlandic and who was not. In the Home Rule period, however, the Danes kept a much lower profile, and young people with a Danish background did not really feel that they were entitled to see the country as their own, even if they had been raised there (Mondrup 2003, Gad 2005, Thisted 2005). Similarly, Greenlanders who did not speak Greenlandic were plagued by feelings of guilt. In recent years these issues have begun to be addressed in a general debate, and Julie's choice of choir members actively entered this negotiation about who can be considered a member of the Greenlandic community. The *Julie AllStars* choir included the whole range of attachment, from a woman whose great-grandmother was Greenlandic to so-called "half" and "full" Greenlanders.[7] One participant was born in Denmark to Greenlandic parents, one was born in Greenland to Danish parents, and another was born in Greenland to American parents. He certainly did not look Greenlandic, but his Greenlandic name marked his attachment with the country. In regards to language skills, the group was similarly heterogeneous, and although the choir consequently used Danish as the common language, everybody was encouraged to use Greenlandic to some extent; similarly everybody had to possess some level of English skill, since most of the songs they performed were in English.

Julie's choice to introduce herself with an English song was hardly a coincidence. While the other choirmasters chose to introduce themselves with one of their own songs in Danish, Julie did her song *Moment's Bliss*. In this way, she signaled a cosmopolitan outlook that is rarely associated with Greenland in a Danish context, but which is in fact an important aspect of life in late-modern Greenland. The song also served to mark Julie's position in Danish culture, especially to anyone who followed *2900 Happiness*, a Danish soap opera that ran over three seasons with 142 episodes, starting in 2007, and which used this song as the title track. For the first show, Julie had also chosen the Aretha Franklin/George Michael song, *I knew you were waiting*, a fairly mainstream choice. The costumes that the choir used did not have a particularly Greenlandic character, except for the word "Asanninneq" [love] that was emblazoned in large print across Julie's back, and the word "Inuit" on the lead singer Nina's blouse. *Inuit* is of course the word that the people characterized by others as "Eskimos" use about themselves. Directly translated, the word simply means "people" and the outfits played on this double meaning. The choir's T-shirts featured slogans encouraging people to protect nature, children, themselves and each other, expressed in a mix of English, Danish and Greenlandic. Thus, the slogans addressed Inuit people as well as people in general. This aspect also emphasized the global outlook. The outfits were never discussed, not in this initial episode nor in any of the subsequent episodes, and strangely, there were never any questions about it in any of the many interviews with the artists. In Julie's choir, the choir members' outfits and makeup were in fact essential elements in the negotiation and reinterpretation of modern Greenlandic identity that the selection of songs throughout the program represented.

Cultural Heritage and Identity

In the second episode the Greenlandic choir also sang in English, but the first song (Nabiha: *Deep Sleep*) included a Greenlandic singing game. The little song was elegantly integrated into the performance, and the show's producers did nothing to highlight it. On the other hand, both in this and the first episode there was much talk about the phenomenon of traveling between two places. This theme had taken on particular prominence because a volcanic eruption in Iceland was preventing all air travel into and out of Nuuk. Thus, one of the two lead singers, Mads Lumholt, was stranded in Nuuk, and the other lead singer, Nina Kreutzmann Jørgensen, had had to do the duet in the previous week's Aretha Franklin song on her own. Mads made it to the second episode, but only barely. In fact he landed in Copenhagen Airport less than thirty minutes before the show began. Of course he was given a chance to talk about the journey, which included a dramatic four hundred kilometer boat ride north to Sisimiut followed by a snow scooter ride to reach the airport in Kangerlussuaq.

That evening's main Greenlandic figure, however, was not Mads but Nina, thirty-two years old and a schoolteacher in Nuuk. Probably in an attempt to make the program more interesting and add a stronger "X factor" element, the producers had chosen to focus on selected members of the choir. From the outset, each choirmaster was asked to pick two lead singers, and in the voting procedure the choirmaster whose choir had the lowest score would have to choose between the two. When a choirmaster lost both lead singers, the choir was out of the competition. In the second episode, the viewers learned more about Nina, who had a husband and two children back in Nuuk and thus had no trouble finding the emotions within herself to carry her interpretation of Alicia Keith's song *Try sleeping with a broken heart.* Julie interpreted the song as a metaphor for being far away from home and having to face yet another lonely night without one's loved ones. Nevertheless, she also toned down the topic: "Det er noget vi lever med, og det er naturligt for os, og så er det OK ikke?" [It's something we live with, and it is natural for us, so it's OK.] Thus, the two Greenlandic songs were tied together by the theme of longing: longing for the Greenland of one's childhood, expressed in the cheerful children's rhyme and singing game, and longing for one's family, expressed in the portrait photos that each of the choir members had with them on stage. Naturally, this theme struck a chord with the Greenlandic audience, and the Danish audience found the message sympathetic. And Julie did not have to send any of her lead singers home that week.

In episode three, the Greenlandic aspect was toned down considerably. The theme this time was love. The choir sang Gavin DeGraw's *In love with a Girl* and Sara Bareille's *Love Song,* and the focus was on the two lead singers' personal presence and their love of music. Episode four began on a similar note with a song by The Script, *Breakeven,* but in the second half of the show the Greenlandic aspect was reintroduced, as Julie did the Lady Gaga song *Bad Romance* with Greenlandic chanting, *aya ayayaya,* and Mask Dance.

Mask Dance is one of the first things that Danes associate with Greenlandic culture. The dancers use dramatic makeup and pull grotesque faces by putting distenders into their mouths. Using grotesque writhing and sounds the dancers mimic spirits. The effect relies especially on a surprising aesthetics that is both frightening and beautiful, and on the discomfort that occurs when the dancers get uncomfortably close to audience members, violating people's personal space and sense of privacy. Another important element of the Mask Dance is humor. In the old days when hard times hit, and people needed magic and entertainment to find the strength to go

Fig. 1: Julie AllStars performing "Bad Romance" (Photo by Henrik Ohsten).

on, Mask Dance was an important ritual. In a toned-down form but still including features such as dressing up in the clothes of the opposite sex, the custom survived throughout the 1800s and 1900s on the west coast of Greenland in the form of the so-called *mitaartut*, which unfold between New Year's Eve and Epiphany (sixth of January) (Kleivan 1960, Kleivan and Sonne 1985, Kielsen 1996). Modern Mask Dance, however, is based on the East Greenlandic variant *uaajeerneq*, which was rediscovered by the Greenlandic artists associated with the Tuukkaq Theater in the early 1970s in part thanks to the writings of Eskimologist William Thalbitzer (1873-1958) (Thisted 2008). The Tuukkaq Theater and its associated acting school were in themselves international and globalized institutions that were initially aimed at Greenland but were soon reinvented as world theater or theater of indigenous peoples.[8] From a religio-historical or ethnographic point of view, Mask Dance expressed a new tradition, both with regard to the actors' interpretation of the meaning elements of the dance and with regard to the entirely new context of the performances. To the actors, however, the revival of Mask Dance was a ritual that linked them more closely to their forefathers and their pre-Christian culture (Thisted 2008). Many of the Greenlanders who were involved at the time still feel that way. As one of the members of *Julie AllStars*, Miki Jacobsen, expressed it when he was asked to explain the masks after the performance, "Det sorte: det ukendte; det røde: liv og død; stregerne, det der fremstår lyst: mit skelet, altså et billede på mine forfædre." [The black: the unknown; the red: life and death; the lines, the elements that appear light: my skeleton— that is, an image of my ancestors.][9]

For younger people who were not involved in the process during the 1970s and 80s, when Mask Dance became an important part of the political awakening and the burgeoning ethnic awareness, Mask Dance is not similarly associated with spirituality or ideology. To them, it is something that young people staying in Denmark can do to make money by performing at corporate events or private parties or even as street performance. To young Greenlanders, Mask Dance is part of their Greenlandic cultural heritage, something that by no means defines them, but with which they may choose to identify; it was in this sense that Julie included it. An introduction to the song included a clip from the choir's practice room at Nordatlantens Brygge in Copenhagen. In the clip Julie said,

> Det er jo vigtigt for mig, selvfølgelig, at få lidt det med, at det *er* Greenland, vi stiller op for, og det er der vi kommer fra, og hele mit kor er – mere eller mindre – Greenlandsk.

> [It's important to me, of course, to touch on the fact that it *is* Greenland we represent, that's where we come from, and my whole choir is – more or less – Greenlandic.]

Next in the clip, we see Julie instruct the choir in transferring the Lady Gaga song to what Julie characterizes as "our culture, our traditions and our history from Greenland." At the same time, she spells it out to the interviewer and the viewers that this has to do with *cultural heritage*: "Maskedans er en ældgammel grønlandsk ting. Den stammer tilbage fra gamle, gamle dage, det er ikke noget, vi har i det moderne samfund i dag, det er en del af kulturhistorien." [Mask Dance is an ancient Greenlandic tradition. It dates back to the old, old days; it's not something that we do in modern society today, it's a part of cultural history.] In this manner Julie takes on the role of cultural translator to the Danish viewers, who may have had their expectations met, but who were also discreetly encouraged to give up their romanticized notions of Greenland and acknowledge Greenland as a modern society. In relation to the Greenlandic audience, by placing Mask Dance in a new and surprising context, she breathes new life into an artistic expression that was frozen in the form it acquired back in the 1970s. The song was perfect for lead singer Nina's voice and once again secured *Julie AllStars* continued survival in the contest.

Similarly, Drum Song was incorporated into Mads Lumholt's performance of the George Michael song *Killer* in episode six. The choir wore a modernized version of the Greenlandic national costume—which in fact dates back to a much more recent era than Drum Song. Once again, there was no intention of offering an ethnographically correct version of the tradition; instead the goal was to incorporate it in an ultramodern, globalized expression. "Is Drum Song something you grew up with?" asked the hostess of the show. Mads replied that, sure it was; his mom teaches Drum Song, so at times it had been a fairly intense part of his everyday life. She then asked Julie the same question, and Julie replied, "Ja altså, både og. På et tidspunkt i løbet af folkeskolen havde vi sådan noget tema noget hen over nogle uger, hvor jeg faktisk blev undervist i trommesang af Mads' mor." [Well, yes and no. At some point in elementary school, we did this theme sort of thing that lasted a few weeks, when I actually took Drum Song lessons from Mads' mom.] Spurred on by the hostess, the audience in the studio now demanded to see Julie herself use the drum, and judging from her performance she had practiced since her school days! For some time in fact, there has been a certain degree of skepticism in Greenland about the use of the drum, as many young people feel that it paints the wrong picture of Greenland and Greenlanders that locks them into the notion of "authenticity". At the same time, there is considerable interest in the old traditions also among the young. Thus, a performance such as Julie's may help others hold onto some of the old ways without fear of being labeled reactionary, nationalistic and out of touch with the modern world.

Fig. 2: Julie performing the Drum Song (Photo by Henrik Ohsten).

Language and Identity

Since both Mask Dance and Drum Song are such a perfect match for most Danes' expectations of what goes into a "Greenlandic event," there was nothing too risky about any of these performances. It was with the song *Silarsuaq takuiuk*, which opened episode five, that Julie really raised the stakes. Greenlandic culture served with the evening coffee right in the middle of primetime without any mitigating exoticism: that was a different experience indeed for the Danish audience. *Silarsuaq takuiuk* could only be seen as representative of a foreign language and a partially foreign culture, outside Danish comprehension and control. Even if all of Greenland was watching the show, with a total population of just over 56,000, it was obvious that the Greenlandic vote alone would not be enough to carry the choir through. Indeed, the hostess commented that this was a brave move!

The situation was further complicated by the fact that the song was to be performed by Mads Lumholt, who does not have Greenlandic as his mother tongue, even though it is definitely his mother's language. Mads Lumholt's mother is the Greenlandic singer and choirmaster Pauline Lumholt, who is a trained opera singer, and who has been one of the driving forces in preserving

Drum Song as a living tradition. Mads Lumholt's late father was Danish, but for many years he served as a priest in Greenland with a diocese that included the northernmost district, Avanersuaq, also known as Thule. While West Greenland was colonized already in the 1700s, the missionaries and the traders did not arrive in Thule until the early 1900s. Hence, the original traditions survived the longest there and on the east coast, which was colonized in the late 1800s. It was in Thule that Pauline Lumholt originally learned Drum Song. As Mads Lumholt, who was born in 1971, explained on the show, he spent much of his childhood in Denmark, and his parents wanted their children to have "one solid language." This statement reflects concerns at the time that bi- or multilingual children would wind up "multi-semi-lingual," without a firm grasp on any language. At the time, people did not know what we know now about children's capacity for learning multiple languages. Additionally there has at times been tremendous pressure on people to speak Greenlandic "properly"; this insistence reflects a perception of languages as distinct entities, essences that, like cultures and identities, should be kept as free of "foreign influences" as possible.[10] Some people zealously monitor language use among the young and rebuke the creative use of code shifting, language mixing, and innovation under influence from other languages, although these features in fact mark the status of Greenlandic as a living language. Children of mixed parentage are under especially close watch and, for some time at least, they were constantly being told that they were not Greenlandic enough, and that their Greenlandic was not good enough. Thus, the hostess of the show was right in more than one regard when she said that it was brave of Julie to let Mads sing in Greenlandic.

In the clip from the practice room that introduced the song, Mads Lumholt explained that although he does speak some Greenlandic and has OK pronunciation, he does have trouble with the nuances. He emphasized that with this particular song, it was crucial to get it right, because *Silarsuaq takuiuk* is "a classic" that people love. Siiva Fleischer, lead singer in the band Zikaza, which was very popular in the 1980s and 1990s and successors to the 1970s band Sume in which Julie Berthelsen's father had been a member, wrote the song. It is a beautiful tune with beautiful lyrics about being aware of nature and man's connectedness with the universe. The song is often used as the closing song at concerts and other events, and most Greenlanders know the words more or less by heart. It is certainly a classic in modern Greenlandic music, with which Nina, Mads and Julie, all "children of Home Rule," had grown up.

Fig. 3: Mads Lumholdt peforming Silarsuaq takuiuk (Photo by Henrik Ohsten).

It was quite apparent that all the Greenlanders in the studio were profoundly moved when the song was over—Mads, Julie, the choir and the audience. The hostess asked for an explanation from both Mads and Julie, but only got some niceties about love. "Come on, I kan da ikke først stå og synge noget på grønlandsk, som vi andre ikke forstår, og så ikke forklare det bagefter. I lukker os jo fuldstændig ude!" [Come on! You can't just do a song in Greenlandic that the rest of us don't understand and then not tell us what it's about. You're shutting us out!] the hostess protested, on her own behalf and on behalf of the Danish viewers. However, the point is that the Greenlanders were probably not moved because of the content of the song. The main thing was the fact that the words were Greenlandic. For one thing, it is always moving to hear one's own language when one is far away from home. And furthermore, everybody in the studio had just seen the clip from the practice room on the big screen and was touched and relieved that Mads had risen to the challenge. With this performance, Julie illustrated the powerful symbolic and emotional role of the Greenlandic language to the Greenlanders, even those who do not have a full or even much of a grasp of the language. And last but not least, with this performance, the Greenlandic representation in the program was fully on "Greenlandic terms." There was an unmistakable sense of a "first" about it. Granted, Her Majesty Queen Margrethe II always includes the Faroese and Greenlandic peoples in her New Year's address. And granted, Danish television does have an annual program called "Christmas Greetings for Greenland."[11] But both of those have a ritualized character and thus carry a sense of obligation. Furthermore, "Christmas Greetings for Greenland" is an isolated feature in the programming schedule. This was different.

With *Silarsuaq takuiuk* the Greenlanders sent a clear and unmistakable message: Greenlandic is the main language of our country, so this is part and parcel of our presence. Take it or leave it! Whether Julie could have pulled it off without having an ace up her sleeve, we will never know. If some viewers had felt that this was over the top, the mood definitely turned with the second act of the evening when Julie sent Nina on stage with a crisp and perfect version of *Barndommens gade* [Childhood's Street]. Note that this was the first (and only) time that the Greenlandic choir sang in Danish.[12] *Barndommens gade* is a core aspect of Danish culture. The lyrics for the song are a poem written by the Danish poet Tove Ditlevsen (1917-1976). The poem became known and embraced by everyone in Denmark when singer and composer Anne Linnet put it to music, along with several other poems by Ditlevsen, for the film version of her eponymous novel from 1943. Exactly as with *Silarsuaq takuiuk*, this is a song that most Danes know more or less by heart. With this song, Julie and her choir said that Denmark *is* a part of Greenland. We know the Danish tradition as well as any of you – we just know something else as well! That evening's vote was probably the one that the Greenlandic choir was most uncertain about. Aalborg was mentioned as the first choir to go on to the final, and judging by the faces of the choir members, they were already preparing to see Julie have to choose between her lead singers. But that is not what happened. Instead, the viewers chose to eliminate Århus from the competition.

Fig. 4: Nina performing "Barndommens Gade" (Photo by Henrik Ohsten).

Representation and Acknowledgement

As representatives not only of a town but also of a country and an ethnicity, the Greenlandic choir was under particular pressure. The contestants were fully aware of the rather unique opportunity that the program presented them with on behalf of Greenland, as Nina explained in episode six:

> Jeg tror det er rigtig, rigtig vigtigt for Nuuk og for Grønland at følge med i det her, fordi vi bliver repræsenteret som Grønland og vi bliver repræsenteret som Nuuk, og det er jo meget sjældent, vi har fået lov til det. Det er nu vi kan vise under det grønlandske navn og under vores eget flag, at vi også har noget at give af. Jeg synes godt, man kan sammenligne det med noget landskampstemning.

> [I think it's really, really important for Nuuk and for Greenland to take part in this, because we're represented as Greenland, and we're represented as Nuuk, and it's so rare that we get to do that. This is our chance to show, in the name of Greenland and

under our own flag, that we too have something to offer. I think you can compare this to a national soccer final.]

Her statement reflects the fact that Greenland, as part of the Danish realm, is rarely allowed to take part in international competitions under its own name, something that has been a major source of discontent not least in connection with sports contests. When Julie mentioned that it was important to note that the choir was representing Nuuk and Greenland, she probably had a different dimension of the representation in mind: the contribution that she and the choir were making to the image of Greenland and Greenlanders.

In Denmark there are two prevailing versions of "Greenland." In the "Sunday version," which comes out on festive or solemn occasions and in official contexts, Greenland is lauded for its proud traditions, its beautiful landscape, and the harmonious relations within the Danish realm. In the everyday version, Greenlanders are stereotyped as losers, dependent on Danish subsidies, alcoholics and "lost in translation" in the modern world. Nuuk in particular has a reputation in the Danish public as a sort of "spoiled space," which stems in part from a number of documentaries that set out to look "beyond the scenic idyll" and draw out "the aspects that don't fit into the postcard image," as the most recent of these documentaries *Flugten fra Greenland* [Escape from Greenland] phrased it (Heilbut 2007). The documentary claimed that young educated Greenlanders with degrees are fleeing Greenland because it holds no future for them and because they feel defeated by the cocktail of social problems, incompetence, and corruption that the Home Rule government produced.[13]

Julie and her Greenlandic choir were determined to present a different picture, and in this they received helpful support from the producers who gave them every opportunity to appear themselves in situations as competent parents and responsible citizens capable of handling their daily jobs in addition to the hard work involved in the "AllStars" program.[14] As mentioned earlier, the prize for winning the competition was a sum of money, earmarked for a preselected charity. Julie had decided that if her choir won, the prize money would go to Nanu, an organization that seeks to establish shelters and support centers for children all over Greenland. Thus, neither the program nor the choir was in denial about the presence of major social problems in Greenland. What was so crucially different about this program was that the question had been detached from the usual context, inherited from the colonial era, where a dysfunctional, abnormal and underdeveloped "them" is described, assessed and chastised by a normative, highly functioning and civilized "us." Denmark, however, has social problems of its own. If Rasmus Nøhr and Nørrebro had won, the prize money would have gone to a foundation that sends underprivileged inner-city youths on skiing trips in Norway. Johnson had decided that the money would go to The National Council for the Unmarried Mother and Her Child in Århus, which once assisted his own mother, and Niarn was hoping to pass the money on to the "Social Commandos" in Aalborg, an organization that helps youths recover from a life of crime. In this respect too, then, the premise of the show was based on the sort of equality that the Act of Greenland Self-Government established as the guiding principle in the shared realm.

Self-Government places new demands on the Danes. That was evident in the attitude of the hostess, which changed as the competition progressed. Danes are often a little awkward around Greenlanders, especially in public contexts. Colonial history is heavy baggage, and many people are worried about saying something inappropriate. There is a tradition for Danes to laugh when they hear Greenlandic spoken, and maybe that is why Danish television hosts think it is clever to use Greenlandic as a sort of ice-breaker to release the tension with a liberating laugh. The Danish hosts in the television show *Christmas Greetings for Greenland* have relied on this tradition for years. The "AllStars" hostess tried to do the same. In the first episode, while Mads was stuck back in Nuuk due to the volcanic ash cloud, she suggested that Nina send him a greeting in Greenlandic. "Maasinnguaq—Tallimanngorpat takuss!" [Dear Mads, see you on Friday!] said Nina. The hostess laughed: "Jamen det var da præcis det, jeg ville have sagt!" [Well, you took the words right out of my mouth!]. From a Greenlandic perspective, however, there is nothing liberating about that sort of joke, and Julie immediately code-shifted the greeting for Mads back into Danish. A couple of Fridays later, the hostess had dropped this approach completely and had actually learned to say, "Welcome" in Greenlandic. As the show progressed, everything became much more relaxed, and when the hostess later introduced Nuuk as "Byen hvor det er *street* at have en snescooter" [The town where having a snow scooter buys you *street cred*], there was no sting or sarcasm in her comment. Nuuk was presented on level with Århus, which Johnson referred to as "Soul City," and Aalborg, "Cement City," a nickname that played on its reputation as a "tough" place (and the presence of the local cement factory). In this way, the show helped generate interest and curiosity about modern Nuuk as something other and more than just a big slum area surrounded by breathtaking scenery.

Group Membership and Community

The presentation of the *Julie AllStars* choir as a multiethnic community based on equality was not completely seamless, also evident in Julie's statement above that her entire choir was Greenlandic—"more or less". Being Greenlandic is not either/or but a matter of degree, and it was easy to see how the strong emphasis on cultural heritage created an inner circle and an outer circle in the otherwise solid group, at least in situations that revolved around powerful ethnic symbols such as the drum, language and food. On several occasions during the program series, the viewers saw the choirs engaged in various forms of communal meals. One particular clip of the Greenlandic choir held special significance. Julie, Nina and Mads had prepared a surprise for the choir: Greenlandic provisions. Food is, of course, one of the key markers of cultural identity and social cohesion, and is often an element in establishing boundaries between cultures and ethnicities. This obtains for Greenland as well where certain products, primarily from marine mammals, are considered particularly "Greenlandic," especially when served and eaten raw (Petersen 1985, Roepstorff 1997, Olsen 2010). There is a special word for this: *kalaalimernit*. The Danish term "grønlandsk proviant" [Greenlandic provisions] is one of the many unique terms that characterize Danish language use in Greenland. Showing appreciation for Greenlandic provisions signals one's attachment to Greenland, and being invited to take part in such a meal is the ultimate sign of inclusion, especially when it takes place in a private setting. By demonstrating his familiarity with Greenlandic provision, Mads was able to demonstrate his attachment to Greenland, and it is probably no coincidence that this clip was included in the presentation of the rehearsals for *Silarsuaq takuiuk*. This scene bolstered his credibility as a Greenlander which might have otherwise been called into question when he (subsequently) admitted that he was not fluent in Greenlandic. By contrast, one of the other members of the choir, who had a weaker attachment to Greenland, was more reluctant to put *mattak*, raw whale hide, and dried cod fish with raw blubber into her mouth. "Der skal tygges godt" [You need to chew it well], Mads explained, and thus the scene resembled a sort of initiation rite.

This scene was just one among many where Julie emphasized the strong sense of community in her choir. This sense of community was something that the other contestants continually emphasized as the Greenlanders' main advantage: the strong team spirit in the choir, where everybody trusted each other and "had each other's back." In this way, Julie managed to turn the choir into an image of an ideal Greenlandic community, one based on inclusion rather than exclusion. In Julie's vision, the dual allegiance to the Inuit, the "fellow tribesmen," in the west and the Scandinavians in the east was further expanded. Consequently, the issue of identity was, in principle, completely detached from the issue of roots and parentage. Instead, the emphasis was placed on with whom and with what an individual chooses to identify and feel solidarity. Throughout the competition, Julie stuck to the line she had established with the code word "attachment" in her call for the open audition. Of course, attachment comes naturally if one has been born and raised in a particular place and one's family is in that place. But it is also something that one can develop as a result of one's personal history and choices. That is why the Danish teacher, who had lived and worked in Nuuk for six years, was able to join the community of the choir on equal terms with the Greenlandic teacher who had lived there her whole life. The success of the choir demonstrated the power of this openness. The most crucial aspect of the presentation of *Julie AllStars* was exactly this merger of the multi-ethnic and the *Zusammengehörigkeitsgefühl* or sense of community that is considered the core of the nation state, because it serves as the basis for the sympathy and trust needed to make the citizens mutually identify with each other (Brubaker and Cooper 2000). As a nation, Greenland cannot be seen only as a scenic paradise for tourists and adventurers. Its image must include that of a functioning modern society that is capable of managing its own affairs—the kind of society that Greenlanders would want to live in, and which is open to the outside world and capable of attracting strong, new citizens, companies and investment.

Fig. 5: Winners! (Photo by Henrik Ohsten).

Indeed, no Greenlander could fail to grasp what the *Julie AllStars* project was about—one need only consider the phrase "A new start for Greenland!" that was quoted in the beginning of this article. Or, as the former chairman of Inatsisartut (Greenland's par liament) Lars Emil Johansen expressed it: "Det betyder meget for den grønlandske selvforståelse og den grønlandske at der er endnu et område, hvor *vi* kan!" [It means a lot for Greenlandic self-awareness and Greenlandic self-esteem that there is one more area where *we* are capable!] (episode 7).[15] Note the phrase "one more area." Here Lars Emil Johansen attempts to dampen the general impression of surprise over the choir's success and to point out that the Greenlanders have had their fair share of successes.

Conclusion

As discussed here, the Greenlandic nation (state) was not held up as an issue in the "AllStars" program, neither by the Greenlanders nor by the producers. The Greenlanders are now in a position to discuss the premises for the nation, rather than debate its existence, something which is now taken for granted. Greenlandic nationalism today is "trivial" in the sense that it is unmarked (Billig 1995). Nation building is a never-ending process. With her critical approach to the ethnicity-based concept of the nation that, with few exceptions, has dominated the Greenlandic discourse, Julie and her choir played an important role at an early stage of Greenlandic self-government. The nation model that was imported to Greenland via Denmark was ethnically and culturally based (Thisted 1990 and 2011; Langgård 2011). The post-colonial confrontation in Greenland was an unambiguously nationalist endeavor in the struggle to establish an ethnically based nation. In a sense, the Act on Greenland Self-Government meets this demand, although the Act, which is written in Danish, only mentions "the people of Greenland." The word *Inuit* is not mentioned, but in a Greenlandic context, "the people of Greenland" will be seen as identical in meaning to *kalaallit*, the same word as in the Greenlandic name for Greenland: *Kalaallit Nunaat*, literally: the land of the Greenlanders. The recommendations of the Greenlandic-Danish commission on Greenlandic self-government emphasized that "a people" should be defined as "a group of individuals who based on objective and subjective criteria possess characteristics that set them apart from other peoples" (Grønlandsk-dansk Selvstyrekommissions betænkning om Selvstyre i Grønland 2008, 29).[16] Greenland has, in this regard, inherited the self-understanding of the ethnicity-based nation, and consequently its issues concerning the inclusion and exclusion of citizens in the national community.

Precisely because Greenland wants to become a valid nation, the term "indigenous peoples" is not mentioned in the Act on

Greenland Self-Government (Johansen 2008). Yet, for a number of years, Greenland has been associated with these peoples, first by outsiders, who categorized them as "primitive," later in the nation's own identification in the form of membership and participation in various international forums for "indigenous peoples." Identifying with the category of indigenous peoples, the Greenlanders have associated themselves with a very powerful narrative. However, this narrative certainly has its limitations. One of them is that indigenousness is more or less always associated with nature, illiteracy and primitivism and huge social problems due to an inability to accommodate to the modern world—the so-called "fatal impact" or "pure or poor" syndrome. One of the most crucial tasks for the new Greenland is to negotiate and alter this image and to create a series of new, positive self-images that align with the ambitions of education, progress and full independence. In this regard, the "AllStars" program provided a branding of the nation that no money could buy. Identity is based on narrative and narration—the stories you tell about yourself and others, and the stories others tell about you in relation to themselves. That also works on a national level. The trick is to take active part in this narration: to tell rather than to be told. The young Greenlanders are fully aware of this and of the premises at play in the globalized world, where identity meets management jargon in expressions such as "competitive identities" (Anholt 2007).

When young Greenlanders incorporate elements from their cultural tradition in a show such as "AllStars," they are in no way seeking shelter from a globalized world. On the contrary, they are turning to tradition in order to fashion their own contribution in a world where local culture still constitutes substantial cultural capital. In literature, poetry, music, film and all sorts of media representations, Greenlanders are currently renegotiating their identity. But this is nothing new. Greenlandic history reveals how Greenlanders have continuously translated themselves to accommodate new environments and opportunities: from "heathens" into Christians, from colonial subjects into equal citizens within the Danish realm, and later into indigenous people with Home Rule (Thisted 2011). With *Julie AllStars*, Greenlandic self-government came into its own, and this event is just one example of the way in which Greenlanders actively engage in creating new images and visions for themselves as a people and for Greenland as a nation.

Notes

[1] Most people outside Greenland associate the country with the old hunting culture. Today, however, the hunting culture actually represents only a small percentage of the country's revenue (Rasmussen 2005). 84% of the population lives in urban communities, 28% of the total population lives in Nuuk (total population: 56,615, in towns 47,857, in Nuuk 15,862, all numbers January 2011).

[2] For a (very abbreviated) version see H.J. Rink: *Tales and Traditions of the Eskimo,* London 1875, online. www.sacred-texts.com

[3] The birthplace criterion was introduced in 1964 to replace previous systems, which specified different pay for the same work for Danes and Greenlanders, respectively, in Greenland. The criterion applied to employees of the state and specified that anyone who was born in Greenland or who took up residence here before their fifth birthday would be paid less and have fewer privileges than Danes. To the Greenlanders, this arrangement demonstrated that they were not in fact considered equal citizens in the Danish state. The criterion was abandoned as far as pay was concerned in 1989 and in relation to other terms of employment in 1991.

[4] The Act will not be discussed in detail here. The full text of the Act is available on the website of Greenland's Government: www.nanoq.gl.

[5] The Home Rule Act specified Greenlandic as the main language of Greenland, but Greenlandic was ranked as equal to Danish in government affairs. Similarly, Danish was safeguarded with the phrase "Danish must be thoroughly taught" (Chapter 2, § 9). The Act on Greenland Self-Government establishes Greenlandic as the country's official language (Chapter 7, § 20). The Act on Greenland Self-Government does not mention Danish.

[6] This and all subsequent quotations from the program have been translated by the author.

[7] Obviously, such terms make no sense. Nevertheless, everybody knows what they imply, and they have been widely used but also widely debated, and today they are always used in quotes.

[8] The Tuukkaq Theater was founded in the town of Fjaltring in western Jutland (Denmark), and the acting school existed from 1975 to 1993. The theater was based on body language, masks and miming, inspired by Eugenio Barba and the Danish Odin Theater. The Greenlandic spin-off of Tuukkaq, *Silamiut*, was founded in 1984 in Nuuk.

[9] Miki Jacobsen was born in 1965 and was the oldest member of the Greenlandic choir.

[10] In Greenland, of course, the reaction should also be seen in relation to the "Danification" that looked poised to threaten the survival of Greenlandic for a time in the 1960s and 1970s.

[11] "Julehilsen til Grønland" began as a radio show in 1932 that turned into a TV show in 1985.

[12] Gad 2009 makes the provoking suggestion that Greenland get on with acquiring post-post-colonial status by replacing Danish with English. Julie's language choices, however, should probably not be seen as support of that position. On the contrary, the choir demonstrated that Danish and English do not have to represent mutually exclusive options; instead, the current situation points to three simultaneously relevant languages: Greenlandic, Danish and English.

[13] The documentary became the target of strong criticism (Gant 2009), also in the Greenlandic press, and triggered a protest demonstration in Copenhagen. It is the first time that Greenlanders have objected so openly to Danish representations, which is in itself an indication that the balance of power has shifted.

[14] In this sense, the show is a good example that the popular media are far from one-sided, producing exclusively negative images of minorities; in fact they can also be actively used by minority groups to negotiate power relations and challenge stereotypes.

[15] Lars Emil Johansen was one of the leading forces behind Greenlandic Home Rule and chaired the Self-Government Commission's working group on constitutional and international law. He hopes for a fully

independent Greenland, in free association with Denmark, see Johansen 2008.

16 This expression was used in order to have the Greenlanders accepted as a people pursuant to international law. Included in the democratic process, of course, are the people who actually live in the country. Anyone who holds Danish citizenship (and meets the relevant age requirements etc.) acquires the right to vote after six months' stay in Greenland.

References

Aarne, Antti. 1911. *Finnische Märchenvarianten*. FF Communications 5. Hamina: Suomalainen Tiedeakatemia.

Abrahams, Roger D. 1993. Phantoms of Romantic Nationalism in Folkloristics. *Journal of American Folklore* 106: 3-37.

Abrams, Meyer H. 1971. *The Mirror and the Lamp: Romantic Theory and the Critical Tradition*. New York: Oxford University Press.

Adam af Bremen. 1978. *Beskrivelse af øerne i Norden*. Edited and translated by Allan Lund. Aarhus: Wormianum.

Agnar Helgason et al. 2000a. Estimating Scandinavian and Gaelic Ancestry in the Male Settlers of Iceland. *American Journal of Human Genetics* 67: 697-717.

Agnar Helgason et al. 2000b. mtDNA and the Origin of the Icelanders: Deciphering Signals of Recent Population History. *American Journal of Human Genetics* 66: 999-1016.

Agnar Helgason et al. 2001. mtDNA and the Islands of the North Atlantic: Estimating the Proportions of Norse and Gaelic Ancestry. *American Journal of Human Genetics* 68: 723-737.

Ahlbäck, Tore, ed. 1987. *Saami Religion: Based on Papers Read at the Symposium on Saami Religion, Held at Åbo, Finland, on the 16th-18th of August 1984*. Scripta Instituti Donneriani Aboensis 12. Åbo, Finland: Donner Institute for Research in Religious and Cultural History.

Albro, Robert. 2005. The Challenges of Asserting, Promoting, and Performing Cultural Heritage. *Theorizing Cultural Heritage* 1: 2-8.

Almqvist, Bo. 1961. Um atkvæðaskáld. *Skírnir* 135: 72-98.

Almqvist, Bo. 1991a. Waterhorse Legends. *Béaloideas* 59: 107-120.

Almqvist, Bo. 1991b. *Viking Ale: Studies on Folklore Contacts Between the Northern and Western Worlds*. Aberystwyth: Boethius Press.

Alver, Bente G. 1989. Concepts of the Soul in Norwegian Tradition. In *Nordic Folklore: Recent Studies*. Edited by Reimund Kvideland and Henning K. Sehmsdorf. Pp. 110-27. Bloomington and Indianapolis: Indiana University Press.

Alver, Brynulf, Olav Bø, Reimund Kvideland, and Mortan Nolsøe, eds. *Ridder Skau og Jomfru Dame: eventyr frå Ringerike*. Vol. 2, Norsk eventyrbibliotek. Oslo: Det Norske samlaget.

Amalia. *Märchenlexikon*. 2009. Die schwarze Madonna 710. Online.

Amundsen, Arne Bugge. 2010-2011. Clerical Culture and Nation Building Four Norwegian Nineteenth Century Examples. Online.

405

Andersen, Bjørn, ed. 2003. *Danske Lov 1683.* Søborg: BA forlag.

Anderson, Benedict. 1991. *Imagined Communities: Reflections on the Origin and Spread of Nationalism.* 2nd ed. London: Verso.

Anderson, Rasmus B. 1874. *America Not Discovered by Columbus: A Historical Sketch of the Discovery of America by the Norsemen in the Tenth Century.* Chicago: S. C. Griggs.

Anderson, Rasmus B. [1892]. *Hvor var Vinland?* Madison: Amerika's forlag.

Andersson, Otto. 1937. Kalevalameter—fornyrdislag. *Budkavlen* 16: 84-100.

Andersson, Theodore M. 2006. *The Growth of the Medieval Icelandic Sagas (1180-1280).* Ithaca and London: Cornell University Press.

Andrén, Anders. 1993. Doors to Other Worlds: Scandinavian Death Rituals in Gotlandic Perspectives. *Journal of European Archaeology* 1:33-56.

Andrén, Anders. 2006. A World of Stone: Warrior Culture, Hybridity, and Old Norse Cosmology. In *Old Norse Religion in Long-term Perspectives. Origins, Changes, Interactions.* Edited by Anders Andrén, Kristina Jennbert, and Catherina Raudvere. Pp. 33-38. Vägar till Midgård 8. Lund: Nordic Academic Press.

Andrén, Anders. 2007. Behind Heathendom: Archaeological Studies of Old Norse Religion. *Scottish Archaeological Journal* 27: 105-138.

Andrén, Anders. 2010. Vem lät bygga kyrkorna på Gotland? *Saga och sed* 2009: 31-59.

Anholt, Simon. 2007. *Competitive Identity: The New Brand Management for Nations, Cities and Regions.* Hampshire and New York: Palgrave Macmillan.

Appadurai, Arjun. 1996. *Modernity at Large: Cultural Dimensions of Globalization.* Public Worlds 1. Minneapolis: University of Minnesota Press.

Arngrímur Fr. Bjarnason. 1954-1959. *Vestfirzkar þjóðsögur.* 3 vols. Reykjavík: Ísafoldarprentsmiðja.

Árni Björnsson. 1996. *Merkisdagar í mannsævinni.* Reykjavík: Mál og menning.

Asbjørnsen, Peter Christen, and Moe, Jørgen. 1995. *Folkeeventyr samlet af P. Chr. Asbjørnsen og Jørgen Moe.* 2 vols. Larvik: Forlaget LibreArte.

Asbjørnsen, Peter Christen. 1861. Darwins nye skabningslære. *Budstikken* 2-3: 65-77. (written under pseudonym Clemens Bonifacius).

Asbjørnsen, Peter Christen. 1879. *Norske Folke- og Huldre-Eventyr i Udvalg. Med illustrationer efter Originaltengninger af P.N. Arboe, H. Gude, V. St. Lerche, Eilif Peterssen, A. Schneider, Otto Sinding, A. Tidemand, og E. Werenskiold.* Copenhagen: Gyldendal.

Asbjørnsen, Peter Christen, and Johann Georg Theodor Grässe. 1858. *Nord und Süd: ein märchen-strauss.* Dresden: C.C. Reinhold & Söhne.

Asbjørnsen, Peter Christen, and Jørgen Moe. 1960. *Norwegian Folk Tales.* Translated by Pat Shaw Iverson and Carl Norman. New York: Pantheon Books.

Asbjørnsen, Peter Christen, and Jørgen Moe. 1967. *Folke- og Huldreeventyr, utvalg og innledning av Johan Borgen.* Norges nasjonalliteratur. Oslo: Gyldendal.

Asbjørnsen, Peter Christen. 1850. *Juletræet: en Samling av norske Folke- og Børne Eventyr: fortalte af P.C. Asbjørnsen med 22 Ill. efter Originaltegninger af Johan Eckersberg.* Christiania: A. Dzwonkowski.

Asbjørnsen, Peter Christen. 1851. *Juletrold, udvalgte Folke- og Børne Eventyr; oversatte af P. Chr. Asbjørnsen, med Illustrationer af Johan Eckersberg.* Christiania: A. Dzwonkowski.

Ásdís A. Arnalds, Ragna Benedikta Garðarsdóttir, and Unnur Diljá Teitsdóttir. 2008. *Könnun á íslenskri þjóðtrú og trúarviðhorfum.* Reykjavík: Félagsvísindastofnun Háskóla Íslands.

Bäckman, Louise, and Åke Hultkrantz, eds. 1985. *Saami pre-Christian Religion: Studies on the Oldest Traces of Religion Among the Saamis.* Acta Universitatis Stockholmiensis. Stockholm Studies in Comparative Religion 25. Stockholm: Stockholms universitet / Almqvist & Wiksell.

Bahrdt, Hans Paul. 1961. *Die moderne Grossstadt: soziologische Überlegungen zum Städtebau.* Reinbek bei Hamburg: Rowohlt.

Bandle, Oskar et al., eds. 2005. *The Nordic Languages: An International Handbook of the History of North Germanic Languages.* Berlin: De Gruyter.

Barry, Phillips. 1914. The Transmission of Folk-Song. *Journal of American Folklore* 27: 67-76.

Barry, Phillips. 1934. Das Volk dichtet nichts. *Bulletin of the Folk-Song Society of the Northeast* 7: 4.

Barry, Phillips. 1961. The Part of the Folk Singer in the Making of Folk Balladry. In *The Critics and the Ballad.* Edited by MacEdward Leach and Tristram P. Coffin. Pp. 59-76. Carbondale: Southern Illinois University Press.

Barthes, Roland. 1972. *Mythologies.* Translated by Annette Lavers. London: Paladin.

Baudou, Evert. 1985. Archaeological Research and the History of the Saamish Religion. In *Saami Pre-Christian Religion.* Edited by Louise Bäckman and Åke Hultkrantz. Pp. 29-41. Uppsala: Almqvist & Wiksell.

Baudrillard, Jean. 1994. *Simulacra and Simulation.* Ann Arbor: University of Michigan Press.

Bauman, Richard. 1986. *Story, Performance and Event: Contextual Studies of Oral Narrative.* Cambridge: Cambridge University Press.

Beck, Heinrich. 1993. *Wortschatz der altisländischen Grágás (Konungsbók)*. Abhandlungen der Akademie der Wissenschaften zu Göttingen. Philologisch-Historische Klasse. Dritte Folge 205. Göttingen: Vandenhoeck & Ruprecht.

Belier, Wouter W. 1991. *Decayed Gods. Origin and Development of Georges Dumézil's 'Idéologie Tripartie.'* Leiden: Brill.

Bellows, Henry Adams, ed. 2004. *The Poetic Edda: The Mythological Poems*. Mineola, NY: Courier Dover Publications.

Bendix, Regina. 1997. *In Search of Authenticity: The Formation of Folklore Studies*. Madison: University of Wisconsin Press.

Bendix, Regina. 2000. Heredity, Hybridity and Heritage from One Fin-de-Siècle to the Next. In *Folklore, Heritage Politics and Ethnic Diversity*. Edited by Pertti J. Anttonen. Pp. 37-54. Botkyrka: Multicultural Centre.

Bennett, Gillian. 1984. Women's Personal Experience Stories of Encounters with the Supernatural: Truth as an Aspect of Storytelling. *Arv* 40: 77-87.

Bennett, Tony. 2000. Acting on the Social: Art, Culture and Government. *American Behavioral Scientist* 43: 1412-1428.

Benson, Stephen. 2003. *Cycles of Influence: Fiction, Folktale, Theory*. Detroit: Wayne State University Press.

Beowulf. 1954. Translated by Björn Collinder. Stockholm: Natur och kultur.

Bergersen, Robert. 1997. *Vinland Bibliography: Writings Relating to the Norse in Greenland and America*. Ravetrykk 10. Tromsø: Universitets-biblioteket.

Bhabha, Homi K. 1994. Of Mimicry and Man: The Ambivalence of Colonial Discourse. In *The Location of Culture*. Pp. 85-92. London and New York: Routledge.

Bibire, Paul. 1986. Freyr and Gerðr: The Story and its Myths. In *Sagnaskemmtun: Studies in Honour of Hermann Pálsson*. Edited by Rudolf Simek et al. Pp. 19-40. Wien: Böhlau.

Billig, Michael. 1995. *Banal Nationalism*. London: Sage Publications.

Bjarni Aðalbjarnarson, ed. 1945. *Heimskringla 2*. Íslenzk fornrit 27. Reykjavík: Hið íslenzka fornritafélag.

Bjarni M. Gíslason. 1940. Edda Finnlands. *Eimreiðin* 46: 309-320.

Björn Þorsteinsson and Guðrún Ása Grímsdóttir. 1989. Norska öldin. In *Saga Íslands* IV. Edited by Sigurður Lindal. Pp. 61-258. Reykjavík: Sögufélag.

Bjørn, Claus, Troels Dahlerup, S. P. Jensen and Erik Helmer Pedersen, eds. 1988. *Det danske landbrugs historie*. 4 vols. Odense: Landbohistorisk selskab.

Black, Henry Campbell et al. 1991 [1891]. *Black's Law Dictionary: Definitions of the Terms and Phrases of American and English Jurisprudence, Ancient and Modern.* 6th ed. St. Paul, MN.: West.

Blair, John. 2005. *The Church in Anglo-Saxon Society.* Oxford: Oxford University Press.

Blomkvist, Torsten. 2002. *Från ritualiserad tradition till institutionaliserad religion: strategier för maktlegitimering på Gotland under järnålder och medeltid.* PhD Diss., Uppsala universitet, Department of Theology.

Boer, Richard C. 1922. *Die Edda mit historisch-kritischem Kommentar.* 2 vols. Haarlem: H. D. Tjeek Willink & Zoon.

Böldl, Klaus. 2005. *Eigi einhamr: Beiträge zum Weltbild der Eyrbyggja und anderer Isländersagas.* Ergänzungsbände zum Reallexikon der Germanischen Altertumskunde 48. Berlin and New York: De Gruyter.

Bosley, Keith. 1977. Translator's preface. In *Finnish Folk Poetry - Epic: An Anthology in Finnish and English.* Edited by Matti Kuusi, Keith Bosley and Michael Branch. Pp. 17-20. Helsinki: Finnish Literature Society.

Bottigheimer, Ruth B. 1990. Marienkind (KHM 3): A Computer-Based Study of Editorial Development and Stylistic Development Within Grimms' Tales from 1808 to 1864. *Arv* 46: 7-31.

Bottigheimer, Ruth B. 2009. *Fairy Tales: A New History.* Albany, N.Y.: Excelsior Editions / State University of New York Press.

Boyer, Pascal. 2001. *Religion Explained: The Evolutionary Origins of Religious Thought.* New York: Basic Books.

Boylan, Alexis. L., ed. 2011. *Thomas Kinkade: The Artist in the Mall.* Durham and London: Duke University Press.

Braadland, Jan Faye. 2001. Andreas Faye: Elaboration (NBL Article). Online.

Brandt, Margit. 1974. *Registrant over Evald Tang Kristensens samling af eventyr.* NIF Rapporter. Åbo: Nordisk Institut for Folklore.

Brennu-Njáls saga. 1954. Edited by Einar Ólafur Sveinsson. Íslenzk fornrit 12. Reykjavík: Hið íslenzka bókmenntafélag.

Brink, Stefan, ed. 1996. *Jämtlands kristnande / The Christianization of the Province of Jämtland.* Uppsala: Lunne böcker.

Brink, Stefan. 2007. How Uniform Was the Old Norse Religion? In *Learning and Understanding in the Old Norse World: Essays in Honour of Margaret Clunies Ross.* Edited by Judy Quinn et al. Pp. 105-136. Turnhout: Brepols.

Broadbent, Noel. 2004. Saami Prehistory, Identity and Rights in Sweden. Presented at *The Third Northern Research Forum.* Yellowknife, Canada.

Brown, Michael F. 2003. *Who Owns Native Culture?* Cambridge: Harvard University Press.

Brown, Michael F., and Margaret M. Bruchac. 2006. NAGPRA from the Middle Distance: Legal Puzzles and Unintended Consequences. In *Imperialism, Art, and Restitution*. Edited by John Henry Merryman. Pp. 193-217. Cambridge: Cambridge University Press.

Brubaker, Rogers and Frederick Cooper. 2000. Beyond 'Identity'. *Theory and Society* 29: 1-47.

Bruun, Niels W. and Allan Lund, eds. 1974. *P. Cornelii Taciti: De origine et situ Germanorum*. Aarhus: Wormianum.

Buisson, Ludwig. 1976. *Der Bildstein Ardre VIII auf Gotland*. Abhandlungen der Akademie der Wissenschaften in Göttingen. Philologisch-historische Klasse, Dritte Folge 102. Göttingen.

Bø, Olav, Ronald Grambo, Bjarne Hodne and Ørnulf Hodne. 1981. *Norske segner: segner i utval*. Oslo: Norske samlaget.

Callon, Michel, Andrew Barry, and Don Slater. 2002. Technology, Politics and the Market: An Interview with Michel Callon. *Economy and Society* 31: 285-306.

de Certeau, Michel. 1984. *The Practice of Everyday Life*. Berkeley: University of California Press.

Chase, Martin, ed. 2005. *Einarr Skúlason's* Geisli: *A Critical Edition*. Toronto: Toronto University Press.

Chesnutt, Michael. 1999. The Three Laughs: A Celtic-Norse Tale in Oral Tradition and Medieval Literature. In *Islanders and Water Dwellers: Proceedings of the Celtic-Nordic-Baltic Folklore Symposium Held at University College Dublin, 16-19 June 1996*. Edited by Patricia Lysaght et al. Pp. 37-49. Dublin: DBA Publishers.

Christiansen, Palle Ove. 1996. *A Manorial World: Lord, Peasants and Cultural Distinctions on a Danish Estate, 1750-1980*. Oslo and Boston: Scandinavian University Press.

Christiansen, Reidar Th. 1959. *Studies in Irish and Scandinavian Folktales*. Copenhagen: Rosenkilde and Bagger.

Christiansen, Reidar Th. 1992. *The Migratory Legends: A Proposed List of Types with a Systematic Catalogue of the Norwegian Variants*. FF Communications 175. Helsinki: Suomalainen Tiedeakatemia.

Christiansen, Reidar Th., ed. 1968 [1964]. *Folktales of Norway*. Translated by Pat Shaw Iverson. Folktales of the World. Chicago: University of Chicago Press.

Clifford, James. 2002. *The Predicament of Culture: Twentieth-Century Ethnography, Literature, and Art*. Cambridge: Harvard University Press.

Clodd, Edward. 1905. *Animism: The Seed of Religion*. London: Archibald Constable & Co.

Clunies Ross, Margaret. 1994. *Prolonged Echoes: Old Norse Myths in Medieval Northern Society*, vol. 1. Odense: Odense University Press.

Clunies Ross, Margaret. 1998. Myths of Settlement and Colonisation. In *Prolonged Echoes: Old Norse Myths in Medieval Northern Society*. Vol. 2, *The Reception of Norse Myths in Medieval Iceland*. Pp. 122-57. The Viking Collection 10. Odense: Odense University Press.

Clunies Ross, Margaret, ed. 2007. *Poetry on Christian Subjects*. 2 vols. Skaldic Poetry of the Scandinavian Middle Ages, vol. 7. Turnhout: Brepols.

Coe, Cati. 1999. The Education of the Folk: Peasant Schools and Folklore Scholarship. *Journal of America Folklore* 113(447): 20-43.

Cohen, Eric. 1979. A Phenomenology of the Tourist Experience. *Sociology* 13: 179-201.

Collinder, Björn. 1949. *The Lapps*. Princeton: Princeton University Press for the American Scandinavian Foundation, New York.

Conrad, JoAnn. 2000. Tracking the Ogre: The Politics of Shape Shifting. *Ural-Altaische Jahrbucher* 16: 56-75.

Cook, Robert. 2004. Jónas á ensku. *Skírnir* 178: 239-255.

Crawshaw, Carol and John Urry. 2005. Tourism and the Photographic Eye. In *Touring Cultures Transformation of Travel and Theory*. Edited by Chris Rojek and John Urry. Pp. 175-195. London and New York: Routledge.

Culler, Jonathan D. 1988. The Semiotics of Tourism. In *Framing the Sign Criticism and Its Institutions*. Pp. 153-167. Norman: University of Oklahoma Press.

DaCosta Holton, Kimberly. 2005. *Performing Folklore: Ranchos Folcloricos from Lisbon to Newark*. Bloomington: Indiana University Press.

Danielsson, Tommy. 2002. *Hrafnkels saga eller Fallet med den undflyende traditionen*. Hedemora: Gidlund.

Danmarks folketing. 1857. *Næringslov*. Copenhagen.

Davidson, W. Phillips. 1983. The Third-Person Effect in Communication. *Public Opinion Quarterly* 47: 1-15.

Davis, Asahel. 1840. *A Lecture on the Discovery of America by the Northmen, Five Hundred Years Before Columbus*. 5th ed. Boston: Bartlett.

Dégh, Linda. 1962. *Märchen, Erzähler und Erzahlgemeinschaft; dargestellt an der ungarischen Volksüberlieferung*. Deutsche Akademie der Wissenschaften zu Berlin. Veröffentlichungen des Instituts für Deutsche Volkskunde 23. Berlin: Akademie-Verlag.

Dégh, Linda. 1995. *Narratives in Society: A Performer-centred Study of Narration*. FF Communications 255. Helsinki: Suomalainen Tiedeakatemia.

Degnbol, Helle et al., eds. 1989. *A Dictionary of Old Norse Prose / Ordbog over den norrøne prosasprog*. Ongoing. Copenhagen: The Arnamagnæan Commission.

Detter, Ferdinand. 1894. Der Baldrmythus. *Beiträge zur Geschichte der deutschen Sprache und Literatur* 19: 495-516.

Ditlevsen, Tove. 1943. *Barndommens gade*. Copenhagen: Athenæum.

Dorson, Richard. 1964 [1968]. Foreword. In *Folktales of Norway*. Edited by Reidar Th. Christiansen. Pp. v-xviii. Chicago: University of Chicago Press.

Dorson, Richard. 1966. The Question of Folklore in a New Nation. *Journal of the Folklore Institute* 3: 277-298.

Dronke, Ursula. 1997. *The Poetic Edda. Vol. 2, Mythological Poems*. Oxford: Clarendon Press.

Dumézil, Georges. 1959. *Les dieux des Germains: essai sur la formation de la religion scandinave*. Mythes et religions 38. Paris: Presses universitaires de France.

Dumézil, Georges. 1971. *Mythe et epopée. Vol. 2, Types épiques indo-européens: un héros, un sorcier, un roi*. Paris: Gallimard.

Dumont, Louis. 1986. *Essays on Individualism: Modern Ideology in Anthropological Perspective*. Chicago: University of Chicago Press.

Dundes, Alan. 1962. From Etic to Emic Units in the Structural Study of Folktales. *Journal of American Folklore* 75: 95-105.

Dundes, Alan 1969. The Devolutionary Premise in Folklore Theory. *Journal of the Folklore Institute* 6: 5-19.

Dundes, Alan. 1971. Folk Ideas as Units of Worldview. *Journal of American Folklore* 84: 93-103.

Dundes, Alan. 1980 [1964]. *The Morphology of North American Indian Folktales*. FF Communications 195. Helsinki: Suomalainen Tiedeakatemia.

Dundes, Alan. 1981. *The Evil Eye: A Casebook*. Madison: The University of Wisconsin Press.

Dybdahl, Vagn. 1982. *Det nye samfund på vej 1871-1913*. Dansk socialhistorie 5. Copenhagen: Gyldendal.

Edda: Die Lieder des Codex Regius nebst verwandten Denkmälern. 1927. Edited by Gustav Neckel and Hans Kuhn. 2 vols. Heidelberg: Winter.

Edda: Die Lieder des Codex Regius nebst verwandten Denkmälern. 1962. Edited by Gustav Neckel and Hans Kuhn. 3rd ed. 2 vols. Germanische Bibliothek. 4. Reihe: Texte. Heidelberg: Winter.

Eddadigte. 1961-71. Edited by Jón Helgason. 3 vols. Nordisk filologi, serie A, tekster. Copenhagen: Munksgaard.

Eddan jumalrunot. 1982. Translated by Aale Tynni. Porvoo: Söderström.

Eddan sankarirunot. 1980. Translated by Aale Tynni. Porvoo: Söderström.

Eggert Ólafsson and Bjarni Pálsson. 1975. *Travels in Iceland 1752-1757*. Translator not named. Reykjavík: Örn og Örlýgur.

Egils saga Skalla-Grímssonar. 1933. Edited by Sigurður Nordal. Íslenzk fornrit 2. Reykjavík: Hið íslenzka fornritafélag.

Einar Ól. Sveinsson. 1934. Formáli. In *Laxdæla saga*. Íslenzk fornrit 5. Reykjavík: Hið íslenzka fornritafélag.

Einar Ól. Sveinsson. 1971. *Njáls saga: A Literary Masterpiece.* Edited and translated by Paul Schach. Lincoln: University of Nebraska Press.

Einar Ól. Sveinsson. 2003. *The Folk-stories of Iceland.* Edited by Anthony Faulkes. Translated by Benedikt Benedikz. Revised by Einar G. Pétursson. Viking Society for Northern Research Text Series 16. London: Viking Society for Northern Research.

Ekroll, Øystein. 2007. The Shrine of St Olav in Nidaros Cathedral. In *The Medieval Cathedral of Trondheim: Architectural and Ritual Constructions in Their European Context.* Edited by Margrete Syrstad Andås et al. Pp. 147-207. Turnhout: Brepols.

Den eldre Gulatingslova. 1994. Edited by Bjørn Eithun, Magnus Rindal and Tor Ulset. Riksarkivet. Norrøne tekster 6. Oslo: Riksarkivet.

Eliade, Mircea. 1963. *Patterns in Comparative Religion.* Translated by Rosemary Sheed. New York: The New American Library.

Eliade, Mircea. 1964. *Shamanism: Archaic Techniques of Ecstasy.* Translated by Willard Trask. Princeton: Princeton University Press.

Ellis Davidson, H. R. 1964. *Gods and Myths of Northern Europe.* London and New York: Penguin Books.

Elviken, Andreas. 1931. The Genesis of Norwegian Nationalism. *The Journal of Modern History* 3: 365-391.

Engström, Johan. 1984. *Torsburgen: tolkning av en gotländsk fornborg.* PhD Diss., Uppsala universitet. Aun 6. Uppsala: Institutionen för arkeologi.

Enzensberger, Hans Magnus. 1996. A Theory of Tourism. *New German Critique* 68: 117-135.

Eriksen, Anne. 2009. Museum: beretninger og betydninger. Keynote lecture at the *31st Nordic Ethnology and Folklore Conference.* August 21, 2009. Helsinki.

Eskeröd, Albert. 1947. *Årets äring: etnologiska studier i skördens och julens tro och sed.* Stockholm: Nordiska museet.

Espada, Arcadi. Interview with Juan Goytisolo. *La espia del sur.* Online.

Expert Criticises Copyright Bill. 2005. *GhanaMusic.Com.* Online.

Eyrbyggja saga. 1935. Edited by Einar Ól. Sveinsson and Matthías Þórðarson. Pp. 1-184. Íslenzk fornrit 4. Reykjavík: Hið íslenzka fornritafélag.

Falnes, Oscar J. 1933. The Folk and Fairy Tales. In *National Romanticism in Norway.* Pp. 214-236. New York: Columbia University Press.

Faulkes, Anthony, ed. 2005. Snorri Sturluson. *Edda: Prologue and Gylfaginning.* London: Viking Society for Northern Research.

Feifer, Maxine. 1985. *Going Places: The Ways of the Tourist from Imperial Rome to the Present Day.* London and New York: Macmillan.

Feld, Steven. 2000. A Sweet Lullaby for World Music. *Public Culture* 12: 145-171.

Finnur Jónsson, ed. 1908-15. *Den norsk-islandske skjaldedigtning.* Vols. A 1-2 and B 1-2. Copenhagen: Gyldendal. Reprinted 1967 (A) and 1973 (B). Copenhagen: Rosenkilde & Bagger.

Finnur Jónsson. 1931. *Lexicon Poëticum Antiquæ Linguæ Septentrionalis: Ordbog over det norsk-islandske skjaldesprog oprindelig forfattet af Sveinbjörn Egilsson.* 2nd ed. Copenhagen: Møller / Atlas bogtryk. Reprinted 1966.

Fjellström, Phebe. 1985. Sacrifices, Burial Gifts, and Buried Treasures: Function and Material. In *Saami Pre-Christian Religion.* Edited by Louise Bäckman and Åke Hultkrantz. Pp. 43-60. Uppsala: Almqvist & Wiksell.

Fleck, Jere. 1970. Konr—Óttarr—Geirrøðr: A Knowledge Criterion for Succession to the Germanic Sacred Kingship. *Scandinavian Studies* 42: 39-49.

Flinn, John. 2005. Solvang Butters Up Visitors with Pastry, Kitsch. *San Francisco Chronicle.* February 27, 2005. Online.

Foster, George. 1965. Peasant Society and the Image of Limited Good. *American Anthropologist* 67: 293-315.

Foster, George. 1966. Foster's Reply to Kaplan, Saler, and Bennett. *American Anthropologist* 68: 210-214.

Foucault, Michel. 1977. What is an Author? In *Language, Counter-Memory, Practice: Selected Essays and Interviews.* Edited by Donald F. Bouchard. Pp. 113-38. Ithaca: Cornell University Press.

Frank, Roberta 2007. The Lay of the Land in Skaldic Praise Poetry. In *Myth in Early Northwest Europe.* Edited by Stephen O. Glosecki. Pp. 175-196. Tempe, Arizona: Arizona Center for Medieval and Renaissance Studies / Turnhout: Brepols.

Friis-Jensen, Karsten and Peter Zeeberg. 2005. *Saxo Grammaticus Gesta Danorum: Danmarkshistorien.* 2 vols. Copenhagen: Det danske sprog- og litteraturselskab / Gad.

Fritzner, Johann. 1883-96. *Ordbog over det gamle norske sprog.* 3 vols. Kristiania (Oslo): Den norske forlagsforening. 4th ed. 1973. Oslo: Universitetsforlaget.

Frow, John. 1991. Tourism and the Semiotics of Nostalgia. *October* 57: 123-151.

Früh, Sigrid and Kurt Derungs. 2003. *Schwarze Madonna im Märchen: Mythen und Märchen von der Schwarzen Frau.* Zürich: Unionsverlag.

Fussell, Paul. 1980. *Abroad: British Literary Traveling Between the Wars.* New York: Oxford University Press.

Fussell, Paul. 1983. *Class: A Guide Through the American Status System.* New York: Summit Books.

Gad, Ulrik P. 2005. *Dansksprogede grønlænderes plads i et Grønland under grønlandisering og modernisering.* Eskimologis skrifter 19. Copenhagen: Københavns universitet, Afdeling for eskimologi og arktiske studier.

Gad, Ulrik P. 2009. Post-colonial Identity in Greenland? When the Empire Dichotomizes Back—Bring Politics Back In. *Journal of Language & Politics* 8: 136-158.

Gallen-Kallela, Akseli. 1953. Ajatuksia. *Kalevalaseuran vuosikirja* 33: 40-45.

Gamwell, Lynn. 2002. *Exploring the Invisible: Art, Science, and the Spiritual.* Princeton and Oxford: Princeton University Press.

Gant, Erik 2009. Om det gådefulde og diabolske i dansk grønlandspolitik. In *Et postkolonialt Danmark.* Edited by Ingemai Larsen and Kirsten Thisted. Special Issue of *TijdSchrift voor Skandinavistiek* 30: 195-223.

Gauti Kristmannsson. 2005. *Literary Diplomacy.* Frankfurt am Main: Peter Lang.

Gering, Hugo, ed. 1896. *Die Edda: Die Lieder der sogenannten älteren Edda; nebst einem Anhang, die mythischen und heroischen Erzählungen der Snorra Edda.* Leipzig: Bibliographisches Institut.

Gering, Hugo, and Barend Sijmons. 1931. *Kommentar zu den Liedern der Edda.* 2 vols. Halle an der Saale: Buchhandlung des Waisenhauses.

Gislestam, Torsten, ed. 1994. *C. G. G. Hilfelings gotländska resor 1797 och 1799.* Visby: Gotlands fornsal.

Gísli Sigurðsson. 1988a. *Gaelic Influence in Iceland: Historical and Literary Contacts; A Survey of Research.* Studia Islandica 46. Reykjavík: Bókaútgáfa Menningarsjóðs.

Gísli Sigurðsson. 1988b. Halldór K. Laxness in Manitoba. *Lögberg-Heimskringla* 8.

Gísli Sigurðsson. 1990. On the Classification of Eddic Heroic Poetry in View of the Oral Theory. In *Poetry in the Scandinavian Middle Ages.* Edited by Teresa Pàroli. Pp. 245-255. Spoleto: Centro Italiano di studi sull'alto medioevo.

Gísli Sigurðsson, ed. 1998. *Eddukvæði.* Reykjavík: Mál og menning.

Gísli Sigurðsson. 2002a. What Does a Story Tell? Eddi Gíslason's (1901-1986) Personal Use of Traditional Material. *Canadian Ethnic Studies* 34: 79-89.

Gísli Sigurðsson. 2002b. Þjóðsögur Vestur-Íslendinga. In *Úr manna minnum: greinar um íslenskar þjóðsögur.* Edited by Baldur Hafstað and Haraldur Bessason. Pp. 169-190. Reykjavík: Heimskringla.

Gísli Sigurðsson. 2004. *The Medieval Icelandic Saga and Oral Tradition: A Discourse on Method.* Translated by Nicholas Jones. Cambridge, MA: Harvard University Press. Originally published as *Túlkun Íslendingasagna í ljósi munnlegrar hefðar: tilgáta um aðferð.* Rit 56. Reykjavík: Stofnun Árna Magnússonar á Íslandi, 2002).

Gjerset, Knut. 1915. *History of the Norwegian People.* 2 vols. New York: Macmillan.

Glick, Thomas. 1974. *The Comparative Reception of Darwinism.* Chicago: University of Chicago Press.

Goffman, Erving. 1986. *Frame Analysis: An Essay on the Organization of Experience.* Boston: Northeastern University Press.

Grágás. Konungsbók. 1974 [1852]. Edited by Vilhjálmur Finsen. Odense: Odense universitetsforlag.

Grágás. Staðarhólsbók. 1879. Edited by Vilhjálmur Finsen. Copenhagen: Gyldendalske boghandel.

Grágás. 1980. In *Laws of Early Iceland: Grágás, the Codex Regius of Grágás, with Material from Other Manuscripts.* Translated by Andrew Dennis, Peter Foote and Richard Perkins. University of Manitoba Icelandic Studies 3. Winnipeg: University of Manitoba Press.

Greenfield, Jeanette. 1996. *The Return of Cultural Treasures.* 2nd ed. Cambridge: Cambridge University Press.

Grettis saga Ásmundssonar. 1936. Edited by Guðni Jónsson. Íslensk fornrit 7. Reykjavík: Hið íslenzka bókmenntafélag.

Grigg, David. 1980. *Population Growth and Agrarian Change.* Cambridge: Cambridge University Press.

Grimm, Jacob and Wilhelm Grimm. 1812-1815. *Kinder- und Hausmärchen, gesammelt durch die Brüder Grimm.* Berlin: Realschulbuchhandlung.

Grimm, Jacob, Wilhelm Grimm and Herman Friedrich Grimm. 1816-1818. *Deutsche Sagen.* Berlin: Nicolaischen Buchhandlung.

Grimm, Jacob and Wilhelm Grimm. 1916. Jacob og Wilhelm Grimm's brev til P. Chr. Asbjørnsen og Jørgen Moe. In *Til Gerhard Gran, 9. December 1916, fra venner og elever.* Edited by Anders Krogvig. Pp. 175-185. Kristiania: Aschehoug.

Groenke, Ulrich. 2005. Kalevala—Stabreim: Zur Verisländischung des Kalevala. In *Hyvä kello kauas kuuluu.* Edited by Gerson Klumpp and Ingrid Schellbach-Kopra. Pp. 117-124. Hamburg: Buske.

Grønlandsk-dansk selvstyrekommissions betænkning om selvstyre i Grønland. April 2008. Online.

Grønvik, Ottar. 1985. *Runene på Eggjasteinen: en hedensk gravinnskrift fra slutten af 600-tallet.* Oslo: Universitetsforlaget.

Guðni Jónsson, ed. 1940-1947. *Íslenskir sagnaþættir og þjóðsögur.* 12 vols. Reykjavík: Ísafoldarprentsmiðja.

Guðni Jónsson, ed. 1954. *Fornaldarsögur Norðurlanda* 1-4. Reykjavík: Íslandingasagnaútgáfan.

Guðrún Nordal. 2001. *Tools of Literacy: The Role of Skaldic Verse in Icelandic Textual Culture of the Twelfth and Thirteenth Centuries.* Toronto: University of Toronto Press.

Guðrún Nordal. 2005. Attraction of Opposite: Skaldic Verse in *Njáls saga.* In *Literacy in Medieval and Early Modern Scandinavian Culture.* Edited by Pernille Hermann. Pp. 211-36. Odense: University Press of Southern Denmark.

Guðrún Nordal. 2008. The Dialogue Between Audience and Text: The Variants in Verse Citations in *Njáls saga*'s Manuscripts. In *Oral Art Forms and Their Passage into Writing*. Edited by Else Mundal and Jonas Wellendorf. Pp. 185-202. Copenhagen: Museum Tusculanum Press.

Guerber, Hélène Adeline. 1895. *Myths of Northern Lands: Narrated with Special Reference to Literature and Art*. New York: American Book Company.

Gundersen, Dag. 1967. *Fra Wergeland til Vogt-komiteen*. Oslo: Universitetsforlaget.

Gunnar Karlsson. 2000. *Iceland's 1100 Years: History of a Marginal Society*. London: Hurst and Company.

Gunnell, Terry. 1998. The Return of Sæmundur: Origins and Analogues. In *Þjóðlíf og þjóðtrú: ritgerðir helgaðar Jóni Hnefli Aðalsteinssyni*. Edited by Terry Gunnell, Jón Jónsson and Valdimar Tr. Hafstein. Pp. 87-111. Reykjavík: Þjóðsaga.

Gunnell, Terry. 2000. The Season of the *Dísir*: The Winter Nights and the *Dísablót* in Early Scandinavian Belief. *Cosmos* 16: 117-149.

Gunnell, Terry. 2001. Mists, Magicians and Murderous Children: International Migratory Legends Concerning the "Black Death" in Iceland. In *Northern Lights: Following Folklore in North-Western Europe: Essays in Honour of Bo Almqvist*. Edited by Séamas Ó Catháin. Pp. 47-59. Dublin: University College Dublin Press.

Gunnell, Terry. 2004. The Coming of the Christmas Visitors: Folk Legends Concerning the Attacks on Icelandic Farmhouses Made by Spirits at Christmas. *Northern Studies* 38: 51-75.

Gunnell, Terry. 2005. An Invasion of Foreign Bodies: Legends of Washed Up Corpses in Iceland. In *Eyðvinur: heiðursrit til Eyðun Andreassen*. Edited by Malan Marnersdóttir, Jens Cramer and Arnfinnur Johansen. Pp. 70-79. Tórshavn: Føroya fróðskaparfelag.

Gunnell, Terry. 2007. How Elvish were the *Álfar*? In *Constructing Nations, Reconstructing Myth: Essays in Honour of T. A. Shippey*. Edited by Andrew Wawn, Graham Johnson and John Walter. Pp. 111-130. Turnhout: Brepols.

Gunnell, Terry. 2010a. From Daisies to Oak Trees: The Politics of Early Folktale Collection in Northern Europe. *Folklore* 121: 12-37.

Gunnell, Terry. 2010b. Sagnagrunnur: A New Database of Icelandic Legends in Print. *Folklore: Electronic Journal of Folklore* 45: 151-162.

Gunnell, Terry. Forthcoming. How High Was the High One? The Role of Óðinn in Pre-Christian Icelandic Society. *Myth and Theory in the Old Norse World*. Edited by Stefan Brink. Turnhout: Brepols.

Gustavson, Helmer and Thorgunn Snædal Brink. 1981. Runfynd 1980. *Fornvännen* 76: 186-202.

Haase, Donald, ed. 2008. *The Greenwood Encyclopedia of Folktales and Fairy Tales*. Westport, CT: Greenwood.

Hafstein, Valdimar Tr. 2004a. The Politics of Origins: Collective Creation Revisited. *Journal of American Folklore* 117: 300-315.

Hafstein, Valdimar Tr. 2004b. *The Making of Intangible Cultural Heritage: Tradition and Authenticity, Community and Humanity*. Unpublished Ph.D. dissertation, University of California, Berkeley.

Hafstein, Valdimar Tr. 2009. Intangible Heritage as a List. In *Intangible Heritage*. Edited by Laurajane Smith and Natsuko Akagawa. Pp. 91-111. London: Routledge.

Hagen, Rune Blix. 2006. Sami Shamanism: The Arctic Dimension. *Magic, Ritual, and Witchcraft* 1: 227-233.

Hallfreður Örn Eiríksson and Marjatta Ísberg, eds. 1987. *Thorgeirin härkä: Islantilaisia kansankertomuksia*. Translated by Marjatta Ísberg. Helsinki: Suomalaisen Kirjallisuuden Seura.

Handler, Richard. 1988. *Nationalism and the Politics of Culture in Quebec*. Madison: Wisconsin University Press.

Haney, Jack V., ed. 2001. *Russian Wondertales*. 2, *Tales of Magic and the Supernatural*. The Complete Russian Folktale, vol. 4. Armonk, NY: M. E. Sharpe.

Hannes Þorsteinsson. 1912. Nokkrar athuganir un íslenzkrar bókmenntir á 12. og 13. öld. *Skírnir* 86: 339-357.

Hansen, Hans. 1932. *P. C. Asbjørnsen*. Oslo: Aschehoug.

Hansen, William. 1996. The Protagonist on the Pyre: Herodotean Legend and Modern Folktale. *Fabula* 37(3/4): 272-285.

Harries, Elizabeth Wanning. 2001. *Twice Upon a Time: Women Writers and the History of the Fairy Tale*. Princeton: Princeton University Press.

Harris, Marvin. 1968. *The Rise of Anthropological Theory*. New York: Harper and Row.

Hastrup, Kirsten. 1990. *Nature and Policy in Iceland: An Anthropological Analysis of History and Mentality*. Oxford: Clarendon Press.

Haugan, Jørgen. 1991. *400-årsnatten: norsk selvforståelse ved en korsvei*. Oslo: Universitetsforlaget.

Haugen, Einar I. 1937. A Critique and a Bibligraphy of the Writings of Rasmus B. Anderson. *The Wisconsin Magazine of History* 20: 255–269.

Hedeager, Lotte. 1997. *Skygger af en anden virkelighed: oldnordiske myter*. Copenhagen: Samleren.

Heilbut, Poul Erik, dir. 2007. *Flugten fra Grønland*. Copenhagen: DR1.

Heimskringla 1-3. 1941(1979)-1951. Edited by Bjarni Aðalbjarnarson. Íslenzk fornrit 26-28. Reykjavík: Hið íslenzka fornritafélag.

Helgi Guðmundsson and Árngrímur Fr. Bjarnason. 1933-49. *Vestfirzkar sagnir*. 3 vols. Reykjavík: Fagurskinna.

Heller, Rolf. 1976. *Die Laxdæla saga: Die literarische Schöpfung eines Isländers des 13. Jahrhunderts.* Akademie-Verlag: Berlin.

Hermann Pálsson. 1996a. *Keltar á Íslandi.* Reykjavík: Háskólaútgáfan.

Hermann Pálsson, ed. 1996b. *Völuspá: The Sibyl's Prophecy.* Edinburgh: Lockharton Press.

Hermann Pálsson. 1997. *Úr landnorðri: Samar og ystu rætur íslenskrar menningar.* Reykjavík: Bókmenntafræðistofnun Háskóla Íslands.

Hesse, Carla. 1991. Enlightenment Epistemology and the Laws of Authorship in Revolutionary France, 1777-1793. In *Law and the Order of Culture.* Edited by Robert Post. Pp. 109-137. Berkeley: University of California Press.

Heusler, Andreas. 1911. *Das Strafrecht der Isländersagas.* Leipzig: Von Duncker & Humblot.

Hodne, Fritz. 1981. *Norges økonomiske historie 1815-1970.* Oslo: Cappelen.

Hodne, Ørnulf. 1979. *Jørgen Moe og folkeeventyrene: en studie i nasjonalromantisk folkloristikk.* Oslo: Universitetsforlaget.

Hoel, Sigurd. 1948. Eventyrene våre. In *Tanker fra mange tider.* Reprinted in 1963 in *Essays i utvalg.* Edited by Nils Lie. Pp. 100-110. Oslo: Gyldendal.

Höfler, Otto. 1934. *Kultische Geheimbünde der Germanen.* Frankfurt am Main: M. Diesterweg.

Höfler, Otto. 1961. *Siegfried, Arminius und die Symbolik: Mit einem historischen Anhang über die Varusschlacht.* Heidelberg: Winter.

Holbek, Bengt. 1987 [1998]. *Interpretation of Fairy Tales: Danish Folklore in a European Perspective.* FF Communications 239. Helsinki: Suomalainen Tiedeakatemia.

Hollander, Lee M. 1986. *The Poetic Edda.* Austin: University of Texas Press.

Holmbäck, Åke and Elias Wessén, eds. 1943. *Skånelagen och Gutalagen.* Svenska landskapslagar 4. Stockholm: H. Geber.

Holmberg, Maj-Lis. 1959. Kalevalaa islanniksi. *Kalevalaseuran vuosikirja* 39: 111-129.

Holmberg, Maj-Lis. 1961. Karl Ísfelt [sic] kuollut. *Kalevalaseuran vuosikirja* 41: 377-379.

Holmberg, Maj-Lis. 1964. Kalevalan islanninnos. *Kalevalaseuran vuosikirja* 44: 330-334.

Holmberg, Uno. 1915. *Lappalaisten uskonto.* Suomensuvun uskonnot 2. Porvoo: Söderström.

Holtsmark, Anne. 1964. *Studier i Snorres mytologi.* Det Norske videnskapsakademi i Oslo, 2 Hist.-filos. klasse, n. s., 4. Oslo: Universitetsforlaget.

Holtsmark, Anne. 1968. Reginnaglar. *KLNM* 13: cols. 712-713.

Hom Cary, Stephanie. 2004. The Tourist Moment. *Annals of Tourism Research* 31: 61-77.

Honko, Lauri. 1964. Memorates and the Study of Folk Beliefs. *Journal of the Folklore Institute* 1(1/2): 5-19.

Honko, Lauri. 2000. Introduction. In *Thick Corpus, Organic Variation and Textuality in Oral Tradition*. Edited by Lauri Honko. Studia Fennica Folkloristica 7. Pp. 3-28. Helsinki: Finnish Literature Society.

Honko, Lauri. 2001. Copyright and Folklore. Paper read at the National Seminar on Copyright Law and Matters, Mangalore University, Mangalore, Karnataka, India, on February 9, 2001. *FF Network* 21: 8-10.

Howser, Huell. 2002. Roadtrip with Huell Howser: Solvang. *Roadtrip with Huell Howser*. Video. [Los Angeles]: Huell Howser Productions.

Hrómundar saga Gripssonar. 1944. In *Fornaldarsögur Norðurlanda* 2. Edited by Guðni Jónsson and Bjarni Vilhjálmsson. Pp. 271-286. Reykjavík: Bókaútgáfan Forni.

Hubert, Henri and Marcel Maus. 1899. Essai sur la nature et la fonction du sacrifice. *L'Année sociologique 2: 29-138.*

Huggert, Anders. 2000. A Church at Lyckselet and a Sacrificial Site on Altarberget: The Two Worlds of the Saami. *Acta Borealia* 17: 51-75.

Huld: safn alþýðlegra fræða íslenzkra. 1935-1936. Edited by Hannes Þorsteinsson, Jón Þorkelson et al. 2nd ed. 2 vols. Reykjavík: Snæbjörn Jónsson.

Hult, Marte Hvam. 2003. *Framing a National Narrative: The Legend Collections of Peter Christen Asbjørnsen*. Detroit: Wayne State University Press.

Hult, Marte Hvam. 2008. Scandinavian Tales. In *The Greenwood Encyclopedia of Folk Tales and Fairy Tales*. Edited by Donald Haase. Pp. 832-841. Westport, Conn.: Greenwood Press.

Hultgård, Anders, ed. 1997. *Uppsala och Adam av Bremen*. Nora: Nya Doxa.

Hultkrantz, Åke. 1985. Reindeer Nomadism and the Religion of the Saamis. In *Saami Pre-Christian Religion*. Edited by Louise Bäckman and Åke Hultkrantz. Studies in Comparative Religion 25. Pp. 11-28. Stockholm: Acta Universitatis Stockholmiensis.

Hultkrantz, Åke. 1987. On Beliefs in Non-Shamanic Guardian Spirits Among the Saamis. In *Saami Religion*. Edited by Tore Ahlback. Pp. 110-123. Uppsala: Almquist & Wiksell.

Hurston, Zora Neale. 1999. Characteristics of Negro Expression. In *Signifyin', Sanctifyin', and Slam Dunking: A Reader in African American Expressive Culture*. Edited by Gena Dagel Caponi. Pp. 293-308. Amherst: University of Massachusetts Press.

Hustvedt, Lloyd. 1966. *Rasmus Bjørn Anderson: Pioneer Scholar*. Authors Series 2. Northfield: Norwegian-American Historical Association.

Hvidt, Kristian and Olaf Olsen. 1990. *Gyldendal og Politikens Danmarkshistorie 11: 1850-1900*. Copenhagen: Gyldendal.

Hyvärinen, Matti, Lars-Christer Hydén, Marja Saarenheimo and Maria Tamboukou, eds. 2010. *Beyond Narrative Coherence*. Amsterdam and Philadelphia: John Benjamins.

Hyvönen, Jouni. 2005. Vanhan Kalevalan Vipusessa käynti -runon loitsujakson tekstualisointi: Elias Lönnrotin tekstualisointistrategiat. Unpublished licentiate thesis, University of Helsinki.

Hølaas, Odd, ed. 1957 [1945]. *Theodor Kittelsen i tekst, tegninger og malerier.* Oslo: Gyldendal.

Hølaas, Odd. 1962. *Troll i Norge som Th. Kittelsen så dem.* Oslo: Forlaget Norsk Kunstreproduksjon Stenersen.

Ilomäki, Henni. 1998. Kalevala in Translation. *FF Network* 16: 2-7.

Islannin Edda-runoja. 1934. Translated by Alku Siikaniemi. Helsinki.

James, Edwin O. 1962. *Sacrifice and Sacrament.* London: Thames and Hudson.

Jaszi, Peter. 1994. On the Author Effect: Contemporary Copyright and Collective Creativity. In *The Construction of Authorship: Textual Appropriation in Law and Literature.* Edited by Martha Woodmansee and Peter Jaszi. Pp. 29-56. Durham: Duke University Press.

Jensen, Ernst. 2001. *Langt væk hjemmefra—grønlandske børn på skoleophold i Danmark i 1960'erne og 1970'erne.* Nuuk: Atuagkat.

Joerges, Bernward. 1999. Do Politics Have Artefacts? *Social Studies of Science* 29: 411-31.

Johansen, Hans Chr. 1979. *En samfundsorganisation i opbrud 1700-1870.* Dansk socialhistorie 4. Copenhagen: Gyldendal.

Johansen, Lars Emil. 2008. Det grønlandske folk, Det grønlandske sprog: Grønlands adgang til selvstændighed. Public address, Nuuk, June 18, 2008. Online.

Johnsen, Birgit Hertzberg. 2010. Norwegian Folktales and Legends. Online.

Johnsen, Oscar A. and Jón Helgason ed. 1941. *Saga Óláfs konungs hins helga: Den store saga om Olav den hellige efter pergamenthåndskrift i Kungliga biblioteket i Stockholm nr. 2 4to med varianter fra andre håndskrifter.* 2 vols. Det norske historiske kildeskriftfond skrifter 47. Kristiania (Oslo): Dybwad.

Jón Árnason. 1954-1961. *Íslenzkar þjóðsagnir og æfintýri.* Edited by Árni Böðvarsson and Bjarni Vilhjálmsson. 6 vols. Reykjavík: Þjóðsaga.

Jón Halldórsson. 2005. *Atriði ævi minnar: bréf og greinar.* Edited by Úlfar Bragason. Reykjavík: Háskólaútgáfan.

Jón Helgason. 1944. Að yrkja á íslenzku. *Tímarit Máls og menningar* 5: 217-251.

Jón Hnefill Aðalsteinsson. 1998. *A Piece of Horse Liver: Myth, Ritual and Folklore in Old Icelandic Sources.* Reykjavík: Háskólaútgáfan / Félagsvísindastofnun.

Jón Sigurðsson et al., eds. 1848-87. *Edda Snorra Sturlusonar: Edda Snorronis Sturlaei.* 3 vols. Copenhagen: Legatum Arnamagnaeanum. Reprinted Osnabrück: Zeller 1966.

Jón Thorarensen. 1971. *Rauðskinna hin nýrri: þjóðsögur, sagnaþættir, þjóðhættir og annálar.* 3 vols. Reykjavík: Þjóðsaga.

Jón Þorláksson. 1956. *Þjóðsögur og munnmæli.* Reykjavík: Bókfellsútgáfan.

Júlíana Magnúsdóttir. 2008. Saga til næsta bæjar: sagnir, samfélag og þjóðtrú sagnafólks frá austurhéraði Vestur-Skaftafellssýslu. Unpublished M.A. thesis. University of Iceland.

Jæger, Henrik. 1896. Tredie tidsrum: 1845-1857; Folkedigtningens herredømme i literaturen. In *Illustreret norsk literaturhistorie 2:1.* Kristiania: Hjalmar Biglers forlag.

Jørgensen, Harald. 1940. *Studier over det offentlige Fattigvæsens historiske Udvikling i Danmark i det 19. Aarhundrede.* Copenhagen: Institutet for historie og samfundsøkonomi i kommission hos Gyldendal.

Kaivola-Bregenhøj, Anniki. 1996. *Narrative and Narrating: Variation in Juho Oksanen's Storytelling.* FF Communications 261. Helsinki: Suomalainen Tiedeakatemia.

Kalevala, or, Poems of the Kaleva District. 1963. Compiled by Elias Lönnrot. A prose translation with foreword and appendices by Francis Peabody Magoun, Jr. Cambridge: Harvard University Press.

Kalevala. 1908. Translated by Ferdinand Ohrt. Copenhagen: Gyldendal.

Kalevala. 1948. Translated by Björn Collinder. Stockholm: Bokverk.

Kalevala. 1957-1962. Translated by Karl Ísfeld. Reykavík: Bókaútgáfa Menningarsjóðs.

Kalevala: The Land of Heroes. 1907. Translated by W. F. Kirby. London: J. M. Dent.

Kaplan, David and Benson Saler. 1966. Foster's "Image of Limited Good": An Example of Anthropological Explanation. *American Anthropologist* 68: 202-206.

Kaplan, Merrill. 2003. On the Road to Realism with Asbjørnsen and Moe, *Peer Gynt,* and Henrik Ibsen. *Scandinavian Studies* 75: 491-508.

Karsten, Rafael. 1955. *The Religion of the Samek: Ancient Beliefs and Cults of the Scandinavian and Finnish Lapps.* Leiden: Brill.

Kaukonen, Väinö. 1979. *Lönnrot ja Kalevala.* Helsinki: Suomalaisen Kirjallisuuden Seura.

Kelchner, Georgia Dunham. 1935. *Dreams in Old Norse Literature and Their Affinities in Folklore.* Cambridge: Cambridge University Press.

Kershaw, Kris. 2000. *The One-Eyed God: Odin and the (Indo-)Germanic Männerbünde.* Journal of Indo-European Studies Monograph 36. Washington D.C.: Journal of Indo-European Studies.

Ketilsson, Eli. 1993. *Norway: Home of the Trolls.* [Illustrated by] Theodor Kittelsen. Translated by Joan Fuglesang. Jar, Norway: Medusa.

Kielsen, Lene. 1996. *Mitaartut:* An Inuit winter festival in Greenland. *Études / Inuit / Studies* 20: 123-129.

Kirshenblatt-Gimblett, Barbara. 1998. *Destination Culture: Tourism, Museums, and Heritage.* Berkeley: University of California Press.

Kirshenblatt-Gimblett, Barbara. 2004. Intangible Heritage as Metacultural Production. *Museum International* 56(1-2): 52-65.

Kittelsen, Theodor. 1957. *Theodor Kittelsen i tekst, tegninger og malerier.* Oslo: Gyldendal.

Kjellström, Rolf. 1985. Piles of Bones, Cult-places, or Something Else? In *Saami Pre-Christian Religion.* Edited by Louise Bäckman and Åke Hultkrantz. Pp. 115-120. Uppsala: Almqvist & Wiksell.

Kjellström, Rolf. 1987. On the Continuity of Old Saami Religion. In *Saami Religion.* Edited by Tore Ahlbäck. Pp. 24-33. Uppsala: Almqvist & Wiksell.

Klein, Barbro. 2006. Cultural Heritage, the Swedish Folklife Sphere, and the Others. *Cultural Analysis* 5: 58-80.

Kleivan, Inge. 1960. Mitaartut: Vestiges of the Eskimo Sea-woman Cult in West Greenland. In *Meddelelser om Grønland udgivne af kommissionen for videnskabelige undersøgelser i Grønland* 161(5). Pp. 1-30. Copenhagen: C. A. Reitzels forlag.

Kleivan, Inge and Birgitte Sonne. 1985. *Eskimos, Greenland and Canada.* Iconography of Religions 8: 2. Leiden: Brill.

Klintberg, Bengt af. 2010. *The Types of the Swedish Folk Legend.* FF Communications 300. Helsinki: Suomalainen Tiedeakatemia.

Kock, Ernst A. 1923-1944. *Notationes Norrœnæ: anteckningar till Edda och skaldediktning.* Lunds universitets årsskrift, n. s., sec. 1. Lund: Gleerup.

Kock, Ernst A., ed. 1946-1950. *Den norsk-isländska skaldediktningen.* 2 vols. Lund: Gleerup.

Koefoed, Holger og Einar Økland. 1999. *Th. Kittelsen: kjente og ukjente sider ved kunstneren.* Oslo: Stenersen.

Kollmann, Wolfgang. 1969. The Process of Urbanization in Germany at the Height of the Industrialization Period. *Journal of Contemporary History* 4: 59-76.

Kreutzer, Gert. 1987. *Kindheit und Jugend in der altnordischen Literatur.* Münstersche Beiträge zur deutschen und nordischen Philologie 2. Münster: Kleinheinrich.

Kreutzer, Gert. 1993. Der Held als Kind, das Kind als Held. In *Arbeiten zur Skandinavistik: 10. Arbeitstagung der deutschsprachigen Skandinavistik, 22.-27.9.1991 am Weißenhäuser Strand.* Edited by Bernhard Glienke and Edith Marold. Pp. 158-66. Texte und Untersuchungen zur Germanistik und Skandinavistik 32. Frankfurt am Main: Peter Lang.

Kristiansen, Kristian. 2001. Rulers and Warriors: Symbolic Transmission and Social Transformation in Bronze Age Europe. In *From Leaders to*

Rulers. Edited by Jonathan Haas. Pp. 85-105. New York: Kluwer Academic.

Kristiansen, Kristian. 2004. Institutioner og materiel kultur: tvillingherskerne som religiøs og politisk institution under bronzealderen. In *Ordning mot kaos: studier av nordisk förkristen kosmologi.* Edited by Anders Andrén et al. Pp. 99-122. Lund: Nordic Academic Press.

Kristján Eldjárn. 1974. Þórláksskrín í Skálaholti. Samtíningur um glataðan forngrip. *Árbók hins íslenzka fornleifafélags 1973*: 19-42.

Kristján Eldjárn. 2000. *Kuml og haugfé úr heiðnum sið á Íslandi.* Edited by Adolf Friðriksson. 2nd ed. Reykjavík: Mál og menning / Fornleifastofnun Íslands / Þjóðminjasafn Íslands.

Kuruk, Paul. 1999. Protecting Folklore Under Modern Intellectual Property Regimes: A Reappraisal of the Tensions Between Individual and Communal Rights in Africa and the United States. *American University Law Review* 48: 769-849.

Kuusi, Matti, Keith Bosley and Michael Branch, eds. 1977. *Finnish Folk Poetry—Epic: An Anthology in Finnish and English.* Helsinki: Finnish Literature Society.

Kuusi, Matti. 1983. Edda suomeksi. *Parnasso* 33: 250-252.

Kvideland, Reimund. 1999. Peter Christen Asbjørnsen: utdypning. In *Norsk bibliografisk leksikon* 1: 106–120.

Kvideland, Reimund and Henning K. Sehmsdorf, eds. 1988. *Scandinavian Folk Belief and Legend.* Minneapolis: University of Minnesota.

La Farge, Beatrice and John Tucker. 1992. *Glossary to the Poetic Edda: Based on Hans Kuhn's Kurzes Wörterbuch.* Heidelberg: Winter.

Labov, William and Joshua Waletzky. 1967. Narrative Analysis. In *Essays on the Verbal and Visual Arts.* Edited by June Helm. Pp. 12-44. Seattle: University of Washington Press.

Läffler, L. Frits. 1908. Till 700-årsminnet af slaget vid Lena (31 januari 1208). 3. Ett stadgande i gutasaga, som ytterst föranledts af slaget vid Lena: en laghistorisk undersökning. *Fornvännen* 3: 137-177.

Lagerfeld, Steven. 1986. The Reading Revolution. *The Wilson Quarterly* 10: 104-115.

Lahelma, Antti. 2008. Communicating with "Stone Persons": Anthropomorphism, Saami Religion and Finnish Rock Art. In *A Touch of Red: Archaeological and Ethnographic Approaches to Interpreting Finnish Rock Paintings.* Doctoral dissertation. University of Helsinki, Faculty of Arts, Institute for Cultural Research. *Iskos* 15. Pp. 121-142. Helsinki: Finnish Antiquarian Society.

Landnámabók. 1968. In *Íslendingabók: Landnámabók.* Edited by Jakob Benediktsson. Pp. 29-397. Íslenzk fornrit 1. Reykjavik: Hið íslenzka bókmenntafélag.

Langgård, Karen 2003. Magt og demokrati—og sprog. In *Demokrati og magt i Grønland.* Edited by Gorm Winther. Pp. 215-235. Aarhus: Aarhus universitetsforlag.

Langgård, Karen. 2011. Greenlandic Literature from Colonial Times to Self-government. In *From Oral Tradition to Rap: Literatures of the Polar North.* Edited by Karen Langgård and Kirsten Thisted. Pp. 121-190. Nuuk: Ilisimatusarfik / Atuagkat.

Langgård, Per. 1992. Grønlandsksproget—tosproget—grønlandsksproget: nogle tendenser i det dansk-grønlandske sprogmøde blandt Nuuk's skolebørn. *Grønlandsk kultur- og samfundsforskning* 92: 104-128.

Lapidge, Michael. 1999. St. Cuthbert. In *The Blackwell Encyclopaedia of Anglo-Saxon England.* Edited by Michael Lapidge et al. Pp. 131-133. Oxford and Malden, MA: Blackwell Publishers.

Larrington, Carolyne, ed. 1996. *The Poetic Edda.* Oxford: Oxford University Press.

Larsen, Hanne Pico. 2006. Solvang, CA: "The Danish Capital of America": A Little Bit of Denmark, Disney, or Something Else? Unpublished Ph.D. dissertation, Department of Scandinavian, University of California, Berkeley.

Larsen, Henning. 1949. Asbjörnsen: A Bibliographic Note and an Unpublished Letter. *The Journal of English and Germanic Philology* 48: 112-115.

Larsson, Lars and Karl-Magnus Lenntorp. 2004. The Enigmatic House. In *Continuity for Centuries: A Ceremonial Building and its Context at Uppåkra, Southern Sweden.* Edited by Lars Larsson. Uppåkrastudier 10. Stockholm: Almqvist & Wiksell.

Larsson, Lars. 2006. Ritual Building and Ritual Space: Aspects of Investigations at the Iron Age Central Site Uppåkra, Scania, Sweden. In *Old Norse Religion in Long-term Perspective: Origins, Changes, and Interactions.* Edited by Anders Andrén et al. Pp. 248-253. Vägar till Midgård 8. Lund: Nordic Academic Press.

Lassen, Annette. 2008. *Det norrøne og det nationale: studier i brugen af Islands gamle litteratur i nationale sammnenhænge i Norge, Sverige, Island, Storbritannien, Tyskland og Danmark.* Edited by Annette Lassen. Reykjavík: Stofnun Vigdísar Finnbogadóttur.

Laxdæla saga. 1934. Edited by Einar Ól. Sveinsson. Íslenzk fornrit 5. Reykjavik: Hið íslenzka bókmenntafélag.

Laxness, Halldór. 1963. *Skáldatími.* Reykjavík: Helgafell.

Lehiste, Ilse. 1983. The Estonian Translation of the Elder Edda: Problems of Metric Equivalence. *Journal of Baltic Studies* 14: 179-184.

Lehmann, Karl, and Hans Schnorr von Carolsfeld. 1883. *Die Njálssage, insbesonder in ihren juristischen Bestandtheilen: Ein kritischer Beitrag zur altnordischen Rechts- und Literaturegeschichte.* Berlin: R. L. Prager.

Leino, Pentti. 1970. *Strukturaalinen alkusointu suomessa: folklorepohjainen tilastoanalyysi.* Suomen Kirjallisuuden Seuran toimituksia 298. Helsinki: Suomalaisen Kirjallisuuden Seura

Leino, Pentti. 1986. *Language and Metre: Metrics and the Metrical System of Finnish.* Helsinki: Suomalaisen Kirjallisuuden Seura.

Leinonen, Marja. 2007. The Filman Sámi on the Kola Peninsula. In *Topics on the Ethnic, Linguistic and Cultural Making of the Russian North.* Edited by Juhani Nuorluoto. *Slavica Helsingiensia* 32: 138-162.

Lerbom, Jens. 2003. *Mellan två riken: integration, politisk kultur och förnationella identiteter på Gotland 1500-1700.* Studia historica Lundensia 11. Lund: Historiska institutionen vid Lunds universitet.

Liberman, Anatoly. 2004. Some Controversial Aspects of the Myth of Baldr. *alvíssmál* 11: 17-54.

Lidén, Hans-Emil. 1969. From Pagan Sanctuary to Christian Church: The Excavation of Mære Church in Trøndelag. With comments by Wilhelm Holmqvist and Olaf Olsen. *Norwegian Archaeological Review* 2: 3-32.

Lie, Thore. 1985. The Reception of Darwinism in Norway: The Early Years, 1861-1900. *Archive of National History* 12: 153-159.

Lie, Thore. 2000. Fra *The origin of species* til *Arternes oprindelse: Tidsskrift for Den norske lægeforening* Nr. 30(10/120): 3714-3718.

Liebgott, Niels-Knud. 1993. Reliquaries. In *Medieval Scandinavia: An Encyclopedia.* Edited by Phillip Pulsiano and Kirsten Wolf. Pp. 525-526. New York and London: Garland.

Lindow, John, ed. and trans. 1978. *Swedish Legends and Folktales.* Berkeley: University of California Press.

Lindow, John. 1982. Swedish Legends of Buried Treasure. *Journal of American Folklore* 95: 257-279.

Lindow, John. 1994. Bloodfeud and Scandinavian Mythology. *alvíssmál* 4: 51-68.

Lindow, John. 1997. *Murder and Vengeance Among the Gods: Baldr in Scandinavian Mythology.* FF Communications 262. Helsinki: Suomalainen Tiedeakatemia.

Lindow, John. 2001a. *Norse Mythology: A Guide to the Gods, Heroes, Rituals, and Beliefs.* Oxford and New York: Oxford University Press.

Lindow, John. 2001b. *Handbook of Norse Mythology.* Santa Barbara, CA: ABC Clio.

Lindow, John. 2003. Cultures in Contact. In *Old Norse Myths, Literature and Society.* Edited by Margaret Clunies Ross. The Viking Collection, vo. 14. Pp. 89-109. Odense: University Press of Southern Denmark.

Lindow, John. 2004. Talking ships. *Margaret and Richard Beck Lecture.* Nov. 20, 2004. University of Victoria.

Lindow, John. 2008. Changelings, Changing, Re-exchanges: Thoughts on the Relationship between Folk Belief and Legend. In *Legends and Landscape: Articles Based on Plenary Papers Presented at the 5th Celtic-Nordic-Baltic Legend Symposium, Reykjavík 2005*. Edited by Terry Gunnell. Pp. 215-234. Reykjavík: Háskólaútgáfan.

Lindqvist, Sune, ed. 1941-1942. *Gotlands Bildsteine*. 2 vols. Kungl. Vitterhets-, historie- och antikvitetsakademien. Monografier 28. Stockholm: Kungl. Vitterhets historie och antikvitets akademien.

Lindwall, Bo. 1982. Artistic Revolution in Nordic Countries. In *Northern Light: Realism and Symbolism in Scandinavian Painting 1880-1910*. Edited by Kirk Varnedoe. Pp. 35-42. New York: Brooklyn Museum.

Littleton, C. Scott. 1982. *The New Comparative Mythology: An Anthropological Assessment of the Theories of Georges Dumézil*. 3rd ed. Berkeley: University of California Press.

Longfellow, Henry Wadsworth. 1855. *The Song of Hiawatha*. Boston: Ticknor and Fields.

Longfellow, Henry Wadsworth. 1985. *Hiawatha*. Translated by Aale Tynni. Porvoo: WSOY.

Lönnrot, Elias, ed. 1835. *Kalewala, taikka, wanhoja Karjalan runoja Suomen kansan muinosista ajoista*. Helsinki: [Suomalaisen Kirjallisuuden Seura].

Lönnrot, Elias, ed. 1849. *Kalevala*. Helsinki: Suomalaisen Kirjallisuuden Seura.

Lönnroth, Lars. 1976. *Njáls saga: A Critical Introduction*. Berkeley: University of California Press.

Lönnroth, Lars. 1977. *Skírnismál* och den fornisländska äktenskapsnormen. In *Opuscula Septentrionalia: festskrift til Ole Widding 10. 10. 1977*. Edited by Bent Chr. Jacobsen et al. Pp. 154-178. Copenhagen: C. A. Reitzel.

López, Raimundo. 2004. El Condor Pasa: Patrimonio Cultural de la Nacion de Peru. Online.

Lorenz, Gottfried, ed. 1984. *Snorri Sturluson. Gylfaginning. Texte, Übersetzung, Kommentar*. Texte zur Forschung 48. Darmstadt: Wissenschaftliche Buchgesellschaft.

Lukjancenko, Tatjana V. 1985. The Burial Customs of the Kola Saamis. In *Saami Pre-Christian Religion*. Edited by Louise Bäckman and Åke Hultkrantz. Pp. 201-210. Uppsala: Almqvist & Wiksell.

Lundager Jensen, Hans J. and Jens Peter Schjødt. 1994. *Suveræniteten, kampen og frugtbarheden: Georges Dumézil og den indoeuropæiske ideologi*. Aarhus: Aarhus universitetsforlag.

Lunden, Käre. 1992. *Norsk grålysing*. Gjøvik, Norway: Det Norske samlaget.

Lüthi, Max. 1968. *Es war einmal*. Kleine Vandenhoeck-Reihe 136/137. Göttingen: Vandenhoeck & Ruprecht.

Mac Philib, Séamus. 1991. The Changeling (ML 5058): Irish Versions of a Migratory Legend in Their International Context. *Béaloideas* 59: 121-31.

MacCannell, Dean. 1999. *The Tourist: A New Theory of the Leisure Class.* Berkeley and Los Angeles: University of California Press.

MacCannell, Dean. 2001. Tourist Agency. *Tourist Studies* 1: 23-37.

Magerøy, Hallvard. 1948. Glælognskviða av Toraren lovtunge. *Bidrag til nordisk filologi av studerende ved Universitetet i Oslo* 12. Oslo: Aschehoug.

Magnús Bjarnason. 1950. *Þjóðsagnakver.* Reykjavík: Hlaðbúð.

Manneke, Peter. 2005. The Excavations of Havor Ringfort and Its Environs. In, *The Havor Hoard: The Gold, the Bronzes, the Fort.* Edited by Erik Nylén, Ulla Lund Hansen, and Peter Manneke. Kungl. Vitterhets-, historie- och antikvitetsakademiens handlingar. Antikvariska serien 46. Pp. 96-144. Stockholm: Kungl. Vitterhets historie och antikvitets akademien.

Mauss, Marcel. 1954 [1924]. *The Gift.* Translated by Ian Cunnison. New York: Free Press.

McNeill, F. Marian. 2001. *The Silver Bough. Vol. 1, Scottish Folk-lore and Folk-belief.* Edinburgh: Canongate.

McSherry, J. Patrice. 2005. *Predatory States: Operation Condor and Covert War in Latin America.* Lanham: Rowman & Littlefield Publishers.

Meulengracht Sørensen, Preben. 1993. *Fortælling og ære: studier i islændingesagaerne.* Aarhus: Aarhus universitetsforlag.

Miller, William Ian. 1990. *Bloodtaking and Peacemaking: Feud, Law, and Society in Saga Iceland.* Chicago: University of Chicago Press.

Mitchell, Brian R. 1992. *International Historical Statistics: Europe 1750-1988.* New York: Stockton Press.

Mitchell, Steven A. 1983. *Fǫr Scírnis* as Mythological Model: *frið at kaupa. Arkiv för nordisk filologi* 98: 108-22.

Moe, Jørgen. 1898 [1851]. *I Brønden og i Tjærnet.* Christiania: Alb. Cammermeyers forlag.

Moe, Moltke. 1917 [1883-87]. *Eventyrbog for børn: Norske Folkeeventyr af P.Chr. Asbjørnsen and Jørgen Moe, med illustrationer af Th. Kittelsen og Erik Werenskiold, texte revision af Moltke Moe.* Kristiania og Copenhagen: Gyldendalske boghandel, Nordisk forlag.

Moe, Moltke. 1927. Det nationale gjennembrud og dets mænd. In *Moltke Moes samlede skrifter* 3. Edited by Knut Liestøl. Oslo: H. Aschehoug and Co.

Moe, Thorvald. 1977. *Demographic Developments and Economic Growth in Norway 1740-1940.* New York: Arno Press.

Mondrup, Iben. 2003. *De usynlige grønlændere / Kalaallit takussaanngitsut.* Nuuk: Atuagkat.

Moreno, Anthony. El cóndor pasa (si pudiera): Comentario. *Literatura. . . ¡y algo más!* Online.

Mortensen, Lars Boje. 2002. Recent Research in the Legend of Saint Olav. In *Scripturus vitam: lateinische Biographie von der Antike bis in die Gegenwart: Festgabe für Walter Berschin zum 65. Geburtstag.* Edited by Dorothea Walz. Pp. 1011-18. Heidelberg: Mattes.

Moyne, Ernest J. 1957. Parodies of Longfellow's *Song of Hiawatha. Delaware Notes* 30: 93–108.

Moyne, Ernest J. 1963. *Hiawatha and Kalevala: A Study of the Relationship Between Longfellow's "Indian Edda" and the Finnish Epic.* FF Communications 192. Helsinki: Suomalainen Tiedeakatemia.

Mulk, Inga-Maria. 1994. Sacrificial Places and Their Meaning in Saami Society. In *Sacred Sites, Sacred Places.* Edited by David L. Carmichael et al. Pp. 121-131. London: Routledge.

Mullen, Patrick B. 1978. The Folk Idea of Unlimited Good in American Folk Legend. *Journal of the Folklore Institute* 15: 209-220.

Munch, Gerd Stamsø. 1991. Hus og hall: en høvdinggård på Borg i Lofoten. In *Nordisk Hedendom: et symposium.* Edited by Gro Steinsland et al. Pp. 321-333. Odense: Odense University Press.

Mundal, Else. 1974. *Fylgjemotiva i norrøn litteratur.* Universitetsforlaget: Oslo.

Mustanoja, Tauno F. 1964. Kalevalan uusi englanninkielinen käännös. *Kalevalaseuran vuosikirja* 44: 322-329.

Nasjonalmuseet for kunst, arkitektur og design. 2007-2008. *Theodor Kittelsen.* Oslo: Nasjonalgalleriet.

Neckel, Gustav and Hans Kuhn, eds. 1962. *Edda: Die Lieder des Codex Regius nebst verwandten Denkmälern.* 3rd ed. Heidelberg: Winter.

Ney, Agneta. 2007. The Edges of the Old Norse World-View. In *Old Norse Religion in Long-term Perspectives: Origins, Changes, and Interactions: an International Conference in Lund, Sweden, June 3-7, 2004.* Edited by Anders Andrén, Kristina Jennbert and Catharina Raudvere. Pp. 63-67. Lund: Nordic Academic Press.

Nicolaisen, William F. H. 1987. The Linguistic Structure of Legends. In *Perspectives on Contemporary Legend,* vol. 2. Edited by Gillian Bennett, Paul Smith and J.D.A. Widdowson. Pp. 61-76. Sheffield: Sheffield Academic Press.

Nicolson, William. 1892. *Myth and Religion, or, An Enquiry into Their Nature and Relations.* Helsinki: Press of the Finnish Literary Society.

Nielsen, Ann-Lili. 1997. Pagan Cultic and Votive Acts at Borg. In *Visions of the Past: Trends and Traditions in Swedish Medieval Archaeology.* Edited by Hans Andersson, Peter Carelli and Lars Ersgård. Pp. 373-392. Lund Studies in Medieval Archaeology 19. Stockholm: Almqvist & Wiksell.

Njal's Saga. 1960. Translated by Magnus Magnusson and Hermann Pálsson. London: Penguin.

Nordahl, Else. 1996. *Templum quod Ubsola dicitur... i arkeologisk belysning.* Aun 22. Uppsala: Department of Archaeology, Uppsala University.

Nordic Council of Ministers and the Arts Council of Great Britain. 1986. *Dreams of a Summer Night: Scandinavian Painting at the Turn of the Century.* Arts Council of Great Britain.

Norges offisielle statistikk. 1949. *Statistiske oversikter, 1948.* Oslo.

North, Richard. 1997. *Heathen Gods in Old English Literature.* Cambridge Studies in Anglo-Saxon England 22. Cambridge: Cambridge University Press.

Noyes, Dorothy. 2003. Group. In *Eight Words for the Study of Expressive Culture.* Edited by Burt Feintuch. Pp. 7-41. Urbana: University of Illinois Press.

Noyes, Dorothy. 2006. The Judgment of Solomon: Global Protections for Tradition and the Problem of Community Ownership. *Cultural Analysis* 5: 27-55.

Noyes, Dorothy. 2009. Hardscrabble Academies: Toward a Social Economy of Vernacular Invention. *Ethnologia Europaea* 39: 41-53.

Nylén, Erik and Jan Peder Lamm. 2003. *Bildstenar.* Stockholm: Gidlund.

O'Donoghue, Heather. 2003. What has Baldr to do with Lamech? The Lethal Shot of a Blind Man in Old Norse Myth and Jewish Exegetical Traditions. *Medium Ævum* 72: 82-107.

Ó hÓgáin, Dáithí. 2006. *The Lore of Ireland: An Encyclopedia of Myth, Legend and Romance.* Cork: The Collins Press.

Oddur Björnsson and Jónas Jónasson. 1977. *Þjóðtrú og þjóðsagnir.* Akureyri: Oddur Björnsson.

Oehlenschläger, Adam Gottlob. 1807. *Nordiske Digte.* Copenhagen: Andreas Seidelin.

Ögmundur Helgason. 2004. *Galdrakver: ráð til varnar gegn illum öflum þessa og annars heims.* 2 vols. Reykjavík: Landsbókasafn Íslands, Háskólabókasafn.

Ólafur Davíðsson. 1940-1943. *Galdur og galdramál á Íslandi.* Reykjavík: Sögufélag.

Ólafur Daviðsson. 1978-1980. *Íslenzkar þjóðsögur.* Edited by Bjarni Vilhjálmsson and Þorsteinn Jónsson. 4 vols. Reykjavík: Þjóðsaga.

Ólafur Halldórsson. 1985. Introduction. In *Eríks saga rauða: texti Skálholtsbókar AM 557 4to.* Íslenzk fornrit 4, addition. Pp. 333–399. Reykjavík: Hið íslenzka fornritafélag.

Ólína Þorvarðardóttir 2000: *Brennuöld: galdar og galdratrú í málaskjölum og munnmælum.* Reykjavík: Háskólaútgáfan.

Olsen, Magnus. 1909. Fra gammelnorsk myte og kultus. *Maal og Minne.* 1: 17-36.

Olsen, Nutuk Lund. 2010. *Kalaalimernit—en immatriel kulturarv.* *Tidsskriftet Grønland* 3: 218-227.

Olsen, Olaf. 1965 [1966]. Hørg, hov og kirke: historiske og arkaeologiske vikingetidsstudier. *Aarbøger for nordisk oldkyndighed og historie* 1965. Pp. 1-307. Reprint Copenhagen.

Olsson, Ingemar. 1996. *Gotländska ortnamn.* Visby: Ödins förlag.

Ordower, Henry. 1991. Exploring the Literary Function of Law and Litigation in *Njál's saga. Cardozo Studies in Law and Literature* 3: 41-61.

Oring, Elliott. 1990. Legend, Truth, and News. *Southern Folklore* 47: 63–77.

Oring, Elliot. 2008. Legendry and the Rhetoric of Truth. *Journal of American Folklore* 121: 127-166.

Oring, Elliott. *Forthcoming.* Thinking Through Tradition. In *Just Folklore: Analysis, Interpretation, Critique.* Pp. 219-238. Los Angeles: Cantilever Press.

Ortiz, Carmen. 1999. The Uses of Folklore by the Franco Regime. *Journal of American Folklore* 112: 479-496.

Oruro Carnival. *Masterpieces website.* UNESCO. Online.

Orkneyinga saga. 1965. Edited by Finnbogi Guðmundsson. Íslenzk fornrit 24. Pp. 1-300. Reykjavik: Hið íslenzka bókmenntafélag.

Østerund, Øyvind. 1986. Nasjonalstaten Norge: en karakteriserende skisse. In, *Det Norske samfunn.* Edited by Lars Alldén, Natalie Rogolf Ramsøy, and Mariken Vaa. Pp. 7-32. Oslo: Gyldendal.

Øverland, Orm. 2000. *Immigrant Minds, American Identities: Making the United States Home, 1870–1930.* Urbana and Chicago: University of Illinois Press.

Oxford English Dictionary. 1989. Oxford: Oxford University Press.

Palmenfelt, Ulf. 1993. On the Understanding of Folk Legends. In *Telling Reality: Folklore Studies in Memory of Bengt Holbek.* Edited by Michael Chesnutt. Pp. 143-167. Copenhagen and Turku: Nordic Institute of Folklore.

Palmenfelt, Ulf. 2009. Dominant Units in Life History Narratives. Paper presented at the *ISFNR Congress in Athens*, Greece, June 2009.

Parker Pearson, Michael. 2003. *The Archaeology of Death and Burial.* 2nd ed. Stroud: The History Press.

Parpola, Asko. 2004. Old Norse *Seið(r)*, Finnish *Seita* and Saami Shamanism. In *Etymologie, Entlehnungen und Entwicklungen: Festschrift für Jorma Koivulehto zum 70. Geburtstag.* Edited by Irma Hyvärinen, Petri Kallio, Jarmo Korhonen, and Leena Kolehmainen. Pp. 235-273. Helsinki: Société Néophilologique.

Patterson, Lyman Ray. 1968. *Copyright in Historical Perspective.* Nashville: Vanderbildt University Press.

Pentikäinen, Juha. 1968. Grenzprobleme zwischen Memorat und Sage. *Temenos* 3: 136-167.

Pentakäinen, Juha. 1978. *Oral Repertoire and World View: An Anthropological Study of Marina Takolo's Life History.* FF Communications 219. Helsinki: Suomalainen Tiedeakatemia.

Pentakäinen, Juha. 1989. The Dead Without Status. In *Nordic Folklore: Recent Studies.* Edited by Reimund Kvideland and Henning K. Sehmsdorf. Pp. 128-134. Bloomington and Indianapolis. 128-34.

Pentikäinen, Juha, ed. 1996. *Shamanism and Northern Ecology: Papers Presented at the Regional Conference on Circumpolar and Northern Religion, Helsinki, May 1990.* Religion and Society 36. Berlin: Mouton de Gruyter.

Pentikäinen, Juha. 1997. *Shamanism and Culture.* Helsinki: Etnika Co.

Petersen, Erik. 1992a. Bøger og bogkultur. In *Viking og Hvidekrist: Norden og Europa 800-1200.* Edited by Else Roesdahl. Pp. 216-17. Copenhagen: Nordisk ministerråd.

Petersen, Erik. 1992b. Vínlandsferð Flateyjarbókar: um bókaverði, *Codex Flateyensis* og þjóðlega hégómadýrð. In *Landsbókasafn Íslands: Árbók 1991, n. s. 17.* Translated by Finnbogi Guðmundsson. Pp. 5–25. Reykjavík: Landsbókasafn.

Petersen, Robert. 1985. The Use of Certain Symbols in Connection with Greenlandic Identity. In *Native Power: The Quest for Autonomy and Nationhood of Indigenous Peoples.* Edited by Jens Brøsted et al. Pp. 294-300. Bergen: Norwegian University Press.

Petterson, Olaf. 1987. Old Nordic and Christian Elements in Saami Ideas About the Realm of the Dead. In *Saami Religion.* Edited by Tore Ahlbäck. Uppsala: Almqvist & Wiksell.

Phelpstead, Carl, ed. 2001. *A History of Norway and the Passion and Miracles of the Blessed Ólafr.* Translated by Devra Levingson Kunin. Viking Society for Northern Research, Text Series 13. London: University College.

Phelpstead, Carl, ed. 2008. *A History of Norway and the Passion and Miracles of the Blessed Ólafr.* Translated by Devra Kunin. Viking Society for Northern Research, Text Series 13. Web publication with minor corrections of original edition of 2001. London: University College.

Picard, Eve. 1991. *Germanisches Sakralkönigtum? Quellenkritische Studien zur Germania des Tacitus und zur altnordischen Überlieferung.* Heidelberg: Winter.

Poetic Edda. 1962. Translated by Lee M. Hollander. Austin: University of Texas Press.

Den poetiska Eddan. 1957. Translated by Björn Collinder. Stockholm: Forum.

Pollock, Sir Frederick and Frederic William Maitland. 1898 [1895]. *The History of English Law Before the Time of Edward I.* Vol. 1. 2nd ed. Cambridge: Cambridge University Press. Reprinted 1968.

Popp, Daniel. 1977. *Asbjørnsen's Linguistic Reform.* Oslo: Universitetsforlaget.

Poulot, Dominique. 2006. *Une histoire du patrimoine en Occident, XVIIIe-XXIe siècle: du monument aux valeurs*. Le noeud gordien. Paris: Presses universitaires de France.

Prescott, Andrew. 2002. *The Benedictional of St Æthelwold: A Masterpiece of Anglo-Saxon Art. A Facsimile*. London: The British Library.

Pressouyre, Léon. 2001. Cultural Heritage and the 1972 Convention: Definition and Evolution of a Concept. In *African Cultural Heritage and the World Heritage Convention: Second Global Strategy Meeting*. Edited by Bertrand Hirsch, Laurent Lévi-Strauss and Galia Saouma-Forero. Pp. 56-64. Paris: UNESCO.

Price, Neil S. 2002. *The Viking Way: Religion and War in Late Iron Age Scandinavia*. Aun 31. Uppsala: Department of Archaeology and Ancient History.

Proclamation Program Website: UNESCO. Culture. Intangible Heritage. Proclamation Programme. Online.

Propp, Vladimir I. A. 1928. *Morfologija skazki*. Leningrad: Academia.

Pushkin, Aleksandr. 1964. *Eugene Onegin: A Novel in Verse*. Translated by Vladimir Nabokov. New York: Bollingen Foundation.

Qvigstad, Just and Georg Sandberg. 1887. *Lappiske eventyr og folkesagn*. Kristiania: Forlagt af Alb. Cammermeyer.

Raffel, Burton. 1989. Translating Medieval European Poetry. In *The Craft of Translation*. Edited by John Biguenet and Rainer Schulte. Pp. 28-53. Chicago and London: University of Chicago Press.

Rasmussen, Rasmus Ole. 2005. *Analyse af fangererhvervet i Grønland*. Roskilde: Roskilde universitet.

Rausmaa, Pirkko-Liisa, ed. 1988. *Suomalaiset kansansadut. 1, Ihmesadut*. Suomalaisen Kirjallisuuden Seura toimituksia 482. Helsinki: Suomalaisen Kirjallisuuden Seura.

Ravila, Paavo. 1931. *Ruijanlappalaisia kielennäytteitä Petsamosta ja etelä-Varangista*. Suomalais-ugrilaisen Seuran toimituksia 61. Helsinki: Suomalais-ugrilainen Seura.

Redfoot, Donald L. 1984. Tourist Authenticity, Tourist Angst, and Modern Reality. *Qualitative Sociology* 7: 291-309.

Republic of Bolivia, Ministry of Foreign Affairs and Religion. 1973. Letter to the Director-General of UNESCO, 24 April 1973. Ref. No. D.G.O.I.1006-79.

Ricoeur, Paul. 2005. *Minne, historia, glömska*. Göteborg: Daidalos.

Ringler, Richard N. 2002. *Bard of Iceland: Jónas Hallgrímsson, Poet and Scientist*. Madison: University of Wisconsin Press.

Rink, Henrik J. 1875. *Tales and Traditions of the Eskimo, with a Sketch of Their Habits, Religion, Language and Other Peculiarities*. Edinburgh and London: William Blackwell and Sons.

Rögnvaldur Pétursson. 1933. Upphaf vesturferða og þjóðminningarhátíð í Milwaukee 1874. *Tímarit Þjóðræknisfélags Íslendinga í Vesturheimi* 15: 66–78.

Röhrich, Lutz. 1964. *Märchen und Wirklichkeit*. Wiesbaden: F. Steiner.

Roepstorff, Andreas. 1997. Den symbolske betydning af *kalaalimernit*. In, *Kalaalimernit: rapport fra seminaret Den sociokulturelle og sundhedsmæssige betydning af kalaalimernit 6. og 7. maj 1997 i Nuuk*. Edited by Klaus Georg Hansen. Pp. 97-106. Nuuk: DIKE og Direktoratet for sundhed og forskning.

Ronalds, Craig and Margaret Clunies Ross. 2001. Thureth: A Neglected Old English Poem and Its History in Anglo-Saxon Scholarship. *Notes and Queries* 48: 359-70.

Rósa Þorsteindóttir. *Forthcoming*. Sagan upp á hvern mann: átta íslenskir sagnamenn og ævintýrin þeirra.

Rose, Mark. 1993. *Authors and Owners. The Invention of Copyright*. Cambridge: Harvard University Press.

Rose, Nikolas. 1999. *Powers of Freedom: Reframing Political Thought*. Cambridge: Cambridge University Press.

Rowlands, Eurys I., ed. 1976. *Poems of the Cywyddwyr: A selection of Cywyddau c. 1375-1525*. Dublin: The Dublin Institute for Advanced Studies.

Rudvin, Mette. 1999. *Norske Folkeeventyr: A Polysystemic Approach to Folk Literature in Nineteenth-Century Norway*. In *Selected Papers of the CETRA Research Seminars in Translation Studies*. Pp. 23-59. Leuven: The Catholic University in Leuven.

Rust, Val D. 1990. The Policy Formation Process and Educational Reform in Norway. *Comparative Education* 26: 13-25.

Røthe, Gunnhild. 2010. *I Odins tid: norrøn religion i fornaldersagaerne*. Hafrsfjord: Saga bok.

Sarajas-Korte, Salme. 1986. Aspects of Scandinavian Symbolism. In *Dreams of a Summer Night: Scandinavian Painting at the Turn of the Century*. Pp. 39-47. London: Arts Council of Great Britain

Schier, Kurt. 1968. Freys und Fróðis Bestattung. *Festschrift für Otto Höfler zum 65. Geburtstag*. Edited by Helmut Birkhan et al. 2 vols. Pp. 389-409. Wien: Verlag Notring.

Schjødt, Jens Peter. 1990a. Det sakrale kongedømme i det førkristne Skandinavien. *Chaos: dansk-norsk tidsskrift for religionshistoriske studier* 13: 48-67.

Schjødt, Jens Peter. 1990b. Horizontale und vertikale Achsen in der vorchristlichen skandinavischen Kosmologie. In *Old Norse and Finnish Religions and Cultic Place-Names*. Edited by Tore Ahlbäck. Scripta Instituti Donneriani Aboensis 13. Pp. 35-57. Stockholm: Almqvist & Wiksell.

Schjødt, Jens Peter. 2004. Kosmologimodeller og mytekredse. In *Ordning mot kaos: studier av nordisk förkristen kosmologi*. Edited by Anders Andrén et al. Pp. 123-133. Lund: Nordic Academic Press.

Schjødt, Jens Peter. 2007. Óðinn, Warriors, and Death. In *Learning and Understanding in the Old Norse World: Essays in Honour of Margaret Clunies Ross*. Edited by Judy Quinn et al. Pp. 137-152. Turnhout: Brepols.

Schjødt, Jens Peter. 2008. *Initiation Between Two Worlds: Structure and Symbolism in Pre-Christian Scandinavian Religion*. The Viking Collection, vol. 17. Odense: University Press of Southern Denmark.

Schjødt, Jens Peter. 2009. Diversity and Its Consequences for the Study of Old Norse Religion. What is It We are Trying to Reconstruct? In *Between Paganism and Christianity in the North*. Edited by Leszek P. Slupecki and Jakub Morawiec. Pp. 9-22. Rzeszôw: Wydawnichtwo Universytetu Rzeszowskiego.

Schjødt, Jens Peter. 2011. The Warrior in Old Norse Religion. In *Ideology and Power in the Viking and Middle Ages*. Edited by Gro Steinsland et al. Pp. 269-295. Leiden: Brill.

Schjødt, Jens Peter. *Forthcoming* a. Reflections on Aims and Methods in the Study of Old Norse Religion. In *Old Norse Religion: Mythological Narratives, Ritual Practices and Regional Distribution*. Edited by Catharina Raudvere and Jens Peter Schjødt.

Schjødt, Jens Peter. *Forthcoming* b. Reconstructing Old Norse Mythology: Source Criticism and Comparative Mythology. In *Myth and Theory in the Old Norse World*. Edited by Stefan Brink. Turnhout: Brepols.

Schulz, Katja. 2007. Eine amerikanische Edda? Von Longfellows 'Song of Hiawatha' und anderen eddischen Eroberungen. In *Þú ert vísust kvenna: Beatrice La Farge zum 60. Geburtstag*. Edited by Klaus von See and Julia Zerneck. Pp. 21-47. Heidelberg: Winter.

Seifert, Edeltraud K. 1952. Untersuchungen zu Grimms Märchen "Das Marienkind". Unpublished dissertation. München: Ludwig Maximilian Universität.

Shand, Peter. 2002. Scenes from the Colonial Catwalk: Cultural Appropriation, Intellectual Property Rights, and Fashion. *Cultural Analysis* 3: 47-88.

Sherkin, Samantha. 2001. A Historical Study on the Preparation of the 1989 Recommendation on the Safeguarding of Traditional Culture and Folklore. In *Safeguarding Traditional Cultures: A Global Assessment*. Edited by Peter Seitel. Pp. 42-56. Washington, DC: Center for Folklife and Cultural Heritage, Smithsonian Institution.

Shumkin, Vladimir. 1996. The Wizards of Lapland and Saami Shamanism. In *Shamanism and Northern Ecology*. Edited by Juha Pentikäinen. Berlin: Mouton de Gruyter.

Sigfús Sigfússon. 1982-1993. *Íslenskar þjóðsögur og sagnir*. Edited by Óskar Halldórsson, Grímur M. Helgason and Helgi Grímsson. 2nd ed. 11 vols. Reykjavík: Þjóðsaga, 1982-93.

Sigurður Nordal. 1940. *Hrafnkatla*. Studia Islandica 7. Reykjavík: Ísafoldarprentsmiðja.

Sigurður Nordal and Þórbergur Þórðarson, ed. 1962. *Gráskinna hin meiri*. 2nd ed. 2 vols. Reykjavík: Þjóðsaga.

Siikala, Anna-Leena. 1990. *Interpreting Oral Narrative*. FF Communications 245. Helsinki: Suomalainen Tiedeakatemia.

Sijmons, Barend. 1906. *Die Lieder der Edda*, 1. Band. 3 vols. Germanistische Handbibliothek 7. Halle an der Saale: Buchhandlung des Waisenhauses.

Siltberg, Tryggve. 1989. Tingsdomarna på Gotland: aristokrati eller storbönder? *Historisk tidskrift* 1989: 375-387.

Simek, Rudolf. 1984. *Lexikon der germanischen Mythologie*. Stuttgart: Alfred Kröner Verlag.

Simek, Rudolf. 1993. *Dictionary of Northern Mythology*. Woodbridge: Brewer.

Simpson, Jaqueline, ed. and trans. 1975. *Legends of Icelandic Magicians*. Cambridge: D. S. Brewer.

Simpson, Jaqueline, ed. and trans. 2004. *Icelandic Folktales and Legends*. 2nd ed. Stroud: Tempus.

Sköld, Tryggve. 1985. On the Origin and Chronology of Saamish (Lappish) Words. In *Saami Pre-Christian Religion*. Edited by Louise Bäckman and Åke Hultkrantz. Pp. 61-67. Uppsala: Almqvist & Wiksell.

Skrydstrup, Martin. 2009. Theorizing Repatriation. *Ethnologia Europaea* 39: 54-66.

Skrydstrup, Martin. 2010. What Might an Anthropology of Cultural Property Look Like? In *The Meanings and Values of Repatriation*. Edited by Paul Turnbull and Michael Pickering. Pp. 59-81. Museums and Collections 2. Oxford and New York: Berghan Books.

Smith, Georgina 1981. Urban Legend, Personal Experience Narrative and Oral History: Literal and Social Truth in Performance. *Arv* 37: 167-173.

Snorri Sturluson. 1911. *Edda: Taruopillinen alkuosa, Gylfin harhanäky (Gylfaginning)*. Porvoo: WSOY.

Snorri Sturluson. 1941-1951. See *Heimskringla 1-3*.

Snædal, Thorgunn. 2002. *Medan världen vakar: studier i de gotländska runinskrifternas språk och kronologi*. Runrön 16. Uppsala: Institutionen för nordiska språk, Uppsala universitet.

Solli, Brit. 2002. *Seid: myter, sjamanisme og kjønn i vikingenes tid*. Oslo: Pax.

Staecker, Jörn. 2004. Hjältar, kungar och gudar: receptionen av bibliska element och av hjältediktning i en hednisk värld. In *Minne och myt:*

konsten att skapa det förflutna. Edited by Åsa Berggren, Stefan Arvidsson and Ann-Mari Hållans. Vägar till Midgård 5. Pp. 41-79. Lund: Nordic Academic Press.

Steinn Steinarr. 1964. Kalevala. In *Kvæðasafn og greinar.* Pp. 273-274. [Reykjavík]: Helgafell. Originally published in *Þjóðviljinn,* 20 November 1949.

Steinsland, Gro. 1991. *Det hellige bryllup og norrøn kongeideologi: en undersøkelse av hierogamimyten i* Skírnismál, Ynglingatal, Háleygjatal *og* Hyndluljóð. Oslo: Solum forlag.

Steinsvik, Tone Sinding, ed. 2007. *Trollbundet av landskapet—Th. Kittelsen 150 år.* Modum: Blaafarveværk press.

Stenberger, Mårten. 1947-1958. *Die Schatzfunde Gotlands der Wikingerzeit.* 2 vols. Kungl. Vitterhets-, historie- och antikvitetsakademien. Monografier 34. Stockholm: Vitterhets historie och antikvitets akademien.

Stenseth, Bodil. 2000. *En norsk elite: nasjonsbyggerne på Lysaker 1890-1940.* Oslo: Aschehoug.

Stewart, Susan. 1991. Notes on Distressed Genres. *Journal of American Folklore* 104: 5-27.

Stewart, Susan. 1994. Scandals of the Ballad. In *Crimes of Writing. Problems in the Containment of Representation.* Pp. 102-131. Durham: Duke University Press.

Stokker, Kathleen. 2009. By Faith Alone? The Black Book, Key to Popular Piety in the Wake of the Reformation. In *The Nordic Storyteller: Essays in Honour of Niels Ingwersen.* Edited by Susan Brantly and Thomas A. DuBois. Pp. 42-60. Newcastle upon Tyne: Cambridge Scholars Publishing.

Ström, Folke. 1983. Hieros gamos-motivet i Hallfreðr Óttarssons *Hákonardrápa* och den nordnorska jarlavärdigheten. *Arkiv för nordisk filologi* 98: 67-79.

Strömbäck, Dag. 1935. *Sejd: textstudier i nordisk religionshistoria.* Stockholm and Copenhagen: H. Gebers and Levin & Munksgaard.

Strömbäck, Dag. 1970 [1928]. Att helga land: studier i Landnáma och det äldsta rituella besittningstagandet. In *Folklore och filologi.* Pp. 135-165. Uppsala: Almqvist & Wiksell.

Strömbäck, Dag. 2000a. The Concept of the Soul in Nordic Tradition. In *Sejd och andra studier i nordisk själsuppfattning.* Edited by Gertrud Gidlund. 2nd ed. Pp. 220-236. Uppsala: Kungl. Gustav Adolfs Akademien för svensk folkkultur.

Strömbäck, Dag. 2000b. *Sejd och andra studier i nordisk själsuppfattning.* Edited by Gertrud Gidlund. 2nd ed. Uppsala: Kungl. Gustav Adolfs Akademien för svensk folkkultur.

Sturlaugs saga starfsama. 1969. In *The Two Versions of* Sturlaugs saga starfsama: *A Decipherment, Edition, and Translation of a Fourteenth Century Icelandic Mythical-Heroic Saga.* Edited and translated by Otto J. Zitzelsberger. Düsseldorf: Michael Triltsch Verlag.

Sundqvist, Olof. 2002. *Freyr's offspring: rulers and religion in ancient Svea society.* Uppsala: Uppsala universitet.

Sundqvist, Olof. In press. 'Religious Ruler Ideology' in Pre-Christian Scandinavia: Some New Perspectives. In *More Than Mythology.* Edited by Catherina Raudvere and Jens Peter Schjødt. Turnhout: Brepols.

Sundt, Eilert. 1850. *Beretning om Fante- eller landstrygerfolket i Norge: et bidrag til kundskab om de laveste samfundsforholde.* Christiania.

Svanberg, Fredrik. 2003. *Decolonizing the Viking Age* 1-2. Acta Archaeologica, Series in 8° No. 43 and Series in 4° No. 24. Stockholm: Almqvist & Wiksell.

Svava Jakobsdóttir. 1980. Reynsla og raunveruleiki: nokkrir þankar kvenrithöfundar. In *Konur skrifa.* Edited by Valborg Bensdóttir, Guðrún Gísladóttir and Svanlaug Baldursdóttir. Pp. 221-230. Reykjavík: Sögufélag.

Svensson, Malin. 2002. Berättelser om andra världskriget: tre människors berättande om andra världskriget. Uppsats för fördjupningskurs (D). Högskolan på Gotland.

Tacitus, Cornelius. 1970. *Germania.* In *Agricola, Germania, Dialogus.* Translated by M. Hutton. Revised by E. H. Warmington. Loeb Classical Library 35. Cambridge: Harvard University Press. London: William Heinemann.

Tangherlini, Timothy R. 1988. Ships, Fogs, and Travelling Pairs: Plague Legend Migration in Scandinavia. *Journal of American Folklore* 400: 176-206.

Tangherlini, Timothy R. 1990. "It Happened Not Too Far From Here...": A Survey of Legend Theory and Characterization. *Western Folklore* 49: 371-390.

Tangherlini, Timothy R. 1994. *Interpreting Legend: Danish Storytellers and Their Repertoires.* Milman Parry Studies in Oral Tradition. New York & London: Garland.

Tangherlini, Timothy R. 1995. From Trolls to Turks: Continuity and Change in Danish Legend Tradition. *Scandinavian Studies* 67: 32-62.

Tangherlini, Timothy R. 1998a. "Who ya gonna call?": Ministers and the Mediation of Ghostly Threat in Danish Legend Tradition. *Western Folklore* 57: 153-178.

Tangherlini, Timothy R. 1998b. Barter and Games: Economics and the Supernatural in Danish Legendry. *Arv* 54: 41-62.

Tangherlini, Timothy R. 2000. "How do you know she's a witch?": Witches, Cunning Folk, and Competition in Denmark. *Western*

Folklore 59: 279-303.

Tangherlini, Timothy R. 2008a. And the Wagon Came Rolling In...: Legend and the Politics of (Self-) Censorship in Nineteenth-Century Denmark. *Journal of Folklore Research* 45: 241-261.

Tangherlini, Timothy R. 2008b. The Beggar, the Minister, the Farmer, his Wife and the Teacher: Legend and Legislative Reform in Nineteenth Century Denmark. In *Legends and Landscape: Articles Based on Plenary Papers Presented at the 5th Celtic-Nordic-Baltic Folklore Symposium, Reykjavík, 2005*. Edited by Terry Gunnell. Pp. 171-196. Reykjavik: University of Iceland Press.

Tangherlini, Timothy R. 2010. Will Work for Food: Legend and Poverty Legislation in Nineteenth Century Denmark. *Western Folklore* 69: 65-83.

Tarkka, Lotte, and Anna-Leena Siikala, eds. 2003. *Dynamics of Tradition: Perspectives on Oral Poetry and Folk Belief; Essays in Honour of Anna-Leena Siikala on Her 60th Birthday 1st January 2003*. Studia Fennica Folkloristica 13. Helsinki: Finnish Academy of Science & Letters.

Tauschek, Markus. 2009. Cultural Property as Strategy: The Carnival of Binche, the Creation of Cultural Heritage and Cultural Property. *Ethnologia Europaea* 39: 67-80.

Tauschek, Markus. 2010. *Wertschöpfung aus Tradition: Der Karneval von Binche und die Konstituierung kulturellen Erbes*. Studien zur Kulturanthropologie / Europäischen Ethnologie 3. Berlin: LIT.

Therman, Erik. 1936. Trolldomens olika innebörd i Eddan och Kalevala. Nya argus 29(18): 243-246.

Thisted, Kirsten. 1990. Nationalfølelse og skriftsprog: en studie i de første grønlandske romaner. *Danske studier* 85: 109-129.

Thisted, Kirsten. 2005. Grey Areas. In *Nordic Voices: Literature from the Nordic Countries*. Edited Jenny Fossum Grønn. Pp. 46-56. Oslo: Nordbok.

Thisted, Kirsten. 2008. Åndernes kraft og kristendommen: fire film om inuits religion. *Tidsskrift for Religionslærerforeningen for Gymnasiet og HF* 2: 26-50.

Thisted, Kirsten. 2011. Greenlandic Oral Traditions: Collection, Reframing and Reinvention. In *From Oral Tradition to Rap: Literatures of the Polar North*. Edited by Karen Langgård and Kirsten Thisted. Pp. 65-120. Nuuk: Ilisimatusarfik /Atuagkat.

Thomas, Gerald. 2003. Meaning in Narrative: A Franco-Newfoundland Version of Aa Th 480 *(The Spinning-Women by the Spring)* and Aa Th 510 *(Cinderella and Cap o'Rushes)*. *Fabula* 44(1/2): 117-136.

Thompson, Stith. 1961. Folklore Trends in Scandinavia. *Journal of American Folklore* 74: 313-320.

Thomson, David. 2001. *The People of the Sea: Celtic Tales of the Sea Folk.* 2nd ed. Edinburgh: Canongate.

Thunmark-Nylén, Lena. 1983. *Vikingatida dosspännen: teknisk stratigrafi och verkstadsgruppering.* Aun 4. Uppsala: Institutionen för arkeologi och antik historia.

Thunmark-Nylén, Lena. 2006. *Die Wikingerzeit Gotlands* 3:1. Stockholm: Kungl. Vitterhets historie och antikvitets akademien.

Torfhildur Þorsteinsdóttir Hólm. 1962. *Þjóðsögur og sagnir.* Reykjavík: Almenna bókafélagið.

Townend, Matthew, ed. *Forthcoming.* Þórarinn loftunga, *Glælognskviða.* In *Skaldic Poetry of the Scandinavian Middle Ages,* vol. 1. *Poetry from the Kings' Sagas 1.* Edited by Diana Whaley. Turnhout: Brepols.

Tranum Kristensen, Rasmus. 2007. Why was Óðinn Killed by Fenrir? A Structural Analysis of Kinship Structures in Old Norse Myths of Creation and Eschatology. In *Reflections on Old Norse Myths.* Edited by Pernille Hermann, Jens Peter Schødt, and Rasmus Tranum Kristensen. Studies in Viking and Medieval Scandinavia 1. Pp. 149-169. Turnhout: Brepols.

Trotzig, Gustaf. 1983. Den gamla och den nya religionen. In *Gutar och Vikingar.* Edited by Ingmar Jansson. Pp. 357-394. Stockholm: Statens historiska museum.

Tschan, Francis J., trans. 2002. *History of the Archbishops of Hamburg-Bremen.* New York: Columbia University Press.

Turi, Johan and Per Turi. 1918-1919. *Lappish texts.* Edited by Emilie Damant-Hatt. Copenhagen: Bianco Lunos bogtrykkeri.

Tynni, Aale, transl. 1960. Viisi skaldia. *Parnasso* 10: 291-294.

Urry, John. 1990. *The Tourist Gaze: Leisure and Travel in Contemporary Societies.* London: Sage Publications Ltd.

Uther, Hans-Jörg. 2004. *The Types of International Folktales: A Classification and Bibliography, Based on the System of Antti Aarne and Stith Thompson.* 3 vols. FF Communications 284. Helsinki: Suomalainen Tiedeakatemia

Valk, Ülo. 2009. Christianization and Folklorization as Discursive Shifts in Genre Formation: the Case of the Estonian Legends. Paper read at the ISFNR Congress in Athens, Greece, June 2009.

Varnedoe, Kirk, ed. 1982a. *Northern Light: Realism and Symbolism in Scandinavian Painting 1880-1910.* New York: The Brooklyn Museum.

Varnedoe, Kirk. 1982b. Nationalism, Internationalism, and the Progress of Scandinavian Art. In *Northern Light: Realism and Symbolism in Scandinavian Painting 1880-1910.* Edited by Kirk Varnedoe. Pp. 13-32. New York: The Brooklyn Museum.

Vaz da Silva, Francisco. 2010. The Invention of Fairy Tales. *Journal of American Folklore* 123: 398-425.

Venuti, Lawrence. 1992. Introduction. In *Rethinking Translation: Discourse, Subjectivity, Ideology*. Edited by Lawrence Venuti. Pp. 1-17. London and New York: Routledge.

Vestfirðinga sögur. 1943. Edited by Björn K. Þorólfsson and Guðni Jónsson. Islenzk fornrit 6. Reykjavík: Hið íslenzka bókmenntafélag.

Vestur-íslenzkar æviskrár, vol. 4. 1972. Edited by Benjamín Kristjánsson. Akureyri: Bókaforlag Odds Björnssonar.

Vésteinn Ólason. 1979. Inngangur. In *Sagnadansar*. Reykjavík: Rannsóknastofnun í bókmenntafræði / Menningarsjóður.

Vésteinn Ólason. 1998. *Dialogues with the Viking Age: Narration and Representation in the Sagas of the Icelanders*. Reykjavík: Heimskringla.Viðar Hreinsson et al., eds. 1997. *Complete Sagas of Icelanders*. Reykjavík: Leifur Eiríksson.

Viðar Hreinsson. 2005. Sex kíló af sögum. Paper presented at Umræðufundur Stofnunar Sigurðar Nordals og Norræna hússins í samvinnu við Bókaútgáfuna Leif Eiríksson um þýðingar og útgáfu á íslenskum fornbókmenntum á skandinavískum málum. May 25, 2005, Norræna húsið, Reykjavík.

Virtanen, Leea. 1994. Women's Songs and Reality. In *Songs beyond the Kalevala: Transformations of Oral Poetry*. Edited by Anna-Leena Siikala and Sinikka Vakimo. Pp. 330-342. Helsinki: Suomalaisen Kirjallisuuden Seura.

Vorren, Ørnulv. 1987. Sacrificial Sites, Types and Function. In *Saami Religion*. Edited by Tore Ahlbäck. Pp. 94-109. Uppsala: Almqvist & Wiksell.

Vries, Jan de. 1956. *Altnordische Literaturgeschichte*. 2 vols. Grundriss der germanischen Philologie. Berlin: De Gruyter.

Vries, Jan de. 1957. *Altgermanische Religionsgeschichte 2*. Berlin: De Gruyter.

Vries, Jan de. 1977. *Perspectives in the History of Religions*. Translated by Kees Bolle. Berkeley: University of California Press.

Vǫlsunga saga: The Saga of the Volsungs; The Icelandic Text According to MS Nks 1824 b, 4°. Translation, introduction and notes by Kaaren Grimstad. Bibliotheca, n. s., vol. 3. Saarbrücken: AQ-Verlag.

Wägner, Wilhelm. 1917. *Asgard and the Gods: The Tales and Traditions of Our Northern Ancestors, Forming a Complete Manual of Norse Mythology*. London: G. Routledge & Sons.

Walker, David M. 1980. *Oxford Companion to Law*. Oxford: Oxford University Press.

Wang, Ning. 1999. Rethinking Authenticity in Tourism Experience. *Annals of Tourism Research* 26: 349-367.

Warmind, Morten. 1999. *Wyrild cyming—veraldar god*: magtens religiøse basis hos germanerne. In *Religion och samhälle i det förkristna Norden: ett symposium.* Edited by Ulf Drobin et al. Odense: Odense Universitetsforlag.

Warner, Marina. 1996. *From the Beast to the Blonde: Fairy Tales and their Tellers.* New York: Farrar, Straus and Giroux.

Wawn, Andrew. 1991. *The Anglo Man: Þorleifur Repp, Philology and Nineteenth-Century Britain.* Studia Islandica 49. Reykjavík: Bókaútgáfa Menningarsjóðs.

Wawn, Andrew. 2000. *The Vikings and the Victorians: Inventing the Old North in 19th-Century Britain.* Cambridge: D.S. Brewer.

Wawn, Andrew. 2001. Victorian Vínland. In *Approaches to Vínland: A Conference on the Written and Archaeological Sources for the Norse Settlement in the North-Atlantic Region and Exploration of America.* Edited by Andrew Wawn and Þórunn Sigurðardóttir. Pr 191–206. Sigurður Nordal Institute Studies 4. Reykjavík: Sigurð Nordal Institute.

Weibull, Lauritz. 1943. En forntida v andring från Gotland. *Scandia* 15: 141-151.

Weiser, Lily. 1927. *Altgermanische Jünglingsweihen und Männerbünde: Ein Beitrag zur deutschen und nordischen Altertums- und Volkskunde.* Baden: Konkordia.

Wellendorf, Jonas. 2006. Homogeneity and Hetrogeneity in Old Norse Cosmology. In *Old Norse Religion in Long-term Perspectives: Origins, Changes, and Interactions: an International Conference in Lund, Sweden, June 3-7, 2004.* Edited by Anders Andrén et al. Pp. 50-53. Lund: Nordic Academic Press.

Wellendorf, Jonas. 2010. The Interplay of Pagan and Christian Traditions in Icelandic Settlement Myths. *Journal of English and Germanic Philology* 109: 1-21.

Wendland, Wend. 2004. Intangible Heritage and Intellectual Property: Challenges and Future Prospects. *Museum International* 56 (221-222): 97-107.

Werenskiold, Marit. Erik Werenskiold: Utdypning. In *Store norske leksikon.* Online.

Whitehouse, Harvey. 2000. *Arguments and Icons: Divergent Modes of Religiosity.* Oxford: Oxford University Press.

Wiggen, Geirr. 2005. A Sociolinguistic Profile of the Nordic Languages in the 19th Century. In *The Nordic Languages: An International Handbook of the History of the North Germanic Languages.* Edited by Oskar Bandle et al. Pp. 1523-1537. Berlin: De Gruyter.

Williams, Raymond. 1977. *Marxism and Literature.* Oxford: Oxford University Press.

Willson, Kendra. 2008. Jónas and the Panther: Translation, Alliteration and Icelandic Identity. *Scandinavian Studies* 80: 313-344.

Wolf, Kirsten. 2001. The Recovery of Vínland in Western Icelandic Literature. In *Approaches to Vínland: A Conference on the Written and Archaeological Sources for the Norse Settlement in the North-Atlantic Region and Exploration of America*. Edited by Andrew Wawn and Þórunn Sigurðardóttir. Pp. 207–219. Sigurður Nordal Institute Studies 4. Reykjavík. Sigurður Nordal Institute.

Woodmansee, Martha. 1994a. *The Author, Art, and the Market. Rereading the History of Aesthetics*. New York: Columbia University Press.

Woodmansee, Martha. 1994b. On the Author Effect. Recovering Collectivity. In *The Construction of Authorship: Textual Appropriation in Law and Literature*. Edited by Martha Woodmansee and Peter Jaszi. Pp. 15-28. Durham: Duke University Press.

Woodmansee, Martha and Peter Jaszi. 1994. Introduction. In *The Construction of Authorship: Textual Appropriation in Law and Literature*. Edited by Martha Woodmansee and Peter Jaszi. Pp. 1-13. Durham: Duke University Press.

Young, Katharine Galloway. 1987. *Taleworlds and Storyrealms: The Phenomenology of Narrative*. Dordrecht: Nijhoff.

Young, Katharine Galloway. 1997. *Presence in the Flesh: The Body in Medicine*. Cambridge: Harvard University Press.

Ziolkowski, Jan. 2010. Straparola and the Fairy Tale: Between Literary and Oral Traditions. *Journal of American Folklore* 123: 377-397.

Yrwing, Hugo. 1978. *Gotlands medeltid*. Visby: Gotlandskonst.

Zipes, Jack. 1999. *When Dreams Came True: Classical Fairy Tales and Their Tradition*. New York: Routledge.

Þorleifur Guðmundsson Repp. 1832. *A Historical Treatise on Trial by Jury, Wager of Law, and Other Co-Ordinate Forensic Institutions, Formerly in Use in Scandinavia and in Iceland*. Edinburgh: Thomas Clark / London: Saunders and Benning.

Þorleifur Guðmundsson Repp. 1849. Ávarp til Heiðarsmönnumárnesinga dags. 28. Sept. 1849. In *Þjóðskjalasafn, Einkaskjöl E 182*.

Þorleifs þáttr jarlsskálds. 1956. Edited by Jónas Kristjánsson. Íslenzk fornrit 9. Pp. 213-229. Reykjavík: Hið íslenzka bókmenntafélag.

Þorsteinn Erlingsson. 1954. *Þjóðsögur Þorsteins Erlingsonar*. Reykjavík: Ísafoldarprentsmiðja.

Þorsteinn M. Jónsson et al. 1964-1965. *Gríma hin nýja*. 5 vols. Reykjavík: Þjóðsaga.

Þorsteins saga hvíta. 1950. Jón Jóhannesson, ed. In *Austfirðingasögur*. Íslenzk fornrit 9. Pp. 1-19. Reykjavík: Hið íslenzka fornritafélag.

Þorsteins þáttr bæjarmagns. 1959. In *Fornaldarsögur Norðurlanda* 4. Edited by Guðni Jónsson. Pp. 319-344. Reykjavík: Íslendingasagnaútgáfan.

Bibliography of
John Lindow's Publications

1973

The Sagas as Ethnographic Documents. *Fyrirlestrar alþjóðlegs fornsagnaþings. Reykjavik 2-8 August 1973*. Edited by Steingrímur Þorsteinsson. Vol. 1, separately paginated. Reykjavík: n.p.

1974

A Note on the Sources of Redundancy in Oral Epic. *Journal of American Folklore* 86: 365-369.

Personification and Narrative Structure in Scandinavian Plague Legends. *Arv* 29-30: 83-92.

1975

Riddles, Kennings, and the Complexity of Skaldic Poetry. *Scandinavian Studies* 47: 311-327.

Review of John Weinstock, ed. 1975. *Saga og språk: Studies in Language and Literature Presented to Lee M.Hollander*. In *Speculum* 50: 366-367.

1976

Comitatus, Individual and Honor: Studies in North Germanic Institutional Vocabulary. University of California Publications in Linguistics 83. Berkeley: University of California Press.

Review of Peter Hallberg. 1975. *Old Icelandic Poetry*. In *Scandinavian Review* 64: 66-68.

1977

A Mythic Model in Bandamanna Saga and its Significance. *Michigan Germanic Studies* 3: 1-9. [Reprinted 1989]

The Two Skaldic Stanzas in Gylfaginning: Notes on Sources and Text History. *Arkiv för nordisk filologi* 92: 106-124.
Review of Michael Jacoby. 1974. *Wargus, Vargr, 'Verbrecher', 'Wolf': Eine sprach- und rechtsgeschichtliche Untersuchung.* Acta Universitatis Upsaliensis, Studia Germanistica Upsaliensia 12. In *Speculum* 52: 382-385.

1978

Swedish Legends and Folktales. Berkeley: University of California Press.
Old Icelandic Þáttr: Early Usage and Semantic History. *Scripta Islandica* 29: 3-44.
Rites of Passage in Scandinavian Legends. *Fabula* 19: 40-61.
Hreiðars þáttr heimska and AT 326: An Old Icelandic Novella and an International Tale Type. *Arv* 34: 152-179.
Review of Klas Östergren. 1977. *Ismael.* In *World Literature Today*: 300-301.
Review of Dag Strömbäck. 1975. *The Conversion of Iceland.* Translated and annotated by Peter Foote. Viking Society for Northern Research, Text Series 6. In *Ethnologica Scandinavica*: 191-192.
Review of Bo Almquist. 1974. *Norrön niddiktning: Traditionshistoriska studier i versmagi, 2: 1-2: Nid mot missionärer; Senmedeltida nidtraditioner.* Nordiska text och undersökningar 23. In *Ethnologica Scandinavica*: 193-195.
Review of Hans Bekker-Nielsen, Peter Foote, Andreas Haarder, and Hans Frede Nielsen, eds. 1977. *Oral Tradition Literary Tradition: A Symposium.* In *Ethnologica Scandinavica*: 195-198.
Review of Oddbjørg Høgset. 1978. *Erotiske folkeeventyr.* In *Ethnologica Scandinavica*: 209-210.

1979

Review of Lisbeth Bendixen. 1977. *Thomas billede.* In *World Literature Today* 53: 133.
Review of Hjalmar Alving, ed. and trans. 1979. *Isländska sagor: Eyrbyggarnas saga; Laxdalingarnas saga.* With introduction by Dag Strömbäck. In *Ethnologica Scandinavica*: 176-177.
Review of Preben Meulengracht Sørensen. 1977. *Saga og samfund: En indføring i oldislandsk literatur.* In *Ethnologica Scandinavica*: 177-178.

Review of Jón Hnefill Aðalsteinsson. 1978. *Under the Cloak: The Acceptance of Christianity in Iceland with Particular Reference to the Religious Attitudes Prevailing at the Time.* Studia Ethnologica Upsaliensa 4. In *Ethnologica Scandinavica*: 178-179.

Review of Anders Grape, Gottfrid Kallstenius, and Olof Thorell, eds. 1977. *Snorre Sturlasson, Edda, II: Uppsala-handskriften DG 11.* In *Speculum* 54: 632-633.

Review of Åke Lejonhuvud. 1978. *Anna och Christian.* In *World Literature Today* 53: 361.

1980

Review of Otto Holzapfel, ed. 1978. *The European Medieval Ballad: A Symposium.* In *Scandinavian Studies* 52: 72-75.

Review of John Greenway. 1977. *The Golden Horns: Mythic Imagination and the Nordic Past.* In *Comparative Literature* 32: 215-218.

Review of Hans Scherfig. 1979. *Den lange dag.* In *World Literature Today* 54: 122

1981

Review of Magnea J. Matthíasdóttir. 1981. *Göturæsiskandidatar.* In *World Literature Today* 55: 127.

1982

Swedish Legends of Buried Treasure. *Journal of American Folklore* 95: 257-279.

Narrative and the Nature of Skaldic Poetry. *Arkiv för nordisk filologi* 97: 94-121.

Review of Brynjulf Alver, ed. 1976. *Sunnafor sør og nordafor nord: Eventyr frå Akershus, Vestfold og Østfold.* Norsk eventyrbibliotek 7; and Reimund Kvideland, ed. 1977. *Glunten og riddar.* Rev: *Eventyr frå Nord-Norge.* Norsk eventyrbibliotek 8. In *Arv* 35: 162-164.

Review of Klaus von See. 1980. *Skaldendichtung: eine Einführung.* In *Speculum* 57: 200-201.

1983

Baldr. *Dictionary of the Middle Ages* 2: 55-56.

Baldrs draumar. *Dictionary of the Middle Ages* 2: 56-57.

Review of David Margolin and Jonathan Wylie. 1981. *The Ring of Dancers: Images of Faroese Culture*. In *Journal of American Folklore* 96: 233-234.

Review of *Michigan Germanic Studies, 7/1: Proceedings of the First International Symposium on Runes and Runic Inscriptions* (Ann Arbor, 1981). In *Speculum* 58: 784-786.

Review of Anthony Faulkes, ed. 1979. *Edda Magnúsar Olafssonar (Laufás Edda); Edda Islandorum: Völuspá: Hávamál: Two Versions of Snorra Edda from the Seventeenth Century*. Stofnun Arna Magnússonar á Islandi rit 13-14. In *Journal of English and Germanic Philology* 8: 116-118.

1984

Review of Omeljan Pritsak. 1981. *The Origin of Rus', I: Old Scandinavian Sources Other Than the Sagas*. In *Scandinavian Studies* 56: 304-306.

1985

Old Norse-Icelandic Literature: A Critical Guide. Co-Editor with Carol J. Clover. Islandica 45. Ithaca: Cornell University Press. [Reprinted 2005].

Mythology and Mythography. In *Old Norse-Icelandic Literature: A Critical Guide*. Edited by Carol J. Clover and John Lindow. Pp. 21-67. Islandica 45. Ithaca: Cornell University Press.

The Male Focus of Scandinavian Household Spirits. In *Papers IV: The 8th Congress for the International Society for Folk Narrative Research*. Edited by Reimund Kvideland and Torunn Selberg. Pp. 35-46. Bergen: Folkekultur.

Fenris Wolf. *Dictionary of the Middle Ages* 5: 47-48.

Gylfaginning. *Dictionary of the Middle Ages* 6: 40.

Háttatal. *Dictionary of the Middle Ages* 6: 113.

Hávamál. *Dictionary of the Middle Ages* 6: 114.

Heimdallr. *Dictionary of the Middle Ages* 6: 113-114.

Huginn and Muninn. *Dictionary of the Middle Ages* 6: 323.

Review of P. H. Sawyer. 1982. *Kings and Vikings: Scandinavia and Europe AD 700-1100*. In *Scandinavian Studies* 57: 110-111.

Review of Joan Rockwell. 1982. *Evald Tang Kristensen: A Lifelong Adventure in Folklore*. In *Scandinavian Studies* 57: 204-206.

1986

Structure and Meaning in Old Norse Literature: New Approaches to Textual Analysis and Literary Criticism. Co-editor with Lars Lönnroth and Gerd Wolfgang Weber. Viking Series 3. Odense: Odense University Press.

Þorsteins þáttr skelks and the Verisimilitude of Supernatural Experience in Saga Literature. In *Structure and Meaning in Old Norse Literature: New Approaches to Textual Analysis and Literary Criticism*. Edited by John Lindow, Lars Lönnroth, and Gerd Wolfgang Weber. Pp. 264-280. Viking Series 3. Odense: Odense University Press.

Software Tools and the Folklore Archive: A Different Perspective. With James A. LaVita. *Computers and the Humanities* 20: 97-106.

Iðunn. *Dictionary of the Middle Ages* 7: 18-19.

Loki. *Dictionary of the Middle Ages* 7: 644-645.

Review of Ulf Eriksson. 1984. *Det gjorda återstår*. In *World Literature Today* 60: 124-125.

Review of Anna Birgitta Rooth. 1981. *L.O.: En analys av en småbrukarhustrus trosvärld*; Anna Birgitta Rooth. 1983. *Från lögnsaga till paradis*. In *Western Folklore* 45: 50-52.

1987

Review of Hans Lagerberg. 1985. *Lästen, eller Nu får det vara nog*. In *World Literature Today* 61: 356.

Norse Mythology and Northumbria: Methodological Notes. *Scandinavian Studies* 59: 308-24. [Reprinted 1989]

Midgard Serpent. *Dictionary of the Middle Ages* 8: 362.

Mímir. *Dictionary of the Middle Ages* 8: 395-396.

Odin. *Dictionary of the Middle Ages* 9: 218-219.

Ragnarök. *Dictionary of the Middle Ages* 10: 248.

Berserkers. *The Encyclopedia of Religion* 2: 115-116.

Fylgjur. *The Encyclopedia of Religion* 5: 460.

Landvættir. *The Encyclopedia of Religion* 8: 437-438.
Valhöll. *The Encyclopedia of Religion* 15: 181-182.
Valkyries. *The Encyclopedia of Religion* 15: 182-183.
Review of Gottfried Lorenz. 1984. *Snorri Sturluson: Gylfaginning. Texte, Übersetzung, Kommentar.* Texte zur forschung 48. Darmstadt: Wissenschaftliche Buchgesellschaft. In *Journal of English and Germanic Philology* 86: 282-283.
Review of Bengt R. Jonsson et al. 1986. *Sveriges medeltida ballader, utgivna av Svenskt Visarkiv, vol. 2: Legendvisor (nr. 37-54) Historiska visor (nr. 55-65).* In *Folk Music Journal* 5: 367-369.

1988

Scandinavian Mythology: An Annotated Bibliography. Garland Folklore Bibliographies, 13; Garland Reference Library of the Humanities, 393. New York and London: Garland Publishing, 1988. xv, 593 pp.
Addressing Thor. *Scandinavian Studies* 60: 119-136.
Scandinavian Mythology. *Dictionary of the Middle Ages* 11: 22-34.
Skáldskaparmál. *Dictionary of the Middle Ages* 11: 323-324.
Snorra Edda. *Dictionary of the Middle Ages* 11: 352-355.
Review of Jan Henrik Swahn. 1986. *Jag kan stoppa ett hav.* In *World Literature Today* 62: 147.

1989

Nordic Narrative Folklore. Issue editor. *Scandinavian Studies* 61(4).
Continuity in Swedish Legend Tradition. *Scandinavian Studies* 61: 375-403.
An Experimental Computer Archiving Scheme with Applications to Folk Narrative Research. With James A. LaVita. *Motif* 8: 1, 4-5.
A Mythic Model in Bandamanna Saga and its Significance. In *Sagas of the Icelanders: A Book of Essays.* Edited by John Tucker. Pp. 241-256. Garland Reference Library of the Humanities 758. New York and London: Garland Publishing.
Norse Mythology and Northumbria: Methodological Notes. In *Anglo-Scandinavian England: Norse-English Relations in the Period before the Conquest.* Edited by John D. Niles and Mark Amodio. Pp. 25-40. Lanham, New York and London: University Press of America. [Reprint of 1987 original]

A Quest for Meaning in Fairy Tales. Review article of Bengt
   Holbek. 1987. *Interpretation of Fairy Tales.* In *Scandinavian Studies*
   61: 404-409.
Review of Solveig Almquist. 1984. *Gengångarföreställningar i*
   svensk folktro i genreanalytisk synpunkt. In *Scandinavian Studies* 61:
   410-411.

1990

Eufemiavisor. *Dictionary of Scandinavian Literature.* Edited by Virpi
   Zuck. Pp. 148-149. New York: Greenwood Press.
Old Norse Poetry. *Dictionary of Scandinavian Literature.* Edited by
   Virpi Zuck. Pp. 457-462. New York: Greenwood Press.
Saxo Grammaticus. *Dictionary of Scandinavian Literature.* Edited by
   Virpi Zuck. Pp. 513-514. New York: Greenwood Press.
Scandinavian Folklore. *Dictionary of Scandinavian Literature.* Edited by
   Virpi Zuck. Pp. 514-519. New York: Greenwood Press.

1991

Manumission Ritual in Old West Scandinavian Law. In *The Audience*
   of the Sagas: The Eighth International Saga Conference. Preprints 2. Pp.
   30-39. Gothenburg: Gothenburg University.
Review of Klaus von See. 1988. *Mythos und Theologie im*
   skandinavischen Hochmittelalter. In *Journal of English and Germanic*
   Philology 90: 377-379.

1992

Loki and Skaði. In *Snorrastefna: 25.-27. júlí 1990.* Rit Stofnunar
   Sigurðar Nordals 1. Edited by Úlfar Bragason. Pp. 130-142.
   Reykjavík: Stofnun Sigurðar Nordals.

1993

Sailing and Interpreting the Ships on the Gotland Stones. *The*
   American Neptune 53: 39-50.
Notes on Bengt Holbek's Interpretation of Kong Lindorm. In
   Telling Reality: Folklore Studies in Memory of Bengt Holbek . Edited

by Michael Chesnutt. Pp. 59-71. Copenhagen Folklore Studies 1; NIF Publications 26. Turku: Nordic Institute of Folklore.

Drápa. *New Princeton Encyclopedia of Poetry and Poetics.* Edited by Alex Preminger and T. V. F. Brogan. Pp. 311. Princeton: Princeton University Press.

Fornyrðislag. *New Princeton Encyclopedia of Poetry and Poetics.* Edited by Alex Preminger and T. V. F. Brogan. Pp. 423. Princeton: Princeton University Press.

Hrynhent. *New Princeton Encyclopedia of Poetry and Poetics.* Edited by Alex Preminger and T. V. F. Brogan. Pp. 539. Princeton: Princeton University Press.

Ljóðaháttr. *New Princeton Encyclopedia of Poetry and Poetics.* Edited by Alex Preminger and T. V. F. Brogan. Pp. 705. Princeton: Princeton University Press.

Old Norse Poetry. *New Princeton Encyclopedia of Poetry and Poetics.* Edited by Alex Preminger and T. V. F. Brogan. Pp. 857-860. Princeton: Princeton University Press.

Skald. *New Princeton Encyclopedia of Poetry and Poetics.* Edited by Alex Preminger and T. V. F. Brogan. Pp. 1154. Princeton: Princeton University Press.

Brands þáttr örva. *Medieval Scandinavia: An Encyclopedia.* Edited by Philip Pulsiano et al. Pp. 56. New York: Garland Publishing.

Freyr and Freyja. *Medieval Scandinavia: An Encyclopedia.* Edited by Philip Pulsiano et al. Pp. 220-221. New York: Garland Publishing.

Halldórs þáttr Snorrasonar. *Medieval Scandinavia: An Encyclopedia.* Edited by Philip Pulsiano et al. Pp. 262-263. New York: Garland Publishing.

Hreiðars þáttr heimska. *Medieval Scandinavia: An Encyclopedia.* Edited by Philip Pulsiano et al. Pp. 302-303. New York: Garland Publishing.

Mythology. *Medieval Scandinavia: An Encyclopedia.* Edited by Philip Pulsiano et al. Pp. 423-426. New York: Garland Publishing.

Stúfs þáttr. *Medieval Scandinavia: An Encyclopedia.* Edited by Philip Pulsiano et al. Pp. 613. New York: Garland Publishing.

Þáttr. *Medieval Scandinavia: An Encyclopedia.* Edited by Philip Pulsiano et al. Pp. 661-662. New York: Garland Publishing.

Ölkofra þáttr. *Medieval Scandinavia: An Encyclopedia.* Edited by Philip Pulsiano et al. Pp. 743-744. New York: Garland Publishing.

1994

Interpreting Baldr, The Dying God. (The 1993 Triebel Lecture). In *The Australian Academy of the Humanities: Proceedings 1993*. Pp. 155-173. Canberra: The Australian Academy of the Humanities. Also in *Old Norse Studies in the New World*. Edited by Geraldine Barnes, Margaret Clunies Ross, and Judy Quinn. Pp. 71-83. Sydney: Department of English, University of Sydney.

The Social Semantics of Cardinal Directions in Medieval Scandinavia. *Mankind Quarterly* 34: 209-224.

Thor's *hamarr*. *Journal of English and Germanic Philology* 93: 485-503.

1995

Nordic Folklore and the Question of Identity. Issue co-editor with Timothy R. Tangherlini. *Scandinavian Studies* 67(1).

Supernatural Others and Ethnic Others: A Millenium of World View. *Scandinavian Studies* 67: 8-31.

Þættir and Oral Performance. In *Oral Tradition in the Middle Ages*. Edited by W. F. H. Nicolaisen. Pp. 179-186. Medieval & Renaissance Texts & Studies 112. Binghamton, New York: Medieval & Renaissance Texts & Studies.

Bloodfeud and Scandinavian Mythology. *alvíssmál: Forschungen zur mittelalterlichen Kultur Skandinaviens* 4: 51-68.

König Lindwurm. With Bengt Holbek. In *Enzyklopädie des Märchens, vol. 8*. Edited by Kurt Ranke, Rolf Wilhelm Brednich, et al. Pp. 159-166. Berlin and New York: de Gruyter.

1996

Thor's Battle with Hrungnir. *alvíssmál: Forschungen zur mittelalterlichen Kultur Scandinaviens* 6: 3-18.

Irish Poetry and Norse dróttkvætt. With Gary B. Holland. In *A Celtic Florilegium: Studies in Memory of Brendan O Hehir*. Edited by Kathryn A. Klar, Eve E. Sweetser, and Claire Thomas. Pp. 54-62. Malden, MA: Celtic Studies Publications.

1997

Murder and Vengeance among the Gods: Baldr in Scandinavian Mythology. FF Communications 262. Helsinki: Suomalainen Tiedeakatemia.

Baldr and Lemminkäinen. *Journal of Finnish Studies* 1: 37-47.

Þrymskviða, Myth and Mythology. In *Germanic Studies in Honor of Anatoly Liberman.* Edited by Martha Berryman, Kurt Gustav Goblirsch, and Marvin Taylor. Pp. 203-212. NOWELE 31/32. Odense: Odense University Press.

Íslendingabók and Myth. *Scandinavian Studies* 69: 454-464.

1998

Kidnapping, Infanticide, Cannibalism: A Legend from Swedish Finland. *Western Folklore* 57: 103-117.

2000

Billings mær. In *Gudar på jorden: Festskrift Lars Lönnroth.* Edited by Stina Hansson and Mats Malm. Pp. 57-66. Göteborg: Gummertz.

Skald Sagas in Their Literary Context 1: Related Icelandic Genres. In *Skaldsagas: Text, Vocation, and Desire in the Icelandic Sagas of Poets.* Edited by Russell Poole. Pp. 218-231. Berlin: de Gruyter.

Medieval Folklore: An Encyclopedia of Myths, Legends, Tales, Beliefs, and Customs. Edited by Carl Lindahl, John McNamara, and John Lindow. Santa Barbara: ABC-Clio.

Berserks. In *Medieval Folklore: An Encyclopedia of Myths, Legends, Tales, Beliefs, and Customs.* Edited by Carl Lindahl, John McNamara, and John Lindow. Pp. 92-93. Santa Barbara: ABC-Clio.

Burgundian Cycle. In *Medieval Folklore: An Encyclopedia of Myths, Legends, Tales, Beliefs, and Customs.* Edited by Carl Lindahl, John McNamara, and John Lindow. Pp. 119-122. Santa Barbara: ABC-Clio.

Scandinavian Mythology. In *Medieval Folklore: An Encyclopedia of Myths, Legends, Tales, Beliefs, and Customs.* Edited by Carl Lindahl, John McNamara, and John Lindow. Pp. 872-876. Santa Barbara: ABC-Clio.

Snorri Sturluson's *Edda*. In *Medieval Folklore: An Encyclopedia of Myths, Legends, Tales, Beliefs, and Customs*. Edited by Carl Lindahl, John McNamara, and John Lindow. Pp. 938-939. Santa Barbara: ABC-Clio.

Thor. In *Medieval Folklore: An Encyclopedia of Myths, Legends, Tales, Beliefs, and Customs*. Edited by Carl Lindahl, John McNamara, and John Lindow. Pp. 975-978. Santa Barbara: ABC-Clio.

Wild Hunt. In *Medieval Folklore: An Encyclopedia of Myths, Legends, Tales, Beliefs, and Customs*. Edited by Carl Lindahl, John McNamara, and John Lindow. Pp. 1036-1037. Santa Barbara: ABC-Clio.

Response to Antonio Vaz da Silva, 'Bengt Holbek and the Study of Meaning in Fairy Tales.' *Cultural Analysis* 1: 11-12.

Interpreting Myth. *Svensk religionshistorisk årsskrift* 9: 64-80.

Thor's Visit to Útgarðaloki. *Oral Tradition* 15: 160-179.

2001

Handbook of Norse Mythology. Santa Barbara: ABC-Clio.

Norse Mythology and the Lives of the Saints. *Scandinavian Studies* 73: 437-456.

Review of *Sami Folkloristics*. Edited by Juha Pentikäinen, in cooperation with Harald Gaski, Vuokko Hirvonen, Jelena Sergejeva, and Krister Stoor. NNF Publications 6. In *Cultural Analysis* 2: 13-15.

2002

Medieval Folklore: A Guide to Myths, Legends, Tales, Beliefs, and Customs. Edited by Carl Lindahl, John McNamara, and John Lindow. Oxford: Oxford University Press.

Norse Mythology: A Guide to the Gods, Heroes, Rituals, and Beliefs. Oxford: Oxford University Press.

The Tears of the Gods: A Note on the Death of Baldr in Scandinavian Mythology. *Journal of English and Germanic Philology* 101: 155-169.

Myth Read as History: Odin in Snorri Sturluson's *Ynglinga saga*. In *Myth: A New Symposium*. Edited by Gregory Schrempp and William Hansen. Pp. 107-123. Blomington: University of Indiana Press.

Review of Ottar Grønvik. 2002. *Håvamål: Studier over verkets formelle oppbygning og dets religiøse innhold.* Det norske Videnskaps-Akademi, Skrifter. II hist.-filos. Kl., ny serie 21. Oslo: Det norske Videnskaps-Akademi. In *International Journal for Germanic Linguistics and Semiotic Analysis* 7: 91-96.

2003

Cultures in Contact. In *Old Norse Myths, Literature and Society.* Edited by Margaret Clunies Ross. Pp. 89-109. The Viking Collection 14. Odense: University Press of Southern Denmark.

2005

Old Norse-Icelandic Literature: A Critical Guide. Medieval Academy Reprints for Teaching. Co-editor with Carol J. Clover. Toronto: University of Toronto Press. [Reprint of 1985 original]

Review of Anu Koskivirta and Sari Forsstrdm, eds. 2002. *Manslaughter, Fornication and Sectarianism: Norm-breaking in Finland and the Baltic Area from Mediaeval to Modern Times.* Translated by Gerard McAlester. Helsinki: Finnish Academy of Sciences and Letters. In *Journal of Interdisciplinary History* 36: 265-266.

Review of Inger Ekremt and Lars Boje Mortensen, eds. 2003. *Historia Norwegie.* Translated by Peter Fisher. Copenhagen: Museum Tusculanum Press. In *Speculum* 80: 1271-1272

2006

Narrative Worlds, Human Environments, and Poets: The Case of Bragi. In *Old Norse Religion In Long-Term Perspectives: Origins, Changes And Interactions: An International Conference in Lund, Sweden June 3-7, 2004.* Edited by Anders Andrén, Kristina Jennbert, and Catharine Raudvere. Pp. 21-25. Vägar till Midagård 8. Lund: Nordic Academic Press, 2006.

Review of Klaus von See et al. 2000. *Kommentar zu den Liedern der Edda,* Band 3: *Götterlieder.* Heidelberg: C. Winter. With Frederic Amory. In *Göttingsche Gelehrte Anzeigen* 258: 100-127.

Review of Lars Levi Læstadius. 2002. *Fragments of Lappish Mythology.* Edited with Introduction and Afterword by Juha Pentikäinen.

Translated by Börje Vähämäki. Beaverton, Ontario: Aspasia Book. In *Journal of American Folklore* 119: 247-248.

2007

Akkerisfrakki: Traditions Concerning Óláfr Tryggvason and Hallfreðr Óttarsson vandræðaskáld and the Problem of the Conversion. *Journal of English and Germanic Philology* 108: 64-80.

Poetry, Dwarfs and Gods: Understanding Alvíssmál. In *Learning and Understanding in the Old Norse World: Essays in Honour of Margaret Clunies Ross*. Edited by Judy Quinn, Kate Heslop, and Tarrin Wills. Pp. 287-305. Medieval Texts and Cultures of Northern Europe 18. Turnhout: Brepols.

Folklore's Debt to the Study of Language: Documenting Folklore and Documenting Language and Dialect in the Nordic Countries. In *Combat pour les langues du monde—Fighting for the world's languages, Hommage à Claude Hagège*. Textes réunis par M. M. J. Fernandez-Vest. Pp. 327-337. Collection Grammaire & Cognition 4. Paris: Ed. L'Harmattan.

Trolls in the Isefjord (A Danish Folktale). With Marijane Osborne. *ANQ* 20: 51-53.

2008

St. Olaf and the Skalds. In *Sanctity in the North: Saints, Lives, and Cults in Medieval Scandinavia*. Edited by Thomas A. DuBois. Pp. 103-127. Toronto: University of Toronto Press.

Changelings, Changing, Re-exchanges: Thoughts on the Relationship between Folk Belief and Legend. In *Legends and Landscape: Plenary Papers from the 5ᵗʰ Celtic-Nordic-Baltic Folklore Symposium, Reykjavík, 15th-18th June 2005*. Edited by Terry Gunnell. Pp. 215-234. Reykjavík: Háskólaútgáfan.

2009

The Strong Housewife: ML 5080. In *The Nordic Storyteller: Essays in Honour of Niels Ingwersen*. Edited by Thomas A. DuBois and Susan Brantley. Pp. 61-78. Newcastle upon Tyne: Cambridge Scholars Publishing.

Mapping Identity in *Bárðar saga*. In *Greppaminni—afmælisrit til heiðurs Vésteini Ólasyni sjötugum*. Edited by Margrét Eggertsdóttir et al. Pp. 247-258. Reykjavík: Hið íslenska bókmenntafélag.

When Njörðr Chose Skaði. In *Romance and Love in Late Medieval and Early Modern Iceland: A Festschrift in Honor of Marianne Kalinke*. Edited by Kirsten Wolf. Pp. 165-182. Islandica 53. Ithaca: Cornell University Library.

2010

Cats and Dogs, Trolls and Devils: At Home in Some Migratory Legend Types. *Western Folklore* 69: 163-179.

Baldr. In *Oxford Dictionary of the Middle Ages*. Edited by Robert E. Bjork. Oxford: Oxford University Press.

Blood Brother. In *Oxford Dictionary of the Middle Ages*. Edited by Robert E. Bjork. Oxford: Oxford University Press.

Folklore and Mythology: Germanic. In *Oxford Dictionary of the Middle Ages*. Edited by Robert E. Bjork. Oxford: Oxford University Press.

Folklore and Mythology: Scandinavian. In *Oxford Dictionary of the Middle Ages*. Edited by Robert E. Bjork. Oxford: Oxford University Press.

Loki. In *Oxford Dictionary of the Middle Ages*. Edited by Robert E. Bjork. Oxford: Oxford University Press.

Midgard Serpent. In *Oxford Dictionary of the Middle Ages*. Edited by Robert E. Bjork. Oxford: Oxford University Press.

Odin. In *Oxford Dictionary of the Middle Ages*. Edited by Robert E. Bjork. Oxford: Oxford University Press.

Ragnarok. In *Oxford Dictionary of the Middle Ages*. Edited by Robert E. Bjork. Oxford: Oxford University Press.

Supernatural Beliefs in Scandinavia. In *Oxford Dictionary of the Middle Ages*. Edited by Robert E. Bjork. Oxford: Oxford University Press.

Thor. In *Oxford Dictionary of the Middle Ages*. Edited by Robert E. Bjork. Oxford: Oxford University Press.

Týr. In *Oxford Dictionary of the Middle Ages*. Edited by Robert E. Bjork. Oxford: Oxford University Press.

Valkyries. In *Oxford Dictionary of the Middle Ages*. Edited by Robert E. Bjork. Oxford: Oxford University Press.

Yggdrasill. In *Oxford Dictionary of the Middle Ages*. Edited by Robert E. Bjork. Oxford: Oxford University Press.

Yule (Jól). In *Oxford Dictionary of the Middle Ages*. Edited by Robert E. Bjork. Oxford: Oxford University Press.

Review of Terry Gunnell, ed. 2007. *Masks and Mumming in the Nordic Area*. Acta Academiae Regiae Gustavi Adolphi 98. Uppsala: Kung. Gustav Adolf Akademien för svensk folklivsforskning. Journal of Folklore Research Reviews. Online.

2011

Meeting the Other: The Cases of Kumlbúa þáttr and Draumr Þorsteins Síðu-Hallssonar. In *Myths, Legends and Heroes: Studies in Old Norse and Old English Literature in Honour of John McKinnell*. Pp. 77-90. Edited by Daniel Anlezark. Toronto: University of Toronto Press.

2012

Skáro á skíði: Völuspá 20 and the Fixing of Fate. Forthcoming in *Mediaeval Scandinavia*.

Some Thoughts on Saxo's Mythography. Forthcoming in *Writing Down the Myths*. Edited by Joseph Nagy. Turnhout: Brepols.

Snorri's Ásynjur. Forthcoming in *Old Norse Mythology and Theory*. Edited by Stefan Brink. Turnhout: Brepols.

Memory and Old Norse Mythology. Forthcoming in *Memory in Old Icelandic Literature*. Edited by Pernille Hermann, Agnes Agnórsdóttir, and Stephen Mitchell. Turnhout: Brepols.

Contributors

Anders Andrén (Stockholm University)

Carol J. Clover (University of California, Berkeley)

Margaret Clunies Ross (University of Sydney)

JoAnn Conrad (Independent Scholar)

Thomas A. Dubois (University of Wisconsin, Madison)

Gísli Sigurðsson (University of Iceland)

Terry Gunnell (University of Iceland)

Merrill Kaplan (The Ohio State University)

Hanne Pico Larsen (Columbia University)

Lars Lönnroth (University of Gothenburg)

Ulf Palmenfelt (Gotland University)

Jens Peter Schjødt (Aarhus University)

Timothy R. Tangherlini (UCLA)

Kirsten Thisted (University of Copenhagen)

Tok Thompson (University of Southern California)

Úlfar Bragason (University of Iceland)

Valdimar Tr. Hafstein (University of Iceland)

Kendra Willson (University of Helsinki)

www.ingramcontent.com/pod-product-compliance
Lightning Source LLC
Chambersburg PA
CBHW051725260326
41914CB00031B/1733/J